ROBERT MANNING STROZIER LIBRARY

TALLAHASSEE, FLORIDA

A GUIDE TO THE
MANUSCRIPTS AND ARCHIVES OF
THE WESTERN RESERVE HISTORICAL SOCIETY

A GUIDE TO THE
Manuscripts
AND
Archives
OF
THE WESTERN RESERVE HISTORICAL SOCIETY

KERMIT J. PIKE
Chief Librarian
The Western Reserve Historical Society

The Western Reserve Historical Society
Cleveland, Ohio
1972

CD
3449
C55
W47

Copyright © 1972 by The Western Reserve Historical Society.
All rights reserved.
Printed in the United States of America.
Library of Congress Catalogue Card Number: 78-170152.
International Standard Book Number: 0-911704-08-6.
The Western Reserve Historical Society Publication Number 124.

CONTENTS

Foreword vii
Introduction xi
Format xvii

PART I: MANUSCRIPTS
    Section A: General Collections 1
    Section B: Special Collections 297
    Section C: Collections on Microfilm . . 311
    Section D: Recent Accessions and Other Collections in Preparation . . 315

PART II: OHIO GOVERNMENT ARCHIVES . . 329
List of Subject Headings 352
Index 353

FOREWORD

Although the Library is but one department of an expanding Western Reserve Historical Society, historically it has been the central core of the Society's interest. While the Library has attained a reputation for its books on Lincoln and the Civil War, its prints and photographs, its runs of early Ohio newspapers, its genealogies, its automotive manuals and instruction books, and, in general, its collection of Americana, it has also acquired wide renown among scholars for its manuscripts.

Credit for initiating an active manuscript-collecting program goes to Wallace H. Cathcart, director of the Society from 1913 until his death in 1942. His immediate successors lacked, as he did, adequate staff, particularly staff with archival training, to arrange and bring under control efficiently the documents that had been accumulated. Until this was done, however, a large portion of the material would remain unserviceable.

As a first step the manuscripts needed to be arranged, boxed, and inventoried in accordance with modern standards of archival procedure. The second step would be the preparation and publication of a guide. A decade ago the task of finding funds, staff, and time appeared herculean. Then suddenly an incident occurred which, however embarrassing it was at the time, proved to be a catalytic agent that would bring the concept to fruition. Dr. Carl Wittke, at the time dean of the Graduate School of Western Reserve University, had assigned a student the task of preparing a doctoral thesis on the life of a Cleveland reformer, Daniel E. Morgan. Morgan's papers were reportedly at the Society, but an extensive search failed to uncover them. When, through Dr. Wittke's efforts, the donor of the papers produced the Society's letter acknowledging their receipt, the search was renewed and the papers were found.

The incident was a *cause célèbre*. It crystallized in the strongest terms the need for effective manuscript control. It became the basis for a successful request to the Cleveland Foundation for a grant to engage a qualified archivist for a three-year period to arrange and inventory records. The discovery of the Morgan papers and the ensuing inventory that was prepared enabled the student, Thomas F. Campbell, to undertake the suggested thesis, which, when published in 1966 by the Press of Western Reserve University, became a steppingstone in his advancement to the post of director of the Institute of Urban Studies of Cleveland State University.

Miraculously the seed money provided by the Cleveland Foundation inspired the development and growth of a manuscript department with a full-time manuscript head and assistants. Over the years order succeeded chaos. When the time came to begin the preparation of the guide, one of the archivists, Kermit Pike, emerged with the skill, dedication, and direction to undertake the task. At the same time that he was preparing the guide, he was successfully obtaining important manuscript collections throughout the Cleveland community and elsewhere. This work is the result of his perseverance.

An important element in the overall library program has been the regular annual subsidy from the Cuyahoga County Commissioners. This subsidy has enabled the Society to expand its service to the community and the general public.

It was not possible to complete the project of preparing the guide without supplementary funds. In addition, funds were necessary to publish the guide. We want to express deep appreciation to the following three foundations that assisted us in the preparation or publication of the guide: the George R. Codrington Foundation, the Harry K. Fox and Emma R. Fox Charitable Trust, and the George Gund Foundation. The funds received from the George Gund Foundation constitute a portion of a larger grant given to improve the availability of all library research materials.

It is the policy of the Board of Trustees of the Western Reserve Historical Society to make freely available to serious students of history the extensive resources of this institution. As a result of the recent processing of manuscripts in the custody of the Society, the use of the collections by students at all local universities and colleges, as well as by other researchers, has more than doubled. The publication and dissemination of this guide will, it is hoped, serve as a further stimulus to historical scholarship.

The processing of the manuscripts and the preparation of the guide come at a time when the Society is acquiring manuscripts relating to the Greater Cleveland area in ever increasing volume. These are preliminary steps toward a third and most important objective, the construction of a modern library building. Such a building will provide much needed space, much better protection, and more satisfactory research facilities.

Frederick C. Crawford, *President*
Meredith B. Colket, Jr., *Director*

January, 1972

INTRODUCTION

Even before the Western Reserve Historical Society was founded in 1867, a coterie of cultured and learned men were concerned with the preservation of the history of Cleveland and of that five-thousand-square-mile region of northeastern Ohio known as the Western Reserve. They actively collected the papers of early settlers and the records of organizations and institutions that had played a part in the growth and development of this region. Much of this material formed the basic collection of the Society, as the early history of the Western Reserve, dating back to the founding of Cleveland in 1796, remained its main focus during the nineteenth century. The interests of the Society expanded during the twentieth century to include a wider range of subjects, including the American Revolution, the Civil War, Shakers, slavery, and abolitionism. The existence of collections in these areas is due largely to the interest and generosity of the Society's trustees, officers, and members who donated their private collections. As a result, the Society's holdings, which are administered by its Library, touch on a wide range of political, military, social, religious, and economic activity outside Cleveland and the Western Reserve.

This guide appears at a time when the Society is developing new programs designed both to assure the preservation of important manuscript and archival sources relating specifically to the history of the Greater Cleveland area during the twentieth century and to meet the expanding needs of researchers from this community's growing educational institutions. As a privately supported organization, the Society relies heavily on special funds for the development of new projects. In September, 1970, the Black History Archives Project was established by a grant through the Cleveland Foundation from the Edith Anisfield Wolf Fund. This grant has enabled the Library to employ additional people to locate manuscripts, archives, newspapers, pictures, and other sources relating to the history of Cleveland's black community. Most of the collections accessioned by this project's staff were received too late for inclusion in this guide.

The same is true for the Library's recently-established ethnic archives project. Based on the need for a multifaceted archives and library program directed toward the many ethnic groups in the Cleveland area, on the significant number of foreign-language newspapers and ethnic-history publications extant in the Library, and on the success of the Library's pilot acquisition program undertaken during the summer of 1971, the Society's board of trustees established an ethnic research center on October 18, 1971. The Society is currently seeking funds to formally organize this project in a manner similar to that used in the Black History Archives Project.

In addition to the accessions made possible by these two projects, the Library's numerous urban history collections, which have also recently been acquired, will be described in a supplement to this guide, or in a series of special publications. We recognize that this guide is the Society's first in 105 years; hopefully another century will not pass before the next. A separate guide, currently being complied, to the manuscripts in the Wallace H. Cathcart Shaker Collection is being considered as the Society's next published finding aid. Funds for undertaking this project were provided by the Shaker Savings Association.

The Society has long recognized the research value inherent in local governmental records and has accessioned such records when they have become available. The Society thus willingly became a charter member of the Ohio Network of American History Research Centers, which was founded by the Ohio Historical Society on July 10, 1970. Under the terms of this charter, the Society is the official archival administrator for records of counties, municipalities, and townships contained within its region, which includes Cuyahoga, Geauga, Lake, Lorain, and Medina counties. Partly in response to the establishment of this network, the Society's holdings of Ohio governmental archives have been separated from its general collection and are reported in Part II of this guide.

Over the years, the Library's collection of manuscripts and archives has not been its only interest. Over 200,000 books, 25,000 volumes of newspapers, and extensive collections of broadsides, prints, and photographs have also been amassed. Among these are numerous printed items such as pamphlets, reports, newsletters, and special publications of organizations whose records are described in the following pages. In many cases, these have been collected and classified in the Library. Consequently, a researcher should also consult the other departments of the Library when seeking source materials relating to any of the individuals or organizations mentioned in this guide.

Little professional work was done with the Society's collections of manuscripts and archives prior to 1960. From that date, there have been at least three staff members in the Library's Manuscript Department arranging collections, preparing registers, and cataloguing. Approximately thirty of these collections are described in Philip M. Hamer, ed., *A Guide to Archives and Manuscripts in the United States* (New Haven: Yale University Press, 1961). Unpublished registers have now been prepared for nearly a hundred collections, twenty-five of which have been reported to the National Union Catalog of Manuscript Collections. The July, 1964, issue of the Society's monthly bulletin, *The Historical Society News* (vol. 18, no. 7), contains descriptions of fifty-three collections for which registers have been prepared. During the past five years new acquisitions have been regularly reported to the appropriate scholarly journals. Many of the collections described in this volume, however, are being publicized for the first time. The Society's attics and basements have been cleared and every major collection in its possession as of December 31, 1970, is reported herein, with three exceptions.

Not included in this guide are the following:

1. The Napoleonic Collection of David Z. Norton, which in-

cludes seventy-six manuscript items. A detailed inventory of this collection is available in the Society.
2. A small number of European manuscripts from the sixteenth, seventeenth, and eighteenth centuries.
3. Several typescripts and manuscripts of unpublished family histories which are housed in the Library's Genealogy Department.

The use of manuscript accession numbers was initiated by the Society in the 1910's. A totally new scheme was introduced in the late 1930's and has been continued to date. The gaps in the MS-number sequence are accounted for, in part, by the fact that these now-vacated numbers were assigned to single documents or very small collections which have been transferred to the Manuscript Vertical File or Oversize Manuscripts, reported in Part I under Special Collections. In other instances, the contents of several numbers, originally part of a single collection but separated for cataloguing purposes, have been brought back together. Occasionally this was not possible because part of a collection had been previously arranged and a detailed inventory prepared (e.g., the papers of Perley Peabody Pitkin, Charles Whittlesey, and Elisha Whittlesey).

Concurrently with the compilation of this guide over the last five years much work was done in sorting, arranging, and re-cataloguing existing collections, as well as accessioning new collections. As late as 1966, there were well over 3,000 "collections" wrapped in brown paper and tied with string. Although this is no longer the case, much processing remains to be done. Consequently, this guide will be less than perfect. Nevertheless, it is hoped that the guide will draw much-deserved attention to the Society's holdings, will better enable it to serve researchers, and will act as a stimulus to its acquisitions program.

Many individuals have contributed to the preparation of this guide. Of key importance has been Meredith B. Colket, Jr. After conceiving the idea for this publication and encouraging one of his fledgling archivists to undertake it, he gave freely of his time every step of the way. Without his constant and expert direction and his infectious enthusiasm, this guide could not have been completed or published. During the past six years, every Library staff member has been called upon for assistance. Their cooperation, especially that of Alma B. Jones, manuscript cataloguer, and Virginia R. Hawley, general reference supervisor, is gratefully acknowledged. A corps of student manuscript processors, particularly Mary B. Bowling, made a significant contribution. Barbara J. Kenny, in addition to typing and retyping each entry through various editorial stages, also labored courageously with the index. Finally, much encouragement was provided by Joyce R. Pike, who also remained cheerful through the innumerable evenings that her husband spent working on the guide.

Kermit J. Pike

FORMAT

The guide entries are divided into two parts, Manuscripts and Ohio Government Archives.

Part I, Manuscripts, is divided into four sections.
    Section A: General Collections, in which entries appear in accession-number sequence.
    Section B: Special Collections, so designated because they are treated by the Library in a manner distinct from the General Collection.
    Section C: Collections on Microfilm, not including the Library's extensive collection of federal population census schedules.
    Section D: Recent Accessions and Other Collections in Preparation, described in brief because they are late additions to the Society's holdings or are not fully processed. For the most part, these have been preliminarily arranged and boxed and are available to researchers.

Part II, Ohio Government Archives, consists of records of Ohio towns, cities, and counties. These have been arranged by county and subdivided by county office; and then arranged alphabetically by town and city.

An effort has been made to keep the descriptions as uniform as possible, and each should be self-explanatory. The name of each collection is followed by identification of the form of the material along with its terminal dates. Occasionally, these dates are followed by dates in parentheses to indicate the period wherein

the bulk of the collection falls. An indication of the size of the collection follows. In addition to an exact item count, the units listed below are most commonly used:
   (a) volume (bound manuscript);
   (b) box (letter- or legal-size archival document box, 5 linear inches);
   (c) ½ box (letter- or legal-size archival document box, 2.5 linear inches);
   (d) folder (archival folder holding 20 to 100 items);
   (e) package (material too large for a document box).
Next, when readily available, appears the name of the donor or other source. This is followed by the collection number. The body of each description contains an account of the types of material within each collection and lists the persons, places, events, and subjects which are referred to.

The availability of unpublished registers is noted below the descriptions of the pertinent collections. When a collection has been reported to the National Union Catalog of Manuscript Collections (NUCMC), the NUCMC item number is given.

PART I: MANUSCRIPTS

SECTION A:
General Collections

1   MANUSCRIPTS RELATING TO THE EARLY HISTORY OF THE CONNECTICUT WESTERN RESERVE, 1795–ca. 1860. 23 volumes of original and/or copies of documents given to the Society or purchased with funds provided by the Cuyahoga County Commissioners, 1867–1871; and bound, 1870–1871. MS 1.

Records relating to the operation of the Connecticut Land Company include the following: proceedings between the company and the state of Connecticut, 1795–1800; articles of association, 1795; report of the Committee on Sale, 1795; minutes and proceedings, 1796–1801; mode of partition of the Western Reserve determined in 1796; accounts between the company and its agents, 1796–1798; reports of the Committee on Partition, 1797, 1809; reports of the Committee on Drafts, 1798 and 1802, and records of the drafts held in 1798, 1799, 1802, 1807, and 1809; reports of the Equalizing Committee, 1798, 1802; list of lands in the Western Reserve mortgaged to the state of Connecticut as collateral surety on its bonds to the School Fund, 1816; and memoranda relating to the Excess Company, undated.

The following surveyors are represented in an assortment of field notebooks made while surveying various tracts of land in the Western Reserve, primarily between 1796 and 1802: Amzi Atwater, Phineas Barker, J. P. Bissell, Abraham Freese, James A. Harper, T. B. Hawley, John Milton Holley, Ezekiel Hover, Joseph Landon, Caleb Palmer, Charles Parker, Nathan Redfield, Warham Shepard, Amos Spafford, Richard M. Stoddard, Abraham Tappan, Moses Warren, and Alfred Wolcott.

Journals of the following early residents are included: John Milton Holley, surveyor, kept while traveling from Salisbury, Connecticut, to Cleveland and back to Salisbury, April–November, 1796; Seth Pease, surveyor, kept while traveling from Suffield, Connecticut, to the Western Reserve (May–September, 1796) and back to Suffield (November, 1796), and while surveying land in the Western Reserve for the Connecticut Land Company (1797–1799) and in the Holland Purchase for the Holland Land Company (1798–1799), 1796–1799; David Hudson, landowner and founder of Hudson, Ohio, kept while traveling from Goshen, Connecticut, to the Western Reserve in 1799; Rev. Thomas Robbins, kept while traveling throughout Ohio, 1803–1806; and Quintus F. Atkins, kept while accompanying Rev. Joseph Badger on a mission to the Wyandot Indians inhabiting the region near the Sandusky River, 1804–1807.

Letters or statements of the following persons contain their responses to letters of John Barr, Charles Whittlesey, and others soliciting information relating to the early history and settlement of the Western Reserve: Amzi Atwater, David H. Beardsley, Gaius Burke, Orlando Cutter, Daniel Dobbins, John S. Edwards, Julius C. Huntington, S. C. Jennings, Levi Johnson, Edward Paine, Augustus Porter, P. R. Spencer, Stanton Sholes, Mrs. Buckley Steadman, Abraham Tappan, and George Tod.

Writings and memoranda of Charles Whittlesey, the Western Reserve Historical Society's first president, include those on topics such as the Kelley family, early maps of Lake Erie, Indian trails in the Western Reserve, the surveying party to the Western Reserve in 1797, the Cuyahoga County Historical Society in 1858, the histories of Brecksville and Tallmadge, and the early history of the states northwest of the Ohio River.

The following persons are represented in biographical sketches: Lorenzo Carter, James S. Clarke, Simon Perkins, Abraham Tappan, Benjamin Tappan, and John Walworth.

Also included are the following items: John Heckewelder's description of northeast Ohio, 1796; record of the partition of Suffield Township, 1802; list of contracts and notes given for lands in the Western Reserve by Turhand Kirtland, 1803; notes by Turhand Kirtland, Eliphalet Austin, and Martin Smith on the exploration of lands west of the Cuyahoga River, 1806; account of taxes paid on city lots in Cleveland, 1807; accounts of the first Cleveland Library Association, 1811–1813; John Barr's lecture on the history of Cleveland, delivered in 1842, and his manuscript history of Cleveland, 1843; an account of Millerism in Cleveland during 1842; an account of the surveys made in 1806 and 1807 of land west of the Cuyahoga River prepared by Abraham Tappan in 1850; Edward Paine's account of the settlement of the Western Reserve, undated; and a copy of the journal of Captain Jonathan Heart, 1st Connecticut Regiment, Continental Army, 1782.

2   FIFTH AVENUE PRESBYTERIAN CHURCH. VESTAL JEWEL SOCIETY. COLUMBUS, O. Records, 1890–1892. 1 volume. MS 2.

Constitution, minutes of meetings, and a list of members of this society which sought to interest young girls in church work.

3   DAVID FORDING (1842–1919). Papers, ca. 1876–1878. ½ box. MS 3.

Letter book containing copies of communications, most of which relate to legal matters, sent by this attorney at law and resident of Alliance, Ohio, to nearly 200 persons throughout the state of Ohio, 1876–1878; and typescript copies of six speeches on historical topics.

4   LUCINDA WHITE BROWN. Diary, March 20–September 20, 1854. 1 volume. MS 4.

Kept on a trip, the purpose of which was "to visit my friends at the west and spend a few weeks among the scenes of my early days." The great-grandfather of Mrs. Brown was one of the first Universalist ministers in Maine, and her husband, Rev. S. J. Brown, was a minister in Perry, New York.

5   ANONYMOUS. Notebook, 1822. 1 volume. MS 5.
Detailed notes taken down during a series of medical lectures, plus a 5-page index to the text.

6   JAMES A. EMMERTON. Autograph Book, 1855. 1 volume. Gift of F. A. Emmerton, 1916. MS 7.
Photographs, biographies, and autographs of both faculty and students from Harvard's class of 1855.

7   METHODIST-EPISCOPAL CHURCH. CHARLESTOWN, O., Records, 1867–1902. 3 volumes. MS 9.
Primarily attendance, subscription, and marital-status records of members of this church, and superintendents' reports of various Sunday school classes. Also included are minutes of quarterly conferences, pastors' reports, and memoranda of the East Ohio Conference, Akron District, Charlestown Charge.

8   CONGREGATIONAL CONSOCIATION OF PORTAGE AND SUMMIT COUNTIES. OHIO. Records, 1841–1851. 1 volume. MS 12.
Constitution, bylaws, and minutes of the organization which was based on the precedent set by the consociated churches in the southern district of Litchfield County, Connecticut. The purpose of this council of churches was "to promote fellowship among themselves, to ordain, install and dismiss Pastors, and to render each other all such assistance in ecclesiastical matters as may be requisite."

9   CHRISTIAN CHURCH. QUINCY, ILL. Records, 1870–1871. 1 volume. Gift of William H. Murray, 1921. MS 14.
Proceedings of the meetings of the building committee and a list of subscribers. C. R. Richardson was chairman of the committee, which included J. S. Fox, D. R. Howard, and H. S. Kemp.

10 STEUBENVILLE FEMALE SEMINARY. STEUBENVILLE, O. Records, 1829–1836. 1 volume. Gift of Mrs. E. J. Donaldson. MS 23.

Select-school book containing a list of students and reports on their attendance, achievement, and behavior.

11 METHODIST-EPISCOPAL CHURCH. RAVENNA, O. Records, 1843–1905. 4 volumes. MS 24.

Predominantly Sunday school records. Three volumes include the attendance, marital status, membership, and financial records of various Sunday school classes. One volume contains the minutes of the meetings of the church's Sunday school board.

12 LOCKWOOD'S CORNERS LITERARY SOCIETY. SUMMIT COUNTY, O. Records, 1874–1878. 1 volume. MS 25.

Constitution, rules of order, minutes, and lists of members of this society.

13 CANTON LADIES ANTI-SLAVERY SOCIETY. CANTON, O. Records, 1836. 1 volume. Gift of W. H. Murray. MS 26.

Preamble and constitution along with the minutes of three meetings.

14 DISCIPLES CHURCH. LADIES AID SOCIETY. RAVENNA, O. Records, 1872–1876. 1 volume. MS 29.

Constitution, minutes of biweekly meetings, and lists of contributing members. This society raised money, food, and clothing for needy families.

15   COURT TEMPERANCE SOCIETY OF THE THIRD JUDICIAL CIRCUIT. RAVENNA, O. Records, 1838–1864. 1 volume. Gift of Mrs. W. H. Beebe. MS 31.

Background, constitution, pledge, membership list, and financial records of this society which was composed of judges, members of the bar, clerks, sheriffs, and their deputies.

16   MARY B. LOVELL. Album, January, 1840. 1 volume. MS 35.

"American Plants copied from Bigelow's Medical Botany" by Mary B. Lovell, Young Ladies Seminary, Keene [N. H.]. Along with a textual description of various plants, there is also a colored hand drawing of each.

17   EASTERN CUYAHOGA COUNTY HORTICULTURAL SOCIETY. EUCLID, O. Records, 1886–1905. 2 volumes. Gift of Mrs. L. B. Hoose. MS 36.

Background, constitution, minutes, and list of members, which include the early officeholders, E. H. Cushman, G. Voorhees, A. P. Stevens, and Mrs. J. W. Maxwell.

18   BENSON JOHN LOSSING (1813–1891). Sketchbook, n.d. 1 volume. Gift of Horace B. Tuttle, 1921. MS 38.

Collection of pencil sketches, watercolor paintings, and crayon drawings depicting places and persons of some historical importance, including scenes from the American Revolution, the War of 1812, and the Civil War.

19   FIRST CONGREGATIONAL CHURCH. RANDOLPH, O. Records, 1846–1899. 4 volumes. MS 40.

The earliest volume of records of the First Congregational Church contains the constitution, financial records, and membership lists, 1846–1885. Two later record books include admission procedures, creed and covenant, rules and regulations, membership lists, baptisms, and minutes, 1855–1887. Also included is a history of the church from 1802 to 1891, written in 1899, followed by a list of the church's 242 members, including the dates they joined and left the congregation.

20 PORTAGE COUNTY BIBLE SOCIETY. RAVENNA, O. Records, 1853–1908. 1 volume. MS 43.

Secretary's book, including the constitution, list of members, and minutes of this society, an auxiliary to the American Bible Society.

21 STAGE OFFICE. RAVENNA, O. Records, 1833–1866. 1 volume. Gift of W. H. Beebe, 1918. MS 44.

Names of passengers, date and place of departure, destination, and other remarks.

22 ELBERT JAY BENTON (1871–1946). Papers, 1918, 1945–1946. 1 box. MS 48.

Correspondence relating to the life of Archibald M. Willard and to the history of Willard's paintings; an unpublished account of "*The Spirit of '76*—How Many Versions?"; and a typescript copy of Benton's article "The Movement for Peace Without a Victory During the Civil War," W.R.H.S. *Tract* No. 99 (1918).

23 DAVID HIGGINS (1761–1842). Diary, 1841–1842. 1 volume. Gift of James G. Gibbs. MS 52.

The diary includes an autobiographical account in the middle of the volume. Rev. David Higgins was born in Haddam, Connecticut; fought with the militia during the Revolution; attended Dartmouth College and graduated from Yale; began preaching in 1786; and then began his travels which took him throughout the East. His writings contain much of his religious thought, and some comments on the religious revivalism of the first third of the 19th century. Some sections in this volume, apparently written by his wife, Eunice Higgins (1762–1843), contain copies of letters and some genealogical data.

24   CONSUL W. BUTTERFIELD (1824–1899). Papers, ca. 1849–1890. 3 boxes. MS 55.

Diaries, research materials, and original manuscript copies or printed editions (with handwritten revisions) of books and articles by Butterfield, historian and editor. Included are six diaries kept on a trip to California, 1849; one diary kept on a trip to San Francisco, 1851; and Butterfield's writings on William Crawford, the Washington-Crawford letters, LaSalle and La Durantaye, Simon Girty, and Jean Nicolet.

25   CLEVELAND CENTRAL HIGH. GRADUATES LITERARY SOCIETY. CLEVELAND, O. Records, 1855–1856. 1 volume. MS 57.

Constitution, bylaws, secretary's book, minutes of meetings, and lists of members.

26   YOUNG WOMEN'S CHRISTIAN TEMPERANCE UNION. SALEM, O. Records, 1889–1891. 1 volume. Gift of Mrs. Cooper, 1915. MS 65.

Secretary's book, including the constitution, pledge, list of members, and minutes of meetings.

27   WESTERN BAPTIST EDUCATION SOCIETY. CINCINNATI, O. Records, 1834–1842, 1848–1855. 3 volumes. Gift of the Estate of George E. Stevens. MS 67.

Constitution, list of officers, copies of letters, annual and financial reports, and minutes of annual, board, and executive meetings of this society which sought to provide an education at the Fairmount Theological Seminary for those wishing to enter the ministry.

28   ISAAC BACKUS (1724–1806). Papers, 1719–1805. 1 folder. Gift of Ambrose Swasey. MS 71.

Primarily letters addressed to and copies of letters sent by Rev. Isaac Backus, Baptist minister and historian. The letters from a variety of correspondents (notably William Richards) span

Backus' life. Also included is a copy made by Backus of an autobiographical account of the conversion of his wife, Susanna Martin (1725–1800); and a draft of a chapter of his *History of New England, with Particular Reference to the Denomination of Christians Called Baptists.*

29   KNIGHTS OF HONOR OF THE STATE OF OHIO. ANCHOR LODGE, NO. 119. ELYRIA, O. Records, 1875–1884. 1 volume. Gift of Eva L. Reefy, 1917. MS 79.

Bylaws, minutes of meetings, and lists of members.

30   GEORGE K. JENKINS. Papers, 1788–1877. 3½ boxes, 2 oversize volumes. Gift of Lillie Jenkins, 1918. MS 100.

Papers accumulated by George K. Jenkins, a Quaker schoolteacher and principal who resided in Mount Pleasant, Ohio, including records of various yearly and monthly meetings of the Society of Friends and other Quaker organizations. Among Jenkins' papers are copies of speeches and other writings on topics such as slavery, tobacco, and patriotism, ca. 1830's; and a journal kept on a trip to various Quaker colonies in Ohio, West Virginia, Indiana, Michigan, and Canada, in which Jenkins recorded his observations on these places as well as on the Wabash and Erie Canal, the Great Lakes, the St. Clair River, and the Free Soil Convention (Columbus, Ohio), April 30 to July 7, 1850.

Relating to Short Creek are minutes of meetings and lists of members, 1828–1836; lists of certificates, 1832–1877, and of marriages, 1832–1876; and the constitution and minutes of the Bible Association, 1847–1851. Records relating to schools in the Mount Pleasant area include a roll of the district school, 1839–1840; school and teachers' daily registers for Mount Pleasant High School, 1842–1858; minutes of the common-school examiners, 1843–1869, and constitution and minutes of the Mount Pleasant Township Sabbath School Union, 1869–1873; register for School District No. 5, 1845–1849; and record book of the Mount Pleasant Friends School Association, established in 1852, 1852–1869. Papers relating to the Free Produce Association, which sought "to promote the use and facilitate the acquirement of goods supplied by free labor," include minutes, inventories, and account books, 1842–1863. Also included are minutes of various meetings in Delaware, New Jersey, Pennsylvania, and Virginia, 1788–1840; minutes of New Garden Monthly Meetings, 1808–1837; minutes of Goshen Preparative Meetings, 1815–1832; an account (11 typescript pages) of the emigration of William Harrison from York County, Virginia, to Mount Pleasant in 1817; minutes of Ohio Yearly Meetings, 1845–1854, and an account book of the Ohio Yearly Meeting Committee on Indian Affairs, 1818–1859; and a memoranda book kept by David Updegraff on visits to Yearly Meetings in Indiana, Maryland, and Pennsylvania, 1849–1860.

31   ELIAS HARMON FAMILY. Papers, 1766–1885 (1795–1860). 14 boxes. Gift of Orrin Harmon, 1909. MS 104.

Correspondence, diaries, financial accounts and receipts, land deeds and memoranda of sales, legal documents, estate papers, powers of attorney, tax records, notebooks, surveys, and other papers relating to the activities of various members of the family of Elias Harmon (1775–1851), who moved to the Western Reserve from Suffield, Connecticut, in 1799 and settled in Mantua, Portage County. Elias Harmon held several public offices and was land agent for many Connecticut residents. Orrin Harmon (b. 1805) was also active in the land business and was surveyor for Portage County. Papers relating to his activities include references to his interest in the Protection Life Insurance Company of Hartford, the Franklin and Warren Railroad, the Pennsylvania and Ohio Canal, and the Independent Knights of Temperance, and in the fur trade and anti-slavery movement. Also included are some receipts and correspondence of Julian Harmon (b. 1835) and some school papers of Martin S. Harmon concerning Allegheny College, Franklin Institute (Ky.), and the Kentucky Military Institute. Although the bulk of this collection deals with land matters, there are frequent references to state and national politics, banking policies, the anti-slavery and anti-masonic movements, and general economic conditions; and a few references to the Millerites, Louis Kossuth's tour of Ohio in 1852, Elisha Whittlesey, and lotteries in the 1830's and 1850's. Unpublished 11-page register available in the Society.

32   SAMUEL BISSELL (1797-1895). Papers, 1797-1895, 1910-1933. 4 boxes. Gift of Mr. and Mrs. Fred L. Bissell, 1933. MS 116.

Sermons, account books, deeds, and other papers relating to the activities of Rev. Samuel Bissell, a Yale-educated Congregationalist minister and founder of the Twinsburg (Ohio) Institute. Specifically included are the following: diary kept on a visit to New Haven, Connecticut, 1819; album of autographs of Bissell's classmates at Yale, 1823; five account books (Twinsburg and Aurora, Ohio), 1825-1845, 1878-1895; six daybooks relating to the Twinsburg Institute, 1825-1875; correspondence with the Office of Indian Affairs, 1825-1895, and other papers concerning Bissell's efforts in behalf of Indian youths, 1847-1850; copies of 172 sermons delivered by Bissell, 1828-1882; and mortgage deeds, financial papers, and ledgers, 1834-1888.

Also included are some letters and receipts of Robert and Thankful Bissell (Samuel's parents) of Aurora, 1797-1855, and some correspondence with the Western Reserve Historical Society and the Samuel Bissell Memorial Library Association of Twinsburg, 1910-1933.

33   WILLIAM D. BICKHAM FAMILY. Papers, 1831-1917. 2 boxes. MS 133.

Autograph album of Maria Bickham and some personal correspondence, 1831-1917; a "Book of Literary Memoranda" by Elizabeth A. Strickle at Hygiea Female Athenaeum, 1846-1860; an account (194-page typescript copy) of William D. Bickham's sojourn in California during 1851; two scrapbooks containing newspaper clippings relating to the Civil War, including articles written by Bickham while he was correspondent for the *Cincinnati Daily Commercial*, 1861, 1863; and a journal recounting the birth and childhood of William Strickle Bickham as kept by his parents from 1856 to 1865.

34   OHIO GOVERNORS. Documents Signed By, 1787–1916. 2 oversize packages. MS 143.
Primarily commissions and other certificates signed by Ohio chief executives from the first governor, Edward Tiffin (1766–1829), to the 48th, Frank B. Willis (1871–1928). Also included are several documents signed by Arthur St. Clair (1736–1818), Governor of the Northwest Territory (1787–1802).

35   BARBER'S BENEVOLENT UNION. CLEVELAND, O. Record Book, 1874–1879. 1 volume. MS 146.
Preamble, constitution, bylaws, and minutes of this organization, the object of which was to assist "its members in sickness and to provide for their interment after death."

36   GENERAL RELIEF COMMITTEE. CLEVELAND, O. Records, 1871. 1 box. Gift of the Committee. MS 151.
Correspondence, shipping orders, lists of donors, and receipts relating to the activities of this committee (and particularly of its chairman, General James Barnett) which centered about the sending of tools, clothing, and food to areas burned out by fire in Michigan and Wisconsin and in Chicago, Illinois.

37   AMERICAN LIBRARY ASSOCIATION. CLEVELAND, O. Records, 1896. 1 folder. MS 152.
Cashbook and vouchers of the local committee of arrangements for the American Library Association's meeting in Cleveland. The financial accounts were recorded by Peter Neff, treasurer of the committee.

38   CLEVELAND INSURANCE COMPANY. CLEVELAND, O. Records, 1831–1865. 1 volume. MS 157.
Book of subscriptions for capital stock in the Cleveland Insurance Company, which was under the original superintendence of Peter M. Weddell, Leonard Case, Horace Perry, John M. Sterling, Edmund Clark, and James S. Clarke. Also included are minutes of

the directors' meetings and poll books of elections held to choose directors.

39   MECHANICS AND CITIZENS INSTITUTE OF CLEVELAND, OHIO. Records, 1857. 1 volume. MS 173.
Constitution and subscriptions of this organization which sought to encourage manufacturing, pursuit of the fine arts, and diffusion of useful knowledge by establishing a library for general circulation. H. B. Tuttle was the secretary.

40   JOSEPH BADGER (1757–1846). Papers, 1823–1841. 12 items. MS 200.
Copies of ten sermons, 1825–1841, delivered by Rev. Joseph Badger, the first missionary to settle in the Western Reserve. In addition to the sermons, most of which were delivered in Gustavus, Trumbull County, Ohio, there are also several pages from his diary concerning the building of a schoolhouse (1823) and a trip through Shawnee Indian country to Wauppaughkanetta (Wapakoneta, Ohio) which include observations on Indian customs and behavior.

Also included are four sermons delivered by Rev. Isaac Van Tassel, 1831–1848.

41   WHIG PARTY. OHIO. Records, ca. 1838. 1 volume. MS 204.
Lists of members in the Whig Party's central committee and committees of vigilance in towns and counties throughout the state of Ohio.

42   LUCIA VAN TASSEL. Notebooks, early 19th c. 2 volumes. MS 211.
Indian (possibly Ottawa) vocabulary and English translation prepared by Lucia Van Tassel (wife of Rev. Isaac Van Tassel) with the help of Lewis King, interpreter. The volumes were unfinished because of her illness and the removal of the Indians.

43   ANONYMOUS. Journal, 1824–1827. Purchased, 1924. MS 212.

This journal was kept by an unknown itinerant preacher who traveled from Princeton, New Jersey, through New York, Connecticut, Massachusetts, Pennsylvania, and Ohio. In Ohio, he preached at Sandusky, Norwalk, Elyria, Cleveland, Painesville, Madison, and several villages in Ashtabula County before leaving the Western Reserve. Included are brief comments on the places he visited, the people he met, and his unusual experiences.

44   MAYFIELD LYCEUM FOR THE PROMOTION OF THE SCIENCES AND ARTS AND USEFUL KNOWLEDGE. MAYFIELD, O. Records, 1843–1845. 1 volume. Gift of S. Prentiss Baldwin. MS 233.

Constitution, list of members, and minutes of this society, whose officers were R. Hall, E. D. Battles, and I. Leuty.

The second half of this volume contains inventories of the accounts and goods belonging to Isaac Leuty & Company which were transferred to the company of Candee & Scribner of New York City, as payment of a debt, 1846.

45   PRESBYTERY OF CLEVELAND. THE WOMEN'S FOREIGN MISSIONARY SOCIETY OF THE PRESBYTERY AND CITY OF CLEVELAND. Records, 1872–1914. 4 volumes. MS 241.

Constitution, names of members, minutes of quarterly and special meetings, and reports from the various sections located throughout Ohio. The object of this society was to assist in sending and sustaining female missionaries in foreign lands. On March 4, 1914, it was formally united with the Woman's Home Missionary Society.

46   ABRAHAM TAPPAN (1779–1855). Papers, 1803–1852. ½ box. MS 259.

Letters and field notes kept by Abraham Tappan while surveying land in the Western Reserve east of the Cuyahoga River, 1803–1805, and west of the Cuyahoga, 1806. Included are nine booklets of notes made while surveying Henry Champion's land in Concord Township (1804), the road from the Muskingum River to Lake Erie (1804), and the road from the mouth of the Grand River to Warren (1804); and eight booklets of notes relating to surveys made west of the Cuyahoga and north of the Tuscarawas River (1806). The letters are addressed to Tappan while he was surveyor and later postmaster (1820–1841) at Unionville, Ohio. Among the correspondents, who discuss land dealings, surveys, and politics in the Western Reserve, are Amzi Atwater, Caleb Atwater, Silas Axtell, Henry Champion, Zalmon Fitch, James A. Harper, Rice Harper, Turhand Kirtland, Edward Paine, Robert B. Parkman, Simon Perkins, Ashbel Walworth, John Walworth, Elisha Whittlesey, and Alfred Wolcott.

47   FIRST UNIVERSALIST CHURCH. BRIMFIELD, O. Records, 1839–1922. 3 volumes. Gift of Julia M. Moulton, 1962. MS 292.

Constitution, lists of members, minutes of regular, annual, and business meetings, and other church and pastoral records.

48   BARTLETT CLAN REUNION. Records, 1882–1894. 1 volume (copy). Gift of the Bartlett Clan Reunion (Mrs. F. O. Snow), 1895. MS 314.

Condensed reports of reunions held in Chester, Chardon, Munson, Strongsville, and Collinwood, Ohio; Collins, Lawton Station, and Kindara, New York; and Pontiac, Michigan.

49   ELROY McKENDREE AVERY (1844–1935). Papers, 1871–1893, and n.d. ½ box. MS 316.

Advertising contracts and several letters relating to the printing and sale of *Cleveland in a Nut-Shell* (Cleveland: Elroy M. Avery, 1893), 1893; four notebooks relating to schoolteaching, undated; and manuscript and typescript notes on the genealogy of the Avery family used by Elroy McKendree and Catherine Hitchcock Avery in compiling *The Groton Avery Clan*, 2 vols. (Cleveland, 1912).

[17]

50   EZRA AND WILLIAM H. LACEY. Papers, 1848–1866. ½ box. Gift of Mrs. Thomas Hardy, 1938. MS 317.

Includes bonds, deeds, and mortgages pertaining to land in Michigan which Ezra Lacey purchased from William Rice, 1848; records of land Ezra Lacey purchased and money he borrowed from William Jennison of Saginaw City, Michigan, 1850–1863; leases from William H. Lacey to various persons, 1859–1861; last will and testament of Ezra Lacey and other estate papers, 1860–1863; cashbook of William H. Lacey, 1860; and mortgage deeds to land in Hambden, Geauga County, Ohio, and Davies County, Missouri, 1863–1866.

51   ARTHUR ST. CLAIR (1736–1818). Papers, 1766–1844 (1790–1818). 1 box. Gift of Alfred T. Goodman, ca. 1871. MS 325.

Financial accounts and receipts, letters, military resolutions, and other documents relating to the activities of Arthur St. Clair, soldier, Pennsylvania political leader, and Governor of the Northwest Territory (1787–1802). The bulk of this collection consists of St. Clair's accounts with merchants, grocers, lawyers, laborers, and the Hermitage Furnace and Mill Creek Iron Works in Ligonier Valley, Pennsylvania. In addition there are 11 scattered letters, 1780–1802; papers relating to the handling of St. Clair's estate, 1818; and some financial accounts and several letters of Daniel St. Clair, Louisa St. Clair Robb, and Robert Graham.

52   JOHN KERR (d. 1823). Papers, 1788–1792, 1800–1822. 4 boxes. MS 330.

Letter and account books, field notes and survey books, and other papers relating to John Kerr of Columbus, Ohio, and the records of various businesses and literary societies with which Kerr was associated. Kerr, a native of Ireland, participated in the movement to have the state capital located in Columbus (opposite Kerr's home city of Franklinton); served on Columbus' first city council in 1816 and as mayor (1818–1819); and acted as agent for a Columbus land syndicate (1813–1815). Specifically included are the following: arithmetic and music books, 1788–1792; diary kept on a trip on the Ohio and Hocking rivers, ca. 1800; field books relating to surveys of land in and around Columbus, 1800–1821; letter and invoice books of John Kerr and Company primarily in account with Alexander McLaughlin, 1801–1807; record books of the Chillicothe Polemic Society, January 25–March 31, 1803, and of the Chillicothe Library, 1804–1813; memoranda books pertaining to the sale of land in Columbus, 1813–1821; survey notes and record book for the Franklinton Turnpike Road Company, 1817–1818; and tax lists for Columbus, 1821, and for Montgomery County, 1822.

53   JOHN WELD BROWN (b. 1828). Letters, 1851–1863, 1866. 1 folder. Gift of Marian L. Whitsey. MS 350.

Letters from John Weld Brown addressed to various relatives (in Cuyahoga County, Ohio, and in Rhode Island) in which he relates his experiences on a journey from Cleveland, Ohio, to Nevada City, California, 1851–1852, and his subsequent activities as a farmer, trader, and gold miner in and around Nevada City, Marysville, and Yuba City, California. Brown's letters touch upon the hardships of the trip by boat to the West, the economic situation in California between 1852 and 1863, and personal and family matters.

54   CLEVELAND CONFERENCE FOR EDUCATIONAL COOPERATION. CLEVELAND, O. Records, 1924–1929. 1 box. MS 362.

Minutes of executive committee and annual meetings, various committee reports, and notices of events sponsored by this organization which sought to stimulate educational activities in Cleveland, primarily by encouraging inter-institutional exchanges of services among its member organizations. These include the Cleveland Museum of Art, Western Reserve Historical Society, Cleveland Public Library, Cleveland School of Art, Cleveland Museum of Natural History, Cleveland Public Schools, and Cleveland Institute of Music. Areas of special interest include adult education, sites and finances, vocational education and guidance, teacher training, and research and graduate instruction. These records were accumulated by Wallace H. Cathcart, who represented the Western Reserve Historical Society.

55   AMERICAN FUR COMPANY. MICHILIMACKINAC, MICH. Records, 1795–1842. ½ box. Gift of A. T. Goodman. MS 371.

Letters addressed to Robert Stuart, agent of the American Fur Company, 1821–1842; papers and letters addressed to Samuel Abbott, notary public in Michilimackinac, relating to trade and Indian affairs; American Fur Company shipping bills, 1834–1839; and various agreements and certificates relating to trade.

56   OHIO & ERIE CANAL. CHILLICOTHE, O. Records, 1848–1883. 1 volume. Purchased. MS 382.

Register of boats on the canal kept by the canal commissioners at Chillicothe.

57   REFORMED PRESBYTERIAN CHURCH. XENIA, O. Records, 1859–1882. 1 volume. MS 383.

Minutes of meetings of the Xenia session of the Associate Synod of North America.

58   MUSKINGUM PRESBYTERY. OHIO. Records, 1861–1887. 1 volume. MS 384.

Minutes of meetings of the Presbytery of Muskingum, which the Associate Synod of North America sought to revive in 1861.

59   SOUTHINGTON PHILOMATHIC SOCIETY. SOUTHINGTON, CONN. Record Book, 1807–1812. 1 volume. Gift of J. Whittlesey Walton, 1898. MS 385.

Constitution and minutes of this debate society. Among the early members were Asoph Whittlesey, Levi Langton, Lemuel Clark,

Chester Brannis, Alphin Clark, Lenos Bronson, and Simeon Bristol.

60   CONGREGATIONAL CHURCH. ECCLESIASTICAL SOCIETY. AUSTINBURG, O. Record Book, 1831–1854. 1 volume. MS 386.

Minutes of meetings, resolutions, and reports pertaining to church matters.

61   ASHTABULA COUNTY FEMALE ANTI-SLAVERY SOCIETY. ASHTABULA, O. Records, 1835–1837. 1 volume. MS 387.

Preamble, constitution, list of members, music notes for various songs, minutes of meetings, and a list of names of memorialists for 1836. An auxiliary to the Ohio Anti-Slavery Society, this organization sought to disseminate information on slavery and to promote advancement of colored people.

62   EAST CLEVELAND LITERARY AND SCIENTIFIC CIRCLE. CLEVELAND, O. Records, 1878–1882. 1 volume. Gift of Mrs. P. H. Sawyer, 1912. MS 388.

Constitution, list of members, and minutes of meetings. The membership included Prof. Charles Penfield, Rev. J. M. Hall, H. H. Hamlen, Julius King, Prof. Z. P. Taylor, Charles Preston, W. C. Wheedon, Elizabeth J. House (secretary), and Myra F. Fenton (secretary).

63   BEDFORD FEMALE BENEVOLENT SEWING SOCIETY. BEDFORD, O. Records, 1848–1851. 1 volume. MS 389.

Constitution, membership lists, dues records, and results of frequent elections for officers. Men were allowed to join soon after this society was founded.

64 BOANERGEAN LODGE. BURTON, O. Account Book, 1855–1857. 1 volume. Gift of the Hitchcock Estate. MS 391.

List of members and account records of members of this lodge.

65 LUTHER RICHARD PRENTISS (1803–1897). Papers, 1832–1852. 1 volume. Gift of Mendon L. Prentiss and Willard C. Prentiss, 1898. MS 394.

Agreement to clean and clear eight acres of land for James Kingsbury in Newburgh, Ohio; deed to lots in Warrensville, Ohio, 1832; docket book of Luther Prentiss, who was justice of the peace in Warrensville Township, 1841–1853; summonses and orders to constables to summon persons, 1847–1852; and miscellaneous receipts for court fees.

66 HENRY W. SMITH. Papers, 1836–1869. 1 folder, 1 volume. MS 397.

Scattered financial papers, tax receipts, certificates, contracts, and letters addressed to Smith, sheriff of Trumbull County, Ohio, and a director of the Pennsylvania and Ohio Canal Company during the 1840's. Also included is a contract concerning land purchased by Henry W. Smith and David Tod from F. Freeman in Warren, Ohio, 1840–1868.

67 AMASA D. SPROAT. Notebook, 1810. 1 volume. Gift of William H. Murray, 1921. MS 398.

Notes taken at medical lectures given by Drs. Benjamin Smith Barton (1766–1815) and Benjamin Rush (1745–1813) at the University of Pennsylvania.

68 FIRST NEW JERUSALEM SOCIETY OF CHILLICOTHE, O. Record Book, 1838–1879. 1 volume. Purchased. MS 399.

Minutes of meetings, list of members, copies of agreements, and letters. The original record book having been destroyed in a fire, the pre-1857 records were recorded from memory by Amasa D. Sproat, secretary of this religious society.

69   MANASSEH CUTLER (1742–1823). Journals, 1787–1807. 2 volumes (copied from originals in 1858 and ca. 1880). MS 400.

The first journal (copied by S. P. Hildreth in 1858) covers the period from June 25 until August 4, 1787, during which time Cutler journeyed from Ipswich, Massachusetts, to New York and Philadelphia while negotiating a contract with Congress for the purchase of lands for the Ohio Company. The second journal (taken from a copy in the possession of Rev. Stephen D. Peet, ca. 1880) covers the period from July 21 to mid-October, 1788, during which Cutler visited the Ohio Company purchase near the junction of the Muskingum and Ohio rivers. Also included in the second volume is a copy of a journal of Rev. Joseph Badger, 1803–1807.

70   JOHN MAY FAMILY. Papers, 1752–1875. 15 boxes. Purchased, 1909. MS 401.

Correspondence, business papers, financial accounts and receipts, speeches, certificates, estate papers, and other materials belonging to various members of this New England family, including John May (1748–1812), soldier, wharfinger, and land agent for the Ohio Company of Associates; Henry Knox May (1780–1865), merchant, shipper, and wharfinger; and Edward Tuckerman May (b. 1824), Boston Custom House agent. The papers of John May, which fill three boxes and cover the period 1752–1821 (1780–1811), reflect his speculations in land in New England and Ohio, his career as an officer in a regiment of Boston militia during the Revolutionary War (particularly during 1780), and his business activities as wharfinger of Union Wharf (May's Wharf) in Boston, but are concerned primarily with his activities as a member and agent for the Ohio Company of Associates from 1780 to 1811. In this latter connection the papers include maps, lists of shareholders, financial reports, correspondence, laborers' accounts, speeches, minutes of meetings, proclamations, and commissions.* His correspondents include James and Elizabeth Bowdoin, Manasseh Cutler, J. P. Cushing, William Ewing, Richard Platt, William Rufus Putnam, Benjamin Tallmadge, Samuel Tenney, and Ebenezer Thayer, Jr.

The papers of Henry Knox May, which fill 11 boxes and cover the period 1794–1847 (1812–1840), relate to both his business and his personal life. His correspondence, financial papers, memoranda, shipping papers, and legal papers present a chronicle of his activities as an agent for New England merchants in Alexandria, Virginia; as a merchant and shipmaster; and as part-owner and wharfinger for Union Wharf in Boston, ca. 1817–1839. Other subjects touched upon here relate to Ohio lands, the Alexandria Canal Company, the Second Church of Boston, local and international shipping, and local and national Whig and National Republican politics. Henry Knox May's correspondents from New England and New York include Josiah Barnard, Levi Bates, N. J. Bowditch, J. P. Cooke, George Fosdick, Nathaniel Goddard, Charles Loring, Theodore Lyman, Edward Tuckerman, Henry Ware, and Isaac Winslow; and from other states, Henry Burke, Abigail Deming, William Fowler, and Joseph W. Riddle.

The Edward Tuckerman May papers fill one box, cover the period 1860–1875, and consist of correspondence, financial papers, railroad passes, and business cards, some of which pertain to his work in the Boston Custom House.

Unpublished 12-page register available in the Society.

* Approximately one-third of the papers relating to the Ohio Company have been published in "Side Lights on the Ohio Company of Associates from the John May Papers," W.R.H.S. *Tract* No. 97 (1917).

71 AMOS TOWNSEND (1821–1895). Papers, ca. 1880. 2 volumes. Gift of Amos Townsend, 1895. MS 407.

List of names of persons residing in Cuyahoga County, arranged according to the township in which they lived, along with the nationality, political affiliation, occupation, and address of each.

Townsend, a wholesale grocer in Cleveland, served as a U.S. representative (1877–1883).

72   HENRY GEROULD (1824–1900). Papers, 1841–1888. 1 box. Gift of the Family of H. Gerould. MS 409.

Three cashbooks of Dr. Henry Gerould, who practiced medicine in Bedford and Cleveland, 1860–1873, and undated; and papers relating to the estates of Thomas J. Clapp and Lorinda Clapp of Cleveland, as executed by Henry Gerould, 1886–1888. Some of the Clapp family papers include land deeds and leases which date back to 1841.

73   WOODLAND AVENUE METHODIST-EPISCOPAL CHURCH. CLEVELAND, O. Record Book, 1874–1886. 1 volume. MS 415.

Lists of names of pastors, members, and probationers, and quarterly conference records (1883–1885).

74   PRESBYTERY OF ELYRIA. ELYRIA COUNTY, O. Record Book, 1864–1866. 1 volume. Gift of E. Bushler. MS 418.

Standing rules and minutes of meetings held in towns throughout this county. These meetings concern activities within this presbytery, relations with other presbyteries, and missionary activities.

75   FIRST CONGREGATIONAL CHURCH. FRANKLIN, O. Records, 1819–1898. 7 volumes. Purchased, 1921. MS 421.

Confession of faith, covenant, articles of practice, minutes of meetings, and list of members (1838) of the First Presbyterian Church (1 volume), 1819–1839, which then became the First Congregational Church, and which now is the Kent Congregational Church; act of incorporation, preamble, names of members, bylaws, and minutes of meetings of the First Congregational Society of Franklin (1 volume), 1832–1892; minutes of general, annual, and special meetings of the First Congregational Church (4 volumes), 1839–1898; records of the Ladies Benevolent Sewing Society of Franklin (1 volume), 1849–1859; and records of the Ladies Aid Society of Franklin, 1857–1861.

76   LEONARD WILSON, *collector*. Papers Relating to the Santiago Campaign, 1898–1907. 2 volumes. Gift of Leonard Wilson, 1911. MS 427.

Letters and report on the situation in Cuba collected by Leonard Wilson, military secretary and aide-de-camp to Major General Joseph Wheeler. In addition to General Wheeler, the correspondents include J. C. Breckenridge, J. H. Dorst, William E. English, E. J. McClernand, Elihu Root, S. S. Sumner, Leonard Wilson, and August Ziegler.

77   OHIO MILITIA. 4TH DIVISION. Records, 1807–1830. 1 volume. Gift of Mrs. H. N. Chittenden, 1873. MS 428.

Orders, class rolls, record of appointments, and court-of-inquiry reports.

78   MRS. FITCH. Journal and Copybook, ca. 1809. 1 volume. MS 429.

Hymns, poems, recipes, sermons, and passages copied from the Bible.

79   "THE BOQUET OF THE SOCIAL BAND," 1844–1846. 1 volume. Gift of the Estate of Solon Severance. MS 434.

Poems and essays submitted to the Cleveland editors of "The Boquet," which was written out in the form of a literary periodical.

80   OHIO UNIVERSITY. ATHENS, O. Journal, 1818–1826. 1 volume. Gift of Wallace H. Cathcart, 1910. MS 436.

Receipts issued for rent payments, 1818–1823; and a record of fines and tuition payments received by Dr. John Brown, treasurer of Ohio University, 1824–1826.

81   UNITED PRESBYTERIAN CHURCH. WEST UNION, O. Records, 1840–1894. 1 volume. Gift of Wallace H. Cathcart, 1910. MS 438.

Resolutions and proceedings of this church which was the Associate Reformed Church until 1860, and which disbanded in 1894.

82   PROTESTANT EPISCOPAL CHURCH. ST. JOHN'S MISSION. CAMBRIDGE, O. Records, 1884–1893. 1 volume. Gift of Burrows Brothers Company, 1914. MS 439.

Minutes of meetings, reports of the executive committee, and correspondence received by the executive committee and Dr. William T. Ramsey, including letters from William Martin Aiken, a Cincinnati architect, regarding the construction of a chapel.

83   MENTOR AND WILLOUGHBY PLAINS TEMPERANCE SOCIETY. OHIO. Records, 1839–1842. 1 volume. Gift of the Estate of Martin E. Gray, 1910. MS 442.

Constitution, list of members, and minutes of meetings.

The second half of this volume contains farm accounts of Martin E. Gray, 1854–1874.

84   LADIES AID SOCIETY OF BROCTON, O. Records, January 14–February 15, 1866. 1 volume. MS 443.

Minutes of meetings, a list of members, and a few poems by members of this society, the object of which was "to furnish physical, moral, and intellectual aid to the colored people, who have recently been in bondage." This society was an auxiliary to the New York National Freedmen's Relief Association.

85   PRESBYTERY OF LORAIN, O. Records, 1836–1839. PRESBYTERY OF ELYRIA, O. Records, 1842–1863. 1 volume. Gift of E. Bushnell. MS 444.

Proceedings of the Presbytery of Lorain until its dissolution and amalgamation with the Presbytery of Huron in 1839. The largest part of this volume contains the proceedings of the Presbytery of Elyria.

86   FRANKLIN CLUB. CLEVELAND, O. Records, 1895–1901. 2 volumes. Gift of the U.S. Marshal, 1907. MS 445.

Minutes of meetings of this club, at which Leon Czolgosz heard Emma Goldman elucidate her anarchical views on May 5, 1901. Four months later Czolgosz assassinated President William McKinley. These volumes were surrendered to the U.S. Marshal by Howard Dennis, and later turned over to the Western Reserve Historical Society.

87   JOHN D. ROCKEFELLER (1839–1937). Memorial Album, September 26, 1905. 1 volume. Gift of John D. Rockefeller. MS 446.

Original copy of the memorial volume issued by the Chamber of Commerce to commemorate a visit paid to Mr. Rockefeller by 300 Cleveland businessmen, including copies of speeches made by Andrew Squire, Liberty E. Holden, and John D. Rockefeller, and the signatures of the 300 visitors.

88   FREEMASONS. MASONIC LODGE NO. 65. NEW LISBON, O. Records, 1822–1833. 1 volume. MS 448.

Bylaws, subscribers, and minutes of meetings.

89 GRAND ARMY OF THE REPUBLIC. DEPARTMENT OF OHIO. TRESCOTT POST NO. 10. SALEM, O. Records, 1868–1874. 1 volume. Gift of Trescott Post No. 10. MS 449.

Minutes of meetings of the Trescott Post. Also included is an 11-page "History of Trescott Post No. 10, Dept. of Ohio, G.A.R.," by J. S. Clemmer, April 6, 1891.

90 JOHN W. NORTHROP. Diary, May 3–November 23, 1864. 2 volumes. Gift of Trescott Post No. 10, Grand Army of the Republic, Salem, O. MS 450.

Detailed account of prison life at Andersonville Prison in Georgia. Northrop, from Salem, Ohio, reports on his battle experiences, capture, and confinement, and on general features of the Civil War. He served in the Ohio Volunteer Infantry, possibly in the 103rd Regiment.

91 OHIO RAILROAD COMPANY. PAINESVILLE AND CLEVELAND, O. Records, 1836–1842. 3 volumes. Gift of G. A. Hyde, 1897. MS 451.

List of subscribers to the capital stock of this company, along with records relating to the purchase of and payment for stock and to the financial disbursements of this company which was organized in 1836 in Painesville. Until it collapsed in 1843, this railroad's financial offices were in Cleveland.

92 SAMUEL L. EGBERT. Account Book, 1830–1836. 1 volume. Gift of Sidney S. Wilson. MS 454.

In account with Asa Archer, Paul Clifford, Samuel Doan, David McDowell, Melancton Miller, Jeremiah Presley, John Presley, Richard Presley, and others.

93   FREDERICK WADSWORTH AND ELISHA WHIT-
          TLESEY. Unpublished Manuscript, ca. 1860. 1 volume.
          Gift of Charles Whittlesey. MS 455.

A "History of Canfield" compiled by Wadsworth and Whittlesey from 1858 to 1860 and written down by Wadsworth. Included are militia, tax, marriage, church, and census records of Canfield, Trumbull County, Ohio.

94   (GEORGE H. SAVAIN?) Daybooks, 1856–1859. 2 vol-
          umes. MS 456.

Remarks recorded while on board the *Lexington* (on the North and South Pacific and Indian oceans), the schooner *Secreto,* and the bark *United States,* all of which were whaling vessels.

95   CLINTON LINE RAILROAD COMPANY. HUDSON,
          O. Records, 1852–1859. 1 volume. Gift of W. A. Ingham,
          1894. MS 463.

Minutes of meetings, bylaws, resolutions, proceedings of board meetings, and a list of stockholders.

96   YDRAD BOAT CLUB. CLEVELAND, O. Records,
          1861–1862. 1 volume. Gift of S. P. Baldwin, 1917. MS
          464.

Constitution, bylaws, and minutes of meetings.

97   MORNING MUSICAL CLUB OF CLEVELAND. Rec-
          ords, 1893–1900, 1914. 3 volumes. Gift of Mrs. L. B.
          Comstock, 1915. MS 465.

Constitution, programs, and minutes of meetings.

98   RUDOLPHUS EDWARDS (1759–1840). Papers, 1794–
          1818, 1821, 1869. 10 items. Gift of Rudolphus Edwards
          II, 1868. MS 466.

Includes seven deeds to tracts of land (mostly in Cleveland), 1794–1814; Edwards' docket book while serving as a justice of the peace, 1815–1818; and a biographical sketch (1869) of Edwards, a merchant in Herkimer County, New York, who settled in Cleveland in 1798 and who was elected Cleveland Township's chairman during its first election in 1802.

99   JERVIS CUTLER (1768-1844). Notebook, 1840's. 1 volume. Gift of the Estate of Caleb Emerson. MS 467.

Descriptions of the Louisiana Bayou country, including Indian life, the rivers, and the settlements; of the state of Ohio and its early settlements; and of other regions along the Mississippi Valley.

100   GRAND ARMY OF THE REPUBLIC. DEPARTMENT OF OHIO. BROUGH POST NO. 359. COLLINWOOD, O. Records, ca. 1900. 1 volume. Gift of the Post, 1909. MS 469.

Personal war sketches of members of Brough Post No. 359, including Joseph L. Baldwin, R. L. Chittenden, Henry M. Frissell, J. F. Herrick, George Carleton Mapes, and Alonzo Waters.

101   MITTLEBERGER SCHOOL. CLEVELAND, O. Records, 1895-1908. 33 volumes. Gift of Augusta Mittleberger, 1908. MS 470.

Daily attendance and grade reports and other records of this private school organized by Augusta Mittleberger in 1877. The school served students—many from outside of Cleveland—from kindergarten to college level until it closed in 1908. Also included are record books of the Happy Thought Society, 1895-1908; physical records of the students, 1892-1902; and registers for the primary grade, 1897-1908.

102   LICKING LAND COMPANY. LICKING COUNTY, O. Records, 1804-1806. 1 volume (manuscript copy). MS 476.

Articles of agreement, regulations, proceedings, and lists of subscribers of this company which bought and settled Granville Township, Licking County, Ohio.

103 MT. LEIGH PRESBYTERIAN CHURCH. WEST UNION, O. Records, 1838–1851. 1 volume. Gift of Wallace H. Cathcart, 1910. MS 477.

Minutes of session meetings including reports of persons examined, certified, suspended, and baptized.

104 WILLOUGHBY COLLEGE. ARCADIAN LITERARY SOCIETY. WILLOUGHBY, O. Record Books, 1875–1884. 3 volumes. Gift of Sidney S. Wilson, 1911. MS 479.

Secretaries' books containing names of members, minutes of meetings, programs, and exercises.

105 PRESBYTERY OF WESTERN RESERVE, OHIO. Records, 1858–1870. 1 volume. MS 482.

Roll of this presbytery and minutes of meetings.

106 LINDA THAYER GUILFORD (1823–1911). Papers, 1855–1906. 1 box, 1 oversize volume. MS 484.

Copies of writings and speeches, notes on early Cleveland schools, letters, newspaper clippings, and a scrapbook concerning Miss Guilford's activities as a teacher at the Cleveland Female Seminary and the Cleveland Academy. In addition to her work in Cleveland schools, Miss Guilford, who settled in Cleveland in 1848, was active in the temperance movement. Relating to this interest are letters addressed to her, 1880–1895; the secretary's book of the Young Ladies Temperance League, 1882–1885; and minutes and newspaper clippings concerning the Young Ladies League for Temperance Education, Cleveland, 1885–1890.

107 IRAD KELLEY (1791–1875). Papers, 1818–1874. 1 box. Gift of Norman E. Hills, 1915. MS 485.

Land deeds and leases, financial accounts and receipts, business papers, insurance policies, newspaper clippings, and some letters addressed to Irad Kelley, a Cleveland merchant, postmaster

(1818), real estate investor, co-owner (with his brother, Datus) of Kelley's Island in Lake Erie, and unsuccessful candidate for the U.S. Congress (1850). Included is a postmaster's record book, 1818–1829; cashbook, 1831–1874; and scrapbook, 1860's. Correspondents include John W. Allen, Millard Fillmore, Alfred Kelley, Datus Kelley, Edwin Kelley, and Elisha Whittlesey.

108 A. F. SMITH. Plantation Records, 1851–1852. 1 volume. Gift of Dr. H. C. Coates. MS 489.

Including inventory of stock and implements, daily record of events, and records of births and deaths of Negroes on the A. F. Smith plantation in Princeton, Mississippi.

109 MEDICAL SOCIETY OF OHIO. 16TH MEDICAL DISTRICT. Records, 1824–1830. 1 volume. Purchased, 1914. MS 492.

Minutes of meetings held in Mount Pleasant, Smithfield, and Steubenville, Ohio.

110 PETER NEFF (1798–1878). Reminiscences, ca. 1840. 1 volume (32 pp.). Purchased, 1914. MS 493.

Neff was at different times a partner of Charles Bird, Henry Bird, and Samuel Nightingale in the hardware business in Baltimore, Maryland, between 1818 and 1828. In 1835, he settled in Cincinnati, Ohio, where he continued in business and was active in banking. His reminiscences contain references to his family, to his personal and business life, and also to his interests while in Cincinnati in the church (Presbyterian) and in temperance.

111 WILLOUGHBY COLLEGE. DELTA KAPPA CHI. WILLOUGHBY, O. Record Book, 1866–1871. 1 volume. Gift of Sidney S. Wilson, 1911. MS 495.

Roll, minutes of meetings, reports, and financial minutes.

112   PRESBYTERY OF GRAND RIVER, O. Records, 1814–1818, 1829–1870. 5 volumes. Gift of Carroll Cutler for the Presbytery of Cleveland, 1876. MS 500.

Copy of the original petition to form the Presbytery of Grand River, annual presbyterial reports, and minutes of meetings held in Euclid, Burton, Hudson, Geneva, Warren, Austinburg, and other cities throughout northeastern Ohio.

113   PRESBYTERY OF PORTAGE, O. Records, 1818–1843. Gift of the Presbytery of Cleveland, 1876. ½ box. MS 501.

Minutes of synod meetings, preamble and regulations, covenant, resolutions, and minutes of regular and annual meetings.

114   NATHAN STARR. Papers, 1821–1846. 1 folder. Gift of Frank F. Starr, 1917, 1932. MS 505.

Deeds and lists of lands in Cuyahoga, Medina, and Summit counties, Ohio, released or sold by Nathan Starr, a sword and gun manufacturer in Middletown, Connecticut, after whom the Summit County community of Western Star was named. Also included are several letters concerning a shipment of gun stocks, 1827, and the construction of the Western Star Seminary in Wadsworth, Ohio, 1844. Correspondents include John W. Allen, Dudley Griswold, and Alfred Kelley.

115   MERRIMAN COOK (d. 1858). Papers, 1786–1860. 1 folder. MS 521.

Land deeds to lots in Cheshire, New Haven County, Connecticut, 1786–1805; miscellaneous account and financial papers, 1791–1840; account book, June–July, 1806; personal correspondence of Elzar, John, and Merriman Cook, 1813–1823; tax-payment receipts from Geauga County, Ohio, 1823–1860; and deeds to land in Burton, Ohio, 1825–1839.

116   WAU LEE. Account Book, 1873–1875. 1 volume. Gift of Wau Lee through Dr. E. Sterling, 1875. MS 522.

Wau Lee was the first Chinese laundryman in Cleveland, Ohio.

117   JOHN M. HENDERSON. Papers, 1818–1850. 1 box. MS 533.

Letters addressed to Dr. Henderson which relate primarily to the Willoughby (Ohio) Medical College and to other matters concerning medical education, and resolutions passed at faculty meetings held at the college, 1835–1838; an account book, 1823–1825; and warrants, subpoenas, and receipts signed by Henderson, justice of the peace in Willoughby, 1834–1850.

118   VIRGINIA MILITIA. Records, 1812–1815. ½ box (copies). MS 534.

Copies of muster rolls, payrolls, general orders, and correspondence, most of which pertains to the activities of various units of the Virginia Militia during the War of 1812.

119   RURAL RETREAT LITERARY SOCIETY. [OHIO?]. Records, 1856–1858. 1 volume. MS 538.

Minutes of meetings. Among the members were Sallie Bonsall, S. J. Firestone, Samuel Galbreath, James Morgan, P. H. Ward, Elijah Whinery, and Joshua Whinery.

120   REGULAR BAPTIST CHURCH. CHARDON, O. Records, 1831–1905. ½ box. MS 542.

Articles of faith, covenant, minutes of meetings, lists of members, and records of deaths in two volumes, 1831–1903; certificates of recommendation, 1844–1903; and miscellaneous minutes of meetings, 1896–1905.

121   GEORGE W. LANDRUM (1830–1863). Letters, 1861–1863. 1 volume (typescript copies bound). Gift of Mrs. Obed J. (Amanda Landrum) Wilson. MS 543.

Primarily letters sent to Landrum's sister, Mrs. Obed J. Wilson, containing descriptions of camp life and of the various military encounters in which Landrum took part during the Civil War, such as Chaplin Hills (Perryville) and Stone River (Murfreesboro). Landrum, born in Augusta, Kentucky, moved to Cincinnati, joined the "Guthrie Grey" Regiment after the firing upon Fort Sumter, and was assigned to the Signal Corps, in which he served until his death at Chickamauga.

122 WOOSTER REGULAR BAPTIST ASSOCIATION. MASSILLON, O. Records, 1840–1881. 1 volume. Gift of Miss Shawn. MS 545.

Constitution, rules of order, and minutes of the 42 anniversary meetings held by this association.

123 OHIO MILITIA. 4TH DIVISION. Record Book, 1809–1867. 1 volume. Purchased, 1921. MS 547.

Muster rolls and returns of the 2nd Brigade under the command of General Reasin Beall; and general orders, minutes of meetings, and rank rolls of officers.

124 A. J. WARNER. Records and Account Book, 1858–1863. 1 volume. Gift of the Warner Family. MS 548.

Quarterly school rolls, 1858–1859; Lewiston, Pennsylvania, farm accounts, 1859; general and current accounts, 1859–1863.

In the back of this volume is a 41-page account of the Battle of Antietam (September 17, 1862) and the Battle of South Mountain (September 14, 1862) written by Warner, who was a participant in these engagements.

125 ANONYMOUS. Copybook, 1843–1849. 1 volume. MS 552.

Copies of articles, containing the author's philosophy of life, prepared for "The Newark [Ohio?] Institute," the "Newark Gazette," and "The Club"; "A Disquisition concerning Religion in General, by Dr. Sherwood, September A.D. 1849."

126 WESTERN ANTI-SLAVERY SOCIETY. [ALLIANCE, O.]. Records, 1857–1864. 1 volume. Gift of William P. Palmer, 1921. MS 554.

Minute book of the executive committee, including the bylaws and the annual reports of the executive committee, which were printed in the *Anti-Slavery Bugle* (Salem, Ohio).

127 GEORGE SOSMAN FAMILY. Papers, 1832–1871. ½ box. Purchased, 1921. MS 555.

Letters and diaries of various members of this family from Chillicothe, Ohio. Included are letters to George and Lucretia Browning Sosman from Wesley Browning, a Methodist (?) minister, and his wife, Phebe, who attended religious conferences in the Midwest and Mississippi Valley region and conducted manual-labor schools among the Indians of the Shawnee and Choctaw nations, 1835–1845; diaries of George Sosman, in which are recorded some comments on his farming activities, 1853, 1858, 1859; a series of letters of John F. Sosman, 73rd Regiment, Ohio Volunteer Infantry, while stationed in Pendleton County, Virginia, April–July, 1862, and his diary kept from October, 1861, until his death in August, 1862; and three diaries of Frank A. Sosman, a clerk and bookkeeper in Chillicothe, 1867–1869.

128 CATHARINE B. SMITH. Albums, 1843–1853. 2 volumes. Gift of Miss Lillie Jenkins. MS 557.

Poems written by or addressed to Catharine Smith, a Quaker and resident of Mount Pleasant, Ohio.

129 JOHN BUTLER. Papers, 1862–1885. ½ box. MS 559.

Journals, diaries, and copies of letters relating to John Butler's activities as a member of the Society of Friends while residing in Salem, Ohio, and while traveling throughout the Midwest. Among the papers are an excerpt from Butler's journal containing an account of an interview that he, as a delegate from the Ohio Yearly Meeting of Orthodox Friends, had with President

Abraham Lincoln concerning the question of drafting Quakers for military service, September, 1862; copies of letters sent to President Lincoln and U.S. Congressman James A. Garfield stating the Society of Friends' opposition to the Civil War and to military conscription, and a short journal kept by Butler while on a trip to Washington, D.C., for the purpose of supporting legislation to exempt Quakers from military service, 1862–1865; an account of a trip to visit friends and relatives in Iowa and Illinois, 1862–1863; a diary kept on a trip to attend the Indiana Yearly Meeting and on subsequent travels through freedmen's camps in the South, 1864; an account of a trip to Kansas to visit Indian agents and tribes, 1869; and a record of the miles traveled and expenses incurred in behalf of Yearly Meetings on Indian matters, 1868–1884.

130   YOUNG MEN'S CHRISTIAN ASSOCIATION. TOLEDO, O. Record Book, 1887–1889. 1 volume. MS 560.
Committee, class, lecture, membership, and junior department records. Also included are some records of the Soul Winner's League, Toledo, Ohio, which was composed of members of the Young Men's Christian Association and which sought "to train Young Men for Christian Work and to engage them in active service for the salvation of unconverted Young Men."

131   THOMAS JAMES & COMPANY. CHILLICOTHE, O. Records, 1831–1834. 1 volume. MS 563.
Shipping receipts of railroads and boats promising delivery of materials from Thomas James & Company.

132   COLLECTION OF ACCOUNT BOOKS, 1770–1920. 54 volumes. Gifts of various persons, combined for ease of access in 1969. MS 565.
Adams Express Company. [Cleveland, O.?]. 1 volume, January–February, 1871.
A. D. Anderson & Company. [Location?]. 1 volume, November 26–December 17, 1860.

Anonymous (wood carder and cloth dresser). [Location?]. 1 volume, 1823–1828.
Anonymous. Jefferson, O. 1 volume, 1824–1854.
Anonymous (merchant). Cleveland, O. 1 volume, 1825–1826.
Anonymous. Mentor and Willoughby, O. 1 volume, 1833–1844.
Anonymous. Painesville, O. 1 volume, 1838–1840.
Baldwin, Edward. Cuyahoga County, O. 1 volume, 1824–1843.
Boughton, George. Trumbull County, O. 1 volume, 1823–1848.
Brough, John (tavern keeper). (Marietta, [O.?]). 1 volume, 1802–1821.
Bunts, Hermes (wool carder). Madison, Lake County, O. 1 volume, 1852–1861.
Clapp, Thomas J. (farmer). [Cuyahoga County, O.?]. 2 volumes, 1844–1871.
Codding, G. M. (d. 1849). Summit County, O. 1 volume, 1838–1852.
Cooper, John (jurist). Easton, Pa. 2 volumes, 1821–1857.
D. W. Anderson & Company. [Location?]. 2 volumes, 1861–1863.
Everett, Azariah (doctor). Cleveland, O. 1 volume, 1854–1874.
Farr, Eliel (civil engineer). Rockport, O. 1 volume, 1820–1842.
Fenton, John. Bloomfield, O. 1 volume, 1845–1857.
Fourth Ward Relief Committee. Cleveland, O. 1 volume, 1863–1865. Also memoranda of lots sold on Woodland Hills in Cleveland, 1882–1895.
Gaylord, E. F. [Cleveland, O.?]. 1 volume, 1848–1877.
George B. Ogden & Company (Great Lakes shipping). Cleveland, O. 1 volume, 1832–1833.
Gridley, A. [Location?]. 1 volume, 1848–1852.
Hayden, M. M. Cleveland, O. 1 volume, 1841–1842.
Head, B. [Location?]. 1 volume, March–November, 1804.
Hogan & Wilson (merchants). Bedford, O. 1 volume, March–July, 1827. Also random notes and meteorological data of James B. Wilson of Willoughby, Ohio, 1840–1880.
Hunt, William S. (farm laborer). Charlestown, O. 1 volume, 1841–1854.
Huntington, Benjamin (1736–1780). Norwich, Conn. 1 volume, 1770–1772.
Kasota (steamboat). Great Lakes. 1 volume, 1885–1890.

Morris, I. G. (farmer). Steubenville, O. 2 volumes, 1856–1870.
Nicholson, John (d. 1800). Philadelphia, Pa. 1 volume, 1793–1796; primarily accounts with Robert Morris (1734–1806).
P. D. Hall & Company. [Location?]. 1 volume, 1862–1870.
Preston, Moses (farmer). Chester, O. 1 volume, 1803–1834.
Renick, George (merchant). Chillicothe, O. 1 volume, 1808–1829.
Renick, George, Jr. (farmer). Chillicothe, O. 1 volume, 1845–1863.
Schnably, Rudolph (d. 1864). West Salem, O. 1 volume, 1848–1866, including an inventory of Schnably's estate.
Shinn, Joshua (schoolteacher). [Location?]. 1 volume, 1822–1869.
Smith, C. L. (construction laborer and storekeeper). Cleveland, O. 1 volume, 1879–1920.
Spafford, Hiram (farmer). Bedford, O. 1 volume, 1839–1851.
Thayer, Almon (shoemaker). Aurora, O. 3 volumes, 1834–1842.
Turney, Asa (farm laborer). Redding, Conn., and the Western Reserve (after 1809). 1 volume, 1786–1832.
Yonts, George (tailor). Ravenna, O. 1 volume, 1814–ca. 1850.

OVERSIZE VOLUMES:

Anonymous (coal and ore mining). Cleveland, O. 1 volume, 1880–1886.
Balyard, John (merchant). Seven Mile, Butler County, O. 1 volume, 1838–1841.
Bentzel, Balser (b. 1774). [Location?]. 1 volume, 1807–1850, written in German script.
Crosby, Abijah (laborer). Lee, Mass., and Euclid, O. (after 1811). 1 volume, 1795–1832.
Cuyahoga Forge. Cleveland, O. 1 volume, 1819–1822.
Fallis, John (farm laborer). [Location?]. 1 volume, 1809–1823.
Gordon, Jonathan. [Location?]. 2 volumes, 1811–1824.
Kinsman & Potter (merchants). [Location?]. 1 volume, 1836–1837.
Merrill, Horace (merchant). Chardon, O. 2 volumes, 1832–1845.
Thayer, Almon (shoemaker). Aurora, O. 1 volume, 1835–1847.
Washburn & Anderson (merchants). Greenwich, O. 1 volume, 1861–1862.
Wright, Sherman (shoemaker). Salem [now Conneaut], O. 2 volumes, 1825–1846.

133   NEWARK AND SHAWNEE COAL & IRON MINING COMPANY. NEWARK, O. Record Book, 1872–1884. 1 volume. MS 567.

Agreements, names of subscribers, minutes of meetings, copies of leases, and bylaws of this company, the name of which was changed in 1878 to the Iron Point Mining Company.

134   OHIO VOLUNTEER INFANTRY. 10TH REGIMENT. Records, 1861–1864. 1 volume. Gift of William P. Palmer. MS 568.

Morning reports and remarks for the month concerning the activities of the various companies within the 10th Regiment.

135   WAR FINANCE CORPORATION. CAPITAL ISSUES COMMITTEE. WASHINGTON, D.C. Report, 1920. 1 volume (typescript). Gift of F. H. Goff, 1920. MS 573.

Detailed statement of the operations of this committee from the date of its organization, May 17, 1918, under the authority of the War Finance Corporation Act, until it was discontinued, December 31, 1918. Frederick H. Goff of Cleveland was vice-chairman of the committee.

136   WOMAN'S VETERAN RELIEF UNION. DEPARTMENT OF OHIO. FINDLAY, O. Roll Book, 1894–1904. 1 volume. MS 575.

Names of women and the soldiers they represent, giving date of muster, company, and regiment, and status of veterans (whether living or dead) at the Elizabeth Neibling Chapter.

137   FIRST FARMER'S CLUB OF BUTLER TOWNSHIP. COLUMBIANA COUNTY, O. Records, 1865–1868. 1 volume. MS 576.

Constitution, bylaws, list of members, and minutes of meetings of this club, which in 1866 became the Farmer's Institute of Butler Township with the goal of "the improvement of its members in a Knowledge of Farming and Kindred subjects."

138 CONVERSATIONAL CLUB OF EAST CLEVELAND. EAST CLEVELAND, O. Records, 1882–1897. 22 volumes. Gift of the Conversational Club of East Cleveland. MS 580.

Constitution, membership roll, and copies of every paper read between 1882 and 1897 before the members of this club, which was founded in 1878.

139 ZALMON FITCH. Papers, 1818–1860. 5 boxes. MS 581.

Contracts, deeds, and business and estate papers of persons for whom Fitch, a prominent Clevelander, was attorney and/or land agent. These include the following residents of Connecticut: Andrew Kingsbury, 1818–1830; Nehemiah Hubbard, 1823–1836; Betsy Storrs, 1823–1831; William Ely, 1825–1840; Joseph, Eliza, and Henry C. Trumbull, 1825–1845; and Asahel Hathaway, 1830–1860. Also served by Fitch were Thompson Blair, Thomas Cowles, Stephen Gales, Daniel Norton, Amelia Shaler, Lemuel G. Storrs, William L. Storrs, Luther Thwing, Henry Walker, and Eliphalet Williams. Also included is some correspondence relating to Fitch as shareholder in the Bank of Cleveland and the Exchange Brokers Company; a one-volume account of the purchase of shares in the Bank of Geauga by Simon Perkins and Zalmon Fitch, 1835–1836; receipts and financial records, 1846–1851; assorted surveys; papers from William H. Potts of Trenton, New Jersey, concerning John Fitch (1743–1789), one of the earliest inventors of the steamboat, including copies of letters from John Fitch to Stacey Potts, 1785–1786, and an essay on John Fitch and the steamboat, 1845.

140 A. C. WILLIAMS. Papers, ca. 1888–1903. ½ box. Gift of Mrs A. C. Williams, 1920. MS 593.

Letters from Arthur B. Deming, an ardent anti-Mormon who labored to secure evidence proving the fraudulent origin of Mormonism, 1900–1903; miscellaneous newspaper clippings on Mormonism; material regarding a protest of anti-Mormons against admitting Reed Smoot into the U.S. Senate, 1903; and notes on

Mormonism belonging to Williams, a resident of Columbus, Ohio. Also included are copies of *Naked Truths About Mormonism* (Oakland, California, 1888).

141   WILLIAM LAW, JR. Papers, 1798–1800. 4 volumes. MS 594.

Journal kept while on a visit to the Western Reserve by William Law, Jr., attorney and land agent for his father, William Law of Cheshire, Connecticut, May–July, October, 1799. William Law owned land in Poland and Burton townships which was managed by his son. William Law, Jr., spent much time in Youngstown and Burton while traveling, often in the company of Turhand Kirtland, to other places in the Western Reserve. Also included are two record books of business transacted, including copies of agreements and indentures, 1799–1800; and the field book of Alfred Wolcott, surveyor of lots in Township No. 1, Range No. 1 (Poland), with field notes of lots drawn in the name of William Law and Andrew Hull, 1798.

142   JONATHAN LAW. Diary, 1802. 9 booklets. MS 597.

Kept on a trip through the Western Reserve, including visits to Burton, Cleveland, Chillicothe, Painesville, Poland, and Warren, Ohio, and other cities between the Reserve and his home in Cheshire, Connecticut.

143   ANONYMOUS. Field Notes, ca. 1800. 26 pages. Gift of Buel Sedgewick, 1869. MS 600.

Field notes for surveys made in Mesopotamia, Trumbull County, and Millsford, New Dorset, and Pierpont, Ashtabula County, Ohio.

144   OHIO VOLUNTEER INFANTRY. 7TH REGIMENT. Records, 1863, 1864. ½ box. Combined from three sources in 1969. MS 640.

Return of Captain Mervin Clark's Company B, September, 1863; morning register, March 1–May, 1864; and an autograph album prepared "In Memoriam of Col. W. R. Creighton and Lt. Col. O. J. Crane. From the Non-Commissioned Officers and Privates of the 7th O.V.I." Creighton and Crane died during battle in Georgia.

145 MARIETTA HISTORICAL ASSOCIATION. MARIETTA, O. Records, 1841. 1 volume. MS 641.

Constitution, officers, and list of members. Most of this volume was used as an account book, 1856–1859, possibly by Caleb Emerson, who was the corresponding secretary of this association.

146 FIRST BAPTIST CHURCH. JEFFERSON, O. Records, 1811–1921. 5 volumes. MS 642.

Covenant, minutes of meetings, and membership lists. There are some newspaper clippings and correspondence pertaining to the church's 100th-anniversary celebration in 1911.

147 LOST CREEK REGULAR BAPTIST CHURCH. LOST CREEK, O. Records, 1816–1896. 3 volumes. Gift of James Webb. MS 645.

Historical records and minutes of meetings from the founding of the church in 1816 until 1896; a church register; and the church covenant, rules, resolutions, and minutes, 1825–1851.

148 NETTLE CREEK BAPTIST CHURCH. CHAMPAIGN COUNTY, O. Records, 1822–1884. 3 volumes. Gift of Mrs. J. M. Stemberger. MS 646.

Minutes of meetings and lists of members of this church which was organized in Mad River Township and which was associated with the Mad River Baptist Association.

149 FIRST REGULAR BAPTIST CHURCH. CLEVELAND, O. Records, 1820–1892, 1901–1916. 4 volumes. Gift of the Reverend Mr. Stone and the Euclid Baptist Church. MS 647.

Articles of faith and practice, covenant, names of members, act of incorporation, constitution, and minutes of regular, annual, and trustee meetings, 1820–1892. Also included is a record book, 1901–1916, of the Euclid Baptist Church's Ladies Aid Society. This volume includes the constitution, bylaws, names of officers and members, and minutes of annual and special meetings.

150 BAPTIST CHURCH. SALEM, O. Records, 1823–1902. 12 volumes. Gift of the J. B. Strawn Family. MS 648.

Primarily volumes of church rolls, treasurers' records, and subscription lists of the Baptist Church of Salem, Ohio, 1867–1902. Also included are two volumes containing the constitution, membership, and minutes of the First Regular Baptist Church from 1823 until 1867 when it disbanded; and the minutes, 1840–1868, of the Second Regular Baptist Church, which joined with the First Regular Baptist Church to form the Baptist Church of Salem.

151 MAD RIVER BAPTIST ASSOCIATION. MISSIONARY COMMITTEE. WESTERN OHIO. Records, 1847–1875. 1 volume. MS 651.

Financial accounts and minutes of committee meetings which were held in several counties, including Champaign, Logan, and Miami.

152 BAPTIST CHURCH. MENTOR AND WILLOUGHBY (O.) PLAINS CONFERENCE. Records, 1836–1848. 1 volume, ½ box. Gift of the Estate of Martin E. Gray, 1910. MS 654.

Confession of faith, covenant, minutes of meetings, membership lists, and a few loose items, including some correspondence and a signed temperance pledge.

153 HANDEL M. SHUMWAY, *collector.* Wolf Scalp Certificates, 1810–1821. ½ box. Gift of Handel M. Shumway, 1893. MS 657.

Certificates issued to various residents of Cuyahoga County for killing wolves.

154 WAR OF 1812. Collection of Papers, 1812–1815. 2 boxes. Accumulated from various sources by the Society. MS 660.

Primarily papers relating to the accounts between the United States and various militia paymasters, 1812–1815. Most of these items are signed by Lieutenant David Clendenin, Paymaster, Poland, Ohio. Also included are regimental orders, correspondence, and other papers concerning military activities in Ohio during the war. Among the correspondents are Jedediah Beard, Charles A. Boardman, John Campbell, Norman Canfield, Ensign Church, William Eustis, Richard Fitch, William H. Harrison, William N. Hudson, Tobias Lear, Wheeler Lewis, Othniel Looker, Rial McArthur, Aaron Norton, Simon Perkins, Richard Rush, Samuel Smith (Maryland), Amos Stoddard, Elijah Wadsworth, Aaron Wheeler, Elijah Whittlesey, and J. Winchester. Also part of this collection are copies of muster, regiment, and pay rolls, lists of soldiers in various companies, and correspondence during or pertaining to the War; a one-volume copy of the "rolls of 18 companies stationed in the Forts of Massachusetts during the War of 1812" and a copy of a "roll of Vermont militiamen who served in the War of 1812"; and assorted newspaper clippings.

155 BAPTIST CHURCH. DOVER, O. Records, 1836–1856. 1 volume. Gift of Mrs. N. B. Hurst, 1911. MS 668.

Names of members, minutes of conference and covenant meetings, and accounts of church expenditures.

156 FREE WILL BAPTIST CHURCH. CHESTER, O. Records, 1863-1904. 1 volume. Gift of the Reverend Mr. Stone, 1913. MS 669.

Names of members and minutes of conference and covenant meetings.

157 HONEY CREEK BAPTIST CHURCH. BETHEL TOWNSHIP, MIAMI COUNTY, O. Records, 1811–1844. 1 volume. Gift of Lee Howells. MS 670.

Membership list and minutes of meetings of this church which was a member of the Mad River Regular Baptist Association.

158 MARION LAWRANCE. Album, 1907. 1 volume. MS 679.

Book of gratitude presented to Marion Lawrance, superintendent of the Sunday school of the Washington Street Congregational Church of Toledo, Ohio, 1876–1907, signed by members of the church.

159 AARON OLMSTED. Field Notes, ca. 1803. 2 volumes (unbound). MS 680.

Aaron Olmsted, original proprietor of Franklin, Portage County, Ohio, arranged to have the surveying of this township commence in 1803.

160 EDWIN DIBELL (b. 1820). Papers, 1841–1893, 1910. 1 box. Gift of E. Dibell, 1910. MS 700.

Primarily letters received by Edwin Dibell, a Baptist minister from Kingsville, Ohio, while he was at Brown University, Providence, Rhode Island; Hamilton Seminary, Madison County, New York; and Newton Theological Institute, Newton Center, Massachusetts, 1841–1856. Among other papers are two account books, 1844–1855; an account of work done by seamen in Providence, Rhode Island, 1847; a series of Dibell's diaries, 1855, 1857, 1861, 1876, 1877, 1879, 1881, 1884, 1887–1889, and 1891–1893; a sketch

[47]

of the town of Kingsville; and an autobiographical account of Dibell's life.

161 ALFRED WOLCOTT. Field Notes and Surveys, 1799–1803, 1811, 1816, 1817. 20 volumes. MS 725.

Notes, surveys, and maps of land in Ashtabula, Batavia, Braceville, Brecksville, Chardon, Coitsville, Concord, Ellsworth, Fowler, Guilford, Howland, Leffingwell, Liberty, Liverpool, Monroe, Newbury, Newton, Parkman, Ravenna, Richfield, Southington, and York, Ohio. The majority of these surveys of land located in the Western Reserve were made by Wolcott for General Simon Perkins.

162 HENRY VANDERBURGH. Papers, 1777–1808. 1 folder. Gift of Dr. Joseph Somes, 1870. MS 732.

General correspondence, 1777–1808, received by Vanderburgh, who was captain in a New York regiment during the Revolutionary War, a judge in the Indiana Territory, and a resident of Vincennes, Indiana. Also included are abstracts and accounts between the United States and Vanderburgh, who provided sundry articles for the Indian Department, 1791; and appointments as commissioner to license retailers in Knox County, Indiana Territory, 1792, and as judge of the Indiana Territory, 1800.

163 AMZI ATWATER. Journal, April 13–December 1, 1796. 90 pages (copy). MS 735.

Description of the Western Reserve as recorded by Atwater, who was an assistant surveyor in Moses Cleaveland's surveying party.

164 TURHAND KIRTLAND (1755–1844). Diary, 1798–1800. 69 pages (copy). MS 737.

Kept on his visits to and his travels throughout the Western Reserve.

165 FREEMASONS. WESTERN STAR LODGE. BOARDMAN, O. Records, 1828–1851. ½ box. MS 745.

Minutes of meetings, resolutions, and election results.

166 JOHN BARR. Papers, 1842–1860, 1873. 1 box. Gift of Mrs. John Barr, 1875. MS 759.

Primarily letters addressed to John Barr, prominent Clevelander and officer of various literary and historical organizations, in answer to his solicitations for information concerning the first settlers to and the early history of Cleveland and the Western Reserve. Correspondents include John Ackley, Amzi Atwater, D. H. Beardsley, Gilman Bryant, Lewis Cass, N. Crookshank, Oliver Culver, D. C. Doan, Thomas Goodman, Julius C. Huntington, Alfred Kelley, and Stanton Sholes. Also included are Barr's reminiscences of Wooster, Ohio, ca. 1873.

167 OVIATT FAMILY. Papers, 1814–1876. 1 box. Gifts of Miss Grace L. Oviatt, 1932, 1942; H. L. Leffingwell, 1953. MS 777.

Deeds, agreements, financial papers, and certificates of Benjamin, Elizabeth L., Heman, Orson M., Marvin, Nathaniel, and Schuyler R. Oviatt. Benjamin Oviatt, from Litchfield, Connecticut, was one of the original settlers of Hudson, Ohio. His brother, Heman, the major focus of this collection, dealt in land in Cuyahoga, Medina, Portage, and Summit counties while a resident of Hudson, Richfield, and Cleveland, Ohio. Schuyler R. Oviatt was treasurer of Summit County in the 1870's, and his report of 1876 is included here. Also included is a catalogue of books in the Richfield Sunday school, 1835; the constitution of the Education Society of Richfield and a list of subscribers, 1847; papers relating to the First Congregational Church of Richfield, 1835–1858; and notes on the history of Richfield.

168   OTTO MILLER (1874–1950). Papers, 1792–1863, 1917–1949. 3 boxes, 1 oversize package. Gift of Otto Miller. MS 783.

Correspondence, certificates, and photocopies of documents relating primarily to the genealogy of Michael Spangler and other English and American ancestors of Otto Miller, a Cleveland businessman and civic leader. Correspondents include Arthur Cochrane, Colonel W. G. C. Probert, Louis Effingham de Forest, Ethel Stokes, and Harry K. Taylor, 1927–1949. Also included is one folder of correspondence with Newton D. Baker, Harry I. Emerson, Edward B. Greene, and Warren G. Harding pertaining to matters arising out of World War I, 1917.

Miller accumulated several series of family letters relating to various ancestors. These include letters from Aaron Woolworth of Bridgehampton, New York, to his parents and brother, Chester Woolworth, of Longmeadow, Massachusetts, 1792–1818; letters to Joseph K. Miller and his wife, Margaret (Spangler) Miller of Cleveland, Ohio, 1823–1863; and letters to Joseph Woolworth of Crawfordville, Indiana, 1851–1852.

169   ANONYMOUS. Field Notes, ca. 1850. 1 volume. MS 784.

Made while surveying land in and around New Lisbon, Columbiana County, Ohio.

170   HENRY C. JONES. Papers, 1860–1881. ½ box. MS 787.

Commissions and citations issued to Jones, who was a notary public, claims and real estate agent, and a lawyer in Salem, Columbiana County, Ohio. Some copies of special orders issued (during the Civil War) to Jones, a first lieutenant in the 12th Regiment, Ohio Volunteer Cavalry, are also included.

171   FIRST BAPTIST CHURCH. WOMEN'S BAPTIST HOME MISSION SOCIETY. ELYRIA, O. Records, 1887–1900. 2 volumes. MS 788.

Minutes of meetings and a list of members (1888) of the Elyria branch of the Women's Baptist Home Mission Society, the object of which was "to cultivate a missionary spirit in this Church [First Baptist], and aid the Women's Baptist Home Mission Society in its work of Christianizing the country."

172 WALLACE HUGH CATHCART (1865–1942). Papers, 1910, 1915, 1920–1921. 1 box. Gift of Wallace H. Cathcart. MS 798.

Correspondence, programs, badges, publicity forms, copies of speeches, and other papers relating to the Cuyahoga County Centennial Celebration (1910), for which Cathcart served on the executive committee; memoranda and newspaper clippings concerning various explorers and explorations of North America, 1910; and letters from William Farrand Felch concerning the Historical Commission of Ohio, of which Felch was executive secretary, 1920–1921.

173 CONNECTICUT (STATE). GENERAL ASSEMBLY. Records, 1801–1803, 1807–1810. 2 volumes (copies). MS 800.

Reports of "the subscribers Managers of the School Fund" to the Connecticut General Assembly, containing bond records.

174 CONNECTICUT LAND COMPANY. HARTFORD, CONN., AND OHIO. Records, 1795–1817. 1½ boxes (some copies). Accumulated from several sources and combined, 1969. MS 802.

An assortment of covenants, bonds, articles of agreement, and indentures involving the directors of the Connecticut Land Company and its shareholders, 1795–1796; scattered financial accounts and receipts, 1796–1807; originals and copies of proceedings of the Company and of the drawings through which the Company's land holdings were divided up among its shareholders, 1798–1817; and several bids and contracts relating to the cutting of a road through the Western Reserve in 1798.

175   SEVERANCE FAMILY. Autograph Albums, 1827–1892. 7 volumes. MS 805.

Including a book of autographs and poems of Mary S. Long, 1827–1843, and a notebook of Solon L. Severance, 1840's.

176   JOHN HECKEWELDER (1743–1823). Diaries, 1786, 1789. 1 volume (translated and copied by Aug. H. Liebert). Gift of C. C. Baldwin, 1894. MS 813.

Diary kept on a journey of John, Sarah, and Anna Heckewelder from the "Cayahoga River" to Bethlehem, Pennsylvania, October 5–November 15, 1786; and a diary kept while journeying with Abraham Steiner from Bethlehem to Pettiquotting near the Huron River and Lake Erie, and back to Bethlehem, April 17–June 20, 1789.

177   WILLIAM H. ECKMAN. Papers, 1870–1880. 3 volumes. Gift of Mrs. William H. Eckman. MS 820.

Includes a journal containing brief notes on Eckman's daily activities, 1858–1877; and a scrapbook containing drawings, sketches, and watercolors by members of the Cleveland Art Club, which was organized in Cleveland in 1876 under the general leadership of Archibald M. Willard. Among those represented in the scrapbook are Otto H. Bacher, George P. Bradley, William H. Eckman, George Grossman, George C. Groll, Otto May, Daniel A. Wehrschmidt, Sion L. Wenban, and Archibald M. Willard.

178   FREEMAN H. MORSE (1807–1891). Papers, 1861–1888. ½ box. Gift of Mrs. Hatch. MS 823.

Papers relating to Morse's activities as U.S. consul in London (1861–1870), including correspondence from Charles Francis Adams, John Bigelow, James D. Bulloch, and William Pitt Fessenden. Also included are copies of affidavits made by seamen aboard the *Alabama* and the *Kearsarge* regarding the sinking of the *Alabama*, June 19, 1864, and a printed letter from Morse to W. L. Putnam of Portland, Maine, concerning Morse's claim of $38,189 against the United States, 1888.

179 FREDERICK KINSMAN (1807–1884). Papers, 1854–1877. ½ box. MS 825.

General correspondence of Kinsman, 1867–1877; accounts, agreements, and mortgage bond receipts relating to the Cleveland and Mahoning Valley Railroad, 1854–1867, of which Kinsman was a director. Frequently mentioned in these papers are Dudley Baldwin, Reuben Hitchcock, Jacob Perkins, Charles L. Rhodes, Charles Smith, and David Tod, all of whom were directors of the railroad.

180 CALVIN PEASE (1776–1839). Papers, 1798–1840. 4 boxes. Gift of Thomas and Charles P. Kennedy, 1927; and others. MS 827.

Correspondence, court dockets and other legal papers, tax and financial records, land deeds and agreements, field notes, and other papers relating to the activities of Calvin Pease, a native of Connecticut who settled in Warren, Ohio, in 1803. An attorney at law, Pease served as a judge of the Third Circuit, Court of Common Pleas (1803–1810), and justice of the Ohio Supreme Court (1816–1830). These papers deal heavily with his legal activities and include court dockets, decisions, depositions, and testimonies. Also included are field notes and lists of lands in the Western Reserve belonging to Gideon Granger (Pease's brother-in-law), early 1800's; and land deeds and agreements and letters concerning land transactions, particularly in Trumbull County, 1817–1840. Other subjects touched upon are the Trumbull & Ashtabula Turnpike Company, 1820's; the proposed joining of the Ohio and Pennsylvania canals, 1833; and the Western Reserve Bank, 1816–1833. Persons involved in litigation brought before Pease include Quintus F. Atkins, Joshua R. Giddings, Gideon Granger, Simon Perkins, Oliver Phelps, and Elisha Whiting.

181 CALEB EMERSON FAMILY. Papers, 1795–1904. 5 boxes, 1 oversize package. Gift of Mrs. E. A. Bailey. MS 830.

Business and personal correspondence, account books, financial papers, speeches, and writings of Caleb Emerson (1779–1853) of

Marietta, Ohio, and other members of his family, including his wife, Mary Dana, and his sons, George D. and William D. Emerson. An attorney at law, Caleb Emerson arrived in Marietta from New York State in 1808; served at the bar for most of his life, including a stint as prosecuting attorney for Washington County, 1815–1821; operated a bookstore and was associated with the *Western Spectator,* ca. 1810–1813; edited the *Marietta Gazette,* 1836; and was active in the Baptist Church from approximately 1820 until his death. The correspondence, which covers mainly the period from 1810 to 1852, touches on all of the aforementioned activities, as well as Emerson's interest in the anti-slavery movement, Marietta College, the Washington Benevolent Society, and the Baptist General Tract Society, but particularly Ohio state and national politics. Included are several account books, 1807–1829; minutes of meetings of the Washington Benevolent Society, 1813–1815; a series of letters from William D. Emerson containing detailed accounts of life in Cincinnati, Ohio, ca. 1830–1850; notes, writings, and speeches on topics such as the history of the Northwest Territory, the settlement of Marietta and of Ohio, the Bible, the Ohio Company, and African colonization, ca. 1830–1852; and letters concerning the arrest of three Ohioans by Virginia for allegedly stealing Negro slaves (Parkersburg Case or Gardner Case), 1845. Among the papers pertaining to Caleb Emerson's family are letters, enlistment certificates, reports, and orders of Captain George D. Emerson, 1st Regiment, Michigan Engineers, 1862–1865; and one volume of records pertaining to the sale of land in Marietta by William D. Emerson, 1880's. Other correspondents include Salmon P. Chase, Thurston Crane, Rebecca Dodge, Paul Fearing, Calvary Morris, Philip H. Nicklin, and Samuel F. Vinton.

182 WAYNE, MEDINA & CUYAHOGA TURNPIKE ROAD COMPANY. CLEVELAND AND MEDINA, O. Records, 1824–1851. 3 volumes. MS 831.

Lists of subscribers, their addresses, and number of shares bought, 1824; and accounts of tolls collected and receipts, 1829–1851.

183 MENTOR LIBRARY COMPANY. MENTOR, O. Records, 1820, 1826–1850. 1 volume. MS 832.

Bylaws, 1820, and account records, 1826–1850, of this book-lending company which was in existence from 1819 to 1859.

184 OHIO GENERAL ASSEMBLY. INVESTIGATING COMMITTEE. Journal, May 18–December 7, 1836. 1 volume. Purchased, 1908. MS 833.

Journal of the proceedings of the examination of the books and vouchers of the canal commissioner and of the canal fund commissioners as ordered by the Ohio General Assembly.

185 ASAPH COLEMAN. Letters, 1811–1818. 11 items. MS 843.

Letters to Dr. Asaph Coleman of Glastonbury, Connecticut, from his son, Asa Coleman of Troy, Ohio, in which he discusses local conditions.

186 JEREMIAH KINSMAN AND ROSWELL ADAMS. Papers, 1804–1851. ½ box. MS 846.

Letters and account statements addressed to Kinsman of Plainfield, Connecticut, and to Adams of Lisbon, Connecticut, from Douglas Putnam, land agent in Marietta, Ohio, 1825–1851; letters from John Kinsman, the founder of Kinsman, Ohio, to his brother Jeremiah, 1804–1807; and surveys of the land of Robert Kinsman, undated.

187 C. M. ELDREDGE. Journal, 1833. 1 volume. MS 859.

Kept on a "tour North, Visiting Montreal & Quebec." In it Eldredge records observations about these two cities, as well as of other towns in Canada, Massachusetts, and Vermont.

188 WILLIAM ELDREDGE. Papers, 1798–1821, 1830–1832. 1 box. MS 870.

Travel journals, land papers, and letters addressed to William Eldredge, a merchant from New London, Connecticut, and landowner in Huron County, Ohio. Included are deeds, lists of proprietors, and lists of lands for sale in the towns of Eldredge and Huron in Huron County, 1798–1821; journal kept on a trip to New Connecticut in the company of Daniel L. Coit and Eben Avery, May 14–July 22, 1806; letters concerning tax matters from John Walworth of Cleveland, January 15–August 1, 1812; and a journal kept on a trip from Cincinnati, Ohio, south through the states of Tennessee, Alabama, Louisiana, and Mississippi, 1830–1832.

189   HASKELL GOLF BALL COMPANY. CLEVELAND, O. Records, 1901–1917. Gift of the Estate of Coburn Haskell, 1945. 2 volumes. MS 879.

One volume containing a record of proceedings, minutes of meetings, and financial statements, 1901–1917; and a journal and ledger book of the company which was founded by Coburn Haskell, who patented an improved rubber-wound core for golf balls in 1899.

190   MEIGS CREEK BAPTIST ASSOCIATION. SOUTHEASTERN OHIO. Records, 1826–1836. 1 volume. Gift of Wallace H. Cathcart. MS 880.

Minutes of 11 annual meetings, including reports on the contributions of member churches, and on other church activities held in various counties in southeastern Ohio.

191   HURON BAPTIST ASSOCIATION. HURON COUNTY, O. Records, 1822–1877. 1 volume. Gift of Wallace H. Cathcart. MS 881.

Minutes of meetings, statistics, contribution tables, and lists of pastors, delegates, and clerks.

192   JAMES A. BRIGGS. Scrapbooks, 1830–1887. 2 volumes. Gift of William F. Holcomb, 1894. MS 882.

Newspaper clippings, some letters and proclamations, a few pictures, and notes written by Briggs. The voluminous number of clippings pertain to Briggs' career as editor of the *Cleveland True Democrat,* and as an attorney in Cleveland and in New York State. While serving as state assessor in New York, Briggs was special correspondent to several newspapers, including the *Cleveland Leader.* An avid temperance advocate and popular speaker, Briggs participated in the movements to convince Abraham Lincoln to accept the nomination of the Republican Party in 1860 and to persuade the Ohio delegation to support Lincoln. Briggs' articles and letters to the editor deal in great measure with contemporary events, politics, and reminiscences of Cleveland.

193   U.S. ARMY. EASTERN DIVISION. ARTILLERY REGIMENT. Orders, 1820–1828. 1 volume. Gift of Mrs. P. M. Hitchcock, 1910. MS 883.

General, departmental, and special orders of Company D.

194   HANNAH HUNTINGTON (1770–1818). Letters, 1791–1811. 51 items. Purchased. MS 884.

Primarily concerning family matters, these personal letters of Mrs. Hannah Huntington are addressed to her husband, Samuel Huntington (1765–1817), jurist, legislator, and Governor of Ohio (1808–1810).

195   KIRTLAND SOCIETY OF NATURAL SCIENCES. CLEVELAND, O. Records, 1869–1881. 3 volumes. Gift of Dr. Elisha Sterling, 1888. MS 888.

Minutes of meetings, notes on birds and some drawings, newspaper clippings, and other items pertaining to the activities of this society. Among the early members were Theodatus Garlick, Jared P. Kirtland, B. A. Stanard, George A. Stanley, Elisha Sterling, and Rufus K. Winslow.

196 CLEVELAND ACADEMY OF NATURAL SCIENCE. CLEVELAND, O. Records, 1845–1858. 1 volume. Gift of Dr. Elisha Sterling, 1888. MS 889.

Constitution, list of members, bylaws, and minutes of meetings of this cultural organization, among whose early members were John W. Allen, Sherlock D. Andrews, William D. Beattie, William Case, J. Lang Cassels, James D. Cleveland, Jacob J. Delameter, Theodatus Garlick, Charles W. Heard, Jared P. Kirtland, Samuel L. Mather, Samuel Starkweather, Elisha Sterling, Charles Whittlesey, Rufus K. Winslow, and Moses C. Younglove.

197 *COLUMBIA NANTUCKET.* Logbook, ca. 1870. 1 volume. Gift of Wallace H. Cathcart. MS 898.

Brief entries concerning this merchant vessel's travels to ports in the South Pacific.

198 COLLECTION OF PAPERS RELATING TO THE LOUISIANA AND MISSISSIPPI DISTRICT, 1768–1803. 2 boxes, 1 package. MS 903.

Primarily surveys and legal documents relating generally to land matters in this region, and specifically to the lands allotted pioneers who settled on the banks of the Mississippi from Natchez to New Orleans. They are signed by various Spanish governors and United States officials, including Esteban Miró, Baron de Garondelet, Manuel Goyoso de Lemos, Carlos Trudeau, and William Dunbar (1749–1810). Included are papers relating to the French settlement of Biloxi.

Also part of this collection are two volumes containing copies of letters and accounts of Charles Hicks, who resided in Florida, 1738–1745.

199 DAUGHTERS OF THE AMERICAN REVOLUTION. OHIO. WESTERN RESERVE CHAPTER. Records, 1891–1917. 1 box. MS 910.

Includes minutes of chapter meetings, 1891–1897; record book of the Committee of Safety, 1897–1898; minutes of the Committee in Charge of Collections for the War Emergency Relief Board, 1898; correspondence and report concerning the promotion of patriotism in public schools, 1898–1900; and the historian's report, consisting of genealogical records of local members.

200   HENRY LOVEJOY AMBLER (1843–1924). Papers, ca. 1871–1911. 2 boxes. MS 920.

Original manuscript and galley proofs for two books written by Dr. Ambler, who practiced dentistry in Cleveland: *Facts, Fads and Fancies About Teeth* (Cleveland: The Helman-Taylor Company, 1899) and the *History of Dentistry in Cleveland, Ohio* (Cleveland: Publishing House of the Evangelical Association, 1911); and copies of several speeches delivered by Dr. Ambler on topics relating to history and dentistry.

201   CUYAHOGA COUNTY UNION CENTRAL COMMITTEE, CLEVELAND, O. Records, 1863. 22 volumes. MS 922.

Canvass books of townships in the county giving names and party affiliation of voters.

202   ABEL LARKIN FAMILY. Papers, 1790–1895. 7 boxes. Purchased, 1921. MS 924.

Correspondence, legal papers, financial accounts and receipts, land deeds and agreements, farm records, and other papers of Abel and Stillman C. Larkin, who at different times resided in Athens, Gallia, and Meigs counties, Ohio. Specifically included are letters, legal papers, and docket books of Abel Larkin, justice of the peace in Gallia County and in Rutland, Meigs County, 1808–1828; account books, 1822–1830, 1837–1843; general and personal letters addressed to Abel, Edwin, Susannah, and Stillman C. Larkin, 1824–1871; a sheriff's fee book, 1840–1849; a subscription list, 1854, and a minute and roll book, 1857–1868, for the Methodist Protestant Church of Chillicothe, Ohio; and Stillman C. Larkin's journals kept on trips to Kansas in 1874, and to

Portland, Oregon, in 1878. Also included are Stillman C. Larkin's account books as treasurer of the Christian Conference of Rutland and treasurer of the ministerial funds in account with the town of Rutland and his 177-page manuscript "Pioneer History of Meigs County."

203   PRESIDENTS OF THE UNITED STATES. Documents Signed By, 1803–1875. Accumulated from various sources. 2 boxes. MS 940.

Land grants and appointments signed by the following U.S. Presidents (or their secretaries): John Adams, Thomas Jefferson, James Madison, James Monroe, J. Q. Adams, Andrew Jackson, Martin Van Buren, John Tyler, Zachary Taylor, Millard Fillmore, Franklin Pierce, James Buchanan, Abraham Lincoln, Andrew Johnson, and Ulysses S. Grant.

204   ENGLISH LUTHERAN CHURCH. MILLERSBURG, O. Records, 1877–1883. 2 volumes. MS 941.

Treasurers' accounts, including a list of subscribers for salaries and other church expenses.

205   CANTEEN CLUB (GOODSHIP ARC). CLEVELAND, O. Logbook, 1918–1919. Gift of Mrs. Charles Hickox, 1919. MS 945.

Containing the comments, cartoons, photographs, and names of boys who visited this canteen established by the American Red Cross during World War I.

206   JOHN M. SCOTT (b. 1824). Papers, ca. 1874–1894. 2 boxes. Acquired, 1921. MS 970.

Primarily typescript copies of speeches delivered by Scott, who resided in Bloomington, Illinois, and served as judge on that state's supreme court (1870–1888). The speeches, some of which are eulogies of prominent men, reflect Scott's interest in the early history and judicial system of Illinois and in the Presbyterian

Church, mound builders, French history, immigration, and the laboring class.

207 METHODIST-EPISCOPAL CHURCH. WEST SALEM, O. Records, 1853–ca. 1864. 1 volume. Gift of Mrs. C. J. Craft, 1916. MS 990.

Minutes of trustee meetings, quarterly conference reports, and lists of subscribers.

208 FOUR-IN-HAND AND TANDEM CLUB COMPANY. CLEVELAND, O. Records, 1902–1908. 1 box, 1 oversize volume. Gift of the Four-in-Hand and Tandem Club, 1908. MS 993.

Articles of incorporation, minutes of meetings, legal papers, and correspondence of this company, the purpose of which was "to furnish facilities for and to promote an interest in four-in-hand and tandem driving and other athletic and outdoor exercises for the amusement, recreation, health and profit of its members, and to acquire and own property convenient therefore." Among the stockholders in this company were Daniel R. Hanna, Howard M. Hanna, A. F. Holden, L. Dean Holden, James H. Hoyt, Edward A. Merritt, Charles A. Otis, James Parmelee, Jacob B. Perkins, William L. Rice, Belden Seymour, and R. H. York.

209 WOMAN'S FOREIGN MISSIONARY JUBILEE COMMITTEE. CLEVELAND, O. Records, 1910–1914. 3 volumes. Gift of Miss S. L. Ball. MS 995.

Minutes of meetings, names and addresses of members, and pamphlets, broadsides, and some correspondence pertaining to the jubilee-year celebration (1911).

210 JAMES BARNABY. Papers, 1842–1865. ½ box. MS 1007.

Assorted papers relating to Salem, Ohio, including a copy of an ordinance creating a board of health and a partnership agreement between Jacob Heaton and James C. Marshall to sell goods, 1842; insurance papers of Benjamin Stanton, 1845–1857; records of the Western Anti-Slavery Society, 1845–1850; letters, military telegrams, vouchers, invoices, shipment statements, and other papers addressed to Captain James Barnaby, Commissary Post, Charleston, West Virginia; an undated speech on temperance; and an essay on the "Supposed Antiquity of the Jews."

211 RICHARD S. COLLUM. Scrapbook, 1892–1903. 1 volume. Gift of John P. Nicholson, 1918. MS 1008.
Letters sent to Collum, secretary of the United Service Club of Philadelphia, Pennsylvania, and others, about activities of the club.

212 R. R. HERRICK. Papers, 1875–1882. ½ box. MS 1009.
Account between the Commercial National Bank and Herrick, mayor of Cleveland, 1875–1876; general correspondence from the mayors of other cities, 1881–1882; and letters from the Committee on Public Buildings relating to the use of city buildings, especially the Armory Hall, by private groups, 1882.

213 U.S. SANITARY COMMISSION. CLEVELAND BRANCH: SOLDIER'S AID SOCIETY OF NORTHERN OHIO. Records, 1860–1878 (1861–1869). 41 boxes, 41 volumes, 1 package. MS 1012.
Correspondence, reports, memoranda, abstracts of weekly and monthly reports, acknowledgments of equipment received, bank drafts, insurance policies, newspaper clippings, and other materials relating in general to the activities of the U.S. Sanitary Commission, but more specifically to those of its Cleveland branch, the Soldier's Aid Society of Northern Ohio (SASNO). The latter was the first of over 500 branches to be permanently organized (April 20, 1861). Under the leadership of its officers, Mrs. Benjamin Rouse, Mrs. John Shelley, Mrs. William Melhinch, Mary Clark Brayton, and Ellen F. Terry, the Cleveland branch

was the model for the institution of other aid societies. Its members participated in the many activities of the Sanitary Commission. These included ministering to the physical needs of soldiers by improving camp hygiene and diets, collecting and disbursing hospital stores, inspecting hospitals and other medical facilities, caring for sick and wounded soldiers, registering and burying the dead, building and supporting a soldier's home, and conducting a special relief system as well as an employment service. Reading material, games, stationery, and free postal service were supplied in an effort to improve soldiers' morale. The major series of unbound papers consists of assorted letters, memoranda, vouchers, registers, and other items concerning the Sanitary Commission, 1860–1878; and acknowledgments of hospital equipment received from SASNO, 1861–1865. The major series of bound papers consists of letters to SASNO from other branches of the Sanitary Commission, 1861–1866; letters from claimants to the Free Claim Agency of SASNO, 1865–1869; correspondence and other documents from various army offices to the Free Claim Agency, 1861–1867; receipt, cash, and memoranda books, 1858–1870; and 41 oversize volumes including registers of SASNO's Bureau of Information and Employment, scrapbooks of newspaper clippings, treasurers' accounts, lists of names, record books of the Special Relief Department of SASNO, invoices and other business papers relating to the Northern Ohio Sanitary Fair (February, 1864), and records of receipts and disbursements of SASNO, 1861–1870. Also included is an undated typescript memoir of Caroline Younglove Abbott concerning the work of SASNO.

Unpublished 21-page register available in the Society.

214   PIONEER ASSOCIATION OF WHITEWATER AND MIAMI VALLEY. ELIZABETHTOWN, O. Records, 1866–1869. 1 volume. Gift of F. F. Prentiss, 1922. MS 1021.

Minutes of meetings, copies of newspaper articles, and lists of pioneers, the latter being defined as "all persons having residence in the North West previously to AD 1825."

215 JOSEPH GASPARD CHAUSSEGROS DE LERY. Journals, 1749–1758. 1 box (copies in French and English). MS 1027.

Journals kept on visits to Detroit and Carillon and to a council of the Five Nations; accounts of the captures of Fort Bull and Fort Oswego and of the progress of the work on the fortification of Quebec. Also included are several newspaper clippings, copies of letters, and correspondence between Charles W. Burrows, A. E. Gosselin, Webb C. Hayes, John T. Mack, and Reuben G. Thwaites concerning the de Lery journals and the Sandoski (Sandusky) forts, 1906–1908.

216 CLEVELAND INSTITUTE. CLEVELAND, O. Records, 1858–1859, 1867–1868. 3 volumes. Gift of Mrs. Craft. MS 1035.

Daybook, 1858–1859; ledger, 1858–1859; and journal, 1867–1868, of this coeducational private school founded in 1859 by Professor Ransom F. Humiston. Also included is a volume containing the constitution, bylaws, and amendments of the Phi Alpha Society, the object of which was "the acquirement of literary culture."

217 ENSIGN CHURCH. Correspondence, 1803–1817. 1 folder. MS 1045.

Personal and business letters sent to Ensign Church and Jerusha Church of Canfield, Ohio, by A. Johnston, Nathaniel Church, and Samuel Church, all of Salisbury, Connecticut.

218 THOMAS B. VAN HORNE. Original Manuscript, 1881. 1 bound volume. MS 1072.

Manuscript copy of the *Life of Major General George H. Thomas* (New York: Charles Scribner's Sons, 1882), the Civil War leader who fought on the Union side. This manuscript varies somewhat from the published edition.

219 LUCIUS VERUS BIERCE (1801–1876). Papers 1838–1839, 1860, 1876. ½ box. MS 1081.

Primarily copies of speeches delivered by Bierce, an attorney at law from Ravenna, Ohio, on such topics as the Firelands, the Mound Builders, and early preachers (Elijah Ellsworth, Timothy Bigelow, and Ammi R. Robbins) in the Western Reserve.

220 GERTRUDE VAN RENSSELAER WICKHAM (1844–1930). Papers, 1887–1911. ½ box. Gift of Katherine V. R. Wickham, 1942. MS 1085.

Primarily letters about dogs, addressed to Mrs. Wickham from famous persons, 1887–1910; and seven letters and assorted newspaper clippings, most of which concern the Cleveland Women's Press Club, 1897–1911.

221 CHESAPEAKE & OHIO RAILROAD COMPANY. Correspondence, 1869–1874. 2 boxes. MS 1089.

Business letters received by H. D. Whitcomb, chief engineer, Richmond, Virginia, January, 1869–March, 1871, and August–October, 1871; letters received by A. H. Perry, general superintendent, C. P. Huntington, president, and J. J. Tracy, treasurer, March–June, 1873, and April–July, 1874.

222 JAMES DUANE DOTY (1799–1865). Papers, 1820–1840. 1 box. MS 1090.

Correspondence, deeds, lists of lots, and legal opinions of Doty, who was a Justice of the Michigan Supreme Court and later Governor of the Wisconsin Territory. Many of his legal opinions concern Indian matters, and the lists and deeds pertain to land in Menasha, Milwaukee, Green Bay, and the Fox River settlements in Wisconsin.

223 JOSHUA STOW. Papers, 1795–1832. ½ box. MS 1100.

Joshua Stow was an original shareholder in the Connecticut Land Company and commissary on the Moses Cleaveland surveying party. Included is a summary of expenses for surveying in the Western Reserve addressed to the directors of the Connecticut Land Company, 1795–1804; letters from Jared Mansfield and Lemuel Storrs, 1808, and from Joseph A. Beebe, Oliver B. Beebe, Leonard Case, and Noah Newton, 1832; letters from Henry Champion, a director of the Connecticut Land Company, concerning the southwestern boundary of the Western Reserve, 1808–1809; and papers concerning the survey of the Firelands by Maxfield Ludlow, 1808.

224 ROBERT McK. ORMSBY. Papers, 1800–1846. ½ box. MS 1102.

Letters received by Ormsby while he was an attorney at law in Bradford, Vermont, and Louisville, Kentucky. Most of these letters, containing local news, were from his relatives in Bradford. Also included are several letters to other members of the Ormsby family and a notebook with scattered entries, 1800–1837.

225 JESSE B. STRAWN (b. 1836). Journals, 1857. 3 volumes. Gift of the Estate of J. B. Strawn, 1922. MS 1103.

Journals kept during 1857 and one volume of personal reminiscences of this resident of Salem, Ohio.

226 SUMNER SOCIETY. DAMASCUS, O. Records, 1858–1860. 1 volume. Gift of the Estate of J. B. Strawn, 1922. MS 1105.

Minutes of meetings of this lecture society, formerly the Philomathian Society.

227 METHODIST-EPISCOPAL CHURCH. WOMAN'S MISSIONARY SOCIETY. BUCYRUS, O. Records, 1871–1888. 1 volume. Gift of the Prentiss Fund, 1922. MS 1121.

Constitution, bylaws, list of members, and minutes of meetings of this society, auxiliary to the Cincinnati branch of the Woman's Foreign Missionary Society of the Methodist-Episcopal Church.

228   GREENVILLE AND WEST MILTON TURNPIKE COMPANY. GREENVILLE, O. Records, 1856–1879. 1 volume (front cover and some pages missing). MS 1123.

Minutes of meetings of the directors, plat and field notes of the turnpike, and a list of shareholders.

229   E. B. FINLEY. Scrapbooks, 1881–1899. 2 volumes. MS 1126.

Scrapbooks containing newspaper clippings concerning the assassination of President James A. Garfield, 1881, and speeches delivered by General Finley, an attorney from Bucyrus, Ohio, and Adjutant General of Ohio.

230   OWL CREEK BANK. MT. VERNON, O. Records, 1816–1820. 2 volumes. MS 1129.

Stock ledger, 1816, and transfer book, 1816–1820.

231   JOHN MORGAN. Papers, 1788–1801. ½ box. Gift of Thomas C. Goss. MS 1138.

Contracts, agreements, and quitclaim deeds pertaining to land in the Western Reserve. Besides Morgan, who resided in Hartford, Connecticut, and was one of the original trustees of the Connecticut Land Company, other parties in these transactions are Daniel L. Coit, Samuel Hinckley, Joseph Howland, Elias Morgan, and Ephraim Root, 1795–1801.

232   BENAJAH WILLIAMS. Papers, 1825–1864. 1 volume. Gift of Mrs. A. C. Williams, 1925. MS 1141.

Primarily personal and family letters addressed to Rev. Benajah Williams, who resided in Ontario and Monroe counties, New York, and later (after 1840) in Chagrin Falls, Ohio. Also included are a few letters addressed to other relatives and some genealogical data.

233   AARON WILCOX (1772-1827) AND MOSES WILCOX (1772-1827). Journal, 1772-1800. 1 volume. Gift of the Estate of Peter Hitchcock, 1925. MS 1142.

Autobiographical account of the lives of these twins, who were born in Killingworth, Connecticut, in 1772, and settled in Summit County, Ohio. In 1819 they gave six acres of land for the public square to the village which was named Twinsburg in their honor.

234   JANE L. CLEVELAND. Letters, 1845-1850. 1 folder. MS 1151.

General and personal letters addressed to Jane L. Cleveland while a resident of Kingsville and Pierpont, Ashtabula County, Ohio, and Penn Line, Crawford County, Pennsylvania. The letters are from Miss Cleveland's relatives, including Chester E. Cleveland.

235   ABNER CROSBY. Diary, 1817-1874. 1 volume (unbound). Gift of Mrs. C. B. McLean, 1926. MS 1157.

Meteorological data and accounts of the daily activities of this resident of Euclid, Ohio.

236   JOSEPH W. GASKILL (b. 1843). Record Book and Diary, 1862-1865. 2 volumes. Purchased, 1925; gift of J. W. Gaskill, 1926. MS 1158.

These volumes relating to the Civil War include a descriptive roll of Company B, 104th Regiment, Ohio Volunteer Infantry, between 1862 and 1865, and a history of that company written by J. W. Gaskill; and Gaskill's diary for 1864, during which time he saw action in Tennessee and Georgia.

237   UNITED BRETHREN IN CHRIST. HOME MISSIONARY SOCIETY. MUSKINGUM DISTRICT, O. Records, 1838-1858, 1892. 1 volume. MS 1159.

Constitution, lists of subscribers, minutes of meetings held in Harrison and Stark counties, and financial records of this society which sought to raise money to defray the costs of sending out missionary preachers.

238   MERCER ACADEMY. MERCER, PA. Records, 1812–1858. 1 volume. MS 1160.

Copy of the act establishing the Mercer Academy, 1812; treasurers' records, 1813–1858; and minutes of trustee meetings, 1829–1833.

239   OHIO VOLUNTEER INFANTRY. 19TH OHIO BATTERY ASSOCIATION. Records, 1862–1915. 3 volumes. Gift of Frank Gilbert, 1926. MS 1163.

Two scrapbooks and one record book containing the history, letters, newspaper clippings, and other data on this battery, recruited originally in Cleveland by Captain J. C. Shields during the Civil War.

240   CHRISTOPHER AND WILLIAM LEFFINGWELL. Papers, 1790–1831. 1 folder. MS 1164.

Correspondence and associated papers concerning Ohio Company land. Among the correspondents of Christopher Leffingwell of Norwich, Connecticut, and William Leffingwell of New Haven, Connecticut, were Wheeler Coit, Samuel H. Parsons, David Putnam, Israel Putnam, Henry Strong, Peter Williams, and Dudley Woodbridge. Also included are field notes for a survey of a township in the Ohio Purchase.

241   McILRATH TAVERN. EAST CLEVELAND, O. Account Book, 1809–1846. 1 volume. Gift of Oliver McIlrath, 1926. MS 1165.

In 1804 Alexander McIlrath opened this tavern which for many decades was an important community center.

242 W. H. MATCHETT. Notebook, February 9–December, 1850. 1 volume. MS 1169.
Includes notes taken during medical lectures by Drs. Jared P. Kirtland and J. Lang Cassels.

243 BURTON ACADEMY CLUB. TRUMBULL COUNTY, O. Records, 1832–1834. 1 volume. Gift of the Estate of Peter Hitchcock, 1926. MS 1171.
Constitution, minutes of meetings, and list of members of this debate society.

244 NATHANIEL SPENCER (1748–1825). Diaries, 1798, 1813. 2 volumes. Gift of Caroline E. Waters, 1919. MS 1179.
Meteorological data and farm activities recorded by Nathaniel Spencer of Claridon, Geauga County, Ohio, formerly of New Hartford, Connecticut.

245 HENRY NEWBERRY. Notebook, 1822. 1 volume. Gift of Mrs. H. S. Newberry and Mrs. H. M. Hitchcock, 1932. MS 1186.
Detailed account of a trip taken from Windsor, Connecticut, to the Western Reserve. Also included is a list of lands laid out to various persons in Windsor, 1733.

246 GEORGE A. MYERS (1859–1930). Correspondence, 1912–1923.* 1 folder (typescript copies). Gift of Andrew Squire, 1927. MS 1199.
Correspondence between James Ford Rhodes, businessman and historian, and George Myers, a prominent leader in Cleveland's Negro community and proprietor of the Hollenden Barber Shop. These letters contain the writers' comments and opinions on notable public figures (Theodore Roosevelt, Marcus A. Hanna, Wil-

liam Howard Taft, and Woodrow Wilson) and on contemporary political issues.

* See John A. Garraty, ed., *The Barber and the Historian: The Correspondence of George A. Myers and James Ford Rhodes, 1900–1923* (Columbus: Ohio Historical Society, 1956).

247   ELISHA WHITTLESEY (1783–1863). Papers, 1804–1863. 83 boxes. MS 1200.
Correspondence, legal papers, speeches, financial accounts and receipts, land deeds and surveys, and other papers relating to the lengthy and varied career of Elisha Whittlesey, who was born in Connecticut and in 1806 moved to the Western Reserve, settling in Canfield, Ohio, where he practiced law intermittently for the next 57 years. In addition to his law career, these papers pertain to his activities as member of the Ohio Militia, 1808–1812; as U.S. Representative, 1823–1838; and as first comptroller of the U.S. Treasury, 1849–1857, 1861–1863. Subjects referred to in the correspondence, which accounts for three-quarters of this collection, include the following: nearly all aspects of the early history and development of the Western Reserve, national and Ohio political issues, local and national campaigns and elections, slavery and abolitionism, canals, banking, agriculture, land development and speculation, railroads, river and harbor improvements, Indian policy, pension claims, financial panics and depressions, postal service, and the Civil War. Specifically referred to are the American Bible Society, American Colonization Society, Cleveland Academy of Natural Sciences, Commercial Bank of Lake Erie, Firelands, Maumee River Valley, Ohio Canal, Western Reserve Bank of Warren, Western Reserve College, and the Whig Party. Correspondents (not including Whittlesey's relatives, from whom there are a significant number of letters) include: Comfort A. Adams, John W. Allen, Paul Anderson, Quintus F. Atkins, Caleb Atwater, Eliphalet Austin, Augustin Averill, Eli Baldwin, George Bancroft, Josiah Barber, John Barr, Mordecai Bartley, Moses Beach, Lucius V. Bierce, David L. Boardman, William Key Bond, E. B. Bostwick, Joel Byington, John C. Calhoun, Harmon Can-

field, Judson Canfield, Leonard Case, Lewis Cass, Luther Chapin, Henry Clay, John M. Clayton, David Clendenin, Lewis Condict, F. A. Conkling, John P. Converse, Eleutheros Cooke, Elliott Cresson, John Crowell, Lewis Dille, James C. Douglas, Theodore Dwight, Heman Ely, Edward Everett, Thomas Ewing, Richard Fitch, Zalmon Fitch, David Foot, Seabury Ford, Nicoll Fosdick, Joshua R. Giddings, Charles Goddard, Horace Greeley, Ralph R. Gurley, Nathan K. Hall, Charles Hammond, John Harmon, Robert Harper, William Henry Harrison, Homer Hine, Peter Hitchcock, Ezekiel Hover, Thomas Howe, Henry Hubbard, David Hudson, John Hutchins, John A. Johnson, Charles Johnston, Alfred Kelley, Daniel Kerr, John Kinsman, Jared P. Kirtland, Darius Lyman, John McLean, Richard Mott, Comfort Mygatt, Eben Newton, Hezekiah Niles, Edward Paine, Samuel W. Parker, Robert B. Parkman, Robert Patterson, Calvin Pease, Simon Perkins, L. M. Phelps, Almon Ruggles, William Russell, Charles Sigourney, J. S. Skinner, John Sloan, Jonathan Sloane, Samuel Starkweather, Elisha Sterling, Lewis B. Sturges, John G. Taliaferro, Benjamin Tappan, Daniel R. Tilden, David Tod, Benjamin F. Wade, Edward Wade, Frederick Wadsworth, Ashbel W. Walworth, Charles A. Wickliffe, Zalmon Wildman, Reuben Wood, William Woodbridge, Levi Woodbury, John Woods, and John C. Wright.

Unpublished 12-page register available in the Society. NUCMC 62-4387

248   OHIO VOLUNTEER INFANTRY. 150TH REGIMENT. Reunion Records, 1894–1927. 2 volumes. Gift of Alexander McIntosh, 1927. MS 1204.

Company rosters, reports, speeches, and minutes of the annual reunions.

249   ROBERT R. SLOAN. Speeches, 1836–1841. 3 volumes. MS 1205.

Copies of speeches delivered by Sloan while he was at Florence Academy and Jefferson College.

250 UNITED PRESBYTERIAN CHURCH. DALTON, O. Records, 1842–1860. 1 volume. MS 1206.

Minutes of session meetings and the subscription list for the minister's salary.

251 OHIO VOLUNTEER INFANTRY. 19TH REGIMENT. Records, 1863–1864. 1 volume. MS 1207.

Inspection reports and statements of the regimental fund.

252 ALEXANDER A. TAYLOR. Autograph Album, January, 1864. 1 volume. MS 1209.

Autographs of prisoners of war in Libby Prison, Richmond, Virginia, collected by Captain Taylor of Cambridge, Ohio. Taylor, who served in Company H, 122nd Regiment, Ohio Volunteer Infantry, was taken prisoner during the battle of Winchester, Virginia, on June 15, 1863.

253 WOMAN'S CHRISTIAN TEMPERANCE UNION. [LAKE COUNTY, O.]. Records, 1916–1924. 1 volume. MS 1210.

Minutes of business, annual, and regular meetings, a membership list for 1922, and some financial records of this local chapter of the Woman's Christian Temperance Union.

254 JAMES CHURCH. Account Book, 1842–1846. 1 volume. Gift of Charles H. Stone, 1927. MS 1211.

Church was a rope dealer in Cleveland, Ohio.

255 ELISHA STERLING. Papers, 1861–1889. 1 folder. MS 1216.

Letters by Sterling, including a number of letters to his granddaughter, Marianne Morgan, Cambridgeboro, Pennsylvania, 1889; Internal Revenue license to carry on the occupation of physician and surgeon in Cleveland, Ohio, 1861; and passports, 1849 and 1855.

256 FIRST PRESBYTERIAN CHURCH OF LAFAYETTE. CHIPPEWA LAKE, MEDINA COUNTY, O. Records, 1853–1883. 5 volumes. Gift of Emily Noyes, 1927. MS 1217.

Minutes of meetings, baptisms, dismissals, and the church register. Also included are the records of the Union Sabbath School, 1877–1881.

257 BEETHOVEN SOCIETY AND SEVILLE MUSICAL ASSOCIATION. SEVILLE, O. Records, 1845–1848, 1860–1875. 1 volume. Gift of Emily Noyes, 1927. MS 1218.

Preamble, constitution, names of members, and minutes of meetings of the Beethoven Society, 1845–1848; and the preamble, constitution, and minutes of meetings of the Seville Musical Association, 1860–1875. The object of these groups was to cultivate the "musical powers" of their members.

258 WINDFALL LYCEUM. MEDINA, O. Records, 1860–1878. 1 volume. MS 1219.

Preamble, constitution, bylaws, names of members, secretary's reports, and minutes of meetings of this discussion group and debate society.

259 DAUGHTERS OF THE AMERICAN REVOLUTION. OHIO. Record Book, 1917–1919. 1 volume. Gift of Mrs. E. L. Harris, 1927. MS 1220.

Guest book for the lodge at Camp Sherman, signed by the hundreds of D.A.R. members from throughout the United States who visited this army cantonment in Chillicothe, Ohio, during World War I.

260 GRAND ARMY OF THE REPUBLIC. POST NO. 568. EDGERTON, O. Records, 1886–1904. 1 volume. Gift of W. H. Hopkins, 1927. MS 1221.

Minutes of post meetings.

261 ROBERT OGLE. Papers, 1835–1861. ½ box. Gift of Robert Ogle, 1927. MS 1222.

Letters, deeds, and legal papers pertaining to Ogle's activities as justice of the peace for various townships (Florence, Superior, Bridgewater) in Williams County, Ohio.

262 KENTON MILLING COMPANY. KENTON, O. Records, 1880–1890. 1 volume. MS 1224.

Charter and minutes of meetings of the board of directors.

263 JAMES WATSON RILEY. Papers, 1835–1869. ½ box. Gift of Miss Lou Riley. MS 1225.

Land deeds, contracts, financial accounts, lists of notes collected, and assorted court papers of Riley, court recorder and later justice of the peace in Celina, Mercer County, Ohio.

264 BROOKLYN CONGREGATIONAL CHURCH. WOMAN'S MISSIONARY SOCIETY. BROOKLYN, O. Records, 1875–1883. 1 volume. MS 1227.

Constitution, names of members, minutes of meetings, and treasurer's annual reports of this society which sought to raise money for missionary activities.

265 METHODIST-PROTESTANT CHURCH. CHILLICOTHE, O. Records, 1854–1861. 2 volumes. MS 1229.

Annual register, constitution, bylaws, and minutes of meetings of the Sabbath school.

266 TRINITY EVANGELICAL LUTHERAN BROTHERHOOD. CIRCLEVILLE, O. Records, 1915–1923. 1 volume. MS 1231.

Minutes of meetings, constitution, bylaws, and signatories to the constitution of this organization which sought to promote "church work and spiritual life; to advance in sociability and to render mutual aid to its members."

267 OHIO MILITIA. 4TH DIVISION. 2ND BRIGADE. 1ST REGIMENT. Records, 1833–1837. 20TH DIVISION. 1ST BRIGADE. 1ST REGIMENT. Records, 1837–1843. 1 volume. MS 1233.

Rank rolls, election results, lists of fines assessed, and other records kept by Colonel Lucius V. Bierce for the 1st Regiment, 2nd Brigade, 4th Division, 1833–1837; and similar records for the 1st Regiment, 1st Brigade, 20th Division, 1837–1843.

268 PERRY H. BABCOCK (1816–1897). Account Book, 1845. 1 volume. Gift of Otto Schmitt, 1928. MS 1234.

Ledger containing accounts of goods shipped between Pittsburgh and Cleveland for the firm of Hubby & Hughes (Cleveland). Also included is a biographical sketch of Babcock and other notes by Mrs. Babcock.

269 B. G. BEYNON. Journal, 1813–1814. 1 volume (243 pp.). MS 1236.

Detailed day-by-day account kept by Lieutenant B. G. Beynon, Royal Marines, who served on board H.M.S. *Menelaus* during the War of 1812. Under the command of Sir Peter Parker, the *Menelaus* participated in the British expedition in Chesapeake Bay and up the Potomac and Patuxent rivers. Beynon and the marines he commanded landed in Baltimore, where they had several encounters with enemy forces.

270 BENJAMIN A. WRIGHT. Account Book, 1862. 1 volume. MS 1244.

Financial record of Wright's accounts with Company B, 39th Regiment, Georgia Volunteers, while stationed at Camp Bartow near Savannah, Georgia.

271 AMELIA CONVERSE. Papers, 1839–1890. ½ box. Gift of Mrs. Samuel P. Baldwin. MS 1247.

Personal diary kept by Miss Converse, daughter of John Phelps Converse and resident of Parkman, Ohio, which deals primarily with illness, death, and other personal tragedies but also touches upon the condition of asylums in Ohio and trips she made around the state (primarily in the 1860's), 1839–1869; and general and personal letters to Miss Converse from various friends and relatives, including Martha Converse, Mary M. Farwell, and Francis Parkman.

272   JESSE BALDWIN. Papers, 1862–1864, 1879–1881. 4 volumes. MS 1248.

Letter books containing copies of letters sent from Youngstown, Ohio, to such persons as Salmon P. Chase, William P. Fessenden, James A. Garfield, Horace Greeley, and John Sherman expressing Baldwin's opinions on the economic (especially monetary) policies of the United States, 1862–1864; copies of letters sent and received, financial accounts, and other records relating to Baldwin's business activities in Boardman, Ohio, 1879–1881.

273   TEMPERANCE SOCIETY. WILLOUGHBY, O. Records, 1836–1842. 1 volume. Gift of Norman E. Hills, 1924. MS 1252.

Minutes of meetings and list of members. Also included in this volume are account records, 1845–1847, of Elijah Murray, a recording secretary of the Temperance Society, and records of the Elijah Murray estate, 1847–1849.

274   OHIO & PENNSYLVANIA YEARLY MEETING OF FREE WILL BAPTISTS. Records, 1880–1917. 1 volume. MS 1253.

Constitution, bylaws, and minutes of meetings of this conference, the object of which was to adjust points of conflict and endeavor "by all possible means to maintain Gospel order, discipline & holiness in its members."

275 *REINDEER.* Logbook, 1826. 1 volume. MS 1254.
Record of the merchant vessel's activities while on the Ohio River.
This volume was also used as "The Illustration Book" of the Family Social School of Mount Pleasant, Ohio, 1854–1858.

276 OHIO WESLEYAN UNIVERSITY. MASONIC CLUB. DELAWARE, O. Records, 1917–1920. 1 volume. MS 1257.
Constitution, charter membership list, new members, bylaws, and minutes of meetings of this fraternal society.

277 DAVID CLENDENIN. Papers, 1809–1817. 1 folder. MS 1266.
Correspondence, legal papers, receipts, and other papers concerning the activities of David Clendenin and of Montgomery and Clendenin & Company of Youngstown, Ohio. Also included is a receipt roll of Lieutenant David Clendenin, a paymaster during the War of 1812.

278 LEMUEL PUNDERSON. Papers, 1812–1826. 1 box. MS 1268.
Contracts and deeds to land in the Western Reserve, correspondence, powers of attorney, and receipts of Punderson while acting as attorney and land agent in Burton, Ohio, for William Ely of Hartford, Connecticut; Henry Thorndike of Fitzwilliam, New Hampshire; and John Wyles of Brimfield, Massachusetts, 1815–1826. Also included is some correspondence from Amzi Atwater, Benjamin Dwight, Asa Gilbert, Silas Hotchkiss, Andrew Hull, Jared Kirtland, Turhand Kirtland, William Lattimore, Charles Parker, Robert B. Parkman, Simon Perkins, and others.

279 ABRAHAM SKINNER (1755–1826). Papers, 1786–1857. 1½ boxes. MS 1270.
Land deeds, financial accounts, estate and other legal papers, but primarily letters addressed to Skinner, a resident of East Hart-

ford, Connecticut, who settled in the Western Reserve in New Market (near Painesville) in 1803 and was a co-founder of Grandon (now Fairport) in 1812. The papers in general relate to Skinner's business and legal activities, primarily to transactions involving land in and around Painesville. Skinner, a merchant, attorney, and land agent, served as counsel to Henry Champion, an original shareholder in the Connecticut Land Company and owner of the land on which was founded the village of Champion (now Painesville) in 1807. Papers also touch on matters relating to the surveying of a road, horse breeding, and the keeping of taverns. Correspondents include Calvin and Eliphalet Austin, William S. Avery, Henry Champion, Julius Deming, Zalmon Fitch, Edward Paine, Robert B. Parkman, Calvin Pease, John Pinney, Benjamin W. Russell, Thomas Skinner, John Walworth, and John W. White.

Unpublished 5-page register available in the Society.

280   JOHN LACEY. Papers, 1776–1780. 1 folder. MS 1271.
Letters to Brigadier General Lacey from various persons concerning his activities during the Revolutionary War.

Also included in this folder are letters and financial accounts of various early settlers in the Western Reserve as well as of Robert Graham and other inhabitants of Ligonier, Pennsylvania; and letters to and from and records of accounts with General Arthur St. Clair, 1792–1806.

281   MASTICK AND TOMLINSON FAMILIES. Papers, 1782–1868. 1 box, 3 volumes. MS 1272.
Benjamin Mastick of Windham, Vermont, and Levi Tomlinson of Derby, Connecticut, moved to Burton, Ohio, early in the 19th century. Intermarriage united their two families, members of which moved to Rockport (now Rocky River), Ohio. This collection consists of personal, general, and business correspondence, much of the latter concerning Levi Tomlinson's activities as land agent for shareholders in the Connecticut Land Company; two account books of Levi Tomlinson and Benjamin Mastick, 1784–

1834; land deeds, agreements, estate papers, legal documents, and financial records concerning Joseph, Benjamin, Benjamin, Jr., Cynthia, Elliot, Asahel, and Edwin B. Mastick, and Levi and Lewis Tomlinson; petitions by citizens of Rockport addressed to the commissioners of Cuyahoga County, and other documents relating to the growth and development of that township; and a letter book of Edwin B. Mastick, 1848–1851.

282   MERRICK ELY. Account Book, 1832–ca. 1870. 1 volume. MS 1274.
Concerns hauling, farming, and related activities of Merrick Ely of Deerfield, Portage County, Ohio.

283   WELLINGTON LITERARY SOCIETY. WELLINGTON, O. Miscellany, 1847–1848. 3 items. MS 1286.
Manuscript copies of "The Visitant," "The Casket," and "The Garland," which were prepared by the members of this women's society whose members sought general improvement in knowledge.

284   SAMUEL S. BALDWIN. Papers, 1806–1810. 2 volumes. Gift of Mrs. Agnes B. Parsons, 1928. MS 1289.
Diary, 1806–1808, and a docket book kept while Baldwin was justice of the peace in Cleveland, 1809–1810.

285   SECOND PRESBYTERIAN CHURCH. FORT WAYNE, IND. Records, 1887–1909. 1 volume. MS 1292.
Minutes of meetings, records of legal proceedings, and committee reports.

286   FEMALE CHARITABLE SOCIETY. CANFIELD, O. Records, 1819–1827. 1 volume. Gift of E. P. Tanner, 1925. MS 1301.
Constitution, minutes of meetings, and lists of members of this society which sought to appropriate funds for "the education of

pious young men for the ministry to the promotion of missions or to the circulation of Bibles & religious Tracts."

287 CANFIELD TEMPERANCE SOCIETY. CANFIELD, O. Records, 1832–1852. 1 volume. Gift of E. P. Tanner, 1925. MS 1302.

Constitution, list of members, and minutes of meetings.

288 PRESBYTERIAN CHURCH OF CHRIST. CANFIELD, O. Records, 1804–1860. 1 volume. Gift of E. P. Tanner, 1925. MS 1303.

Background, confession of faith, covenant, articles of practice, minutes of meetings, and lists of communicants and baptisms.

289 METHODIST-EPISCOPAL CHURCH. ERIE CONFERENCE. KINGSVILLE, O. Records, 1848–1873. 2 volumes. Purchased, 1926. MS 1306.

Minutes of quarterly meetings and trustee, financial, and other church reports.

290 SONS OF TEMPERANCE. HOCKING VALLEY DIVISION NO. 66. LOGAN, O. Records, 1846–1852. 1 volume. Purchased, 1922. MS 1311.

Minutes of division meetings including results of elections of officers, committee reports, and some financial data.

291 GRANGE. SHALERSVILLE, O. Records, 1900–1903. 1 volume. MS 1312.

Minutes of meetings of this subordinate Grange which was organized in 1900. The meetings generally consisted of discussions of farming procedures and musical entertainment.

292 METHODIST-EPISCOPAL CHURCH. NEW LISBON, O. Records, 1836–1865. 1 volume. MS 1313.

Minutes of quarterly conference meetings held in the homes of various persons in New Lisbon and Wellsville until 1845, at which time conferences took place in the church building; and lists of contributors and other financial accounts.

293 DANIEL L. COIT. Papers, 1815–1819. 1 folder. MS 1314.

Land agreements and associated papers concerning sales by Daniel L. Coit of Norwich, Connecticut, to residents of Medina and Portage counties, Ohio.

294 THOMAS BARCLAY. Papers, 1813–1814. 1 folder. Gift of David M. Massie, 1923. MS 1315.

Correspondence among Colonel Barclay, David Collins, and Thomas Hinde, and other documents relative to the handling of British prisoners of war at Chillicothe, Ohio.

295 RICHARD LORD. Papers, 1835–1838. 1 folder. MS 1316.

Papers concerning the formation and activities of the New Harbour Company of Ohio City, Ohio, of which Lord was president. The joint-stock company was formed to promote real estate development in Ohio City, but went bankrupt during the Panic of 1836.

296 ALCINUS WARD FENTON (1839–1923). Papers, 1862–1912. 2 boxes. Gifts of Captain A. W. Fenton, 1923; McGregor Home, 1962. MS 1318.

Letters containing comments on troop movements, camp conditions, and battle experiences written by Captain Fenton while serving in the 6th Regiment, Ohio Volunteer Cavalry, which was stationed in Virginia during most of the Civil War, 1862–1865; two scrapbooks containing the reunion records of the 6th Ohio Cavalry prepared by Fenton, ca. 1884; and one scrapbook of letters and newspaper clippings relating mainly to Fenton's activities as a customs broker, customs inspector, and chairman of the Civil Service Customs Board in Cleveland and his relations with

Charles F. Leach, collector of customs and Republican political leader, who was deposed from his position in the Customs House in 1911 and replaced by Maurice Maschke, 1888–1923. Correspondents in this matter involving political patronage as well as Fenton's fitness for office, ca. 1898–1911, include Theodore E. Burton, James R. Garfield, Leach, and John R. Proctor.

297 THOMAS BOLTON. Papers, 1835–1860. 1 box. MS 1319.

Primarily deeds, leases, and agreements relating to Bolton's land holdings in Cleveland. Also included is one folder of correspondence concerning Bolton's law practice as a partner in the firm of Bolton & Kelley, which he organized with Moses Kelley in 1837; and one folder of letters from Ohio political leaders such as Albert G. Riddle and Norton S. Townshend, 1848–1849.

298 CLARK WEBSTER. Papers, 1801–1849. 1 folder. MS 1320.

General and personal letters received by Webster, a resident of Kingsville, Ashtabula County, Ohio. Also included are some papers relating to other Kingsville inhabitants, including Lemuel Beckwith, Corinna Rice, and Hiram C. Webster.

299 CHRISTOPHER COWAN. Papers, 1784, 1787, 1798, 1815–1826. ½ box. MS 1328.

Letters, agreements, powers of attorney, and other papers concerning the estate of Major Abraham Kirkpatrick of Pittsburgh, Pennsylvania. These papers focus on the disposal of land lying in Ohio's Virginia Military District. Kirkpatrick, who died intestate, was survived by three daughters, Mrs. Charles Shaler, Mrs. Joel Lewis, and Mrs. Christopher Cowan. Correspondents include William Armstrong, William Croghan, Philip Doddridge, Allen Latham, and Charles Shaler.

Also included here is an unsigned letter addressed to Colonel John Newville near Fort Pitt containing diary-like entries made while the writer traveled throughout the area of what is now southern Ohio during June and July, 1784. The writer sketched a map showing the rivers and names of various settlements, including Indian camps.

300   LUTHER M. STRONG. Papers, 1849–1883. 1 box. Gift of John M. Strong, 1924. MS 1329.

Inventories, invoices, official correspondence, quarterly return lists, receipts, and other documents relating primarily to Captain Strong's activities as commanding officer of Company G, 49th Regiment, Ohio Volunteer Infantry, during the Civil War. Also included are a few deeds, speeches, and letters received by Strong, a resident of Tiffin and Kenton, and Ohio State Senator from the 13th District during the 1880's; and some land deeds belonging to members of the Milliman family.

301   N. R. JENNINGS. Papers, 1830–1863. ½ box. MS 1349.

Primarily correspondence, commissions, orders, and other military papers of Major N. R. Jennings, who served as brigade commissary in the Confederate Army under General Leonidas Polk, 1861–1863. Correspondents and persons referred to include Judah P. Benjamin, Thomas S. Dabney, Robert M. Lusher, and John C. Ruggles. Also included are deeds and contracts concerning the sale of slaves and land to James R. Jennings of New Orleans, Louisiana, 1842–1854; and resolutions and minutes of directors' meetings of the New Orleans, Jackson & Great Northern Railroad during the Civil War.

302   SOCIETY OF FRIENDS. OHIO AND PENNSYLVANIA YEARLY MEETING. MINISTERS INSTITUTE. Records, 1900–1910. 1 volume (44 pp.). MS 1351.

Minutes of meetings held in various counties in Ohio and Pennsylvania at which sermons were preached and discussions concentrated on relations with other religious denominations.

303 ANONYMOUS. Journal, 1834. 1 volume. MS 1352.
Account of a trip from Philadelphia, Pennsylvania, to Savannah, Georgia, by land.

304 STEUBENVILLE & RICHMOND PLANK ROAD COMPANY. STEUBENVILLE, O. Records, 1857–1867. 1 volume. MS 1356.
List of stockholders and minutes of meetings.

305 RICHMOND COLLEGE. RICHMOND, O. Records, 1872–1903. 1 volume. Gift of Sheridan B. Pyle. MS 1360.
Matriculation records, including names and addresses of students. This college, a nonsectarian institution incorporated in 1835, was located in Richmond, a small village ten miles northwest of Steubenville, Ohio.

306 METHODIST-EPISCOPAL CHURCH. CHATHAM CIRCUIT, WOOSTER DISTRICT, NORTHERN OHIO CONFERENCE. Records, 1870–1882. 1 volume. MS 1361.
Minutes of financial and quarterly conference meetings held in various cities.

307 VERMILLION INSTITUTE. PHILOPHRONESIAN LITERARY SOCIETY. HAYESVILLE, O. Records, 1846–1851. 1 volume. Gift of Grace Armstrong, 1925. MS 1362.
Membership roll and minutes of meetings.

308 FRANKLIN COLLEGE. NEW ATHENS, HARRISON COUNTY, O. Records, 1831–1842. 2 volumes. Gift of Lillie Jenkins. MS 1363.
Minutes of meetings of the Jefferson Literary Society of Franklin College (a Presbyterian school organized in 1825), 1831–1842;

and list of classes in the mathematics department with the name and standing of each student, 1840–1842.

309 OHIO (STATE). FIFTH DISTRICT. Records, 1864–1866. 1 volume. MS 1364.

Record of pay and allowance to assistant (tax) assessors.

310 OHIO VOLUNTEER INFANTRY. 163RD REGIMENT. Record Books, May–September, 1864. 3 volumes. Purchased, 1926. MS 1365.

Clothing accounts, morning reports of Captain William W. Cockley, and a descriptive roll of Company C. This regiment, composed of various Ohio National Guard units, was organized on May 12, 1864, to serve 100 days.

311 OHIO VOLUNTEER INFANTRY. 187TH REGIMENT. Record Book, March–December, 1865. 1 volume. MS 1372.

Clothing account kept by Captain William W. Cockley. This one-year regiment was organized on March 2, 1865.

312 VALLANDIGHAM AND LAIRD FAMILIES. Papers, 1797–1866. 1 box. MS 1381.

Letters, speeches, financial receipts, legal documents, marriage certificates, land deeds, account book, and other papers relating to the activities of various members of these two families who resided in New Lisbon, Columbiana County, Ohio. Of the Vallandighams, those most frequently referred to are Clement, Clement L., Elizabeth, George, James L., Mary E., and Rebecca. This collection touches primarily upon national, state, and county politics. Of special interest are those items which refer to Clement L. Vallandigham, lawyer and Ohio legislator, who, as a Peace Democrat, was a candidate for governor of Ohio in 1863. Institutions referred to include the New Lisbon Tippecanoe Club, the Democratic Hickory Club of Centre Township (Ohio), and the Presbyterian Church of New Lisbon, for which Clement Vallandigham (father of Clement L.) served as pastor.

Nearly one-half of this material relates to the business and political activities of the Laird family, including John Laird (d. 1824), a lawyer and Ohio State Senator.

313   JOHNSON AND HUMRICKHOUSE FAMILIES. Papers, 1800–1910. 6 boxes. MS 1385.

Papers relating to members of these two early families who settled in Coshocton, Ohio, including the following: business, general, and personal correspondence; land deeds and agreements, plats, field notes, and surveys of land in Coshocton County; inheritance papers; records of the Coshocton Presbyterian Church; deeds and associated papers concerning land holdings in various states, including Illinois, Kansas, and South Dakota; and other papers pertaining to the development of Coshocton County. Individuals mentioned most frequently are James, John, Joseph, and William K. Johnson, and George and Thomas S. Humrickhouse.

314   PETER H. KAISER (1840–1929). Papers, 1900–1927. 1 box. MS 1387.

Correspondence, notebooks, and other papers containing data relating to the 150th Regiment, Ohio Volunteer Infantry, which were gathered by Kaiser, historian of this regiment, 1900–1927; "A Half-Century in Cleveland," which includes Kaiser's observations on topics such as housing, population, railways, industry, and the Cleveland Bar (11 typescript pages), February 2, 1919; and a "History and Evaluation of Soldiers' Relief in Ohio" (119 typescript pages), undated.

315   DAVID L. PERRY. Papers, 1836, 1845–1846. 1 folder. MS 1395.

Primarily letters to Rev. David L. Perry of Bloomington, Illinois, from his son, a soldier, who was stationed for the most part at Camp Rio Grande and at Camargo, Mexico, 1845–1846.

316   URBANA HIGH SCHOOL. ALCYONE LITERARY SOCIETY. URBANA, O. Records, 1916–1919. 1 volume. MS 1403.

Constitution, list of members, and minutes of meetings of this society, the objective of which was to develop proficiency in public speaking.

317   JOSIAH RENICK. Papers, 1828–1857. 1 folder. MS 1405.

Land deeds, indentures, and some other legal papers relating to the activities of Joseph Renick of Pickaway County, Ohio.

318   THEOPHILUS MORGAN. Papers, 1844–1852. 1 folder. MS 1422.

Deeds and associated land papers, tax payment receipts, and some correspondence of Theophilus Morgan, his wife, May, and the administrator of his estate, James Lynn. Morgan lived in Oswego, New York, and Iowa County, Wisconsin.

319   ALLING & BROTHER COMPANY. TWINSBURG, O. Records, 1850–1852. 1 folder. MS 1425.

Correspondence, receipts, vouchers, and manufacturers' advertisements received by Francis A. and George H. Alling, merchants in Twinsburg, Ohio.

320   JOHN McSWEENEY. Record Book, 1878. 1 volume. MS 1428.

Agency partnership and sales records of this insurance agent from Wooster, Ohio.

321   LILLIE TRYON CURTIS. Papers, ca. 1930. ½ box. Gift of Lillie T. Curtis, 1931. MS 1432.

Papers relating to the history of Waite Hill, Lake County, Ohio, including "The Story of Waite Hill" (161 typescript pages); and a collection of photos of members of the Hobart, Howard, Tryon, and Waite families, all early settlers of Waite Hill.

322 LOUISIANA MILITIA. JEFFERSON MOUNTED GUARDS. JEFFERSON, LA. Records, 1860–1862. 83 pages. MS 1451.

Constitution, rules of order, and minutes of meetings of this corps from its inception until the unit left for war.

323 *BALTIC.* Logbook, 1864–1865. 2 volumes. MS 1452.

Log of this Confederate barge which was captained by James E. Leroy and worked near Fort Powell.

324 GEORGE E. STEVENS (1841–1917). Papers, 1905. 1 folder. MS 1454.

Correspondence and newspaper clippings concerning the National Baptist Congress held in Cincinnati in November, 1905. Stevens, the son of Rev. John Stevens, was chairman of the Cincinnati Baptist Social Union, clerk of the Miami Baptist Association, and a prominent bookseller and publisher in Granville, Ohio.

325 JOHN STEVENS (d. 1877). Papers, 1824–ca. 1875. 4 boxes. MS 1455.

Correspondence, financial papers, essays and articles, deeds, newspaper clippings, and other papers relating to the activities of Rev. John Stevens of Cincinnati, who was agent of the American Baptist Missionary Union, editor of the weekly *Cross and Baptist Journal,* and professor at the Granville Literary and Theological Institution (now Denison University). Included is correspondence concerning the operation of the *Cross and Baptist Journal,* fund raising for the American Baptist Missionary Union, circulation of the *Macedonian,* the German Baptist Mission, the Baptist Board of Foreign Missions, the American Baptist Home Mission Society, and the Fairmount Theological Seminary, and relating in general to Baptist missionary activities in Ohio, Kentucky, Indiana, and Pennsylvania, 1830–1870; correspondence, annual reports, minutes of meetings, financial notes, and statements concerning the Western Baptist Education Society and the Ohio Baptist Education Society, 1834–1860; and assorted newspaper clippings and photographs of members of Stevens' family.

About one-third of this collection is composed of papers of other professors who were connected with the Granville Literary and Theological Institution, particularly Rev. John Pratt, a Baptist minister and president of Granville College. These letters and financial papers relate primarily to the activities of the college, the Society for Religious Inquiry, or Baptist affairs in general between 1830 and 1852. Records of the Cincinnati Baptist Missionary Society from its establishment in 1824 include a list of members, convention rules, constitution and bylaws, a list of subscribers, and minutes of board meetings. Correspondents include Edward Bright, Jr., Richard E. Eddy, John S. Kerr, R. E. Pattison, D. A. Randall, and Samuel Trevor.

326   KIRTLAND AND MORSE FAMILIES. Papers, 1779–1909. 9½ boxes, 1 oversize package. Gift of Mary Morse, 1936. MS 1463.

Agreements, land deeds, financial papers, correspondence, shipping records, account books, daybooks, ledgers, and other record books pertaining primarily to the mercantile and shipping interests of various members of these two families, who resided in and around Poland, Ohio. The names mentioned most frequently are Henry T., Jared, Lois, Nancy M., and Turhand Kirtland; Eldredge, Elkanah, Emery, Franklin, and Henry K. Morse. Included are account books of Jared Kirtland, 1792–1838; account book of William Truman, 1803–1838; bills, invoices, receipts, shipping records, and letter copies relating to the Morse and Kirtland Company, 1814–1830; daybooks of Richard Hall, 1821–1831; account books of Elkanah Morse, 1817–1819, 1834–1846; business transactions of E. Morse and Company, 1840; daybooks and ledgers of Henry K. Morse, 1844–1879; account book of Kirtland, Morse, & Company, 1848–1873; records of the estate of Polly

Kirtland, 1848; ledger and checkbook of Edwin Morse, 1852–1854; Poland Mill record book, 1857–1871; and scattered shipping records of the Morse Bridge Company of Youngstown, Ohio. Also included are the following: a biographical sketch of Dr. Jared Potter and several letters addressed to him in Wallingford, Connecticut, 1779–1810; copies (made by Henry K. Morse in 1909) of account books and letters of Turhand Kirtland, 1798–1833, and of memoranda of Henry T. Kirtland, 1798–1873; and a series of letters addressed to L. K. Mansfield of Poland, Ohio, 1840–1877.

327   TUSCARAWAS COAL & IRON COMPANY. CANAL DOVER, O. Records, 1865–1907. 3 volumes, 1 folder. Gift of David T. Craxton. MS 1464.

Ledger, 1865–1907; daybook, 1874–1907; cashbook, 1881–1904; one folder of loose invoices, receipts, and balance sheets.

Also included here are several Tuscarawas County land grants.

328   FIRST CONGREGATIONAL CHURCH. PARMA, O. Records, 1835–1874. 2 volumes. Gift of K. K. Hodgman. MS 1468.

Minutes of church meetings, confession of faith, and lists of members of this church which was organized in 1835, 1835–1874; and minutes of meetings and other records of the First Congregational Church and Society of Parma, 1839–1873.

329   PRESBYTERIAN CHURCH. WILLOUGHBY, O. Records, 1883–1897. 3 folders. Gift of Sidney S. Wilson. MS 1485.

Bills, receipts, treasurer's reports, and contracts and payroll reports for rebuilding the church, 1883–1897; and correspondence concerning efforts to procure a minister to replace Rev. A. J. Waugh, 1890.

Also included here is one folder of contracts, correspondence, receipts, and stock certificates of Martin E. Gray of Willoughby.

330   BENJAMIN F. TAYLOR FAMILY. Papers, 1839–1925. 1 box. MS 1498.

Primarily letters touching upon the careers of Benjamin F. Taylor (1819–1887), Cleveland journalist, artist, and poet; and Lucy E. L. Taylor, member of the Cleveland Board of Education during the first quarter of the 20th century. Specifically included are letters from Taylor while a teacher at Brooklyn (N.Y.) High School to his father, 1840; copies of poems and general correspondence, 1861–1884; original manuscript of a novel, *Theophilus Trent* (1887); and copies of speeches delivered by Lucy E. L. Taylor on a variety of topics relating to history, education, and culture.

331   CHAMBER OF INDUSTRY. CLEVELAND, O. Records, 1912, 1914, 1915. 1 volume. Gift of the Chamber of Industry, 1930. MS 1500.

Records of social events and some financial accounts of this organization which was incorporated in 1907 to promote the general interests of Cleveland's west side.

332   SECOND CREEK NEW HOPE BAPTIST CHURCH. NEW HOPE, O. Records, 1836–1881. 1 volume. Gift of Mrs. Watkins, 1930. MS 1509.

List of members and minutes of meetings.

333   THOMPSON AND TUTTLE FAMILIES. Papers, ca. 1812–1915. 11 boxes. Gift of Mary McArthur Tuttle, 1910 and later. MS 1511.

Correspondence, legal and business papers, speeches, pamphlets and newspaper clippings, biographical and genealogical data, photographs, and other materials relating to various members of these two families residing for the most part in Hillsboro, Ohio. Included are Mary McArthur (Thompson) Tuttle (1849-1916), artist, author, and lecturer; Herbert Tuttle (1846–1894), educator, journalist, and historian; James Henry Thompson (1812–1900), lawyer, jurist, and public servant; and Eliza Jane (Trimble) Thompson (1816-1905), author, temperance crusader, and founder of the temperance movement in 1873. The bulk of this collection consists of the correspondence of Eliza Jane Thompson and Mary McArthur Tuttle with representatives of the national, world, and Ohio organizations of the Woman's Christian Temperance Union and of the temperance publications, *The Union Signal* and the *National W.C.T.U.*, 1873-1903. Other material relates to *Hillsboro Crusade Sketches and Family Records* (1896) by Eliza J. Thompson, her two daughters, and Frances E. Willard; and to the visit of 500 W.C.T.U. delegates to Hillsboro in 1903. Also included are some papers relating to the Trimble family of Ohio, including the manuscript autobiography of Allen Trimble (1783-1870), Ohio legislator and National Republican Governor (1826-1830), who was also active in the Whig Party.

Unpublished 12-page register available in the Society.

334 PROVIDENCE BAPTIST CHURCH. [WARREN COUNTY, O.] Records, 1820-1846. 1 volume. MS 1512.
Covenant, rules, minutes of meetings, and a list of members of this church which was originally organized at Bear Run in Hamilton Township with the assistance of three other Baptist churches in Warren County.

335 JOSIAH FOX (1763-1847). Papers, 1826-1836. 1 folder. Gift of Ernest J. Wessen, 1930. MS 1515.
Correspondence and documents relating to the Society of Friends. Specifically referred to are the Orthodox-versus-Friends controversy within the Ohio Yearly Meeting and the activities of Josiah Fox, Elisha Bates, Elias Hicks, Isaac T. Hooper, and various other Quakers residing in and around Mount Pleasant, Ohio. Included here are the following: a record of the Friends' trial at Steubenville, 1828; a proposal for publishing "Orthodoxy Unmasked or All is Not Gold that Glitters," 1829; and a petition seeking incorporation for the Ohio Yearly Meeting from the Ohio legislature, 1832.

336 NATHAN MOORE. Field Notes, 1798. 1 volume. MS 1521.

Surveys of lots in Campfield (Canfield), Mahoning County, Ohio.

337 FIRST PRESBYTERIAN CHURCH. EAST CLEVELAND. O. Records, 1807–1911. 2 boxes. MS 1528.

Confession of faith, list of charter members, and minutes of session meetings, 1807–1911; constitution and minutes of annual meetings, 1828–1892; record of the suspension and reinstatement of Jedediah D. Crocker, 1830; and the treasurers' book, 1836–1871.

Also included here are copies of the church publication, *Contact*, 1950–1958.

338 ELISHA WHITTLESEY (1783–1863). Papers, 1811–1863. Combined from several sources, 1969. 5 boxes, 2 volumes. MS 1529.

Financial papers, notes and speeches, docket books, newspaper clippings, certificates of appointment, and some letters addressed to Whittlesey, attorney, U.S. Congressman, land speculator, and Whig and Republican political leader. Whittlesey, while residing in Canfield, Ohio, was active in affairs throughout the Western Reserve. Included are three volumes containing "Notes on Law," undated; financial receipts, 1811–1862; a Western Reserve Bank book, 1815–1824; and research notes and speeches on topics such as African colonization, agriculture, the Ohio Militia, and the War of 1812. Subjects referred to in the letters include the Board of Ohio Canal Fund Commissioners, Samuel Brady (Brady's Leap), the estate of Stanley Griswold, and the history of the Western Reserve (especially that of the Firelands and of Canfield). Correspondents include Rev. Joseph Badger, Lyman C. Draper, C. Lancaster, Rev. Isaac Van Tassel, Frederick Wadsworth, and William Wills.

Also included are two volumes containing approximately 140 letters of early Ohio governors, members of the Ohio Constitutional Convention, various state legislators, and soldiers during the War of 1812. Most of these are addressed to Elijah Wadsworth (1747–1817) and touch upon political and military matters in Ohio, but particularly to affairs in the Western Reserve, 1801–1857. Correspondents include: Reasin Beall, Thomas Kirker, Duncan McArthur, Return J. Meigs, Calvin Pease, John Sloane, Benjamin Tallmadge, Benjamin Tappan, Edward Tiffin, Elijah Wadsworth, Frederick Wadsworth, and Thomas Worthington.

339   JAMES BACKUS. Papers, 1791–1833. 2 folders. MS 1548.

General correspondence between members of the Backus family of Norwich, Connecticut, and other members of that family and of the Woodbridge family who emigrated to Marietta, Muskingum, or Norwalk, Ohio. Also included is one folder of Marietta newspaper clippings from the 1880's.

340   NEWCOMB FAMILY. Reunion Records, 1880–1923. 1 volume. Gift of Ozro R. Newcomb, 1931. MS 1553.

Minutes of reunions held throughout Geauga and Cuyahoga counties in Ohio.

341   FIRST UNIVERSALIST CHURCH. UPPER SANDUSKY, O. Records, 1870–1912. 2 volumes. MS 1559.

Subscription list, minutes of meetings, constitution and bylaws adopted in 1880, list of members, and financial records.

342   NEW YORK STATE VOLUNTEERS. 19TH REGIMENT. Records, 1861–1863. 1 volume. MS 1561.

Orders and descriptive roll for Company C.

343   RUFUS SWAIN. Notebook, 1854–1858. 1 volume. MS 1574.

Comments on law recorded by Rufus Swain of St. Louis, Missouri, as well as copies of letters sent by Swain to friends and relatives.

344 JAMES KYSER. Papers, 1849–1879. 1 folder. Gift of Miss Abbie Webb. MS 1575.

Warranty deeds and contracts pertaining to the construction of various buildings in Cleveland.

345 BARTHOLOMEW BROWN. Notebook, 1820–1850. 1 volume. Gift of F. F. Prentiss, 1918. MS 1576.

Copies of sermons delivered by Rev. James Flint in East Bridgewater, Massachusetts, 1820–1821; Bartholomew Brown family records, 1772–1854; and an account of Brown's visit to his daughter, Harriett, and his travels through the Western Reserve, including visits to Cleveland, Chagrin Falls, Warren, and Ravenna, undated.

346 JOHN S. GANO. Papers, 1812–1814. 1 folder. Gift of the Tuttle Company, 1922. MS 1583.

Correspondence and orders of Major General Gano of Cincinnati, later commander in chief of the Ohio Militia in Lower Sandusky during the War of 1812.

347 BETHEL UNION BAPTIST CHURCH. JEFFERSON, O. Records, 1829–1887. 2 volumes. MS 1585.

Minutes of meetings, articles of faith and of practice, covenant, and list of subscribers of this church, organized in 1829 and united with the First Baptist Church of Jefferson in 1833. Also included are scattered legal documents, 1834–1839; the treasurer's book, 1867–1887, of the First Baptist Church and Society of Jefferson; and a 25-page typewritten history of this church by B. J. Lomus.

348 SETH I. ENSIGN. Field Notes, 1806. 1 volume. Gift of the Tallmadge Historical Society, 1872. MS 1588.

Field notes of the original survey of Tallmadge, Ohio, made by Seth Ensign.

349 U.S. POST OFFICE. WILLOUGHBY, O. Records, 1855–1861. 1 volume. MS 1592.
Journal of registered letters received in this office.

350 HOSEA PAUL, JR. Report, 1864. 1 volume. MS 1597.
Report of Hosea Paul, Jr., who was sent as delegate from Cleveland to the U.S. Christian Commission, City Point, Virginia.

351 CLEVELAND LIGHT ARTILLERY ASSOCIATION. CLEVELAND, O. Records, 1856–1914. 4 volumes. MS 1600.
Correspondence, invitations, and acknowledgments, 1856–1914; minutes of meetings, 1870–1912; names of deceased members, biographical sketches, and location of burials in Cleveland's Lakeview Cemetery.

352 ROBERT COCHRAN. Papers, 1830–1858. 1 folder. MS 1602.
Correspondence, contracts, deeds, and financial receipts of Robert Cochran, a resident of Twinsburg, Ohio. Also included are papers concerning the will and estate of John Cochran of Paisley, Renfrewshire, Scotland, 1830–1849.

353 WILLIAM E. HUNT. Papers, late 19th c. ½ box. MS 1609.
Primarily manuscript copies of writings relating to early Presbyterian churches in Ohio, prepared by Hunt, a resident of Coshocton, Ohio. Included are histories of the Hopewell Church, Richland Presbytery; the Presbytery of Steubenville; early Ohio Presbyterian churches; and the Synod of Ohio; and letters (1859) to Hunt from T. R. Crawford concerning the Nottingham Church, Harrison County, Ohio, and from Milo Templeton concerning a church in Marseilles, Wyandot County, Ohio.

354 MEAD FAMILY. Papers, 1760–1850. 1 folder. MS 1615.

Correspondence, deeds, powers of attorney, appointments and certificates, surveys, financial papers, and records of the estates of Hobby, Jabez, Jeremiah, Sarah, Shadrach, and Titus Mead of Greenwich, Fairfield County, Connecticut.

355 OHIO C. BARBER. Papers, 1880–1913. 2 folders. MS 1617.

Barber, a resident of Akron, Ohio, was co-founder (1864) of the Barber Match Company, forerunner of the Diamond Match Company; founder (1891) of the industrial city of Barberton; and president (1907) of the National Sewer Pipe Company. These papers include a draft of the proposed constitution and bylaws for the National Match Company, 188?; certificates of stock ownership and mortgage bonds from various companies, 1899–1908; some general correspondence including single letters from George B. Cortelyou, Marcus A. Hanna, and Booker T. Washington, 1902–1903; statement of the Diamond Match Company, 1907–1908; railroad passes and automobile registration cards, 1908–1913; and newspaper clippings concerning the Barber family and home.

356 EARLY SETTLERS' ASSOCIATION OF CUYAHOGA COUNTY, O. Records, 1890–1891. 1 folder. MS 1623.

Report of the executive committee, financial report, copies of speeches delivered to the association, and some newspaper clippings referring to old settlers.

357 ISAAC MISHIMENS. Account Book, 1833–1847. 1 volume. Gift of Frank Winch, 1924. MS 1627.

Mishimens, of Zanesville, Ohio, kept a detailed account of the activities on his farm, which included an orchard and nursery.

358 OHIO VOLUNTEER INFANTRY. 19TH REGIMENT. Records, 1861–1864. 1 volume. MS 1628.
Roll book kept by Captain Solomon J. Firestone.

359 PRESBYTERIAN CHURCH. MOUNT VERNON, O. Records, 1841–1843. 1 volume. MS 1629.
Minutes of meetings, lists of subscribers for ministers' salaries, and some other financial records.

360 MUSIC BOOKS. 2 volumes. MS 1630.
Volume containing music and words of hymns transcribed in England, ca. 1840; volume labeled *Zoar Gessang-Verein* belonging to Solomon Ackerman, tenor, containing music and words of hymns in German.

361 ANONYMOUS. Diary, 1840–1844, 1850–1852. 1 volume. MS 1633.
Work record and meteorological data kept by a member of the Society of Friends from Columbiana County, Ohio.

362 JONAS D. CATTELL. Scrapbook, 1838–1879. 1 volume. MS 1634.
Copies of extracts of speeches by ministers and congressmen and newspaper clippings collected by Cattell, of Salem, Ohio.

363 COLLECTION OF AUTOGRAPH ALBUMS, 1825–1899. 25 volumes. Gifts of various persons. MS 1636.
Anonymous. 1 vol., 1855–1866 (Lake Cottage, Ind.). Classmates.
———. 1 vol., 1860's [Location?]. Cut signatures of U.S. Presidents, Cabinet officials, and other notable persons.
———. 1 vol., 1876 (Philadelphia). Persons in attendance at the Centennial Exposition.
Bobb, Emma C. 1 vol., 1879–1880 (Columbus, O.). High school classmates.

Brinkerhoff Family. 2 vols., 1876–1885 (Ohio and New York). Classmates and friends.

Butler, Benjamin. 1 vol., 1849–1851, 1858 (Richmond, Ind.). Friends.

Case, Esther. 2 vols., 1875–1876, 1881 (Wooster, O.). Classmates.

Farr, Joseph M. 1 vol., 1850–1851 (Columbus, O.). Members and officers of the Ohio Constitutional Convention.

Gordon, Eleanor. 1 vol., 1825–1826 (Canton, O.). Friends.

Gurley, Mary Alice. 1 vol., ca. 1850's (Delaware, O.). Findlay College classmates.

Kauffman, Catherine. 1 vol., 1848–1853 (Lancaster County, Pa.). Friends.

Lee, Fanny J. 1 vol., 1879–1880 (Cleveland, O.). Classmates at Sterling School.

Lewis, Martha J. 1 vol., 1849–1851 (Dayton, O.). Classmates.

Mason, Mary L. 2 vols., 1875–1876 (Cleveland, O.). Classmates.

Merrell, Catherine. 1 vol., 1826–1827 (New Hartford, Conn., and Canton, O.). Friends.

Potter, Julia. 1 vol., 1831–1840 (Plymouth, Mass.). Friends.

Trowbridge, G. A. 1 vol., 1823–1828 (Canandaigua and Rochester, N.Y.). Friends.

Welch, D. E. 1 vol., 1850–1851 (Columbus, O.). Officers and members of the Ohio Constitutional Convention.

———. 1 vol., ca. 1865 (Washington, D.C.). U.S. congressmen and other public officials.

Wintermute, Lewis H., Jr. 2 vols., 1897–1899 (Washington, D.C.). U.S. representatives to the 55th Congress and other government officials.

364   WINCHESTER FITCH. Papers, 1860–1932. 1 box. Gift of Winchester Fitch, 1931–1946. MS 1637.

Scrapbook (newspaper clippings) kept by Mrs. R. M. N. Taylor, wife of the proprietor of the McHenry House in Unionville, Ohio, 1860–1887; historical address (70 typescript pages) delivered by Edward H. Fitch at the Conneaut Centennial Celebration, July 4, 1896; some correspondence and genealogical data concerning the Coleman, Fitch, Frisbie, Sherwood, Warner, and Weeks families, 1912–1932; 11 volumes of notes on the history of Unionville, Ohio, and one volume of notes for a census of Unionville, 1798–1838, compiled by Fitch, chairman of the historical committee for the Unionville Reunion in 1912.

365   MARIUS R. ROBINSON (1806–1878). Papers, 1830–1865, 1877. 1 box. Gifts of William P. Palmer, 1921; W. C. Boyle, 1927. MS 1660.

Correspondence, speeches and lectures, and newspaper clippings relating to the activities of Rev. Marius R. Robinson, an itinerant lecturer for the American Anti-Slavery Society in Ohio (1836–1839) and later editor of the *Anti-Slavery Bugle* (Salem, Ohio). Relating primarily to slavery, abolitionism, and emancipation, this collection includes copies of lectures and speeches delivered by Robinson, 1830–1865; a scrapbook of newspaper clippings relating to the Anti-Slavery Society of Lane Seminary, Cincinnati, Ohio, and the American Colonization Society, 1830–1850; a notebook of arguments and refutations concerning theological subjects, 1834–1840; correspondence between Robinson and his wife, Emily, 1836–1839; a journal for part of the year of 1840; and a birthday testimonial, July 29, 1877.

Also included is a typescript copy of an article on Robinson by Homer C. Boyle which was published in the *Daily News* (Salem, Ohio), July 31, 1897.

366   SEPARATIST SOCIETY OF ZOAR. TUSCARAWAS COUNTY, O. Papers, 1818–1911. 4 boxes, 4 packages. MS 1663.

Papers (in English and German) relating to this German religious community. Among the English documents are account books, 1818–1820, 1841–1862; banking and other financial papers, 1818–1873; deeds, contracts, and agreements, 1818–1860; post office records, including reports, mails sent, and mails received, 1821–1845; Fairfield Furnace Store records, 1843–1852; subscription lists, 1870–1900; an undated map of Zoar and a petition concerning a road through Zoar; copies of land patents sent to J. K. Johnson of Coshocton, Ohio, 1871; and typed copies and summaries of the "Appraisal of the Zoar Mills," Zoar, Ohio, March 10, 1911, with blueprints of the Society's property.

Among the German documents are a hymn book, letters, a medicine book, prescriptions for medicine, orders, a religious treatise, and copies of sermons, 1840–1860.

Also included are three volumes by Joseph Bimeler: *Die Wahre Separation* . . . , 4 volumes in 2 (1856–1860); *Etwas fürs Herz,* 2 volumes in 1 (1860–[1861]).

367 ANONYMOUS. Notebook, n.d. 1 volume. MS 1667.
Plats in various townships in the Wisconsin counties of Houghton, Marquette, and Ontonagon.

368 NATHANIEL WRIGHT. Papers, 1817–1855. 1 folder. MS 1670.
Correspondence, deeds, and some legal papers belonging to Wright, an attorney in Cincinnati, Ohio.

369 ANONYMOUS. Journal, ca. 1893. 1 volume. MS 1671.
Kept on a tour of California and of other western states.

370 OHIO VOLUNTEER INFANTRY. 171ST REGIMENT. Records, 1864. 2 volumes. MS 1673.
Roster book and clothing and ordnance book for Company K, which was under the command of Captain Peter Hitchcock. This regiment, which consisted of several Ohio National Guard units, was organized at Sandusky, Ohio, on May 7, 1864, to serve 100 days. It served guard duty at Johnson's Island and fought against the forces of Confederate General John H. Morgan in Kentucky during June, 1864.

371   A. H. TWEEDY, *compiler.* Genealogical Data, n.d. 1 box. MS 1674.
Genealogical data on the Tweedy, Turpin, Newman, Hearne, and Fellows families.

372   ROYCE FAMILY. Papers, 1852–1924. 1 folder. Gift of W. D. Royce, 1931. MS 1675.
Papers include descriptive rolls and letters written by Abner Royce of Company H, 55th Regiment, Ohio Volunteer Infantry, while he was stationed at Camp Chase, Ohio, and at various camps throughout Virginia, to his parents, Mr. and Mrs. B. F. Royce of Bloomville, Seneca County, Ohio, 1861–1862; sketchbook of Henrietta L. (Knapp) Royce; papers concerning the activities of the Cleveland division of the American Protective League (which in 1919 became the Loyal American League) for which William D. Royce was an inspector, including a plan of organization, inspector reports, form letters and other correspondence, and a few handbills, 1918–1924; miscellaneous letters, stock certificates, and other family papers, 1852–1909.

373   LEGION OF THE UNITED STATES. Orderly Book, August–December, 1793. 1 volume. Gift of William P. Palmer, 1909. MS 1679.
Record of the U.S. Army Legion in camp at Hobson's Choice and Greenville in the Northwest Territory containing the orders issued by General Anthony Wayne, Commander in Chief.

374   JOHN G. MATHEWS FAMILY. Genealogical Papers, 1919–1935. 1 box. Gift of Mary L. Mathews, 1936. MS 1689.
Correspondence, notes, charts, and newspaper clippings concerning the ancestors of John G. Mathews, who resided in Berea, Ohio.

375 AMZI ATWATER. Field Notes, 1797. 1 volume. Gift of Darwin Atwater, 1870. MS 1693.
Field notes for surveys of land in eastern Cuyahoga County, near Lake Erie (townships 6 and 7, range 11).

376 HALSEY D. MILLER. Diaries, 1870–1872, 1875, 1878. 5 volumes. MS 1695.
An avid churchgoer (Baptist), this Clevelander briefly recorded his daily activities and financial transactions.

377 PHILO SCOVILL. Daybook, 1816–1828. 1 volume. Gift of Mrs. C. Scovill Bemis, 1892. MS 1700.
Scovill came to Cleveland in 1816 from Buffalo, operated a sawmill for a while, was elected county commissioner in 1827, and built, owned, and managed the Franklin House, a hotel on Superior Street, for almost a quarter of a century.

378 BAPTIST CHURCH. MONTVILLE, CONN. Records, 1749–1779, 1779–1801, 1807–1827. 3 volumes. MS 1704.
Minutes of meetings, confession of faith, covenant, and membership lists.

379 FIRST METHODIST-EPISCOPAL CHURCH. WOMAN'S HOME AND FOREIGN MISSIONARY SOCIETY. PORT CLINTON, O. Records, 1905–1910. 1 volume. MS 1707.
Minutes of meetings and members' attendance records.

380 DELTA BUILDING LOAN & SAVINGS COMPANY. DELTA, O. Records, 1895–1900. 1 volume. MS 1715.
Minutes of meetings of the board of directors, A. L. Sargent presiding.

381 BAPTIST CHURCH. HAYESVILLE, O. Records, 1841–1859. 1 volume. Gift of Grace Armstrong, 1925. MS 1721.

Resolutions, articles, covenant, list of members, and minutes of meetings.

382 KELLEY FAMILY. Papers, 1798–1881. 1 box. MS 1723.

Letters, land contracts and deeds, diaries, and other papers relating to members of the Kelley family who owned and developed Kelley's Island in Lake Erie. Included are several letters, 1798–1847; land deeds and other legal papers of Addison, Alfred S., Datus, Hannah, and Sarah Kelley, 1848–1880; a diary of one of the Kelleys, 1854–1855; five diaries kept by Alfred S. Kelley while residing on Kelley's Island and containing some references to local events and comments on the Civil War, 1860–1864; criminal-docket book kept by Addison Kelley, justice of the peace, 1865–1877; statements on the condition of the Kelley's Island Wine Company, 1870–1880; and a diary kept by Hermon A. Kelley while attending school on the island, 1871.

383 ANONYMOUS. Diary, 1822–1859. 1 volume (unbound). Gift of the Library of Adelbert College of Western Reserve University, 1926. MS 1732.

Kept by a resident of Edinburgh, Portage County, Ohio, who spent much time in Canfield. Although containing mostly meteorological data, there is brief mention of trips locating and investigating a road built from Cleveland to the Ohio River, 1823–1825, and trips to Newcastle, Pennsylvania, in 1826 and to Columbus, Ohio, in 1831 and 1832.

384 ST. STEPHEN'S SCHOOL. BOSTON, MASS. Records, 1856. 1 volume. MS 1740.

Journal containing names of students, grades, deportment records, and other information. Thomas H. Evans was apparently the teacher of this school, which was located on Purchase Street.

385 HARRIET TAYLOR UPTON. Papers, 1893–1916. 1 folder. Gift of Mrs. H. T. Upton. MS 1746.

Various letters, telegrams, broadsides, and other documents concerning the activities of the Ohio Association Opposed to Womans Suffrage, Ohio Woman Suffrage Association, and the National Anti-Suffrage Association, 1906–1916. Also included is a 6-page manuscript copy of an article written by Mrs. Caroline McCullough Everhard (president of the Ohio Woman Suffrage Association) at the time the school suffrage law was passed in 1893.

386 BRANCH BIBLE SOCIETY OF BOARDMAN. BOARDMAN, O. Records, 1844–1863. 1 volume. Purchased, 1925. MS 1749.

Constitution, rules, list of members, minutes of meetings, and treasurers' reports of this society (auxiliary to the Trumbull County Bible Society), the object of which was "to aid in giving wider circulation to the Holy Scriptures without note or comment." Meetings were held in the Boardman Congregational Church.

387 BURKE AARON HINSDALE (1837–1900). Papers, 1854–1900. 5 boxes. MS 1772.

Correspondence and other papers relating to Hinsdale's activities as a student, author, and educator, but particularly as a friend and associate of James A. Garfield; president of Hiram College, 1870–1882; superintendent of Cleveland schools, 1882–1886; and professor at the University of Michigan from 1888. That which relates to Garfield includes copies of Hinsdale's speeches and writings, copies of agreements and receipts concerning the publication of Hinsdale's book *The Works of James Abram Garfield* (Boston: James R. Osgood & Co., 2 vols., 1882–1883), and letters in answer to Hinsdale's request for information concerning Garfield's early life and the Republican Convention of 1880. Also included are biographical sketches and obituary notices for Hinsdale, recollections of his early life and ancestry, copies of many of his published articles, school notes and essays, scrapbooks of newspaper clippings, and a series of letters of condolence addressed to Mrs. Hinsdale after her husband's death. Among the many educators, publishers, newspaper editors, and political figures who corresponded with Hinsdale were James B. Angell, A. E. Church, Isaac N. Demmon, Charles W. Eliot, Isaac Errett, Charles Foster, President James A. and Lucretia R. Garfield, E. L. Godkin, W. T. Harris, Benjamin Harrison, C. E. Henry, A. Johnston, George C. Mann, William A. Mowry, A. P. Peabody, A. L. Perry, J. H. Rhodes, Whitelaw Reid, Albion W. Tourgée, and Francis A. Walker.

388 CONGREGATIONAL CHURCH. WAYNE, O. Records, 1826–1841. 1 folder. MS 1777.

Subscription lists to raise money to pay the salary of the pastor, Rev. Ephraim T. Woodruff, and lists of notes, agreements, and receipts. Also included are copies of sermons preached by Woodruff.

389 MARION LOUISE MOORE. Journal, 1831–1860. 1 volume (unbound). MS 1792.

Journal kept by this resident of Williamsfield, Ohio, which includes reports on her domestic problems and her religious ideas.

390 CHRISTIAN CHURCH. BRADFORD, N.H. Records, 1829–1845. 1 volume. MS 1797.

Proceedings concerning the organization of the church, minutes of meetings, and lists of members for various years.

391 DAVID ABBOTT FAMILY. Papers, 1799–1875. ½ box. MS 1804.

Contracts, correspondence, deeds, financial accounts, receipts, and other documents pertaining to the general and business activities of David Abbott, of his son, Benjamin W., and of his grandson, David. David Abbott emigrated from Massachusetts in

1798 and settled in the area which is now Willoughby, Ohio. Having bought 1,800 acres of land on the Huron River in 1808, he moved his family there the following year. Among these papers are some concerning the settlement of the estate of David Abbott (debts to Samuel Hughes), 1820–1840; building plans and various reports of the Presbyterian Society of Milan, Ohio, 1830's; and the preamble and constitution of the Christian Meeting House at Bradford, New Hampshire.

392 ALEXANDER NELSON. Papers, 1830–ca. 1874. 1 folder. MS 1805.

Rev. Alexander Nelson, a Methodist minister, settled in Ann Arbor, Michigan, in 1837, but soon moved into Ohio, where he held teaching positions at Norwalk Seminary, Worthington Female Seminary, and Baldwin Institute between 1838 and 1850. Included here are some papers relating to these assignments, as well as copies of sermons and lectures on subjects such as Benedict Arnold, Western antiquities, Methodism, and the Sabbath. Also inclued is an 18-page address on the Bible delivered before the American Bible Society, and a 33-page autobiographical sketch.

393 WOMEN'S MISSIONARY UNION OF THE CLEVELAND CHURCHES. CLEVELAND, O. Records, 1895–1915. 2 volumes. Gift of Miss Effie Gerould, 1932. MS 1808.

Secretaries' books containing a history of the organization, constitution, reports, and minutes of meetings of this union, the objects of which were to increase members' knowledge of missionary work carried on by all denominations and to stimulate interest in and support for missionary activity.

394 WESTERN RESERVE RAILROAD COMPANY. PORTAGE COUNTY, O. Records, 1879–1882. 1 volume. Purchased, 1932. MS 1810.

List of subscribers, certificates of incorporation, notices, minutes of meetings, and results of an election of officers.

395   C. H. SMITH, FLOUR, GRAIN AND MILL FEED. CLEVELAND, O. Records, 1890–1910. 2 volumes. Gifts of the Estate of Mrs. C. H. Smith, 1932. MS 1814.
Ledger C, 1890–1896; and cashbook, 1907–1910.

396   HENRY DOOLITTLE. Papers, 1849–1864. 2 folders. Purchased, 1932. MS 1818.
Correspondence and contracts concerning business activities engaged in by Doolittle, a contractor in Dayton, Ohio, primarily with the Franklin and Warren Railroad and the Atlantic & Great Western Railroad, 1849–1864. Also included are estimates of work done and materials furnished by Doolittle and others under contract for construction of the Atlantic & Great Western Railroad and the Franklin and Warren Railroad, 1853–1857; and payroll lists and board bills of construction workers on the Eastern Division of the Atlantic & Great Western Railroad, Orangeville, Ohio, 1857–1858.

397   BENJAMIN EXCELL (1820–1904). Ministerial Records, 1852–1884. 1 volume. Gift of Miss Minnie Excell, 1924. MS 1823.
Record of appointments filled, sermons preached, and marriages solemnized by Rev. Benjamin Excell, who had resided in Cleveland and Warren, Ohio, and in Meadville, Pennsylvania. Also included is his license to perform marriages in Ohio.

398   HATTIE J. A. COWING. Papers, 1909–1914. 1 folder. Gift of Mrs. Hattie J. A. Cowing. MS 1825.
Military histories of soldiers from Cuyahoga and Lorain counties who served in the Revolutionary War or the War of 1812 as provided by the Bureau of Pensions of the Department of the Interior respectively to the Western Reserve chapter of the Daughters of the American Revolution and to the Ohio chapter of the National Society of United States Daughters of 1812, 1911–1912. Also included are some miscellaneous items and letters to Mrs. Cowing, an active member in both these organizations.

399   SPOONER FAMILY. Genealogical Material, 1870–1935. 4 boxes. MS 1826.

Memorial of William Spooner, 1637 . . . (1871) by Thomas Spooner; manuscript copy of the "Records of William Spooner and His Descendants" (unpublished); and correspondence of Thomas Spooner and Miss Emily Spooner of Glendale, and later Cincinnati, Ohio, pertaining mostly to the Spooner family genealogy, 1870–1935.

400   ALBERT GALLATIN RIDDLE (1816–1902). Papers, 1835–1902. 5 boxes. MS 1827.

Papers cover Riddle's life as a lawyer, State Representative, U.S. Representative (1861–1863), and author from Ohio. Included are manuscripts of unpublished autobiographical writings, romances, and historical novels; accounts of the life in Cuba, where Riddle spent several months (1863–1864) as U.S. consul to Matanzas; personal papers, commissions, certificates, legal documents, and newspaper clippings; and correspondence from many well-known public and political figures referring to political or legal matters or to Riddle's various writings. Correspondents include Susan B. Anthony, Benjamin F. Butler, Simon Cameron, Salmon P. Chase, Schuyler Colfax, John French, James A. Garfield, Joshua R. Giddings, Ulysses S. Grant, Horace Greeley, Alfred Phelps, James Ford Rhodes, William H. Seward, Moses Coit Tyler, Benjamin F. Wade, and Gideon Welles.

Unpublished 5-page register available in the Society.
NUCMC 62-4396

401   GEORGE WASHINGTON BICENTENNIAL COMMITTEE. CLEVELAND, O. Records, 1932. 3 boxes. MS 1828.

Bank book, cash journal, contribution and committee reports, correspondence, contribution data, minutes of meetings of the executive committee, news releases, newspaper clippings, photos of some committee members, programs, and a report on the

George Washington Bicentennial observance in the elementary schools presented by Julius E. Warren, superintendent of schools in Lakewood, Ohio. Among the correspondents, including some officers of the committee, are Sol Bloom, Harold H. Burton, Harold T. Clark (chairman, finance committee), Horatio Ford (general chairman), Stanley S. Friedman (executive secretary), Albert Bushnell Hart, and Laurence H. Norton (treasurer).

402 WILLIAM FREDERICK DOOLITTLE (1872–1948). Genealogical Papers, 1889–1940. 8 boxes. MS 1829.

Correspondence, charts, memoranda, newspaper clippings, and other papers containing data relating to the genealogy of the Doolittle family. William F. Doolittle, a Cleveland doctor, compiled a 7-part history of *The Doolittle Family in America* (Cleveland, 1901–1908).

403 NATIONAL WAR SAVINGS COMMITTEE. SOUTH CAROLINA. Records, 1917–1919. 7 volumes. Gift of Paul M. Rea. MS 1833.

Robert G. Rhett was state director and Paul M. Rea was vice-director of South Carolina for the National War Savings Committee organized by the Treasury Department in November, 1917, primarily "to raise money [two billion dollars] to prosecute our fight for democracy and decency in the world." These records reflect the efforts of volunteers and salaried employees to sell thrift stamps and war-savings stamps throughout the state. Included are two volumes of correspondence, form letters, requisition forms, bulletins, news releases, and county reports arranged chronologically, 1917–1919; two volumes containing material similar to that in the aforementioned volumes, except arranged by subject headings, e.g., County Chairman, War Savings Society, Bankers, Mayors, Publicity, and Editors; one volume containing graphic reports on state personnel and cumulative weekly sales for each county, and charts comparing amounts collected with quotas established by Washington; one volume of graphic reports of weekly sales for each county; and one volume of literature, e.g., certificates, broadsides, envelopes, and pamphlets, which were received from Washington, D.C., and distributed throughout the state.

404   ISAAC NEWTON PILLSBURY. Papers, 1840–1861. 4 volumes, 2 folders, 1 package. Gift of Ansel Pillsbury, 1896. MS 1851.

Civil engineer of Cleveland (1840–1863), Pillsbury's papers include copies of correspondence among Elias Loomis, Benjamin Tappan, Seth Pratt, and himself, and notes on mathematics and surveying, 1840–1843; notebook of building estimates for bridges and arches while Pillsbury was engineer and superintendent of the 2nd Subdivision of the Cleveland, Painesville & Ashtabula Railroad Company in the 1850's; assorted surveys of tracts of land in Cuyahoga County (primarily in Cleveland), 1850–1860; one volume of private records kept between 1852 and 1860 and containing the results of Cleveland's first charter election and an Ohio City election (1853); surveying and elevation information about various streets in Cleveland and about the Great Lakes; and surveys of the routes of various Cleveland railroads and of the Ohio, Miami, and Sandy & Beaver canals.

405   JOHN S. STRONG FAMILY. Papers, 1816–1856, 1916–1917. 2 boxes. Part of the collection is a gift of Albert Strong, 1933. MS 1853.

John Stroughton Strong (1771–1863) was land agent for Governor Caleb Strong of Massachusetts and Oliver Ellsworth of Connecticut and in 1816 led the party that settled in what was later named Strongsville Township in the Western Reserve. The papers, which pertain primarily to the sale of land and the development of the township, include correspondence, deeds, agreements, bills, memoranda, receipts, and financial accounts. Some of the papers pertain to the business and legal affairs of Emory Strong (1796–1834), who assisted his father in selling land and later became a merchant, and of Warner Strong (1804–1856), merchant, justice of the peace, and postmaster of Strongsville. Also included are some items relating to the Strongsville Centennial Celebration in 1916.

406 NICHOLS AND MERRILL FAMILIES. Papers, 1839–1872. 3 folders. MS 1859.

Dr. John Nichols was a teacher and later superintendent (1847–1853) of the Western Reserve Teachers' Seminary in Kirtland, Ohio. Charles C. Merrill was an associate of Nichols during the latter's term of superintendency. The papers consist primarily of personal and general correspondence from friends or relatives received by these two men or members of their families, residing in either Chardon or Kirtland. Also included are some letters to Nathan Daggett, postmaster of Kirtland, 1840–1848; an agreement between directors of District No. 17 in Kirtland and the trustees of the Western Reserve Teachers' Seminary, undated; and a petition addressed to U.S. Postmaster Francis Granger requesting the removal of Kirtland's incumbent postmaster, undated.

407 SARCHET FAMILY. Papers, 1816–1851. 1 folder. Purchased (Prentiss Fund), 1925. MS 1860.

General correspondence and business and legal papers pertaining to the activities of David, Moses, and Thomas Sarchet and of other residents of Cambridge, Guernsey County, Ohio, such as C. P. and Zaccheus A. Beatty and James M. Bell.

408 PETER M. AND HORACE P. WEDDELL. Papers, 1820–1860. 4 boxes. Gift of Mrs. Walter Rich. MS 1864.

Land deeds and agreements, financial notes and accounts, and other business papers relating to the interests of Peter Martin Weddell (1788–1847), Cleveland merchant and banker, and those of his son, Horace Perry Weddell (1823–ca. 1910). From 1828 to 1845, P. M. Weddell & Company was one of Cleveland's leading merchandising firms. In 1845, construction began on the Weddell House, which, after it opened in 1847, became Cleveland's most famous hotel. In addition to these two enterprises, the papers also concern the Weddells' interest in land in both Cleveland and Newark, Ohio.

409 JOHN HOWARD WEBSTER (1846–1930). Genealogical Data, ca. 1895–1930. 1 box. MS 1865.

Correspondence, charts, notes, and newspaper clippings concerning various branches of the Webster and Perry families, accumulated by John H. Webster, a Cleveland-based lawyer and industrialist. Also included are 250 typescript pages of copies of records from New Hampshire and a biographical sketch of Peter M. Weddell (1788–1847), Cleveland businessman.

410 AMERICAN EXPEDITIONARY FORCE. 37TH DIVISION. Records, 1917–1919, 1923. 4 boxes. Gift of Otto Miller, 1920. MS 1870.

Intelligence reports and maps, index to maps, journals of operation, movement orders, tables of organization, training memoranda and maps, aeronautical reports, plans of offense and defense, bulletins, and field orders pertaining to the division's activities in France and Belgium and primarily when it was commanded by Major General Charles S. Farnsworth, 1917–1918. Also included are historical data on the 37th, histories of other divisions which saw action in Europe, and affidavits and correspondence of Major Edward P. Lawler of the 37th Division Association (Columbus, Ohio) regarding the efforts of the 37th in capturing the village of Montfaucon (September–October, 1918), 1923.

The 37th Division was organized at Camp Sheridan, Alabama, by a War Department order of July 8, 1917. Comprising National Guard troops from Ohio and supplemented by National Army personnel, this division saw action in the Baccarat, Pannes, and Marbache sectors (France), the Meuse-Argonne offensive (France), and the Ypres-Lys offensive (Belgium).

411   CHARLES KNOWLES BOLTON. Reminiscences, 1934. 1 volume. MS 1871.
This antiquarian and librarian of the Boston Athenaeum (1898–1933) reminisces about his experiences in Cleveland (where he was born in 1867) during the last quarter of the 19th century.

412   EPHRAIM BROWN (1775–1845). Papers, 1790–1887. 15 boxes, 17 oversize volumes. MS 1872.
Correspondence, land agreements and deeds, account books, business papers, financial receipts, certificates, and court-docket books of Ephraim Brown, merchant, land agent, postmaster, legislator, abolitionist, and justice of the peace in North Bloomfield, Ohio, and of his son, Ephraim A. Brown (1807–1894), merchant. A native of Westmoreland, New Hampshire, Brown settled in the Western Reserve in 1817; represented the Whig Party in the Ohio State House and Senate, 1820's and 1830's; served as road commissioner of Ohio, 1825; and participated in various business ventures, including the Ashtabula, Warren & Liverpool Railroad and the Trumbull & Ashtabula Turnpike Company, ca. 1830–1843. The papers, which relate to the aforementioned activities, include account books relating to business enterprises such as E. A. Brown & Brothers Company, 1800–1845, 1853–1883; political, business, and personal correspondence, 1801–1845; plans and charts of the township of North Bloomfield, 1814–1820; docket books, 1832–1843; and estate papers, 1845–1848. Also included are some letters and school papers of four of Ephraim and Mary Brown's nine children, 1827–1866. Other correspondents include P. C. Brooks of Boston, John P. Converse, Joshua R. Giddings, Thomas Howe, Marvin Huntington, Rev. Alvan Hyde, Harmon Kingsbury, William A. Otis, Calvin Pease, Simon Perkins, Ebenezer Pierce, Lyman Potter, and Francis Proctor.

413   ASHER MILLER COE FAMILY. Papers, 1830–1934. ½ box. Gift of Asher M. Coe, 1934. MS 1877.
Primarily land deeds of Asher Miller Coe, who settled in North Olmsted, Ohio, in the 1820's, 1836–1854. Among other assorted

family papers are a notebook containing a biographical account of Wait Cornell of Long Mill (Connecticut) and miscellaneous financial accounts, 1830–1860; a 3-page biographical sketch of Asher M. Coe prepared by Asher M. Coe II, ca. 1933–1934; and 12 pages on the "Genealogy of the Coes" and notes on the David Lyman family, undated.

414 ANDREW JACKSON II. Account Books, 1845–1877. 2 volumes. MS 1880.

Account book containing data on the purchase, sale, birth, marriage, and death of slaves at the Hermitage, 1845–1877, and a receipt book of Andrew Jackson II and Sarah Jackson, 1845–1877.

415 IMPROVED ORDER OF RED MEN. HOCKHOCKING TRIBE NO. 58. CAMBRIDGE, O. Records, 1908–1914, 1917–1920. 3 volumes. Purchased, 1934. MS 1885.

Minutes of weekly meetings, price lists of tribal supplies, and financial records of the Cambridge chapter of this secret social, fraternal, and benevolent society which sought to commemorate the culture, history, and tradition of the American Indian.

416 ORDER OF UNITED AMERICAN MEN. GUERNSEY COUNCIL NO. 73. CAMBRIDGE, O. Records, 1907–1911, 1917–1929. 2 volumes. Purchased, 1934. MS 1886.

Minutes of meetings and other records kept by the secretary.

417 WILLIAM B. FASIG. Letter Books, 1891–1892. 2 volumes. MS 1887.

Typescript copies of letters sent by William B. Fasig while acting as secretary of a firm which dealt in the sale of standardbred and thoroughbred horses (probably the Fasig-Tipton Company of Cleveland).

418 C. F. EMERY. Letter Books, 1889–1892. 4 volumes. MS 1888.

Emery, a prominent driver and owner of horses, was also proprietor of Forest City Farm in Randall, Ohio (offices in Cleveland), which dealt in the sale of horses. The letter books include price lists as well as copies of letters, most of which pertain to the sale of horses throughout the United States.

419 GEORGE G. WASHBURN (1821–1898). Papers, 1850–1896. 1 folder. MS 1890.

Letters on business or politics received by Washburn, an Ohio lawyer, journalist, and manager and editor of the Elyria *Democrat* (1856–1890). Correspondents include R. Brinkerhoff, John Brough, Schuyler Colfax, William Dennison, Joseph B. Foraker, Joshua R. Giddings, Rutherford B. Hayes, Henry Howe, James Monroe, John Sherman, Norton S. Townshend, F. S. Washburn, Elisha Whittlesey, and C. P. Wickham.

420 CONGREGATIONAL CHURCH. CHARLESTOWN, PORTAGE COUNTY, O. Records, 1829–1858. 1 volume. MS 1897.

Minutes of a meeting held January 20, 1829, by citizens of Charlestown to consider building a meeting house for the use of the Congregational Church and Society, memorandum of notes and payment of same by the proprietors of the society's meeting house, and an account of the money spent for construction.

421 JOHN AND ASHBEL W. WALWORTH. Papers, 1785–1829. 1½ boxes (some copies). Gifts of Mrs. S. L. Severance; Mrs. Eugene T. Izant, 1970. MS 1901.

Correspondence, financial papers, land deeds, certificates, depositions, petitions, agreements, and other papers relating to the activities of John Walworth (1765–1812) of Groton, Connecticut, who settled in Painesville, Ohio, in 1800 and moved to Cleveland in 1806, and of his son, Ashbel W. Walworth (1790–1844), who spent most of his life in Cleveland. John Walworth held several civil positions while in Cleveland, including those of postmaster and customs collector (1806–1812); Ashbel followed his father as customs collector (1812–1829) and postmaster (1812–1816). Among these papers is a series of summonses from Litchfield County, Connecticut, 1780's; letters, receipts, and abstracts of licenses relating to navigation on Lake Erie, 1809–1817; a letter book relating to land taxes, customs matters at the Port of Cleveland, and post office affairs, 1809–1812; various documents concerning construction of a road (1812) and schoolhouse (1814) in Cleveland, and a lighthouse (1825) at the mouth of the Grand River (Fairport), including a proposal by Jonathan Goldsmith and bills for timber and labor; and financial accounts, notes and lists of notes due, orders to pay, and other papers concerning the operation of the city of Cleveland, 1816–1829. Throughout this collection are references to the sale and ownership of land in the Firelands. Correspondents of John and Ashbel W. Walworth include Hannah Avery, Noyes Barber, William Eldredge, Albert Gallatin, Gideon Granger, Samuel Huntington, Alfred Kelley, Nathaniel Ledyard, Lewis Morgan, Enoch Parsons, Calvin Pease, Simon Perkins, Amos Spafford, Joseph Wakeman, Thomas L. Winthrop, and William Winthrop.

422   ELIZUR WRIGHT, JR. (1804–1885). Letters, 1822–1843. 2 folders (typescript copies made by Frederick C. Waite in 1940 from the originals in the possession of Mrs. Samuel B. Tay of Maynard, Massachusetts). Gift of Frederick C. Waite, 1940. MS 1994.

The first professor of mathematics and natural philosophy at Western Reserve College, Elizur Wright was an active abolitionist and took part in the anti-slavery movement before the Civil War. His father came from Canaan, Connecticut, to Tallmadge, Ohio, in 1810, where he founded the Tallmadge Academy. The letters are primarily from his father, although there are some from his mother (Clarissa), sister (Clarissa), and brother

(James). Topics discussed include daily life in Tallmadge, Western Reserve College, and the anti-slavery movement.

423   BRAXTON BRAGG (1817–1876). Papers, 1833–1876 (1861–1865). 3 boxes, 4 volumes. Gift of William P. Palmer, 1913–1927, combined for ease of access, 1962. MS 2000.

Official and personal letters, and letter books, military reports and orders, telegrams, memoranda, and other papers relating primarily to General Braxton Bragg's Confederate Army campaigns and to his service as advisor to President Jefferson Davis between 1861 and 1865. A few papers concern the Mexican War and Bragg's postwar career as a civil and railroad engineer. Of interest among the papers dating from the Civil War are those concerning Pensacola Harbor, the Army of the Tennessee, and tactics during the battles of Shiloh, Perryville, Murfreesboro (Stone River), and Chickamauga and during the North Carolina campaign. Also included is a journal of George William Brent, 1862–1863; and reminiscences of General Bragg written by Dr. Samuel H. Stout, 1876. Correspondents include Pierre G. T. Beauregard, Judah P. Benjamin, John C. Breckinridge, Robert H. Chilton, Jefferson Davis, Nathan B. Forrest, John B. Hood, Josiah S. Johnston, Joseph E. Johnston, Robert E. Lee, James Longstreet, Leonidas Polk, Samuel H. Stout, Lloyd Tilghman, and Earl Van Dorn.

Unpublished 9-page register available in the Society.
NUCMC 62-4983

424   JOHN CALHOUN. Papers, 1773–1787. 1 folder. Gift of John Calhoun, 1870. MS 2011.

Notebook containing information pertaining to the school committee [Litchfield County, Connecticut], 1773–1782; docket book of John Calhoun, justice of the peace in Washington, Litchfield County, 1781 and 1783; and summonses issued in Washington, 1784–1787.

425 JOHN BALDWIN (1799–1884). Papers, 1827–1902. 3½ boxes. 1 oversize volume. MS 2015.

Account books, land deeds, business contracts, and letters received by John Baldwin, who settled in Berea, Ohio, where for many years he operated a sandstone quarry. The papers relate primarily to his sandstone business and to the manufacture and sale of grindstones; to Baldwin University (now Baldwin Wallace University), which John Baldwin founded in Berea in 1845; and to the Baldwin Public School, founded by John Baldwin in Louisiana in 1867. Specifically included are 13 ledgers and account books, 1841–1873; minutes of a meeting of the trustees of Baldwin Institute, 1846; and John Baldwin's 12-page "Reminiscences: History of Berea," 1874. Besides various members of the Baldwin family, correspondents include Lyman Baker, William Bissell, Peter Merkel, Rev. R. S. Rust, and S. N. Walker.

426 QUINTUS F. ATKINS (1782–1859). Papers, 1803–1804, 1823–1827, 1855–1856, and 1876. 1 box (some copies). Gift of Harvey R. Gaylord, 1876. MS 2018.

Diary, correspondence, business papers, and copies of historical articles written for the *Ashtabula Sentinel* by Atkins, who settled in Morgan Township, Ashtabula County, Ohio, in the fall of 1802 and subsequently was engaged in farming, in supervising the construction of the Maumee and Sandusky Road (1823–1828), and in holding a variety of civil positions, primarily in Ashtabula County. Atkins' diary records his activities in relation to farming, hunting, reading, and worshiping (among those mentioned here are Rev. Joseph Badger, Asa Gillet, George W. and Timothy R. Hawley, Isaac Phelps, Rev. Thomas Robbins, Moses Wilcox, and Aaron Wright), 1803–1804. Also included are papers relating to the construction of the Maumee and Sandusky Road: letters, contracts, land-sale records, commissioner's reports, and stubs of certificates issued to persons agreeing to build a half-mile of the road, 1823–1827; copies (made by H. R. Gaylord, Atkins' son-in-law, in the 1870's) of Atkins' articles published in the *Ashtabula Sentinel* in the 1850's and dealing with the settlement and early history of Ashtabula and events during the War of 1812; and a biographical sketch of Atkins prepared by Gaylord in 1876.

427   WATERS FAMILY. Reunion Records, 1896–1931. 1 volume. Gift of Ethel Waters, 1935. MS 2023.

Minutes of the annual meetings of the descendants of Abner and Lucy Waters held in various cities throughout Ohio.

428   DAVID CLENDENIN. Papers, 1812–1814. 1 box. Gift of Mrs. M. R. Parmelee. MS 2025.

Pay and muster rolls, subsistence accounts, pay vouchers and receipts, morning reports, and abstracts of payments made to the officers and enlisted men who served in various regiments of the Ohio Militia during the War of 1812. These payments, made through the office of David Clendenin, assistant district paymaster of the U.S. Army, of Poland, Ohio, involve companies of dragoons, infantrymen, and riflemen. A small number of documents pertain to the military activities of John Campbell, Return J. Meigs, and William Hull.

429   AUSTIN JOHNSON. Letters, 1842–1864. 15 items. MS 2028.

Letters received by Austin Johnson of Rupert, Bennington County, Vermont; 13 being from his brother, Horace Johnson, of Sandusky, Ohio, and containing his views on contemporary events, including the Civil War.

430   ALBERT BARNITZ. Papers, 1862–1894. 2 boxes. Gift of Mrs. Albert Barnitz, 1935. MS 2031.

Papers dealing primarily with the military activities of Colonel Barnitz, Company G, 2nd Regiment, Ohio Volunteer Cavalry (later 7th U.S. Cavalry), including orders and circulars, muster and pay rolls, quarterly and monthly returns of quartermaster stores, and invoices and vouchers, 1862–1867.

431   METHODIST-EPISCOPAL CHURCH. BELLEVUE, O. Records, 1852–1886. 1 volume. Purchased, 1924. MS 2041.

Historical record, class records, and membership and baptism lists.

432   D. JOHNSON. Account Book, 1848–1861. 1 volume. MS 2042.

Johnson resided in Willoughby, Ohio. Also included in this volume are 14 leaves from an account book of Lewis and Merrick Ely, 1816–1820.

433   ERASTUS AND HENRY K. CUSHING. Papers, 1808–1907. 1½ boxes. Gift of H. K. Cushing, 1918. MS 2045.

Both Erastus Cushing (1802–1893) and his son, Henry Kirke Cushing (1827–1910), were prominent Cleveland physicians. Included here are account books, 1808–1814, 1850–1851; matriculation tickets from the medical departments of various institutions, 1822–1851; notes and letters concerning Dr. Henry K. Cushing's study of portraits of Benjamin Franklin, ca. 1885–1907; a biographical account of Joc-O-Sot (d. 1845), an Indian chief who lived in Cleveland; and other assorted writings and speeches of Dr. Henry K. Cushing.

434   BENJAMIN T. JONES. Papers, 1855–1906. 1 box. Gift of Isaac N. Jones, 1933. MS 2052.

Correspondence, letters of recommendation, memoranda, teacher's certificates, and newspaper clippings dealing with Jones' activities in the field of education, 1868–1906. Jones was a teacher and superintendent of schools in Ashland, Bellaire, and Millersburg, Ohio; professor at Bethany and Buchtel colleges; and finally teacher at various secondary schools in Cleveland. Some of the papers pertain to Jones' participation in the Civil War as a captain in the 120th Regiment, Ohio Volunteer Infantry, 1862–1865.

435 DARIUS ELY (1761–1844). Daybook, 1809–1858. 1 volume. Gift of Mrs. J. Garfield Buell, 1936. MS 2056.
Darius Ely, a farmer and veteran of the American Revolutionary War, resided in Ravenna, Ohio, with his son, Ashley. Many of the entries in this volume relate to the activities of Ashley Ely.

436 OTTO MILLER, *collector*. Andrew Jackson Miscellany. 30 items. Gift of Otto Miller, 1928. MS 2066.
Nine letters to, three letters from, and two letters about Andrew Jackson (1767–1845), and other papers including financial accounts, 1804, 1819, 1833; a list of Jackson's land holdings, 1793–1801; and several estate papers, 1867.

437 JAMES M. PARKER. Daybook, 1840–1841. 1 volume. Gift of Otto Miller. MS 2067.
Entries made by James Parker while employed at Andrew Jackson's plantation.

438 CAMP AND IDDINGS FAMILIES. Papers, 1834–1903. ½ box. MS 2069.
Primarily general and personal letters received by various members of these two related families who for the most part resided in Euclid, Ohio. Correspondents include Ann O. Camp, Henry C. Camp, Hiram Iddings, Hiram A. Iddings, Richard Iddings, and Thomas Asmun.

439 RUBINSTEIN CLUB. CLEVELAND, O. Records, 1909–1912. 1 volume. Gift of Mrs. C. E. Porter, 1936. MS 2070.
Lists of members, minutes of meetings, and some financial records of this musical club which was founded in 1899.

440 CHARLES B. SMITH. Papers, August–November, 1863. 1 folder. MS 2076.

Orders, specifications, letters, and documents pertaining to a court martial in which Lieutenant C. B. Smith, judge advocate at Camp Dennison, Ohio, was involved.

441 GRAND RIVER BAPTIST ASSOCIATION. OHIO. Records, 1817–1842, 1853–1871. 2 volumes. Gift of the Ashtabula Baptist Association through Rev. E. O. Jessup, 1911. MS 2085.

Formation, plan, confession of faith, and minutes of meetings of this association which was originally composed of the churches in Madison, Painesville, Kingsville, Jefferson, Geneva, and Chardon, Ohio, 1817–1842; and treasurer's account book, 1853–1871.

442 GARRETTSVILLE BAPTIST CHURCH. GARRETTSVILLE, O. Records, 1808–1860. 2 volumes. Gift of Mrs. E. Truesdale for the Garrettsville Baptist Church, 1911. MS 2087.

Covenant, declaration of faith, minutes of meetings, and a list of members for 1839.

443 FIRST REGULAR BAPTIST CHURCH. DAYTON, O. Records, 1840–1846. 1 volume. MS 2088.

Accounts between the church and its treasurers and minutes of meetings during this period.

444 STRAIT CREEK BAPTIST ASSOCIATION. SEAMAN, O. Records, 1812–1850. 1 volume. Deposited by L. E. Gayman, Clerk of Adams Baptist Association, 1912. MS 2089.

Minutes of meetings and treasurers' accounts from the founding of this association, which was later renamed the Adams Baptist Association.

445 BASSETT FAMILY. Papers, 1810–1887. 1 folder. Gift of Clayton W. Tyler, 1936. MS 2094.

Includes four contracts of Stephen Jordan of Brookfield, Madison County, New York, 1810–1836; land agreements and deeds to tracts of land in Brooklyn and Rockport, Cuyahoga County, Ohio, and other contracts involving Homer F. and Henry D. Bassett and Charles R. Jordan, 1853–1887; 19 letters, containing personal impressions of the Civil War, from John M. Bassett to his family, written while he was stationed in Pennsylvania, Maryland, and Virginia, 1861–1863.

446 ELI BALDWIN FAMILY. Papers, ca. 1800–ca. 1900. 3 boxes. MS 2097.

Correspondence, diaries, deeds and land agreements, financial accounts, tax records, legal and business papers, and estate papers of members of this family, including Asa, Eli, George S., Henry, Horace, Jesse, Mary, and William Baldwin, all of whom were active in and around Boardman, Mahoning County, Ohio. Most of the material pertains to Eli Baldwin, one of Boardman's first settlers, a land agent, gristmill and distillery operator, and deputy postmaster (1807), and to his son, Jesse Baldwin, also a gristmill operator. Included are diaries of Eli Baldwin, 1801–1804; papers relating to the land holdings and the estate of Elijah Boardman, 1809–1823; documents concerning the settlement of the estate of Robert Patrick, for which Jesse Baldwin was executor, 1858–1889; Common Pleas Court proceedings involving Jesse Baldwin and papers relating to his business interests, e.g., the Cleveland and Mahoning Valley Railroad, 1845–1890. Correspondents include Seth R. Alcott, John Cook, David S. and William W. Boardman, Daniel Fairchild, Thomas J. McLain, Thomas Newport, and David Tod.

447 WILLIAM L. GROSS. Papers, 1856, 1862–1868 (1863–1866). 18 boxes, 1 volume. Gift of William P. Palmer, 1913–1927, combined for ease of access, 1961. MS 2101.

Correspondence, abstracts, orders and receipts, personnel reports, and record books relating to the activities of William L. Gross while he served at the telegraph office in Cairo, Illinois, 1862; at the U.S. Military Telegraph headquarters in Danville, Kentucky, 1863–1865; at the telegraph office of the Military District of the Gulf in New Orleans, Louisiana, 1865–1866; and while he was manager of the Western Union office in Omaha, Nebraska, 1866–1867. This collection reflects the role the telegraph played in the campaigns of the Union Army from Kentucky to Georgia. Specifically included are monthly reports and returns, receipts, lists, rolls, and accounts which provide information on payments made to foremen, operators, repairmen, and laborers working on the telegraph lines, and payments for repairs, forage, stables, and warehouses. Also included are lists of stores, clothing, and camp and garrison equipage; rolls of enlisted men and officers; reports on lines, cables, and other property of the Military Telegraph Line; and orders, instructions, and oaths taken by telegraph operators.

Unpublished 4-page register available in the Society.
NUCMC 62-4239

448 "THE ISLANDER." Manuscript Newspaper, 1860–1878. 17 volumes. Gift of Mrs. Hermon A. Kelley and Norman E. Hills. MS 2116.

Published by the Kelley's Island Literary Society, from 1860 to 1878, on Kelley's Island in Sandusky Bay, Erie County, Ohio, this journal was "devoted to the discussion of questions in the Arts and Sciences, Agriculture and Manufactures, Politics and Morality." Prepared and written during the winter months, issues were read before weekly gatherings of inhabitants of the isolated island. The format resembled that of a contemporary printed newspaper, in that it included reports on current events, editorials and letters to the editors, articles on history, humor, philosophy, religion, and science, and some advertisements. Events of national as well as local significance were mentioned. The recollections or reminiscences of travelers and letters of soldiers participating in the Civil War were also included.

449 KERSHAW FAMILY. Papers, 1869–1896. 9 items. MS 2117.

Deeds and other general papers of members of this family from Kent, Portage County, Ohio, including the letters patent issued to John Kershaw on June 15, 1869, for improvement in harvesters.

450 LUCY A. H. BUNGERT. Papers, 1832–1891. 1 folder. Gift of Mrs. Lyman A. Reed, 1936. MS 2118.

Deeds and land contracts pertaining to tracts primarily in Ashtabula County, Ohio, and involving many individuals, but most frequently Frederick L. Chapman.

451 MEDICAL DEPARTMENTS AND HOSPITALS, UNION AND CONFEDERATE ARMIES. Papers, 1862–1866. 3 boxes. Gift of William P. Palmer, 1913–1927, combined for ease of access, 1962. MS 2121.

These papers relate to the medical departments and hospitals of Union armies along the Atlantic Coast and in Louisiana and to Confederate hospitals in Virginia and Atlanta, Georgia. Included are copies of orders, reports of sick and wounded, lists of dead, invoices and reports of medicines and other hospital supplies and equipment, and some correspondence. Specifically referred to are the activities of the following Confederate surgeons: Robert Battey, 19th Georgia Volunteers; Renley S. Butler, 2nd Florida Volunteers; William A. Carrington, departments of Henrico and of Virginia and North Carolina; and John Payne Logan, Atlanta hospitals; and of the following Union surgeons: Benjamin F. Harrison, New York Independent Volunteers, and Henry M. Kirke, Pennsylvania Volunteers.

Unpublished 4-page register available in the Society.
NUCMC 62-4397

452 UNITED PRESBYTERIAN AND CONGREGATIONAL CHURCH. FARMINGTON, O. Records, 1817–1866. 2 volumes. Gift of F. S. Hart, 1937. MS 2125.

Confession of faith, covenant, list of members, baptisms, and minutes of meetings of this church, apparently formed from the union of the Congregational Church of Christ (founded 1817) and the Centre Presbyterian Church.

453 AQUILA WILEY. Papers, 1861–1901. 1 box. MS 2127.

Correspondence, bounty claims, muster rolls, invoices, and returns, most of which pertain to Wiley's activities in the 41st Regiment, Ohio Volunteer Infantry, 1861–1865. A resident of Wooster, Ohio, Wiley was brevetted to brigadier general in 1865 for his efforts during the battles of Mission Ridge, Stone River, Chickamauga, and Chattanooga. Also included are copies of articles and speeches on various Civil War topics; lists containing names of voters and their political affiliations in Wayne County, Ohio, in the 1890's; and correspondence and maps relating to the activities of the Ohio Chickamauga and Chattanooga National Park Commission, 1893–1901.

454 MATTHEW SCOTT COOK (d. 1882?). Papers, 1815–1883. 3 boxes. MS 2129.

Correspondence, land agreements and deeds, survey and field notes, financial receipts, legal briefs, and other papers of Cook, surveyor, farmer, businessman, Ohio State Representative from 1850 to 1851, uncle of U.S. President Rutherford B. Hayes, and long-time resident of Chillicothe, Ohio. In addition to business interests in Ohio, Indiana, and Kentucky, Cook was involved in Ohio politics in the 1840's and 1850's. Included are the following: a journal kept while working, sometimes as a flatboatman, on the Ohio and Mississippi rivers, and on other waterways in Indiana, Illinois, and Ohio, 1815–1817; memoranda and account books relating to Cook's Paint Creek Farm, 1830–1844; journal kept on a trip to Quebec, Saratoga, and Boston, 1852; several volumes containing meteorological data, 1860–1884; letters from several nephews who served in the Civil War and from his son, Edward T. Cook, Company D, 89th Regiment, Ohio Volunteer Infantry, 1861–1865; and two letter books, 1873–1881. Correspondents include John R. Bailey, C. G. W. Comegys, Samuel Galloway (1811–1872), Rutherford B. Hayes (1822–1893), Isaac Moore, Joseph T. Reynolds, Isaac C. Riggin, and John L. Taylor (1805–1870).

455   ROYAL CHIDESTER FAMILY. Papers, 1797–1876. 1 folder. MS 2134.

General and personal correspondence, financial accounts, and land deeds and agreements involving members of this family, particularly Royal Chidester, the son of William (who settled in Canfield, Trumbull County, Ohio, in 1802).

456   EDWARD E. KELSEY (1840–1927). Record Books, 1857, 1862, 1874–1877. 4 volumes. Purchased, 1928. MS 2135.

Pocket diaries for the years 1857 and 1862 containing brief accounts of the daily activities of Kelsey, a native of La Porte, Ohio, who served in Company C, 7th Regiment, Ohio Volunteer Infantry, during the Civil War. Also included is an account book, 1874–1877; and a geometry notebook, undated.

457   WILLIAM W. RICHARDSON. Diaries, 1862, 1864–1865. 4 volumes. Purchased, 1925. MS 2136.

Diaries kept by Richardson while serving in the 104th Regiment, Ohio Volunteer Infantry. A musician (drummer) in Company I, Richardson served from August, 1862, until June, 1865. These diaries (including two concurrent ones for the year 1864) reflect this regiment's battle activities, as well as Richardson's duties which, in addition to playing in the band, included burying the dead, building fortifications, barbering, and drawing maps.

458 PETER M. HEROLD (b. 1847). Papers, 1901–1911. 4 volumes. Purchased, 1925. MS 2137.

Three private diaries and an index referring to the library and diaries of Peter M. Herold, who settled in Washingtonville, Carroll County, Ohio, in 1898, and operated a shoe shop.

459 JUSTIN G. MORRIS. Papers, 1840–1896. 2 folders. MS 2139.

Account books, letters, land deeds and agreements, receipts, and contracts relating to Morris' activities in the coal business in Steubenville, Ohio.

460 SOLDIERS' AND SAILORS' MONUMENTAL ASSOCIATION OF BELLAIRE, O. Records, 1879–1885. 1 volume. MS 2142.

Minutes of meetings and treasurer's reports of this organization which raised funds from voluntary sources in order to construct a soldiers' monument.

461 RIAL McARTHUR AND R. WARDEN. Field Notes, 1805. 1 volume (copy of original in possession of Schuyler R. Oviatt). Gift of Miss G. L. Oviatt, 1923. MS 2143.

Field notes for a survey of Bath (formerly Wheatfield) Township, Summit County, Ohio.

462 WILLIAM PITT FESSENDEN (1806–1869). Papers, 1837–1869 (1861–1868). 2 boxes. Gift of William P. Palmer, 1913–1927, combined for ease of access, 1962. MS 2145.

Primarily letters from supporters and constituents spanning Fessenden's career during which this attorney at law from Portland, Maine, served in the Maine House of Representatives; in the U.S. Senate (1854–1864, 1865–1868); and as Secretary of the Treasury (1864–1865). These letters deal with the politics (primarily in Maine) of the Whig, Republican, Liberty, and Free Soil parties; with the activities of the anti-slavery and temperance movements; and with Fessenden's activities as chairman of the Senate Finance Committee (1864, 1865). Referred to in this collection are John Appleton, William G. Crosby, Woodbury Davis, Neal Dow, George Evans, Edward Kent, Hiram Ketchum, A. B. Mullen, Allison Owen, and Israel Washburn, Jr.

Unpublished 4-page register available in the Society.
NUCMC 62-4393

463   T. F. NEWMAN, Scrapbook, 1900–1901, 1922. 1 volume. Gift of T. F. Newman, 1922. MS 2146.

Correspondence, newspaper clippings, and the agreement concerning the race between the Cleveland and Buffalo Transit Company's steamer *City of Erie* and the White Star Lines' steamer *Tashmoo*, held in Lake Erie on June 4, 1901.

464   ZEBULON MONTGOMERY PIKE (1779–1813). Letters,* 1801–1811. 14 items. Gift of J. H. Gage, 1870. MS 2150.

Collection of general and personal letters from Zebulon M. Pike to George W., Isabel, Maria, and Major Zebulon Pike.

* Four of these letters were published in W.R.H.S. *Tract* No. 39 (1877).

465   PERLEY PEABODY PITKIN (d. 1891). Papers, 1861–1868, (1862–1864). 9 boxes. Gift of William P. Palmer, 1913–1927, combined for ease of access, 1962. MS 2151.

Official papers, relating primarily to Lieutenant Colonel Perley P. Pitkin's activities as assistant quartermaster for the Army of the Potomac from 1862 through 1864. They involve shipments, receipts, and transfers of supplies and government property for units of the army under Generals George B. McClellan and Ambrose E. Burnside in 1862, Joseph Hooker and George G. Meade in 1863, and Meade and Ulysses S. Grant in 1864. The shipments from army depots were made mostly by the Baltimore and Ohio Railroad if they went by land or by barges and small river and coastal steamers if they were moved via the Potomac or Chesapeake Bay. These shipments included food, forage, and clothing and other equipment for officers and enlisted men. There are also receipts for the payment of laborers and other employees, including slaves (contrabands) within the Union lines. Specifically these papers consist of lists of quartermaster and other supplies received, invoices, receipts, correspondence, abstracts, requisitions and material on contrabands, and carrier receipts.

Unpublished 3-page register available in the Society.
NUCMC 62-4122

466 REGIMENTAL PAPERS OF CIVIL WAR, 1861–1865. 36 boxes, 17 volumes. Gift of William P. Palmer, 1913–1927, combined for ease of access, 1962. MS 2152.

Records of numerous regiments in both the Union and Confederate armies from 30 states. These include military correspondence, official orders, muster rolls, ordnance and quartermaster reports, and casualty lists. In addition to these there are also letters, diaries, and memoirs of soldiers serving in these regiments, and accounts of engagements. Regiments from the following states are represented here: Alabama, Arkansas, Connecticut, Florida, Georgia, Illinois, Indiana, Iowa, Kentucky, Louisiana, Maine, Maryland, Massachusetts, Michigan, Minnesota, Mississippi, Missouri, New Hampshire, New Jersey, New York, North Carolina, Ohio, Pennsylvania, Rhode Island, South Carolina, Tennessee, Texas, Vermont, Virginia, and Wisconsin. The bulk of this collection refers to Ohio regiments, although those from Illinois and Massachusetts are also well represented. The Ohio regiments include the 1st Volunteer Light Artillery (papers of General James Barnett and Captain N. A. Baldwin), 2nd Volunteer Cavalry (papers of Walter P. Austin), 6th Volunteer Cavalry (papers of Alcinus W. Fenton), 7th Volunteer Infantry (papers of William R. Creighton, Mervin Clark and James T. Sterling), 59th Volunteer Infantry (papers of Edwin Perkins),

94th Volunteer Infantry (papers of Lieutenant Frank A. Hardy), 98th Volunteer Infantry (papers of Captain H. A. Thomas), 101st Volunteer Infantry (papers of L. W. Day and Elbert J. Squire), and 115th Volunteer Infantry (papers of Thomas C. Boone). Also included are records of the Cuyahoga County Military Committee, 1861–1868; papers of H. G. Crickmore and J. W. Paine of the 4th U.S. Colored Cavalry, and those of other Negro regiments; and a journal in 14 parts entitled "With Sheridan up the Shenandoah Valley. Leaves from a Special Artists Sketch Book and Diary" by James E. Taylor, containing numerous watercolor drawings of places, events, and persons, as well as accounts of the military engagements of the Army of the Shenandoah under the command of General Philip H. Sheridan, August–December, 1864.

Unpublished 16-page register available in the Society.
NUCMC 62-4389

467   HOMER H. HINE, Jr. Papers, 1837–1900. 2 folders. MS 2155.

Primarily business papers and letters received by Homer H. Hine of Painesville, Ohio, an attorney, who was active in the Grange and in Ohio Republican politics during the 1870's and 1880's.

468   HOMER H. HINE. Papers, 1796–1857 (1802–1835). 1 folder. Gift of Dudley Baldwin, 1870. MS 2155a.

Letters addressed to Homer H. Hine of Youngstown, Ohio, an attorney who was active in local business and state political circles. Correspondents include Samuel Bryson, Samuel Huntington, Allen Trimble, Elijah Wadsworth, and Elisha Whittlesey.

469   ANTHONY WAYNE (1745–1796). Papers, 1792, 1794–1796. 29 items. Gift of Alfred T. Goodman, ca. 1871. MS 2156.

Primarily letters addressed to Major General Anthony Wayne and concerning army personnel and administration as well as the campaign against the Indians which resulted in Wayne's victory at Fallen Timbers in 1794 and the Treaty of Greenville in 1795. Also included is an ordnance return for Fort Garrison, 1794; and a muster roll for Fort Fayette, 1796.

470   SAMUEL TUPPER. Letters, 1807–1812. 1 folder. MS 2159.

Duplicates of letters written by Tupper while he was agent at the U.S. Trading House in Sandusky, Ohio. The letters, addressed to General John Shee or General John Mason, concern business matters at the Trading House and include commentary on the Indian tribes in that area.

471   EAST 105TH STREET CANTEEN. CLEVELAND, O. Records, 1918–1919. 1 volume. Gift of Mrs. Jane T. Ingalls, 1920. MS 2160.

Register of visitors during World War I.

472   LEO WEIDENTHAL (1878–1967). Papers, 1932–1936. 1 folder. Gift of Leo Weidenthal, 1937. MS 2161.

Correspondence and other papers relating to the Spirit of '76 Committee for the Willard Centennial organized in Cleveland in 1935. Weidenthal served as secretary of this committee. Also included are other miscellaneous items pertaining to Archibald M. Willard, the Willard family, and the paintings of Archibald M. Willard in the Western Reserve Historical Society, 1932–1936.

473   JOHN ANDREWS FAMILY. Papers, 1783–1835. 14 items. MS 2165.

Land deeds, receipts, and general and personal letters addressed primarily to Dr. John Andrews of Wallingford, Connecticut.

474 SAMUEL H. STOUT (1822-1908). Papers, 1861-1865 (1863-1864). 7 boxes. Gift of William P. Palmer, 1913-1927, combined for ease of access, 1961. MS 2175.
Correspondence, reports, orders, circulars, and other papers relating to the activities of Dr. Samuel H. Stout in establishing and operating the hospitals of the Confederate Army of the Tennessee. This collection presents a detailed picture of conditions in the Confederate hospitals, primarily those located in Georgia. Specifically included are monthly and weekly reports of supplies of medicines and food, hospital equipment and furnishings, stewards and surgeons, and patients admitted, furloughed, or deceased, as well as data on their ailments and homes. Referred to in this collection are Generals Braxton Bragg, Joseph Eggleston Johnston, and John B. Hood (under whom Dr. Stout served), as well as Drs. Andrew J. Foard and A. J. Flewellen.

Unpublished 4-page register available in the Society.
NUCMC 62-4388

475 CHARLES W. MONROE. Papers, 1865. 2 folders. MS 2185.
Muster and pay rolls, monthly and quarterly returns, receipts, and reports for the 29th Regiment, Michigan Infantry, in which Monroe held the rank of lieutenant.

476 N. A. BALDWIN. Papers, 1863-1865. 2 folders. Gift of Mrs. J. W. Howard, 1937. MS 2214.
Lists, receipts, and returns of quartermaster stores for Battery B, Ohio Volunteer Artillery, which was commanded by Lieutenant Baldwin.

477 WOMAN'S TEMPERANCE SOCIETY OF MORGAN COUNTY. OHIO. Records, 1853-1856. 1 volume. Purchased, 1925. MS 2215.
Constitution and minutes of meetings of this society which sought "to encourage the practice of Total abstinence and desseminate temperance principals in every laudable way."

478   CHARLES E. BOLTON. Estate Papers, 1908. 1 folder. MS 2234.

Abstracts of title to and incumbrances upon the property of the late Charles E. Bolton located in East Cleveland, Ohio.

479   GOETHE-SCHILLER MONUMENT ASSOCIATION OF CLEVELAND, O. Records, 1904–1907, 1927. 2 boxes. Gift of J. Gerlich, 1937. MS 2257.

Correspondence, newspaper clippings, programs, pamphlets, and other records of this association of which J. H. Gerlich was secretary and Ernst J. Siller was president.

480   A. C. VAN DYKE. Genealogical Data, ca. 1915–1920. 1 box. MS 2258.

Notes on the genealogy of members of both the Ohio and Pennsylvania branches of the Billman family as compiled before 1920 by Mr. Van Dyke, sanitary policeman for the city of Wellsville, Ohio.

481   RANDOLPH STONE. Account Book and Diary, 1811–1825. 1 volume. Gift of Laurence H. Norton, 1937. MS 2260.

Financial accounts, 1811–1819, and diary kept by Rev. Randolph Stone, known for his connection with the First Presbyterian Church of Cleveland (later Old Stone Church), while pursuing his missionary labors throughout the Western Reserve for the Missionary Society of Connecticut.

482   COLLECTION OF MATHEMATICS NOTEBOOKS, 1788–1843. 20 volumes. Gifts of various persons. MS 2266.

Anonymous. 1 vol., 1828–1829 (Rome, N.Y.). Arithmetic.
Coe, Elisha. 2 vols., 1778 [Location?]. Arithmetic.
Daggett, Nathan (1802–1891). 1 vol., 1817 (Freetown, [Mass.?]).
    Arithmetic.

Darlington, Carey Allen. 1 vol., 1812–1814 (West Union, O.). Trigonometry, mensuration, and surveying.

Emery, Samuel M. 3 vols., 1788–1805 (Newburyport, [Mass.?]). Arithmetic, bookkeeping.

Fallis, Miriam. 1 vol., 1792 [Location?].

Gordon, William R. 1 vol., 1829 [Location?]. Arithmetic.

Hawley, Abel, Jr. (1775–1864). 2 vols., 1834–1836 (Hannibal Ville, N. Y.). Arithmetic.

Hyatt, Elisha. 1 vol., 1843 (Saltcreek, [O.?]). Mensuration.

Jenkins, George K. 2 vols., ca. 1832 (Mount Pleasant, O.). Arithmetic.

Jones, Catlitt. 1 vol., 1778–1796 [Location?]. Arithmetic.

Reed, Calvin G. (1821–1900). 1 vol., ca. 1840 [Location?]. Arithmetic.

Schillinger, N. I. 1 vol., 1822 (Cincinnati, O.). Arithmetic.

Updegraff, David L. 1 vol., 1808 (Mount Pleasant, O.). Arithmetic.

Wildeson, Henry. 1 vol., 1824 (Baltimore County, Md.). Arithmetic.

483   WOMAN'S CHRISTIAN TEMPERANCE UNION. CUYAHOGA COUNTY, O. Records, 1887–1932. 14 volumes. Gift of Mrs. E. S. Loomis. MS 2271.

Secretaries' books containing minutes of meetings, officer reports, financial accounts and reports, convention programs, and some correspondence.

484   JEFFERSON COUNTY, O. Collection of Deeds, 1805–1830, 1872. 1 folder. MS 2280.

Land indentures and deeds involving many persons from this county.

485   JOHN J. ELWELL (1820–1900). Papers, 1863–1892. 1 folder. Gift of J. R. Nutt, 1918. MS 2285.

Primarily letters received by General Elwell, Civil War veteran and Cleveland attorney, most of which are either from or about

Clara H. Barton (1821–1912), founder of the American Red Cross. Also included is a notebook containing copies of poems and several newspaper clippings.

486   JOHN SOWERS. Diaries, 1853, 1860. 2 volumes. MS 2287.

Daily entries made by Sowers, a tracklayer from Covington, Miami County, Ohio. In 1860, Sowers worked for the Atlantic & Great Western Railroad.

487   ISAAC G. THORNE (b. 1835). Papers, 1862–1901. 1 folder. MS 2296.

Includes commissions, passes, and other papers relating to Thorne's activities as agent of the committee of the Miami Quarterly Meeting of Friends for relief of colored refugees in the Mississippi Valley and as agent for the Western Freed-Man's Commission, 1863–1865; and copies of various letters recommending Thorne for governmental positions, 1892.

488   JOHN McMEEKIN FAMILY. Papers, 1862–1866. 1 folder. MS 2297.

Primarily letters of John McMeekin of the 144th Regiment, Ohio Volunteer Infantry, while he was stationed at Camp Marietta, Ohio, and in various camps in Tennessee, Louisiana, and Mississippi. They are addressed to his mother, Hanna McMeekin of Washington, Fayette County, Ohio.

489   HARVEY RICE (1800–1891). Papers, 1830–1897. Gift of Mrs. Walter P. Rice, 1948; and others. 1 box. MS 2307.

Letters, business papers, land deeds and titles, certificates, and copies of speeches delivered by Harvey Rice, a Cleveland-based lawyer, legislator, businessman, and author. This collection consists primarily of letters relating to the Oliver H. Perry Monument, 1860–1883; and letters, financial records, photographs, and newspaper clippings relating to the construction of the Moses Cleaveland Monument on Cleveland's Public Square, 1886-1888.

490 CLEVELAND CENTENNIAL COMMISSION. CLEVELAND, O. Records, 1895-1896, 1922-1925. 1 box, 1 oversize volume. MS 2317.

Various records relating to the activities of members of this commission which was charged with directing the city's centennial celebration in 1896. Included are the constitution, minutes of meetings, and list of councilors of the Women's Department, 1895-1896; an account book, 1922-1925; and a visitors' register book, July 18-September 11, 1896.

491 THIRD BAPTIST CHURCH. CLEVELAND, O. Records, 1852-1867, 1880-1900. 3 volumes. MS 2335.

Constitution and rules, minutes of meetings, financial reports, and lists of members of this church (formerly the First Baptist Church of Ohio City, Ohio) which disbanded in 1900.

492 WILLOUGHBY COLLEGIATE INSTITUTE. WILLOUGHBY, O. Records, 1858-1911. 1 box. Gift of Sidney S. Wilson, 1916, 1937, 1938. MS 2338.

Constitution and subscription lists, minutes of trustee meetings, reports of school principals, financial accounts and receipts, contracts, and some correspondence relating to this institution of higher learning which was also called Willoughby College or Willoughby University. Incorporated in 1858, it was operated under the Erie Annual Conference of the Methodist-Episcopal Church. Also included are some scattered papers and one volume of records pertaining to the estate of Benjamin Woolsey (one of the original incorporators of this university) and of Mrs. Kezia Woolsey, 1861-1870.

493 WAR EMERGENCY RELIEF BOARD. CLEVELAND, O. Records, 1898. Gift of Mrs. Andrew Squire, 1898; and others. 6 volumes, 2 folders. MS 2339.

Lists of contributions, work done, work returned, and auxiliary societies; receipt book of the committee on appropriations; and some letters addressed to various members of this charitable organization formed under the auspices of the Daughters of the American Revolution to help provide supplies to hospitals caring for American men wounded during the Spanish-American War.

494 JONATHAN TRUMBULL (1740-1809). Papers, 1787-1811. 1 folder. MS 2347.

Correspondence, land deeds and agreements, powers of attorney, and other papers of Trumbull, during the time he was a U.S. Representative and Senator, and Governor of Connecticut, dealing primarily with land matters involving the Ohio Company. Correspondents include Samuel H. Parsons, Jonas Prentice, Rufus Putnam, and Nathaniel Williams.

495 JAMES G. MARTIN & COMPANY. NASHVILLE, TENN. Letter Book, 1820-1822. 1 volume. MS 2349.

Copies of letters sent by various persons connected with this merchant company.

Included in this volume are financial accounts of Willoughby Williams, 1830-1845.

496 WILLOUGHBY UNIVERSITY OF LAKE ERIE. CHAGRIN (NOW WILLOUGHBY), O. Records, 1834-1847. ½ box. MS 2352.

Articles of incorporation and minutes of meetings of the trustees of this institution, the first in the Western Reserve to offer medical education.

497 PHILANDER H. STANDISH (ca. 1835–1918). Papers, 1861–1918. Gift of Miss Myra R. Standish, 1919. 6 boxes. MS 2356.

Correspondence, letters patent, contracts and agreements, notebooks, specifications and price lists for various types of chain, drawings of steam generators and steam plows, time and account books, and other papers relating to the activities of Philander H. Standish, mechanical engineer and inventor. Active in several cities in California, Missouri, and Ohio before settling in Cleveland, Standish was owner or co-owner of several manufacturing companies which were involved in the making of steel chains, including the Standish Chain Company of Cuyahoga Falls, Ohio, early 1880's; the Bimel-Standish Company of St. Mary's, Ohio, 1890's; and the Standish Chain and Manufacturing Company of Kent, Ohio, 1900's. Among the letters patent issued Standish by Russia, the United Kingdom, the United States, Canada, Belgium, Germany, and Sweden were those for his invention of a chain-making machine, a treadle mechanism for sewing machines, and a steam cultivator and for improved methods in tethering horses, welding chain links, and coiling metal rods. The business associates with whom he corresponded include J. B. Carey, president of the Chain Makers National Union.

498 S. A. BOYNTON AND J. A. STEPHENS. Account Books, 1888–1891. 4 volumes. MS 2360.

Account book, 1888–1891, and three daybooks, 1888–1890, of these two Cleveland doctors.

499 JAMES B. DAY. Original Manuscripts. 3 items. Gift of the Author, 1938. MS 2364.

Typescript and manuscript copies of "Nuggets of Gold: A Story of Pioneer Life in Northern and Southern Ontario, Canada" (161 pages), 1936; "Kathie" (29 pages), undated; and "Modern Melodies for Minors" (53 pages), undated.

500 WILLIAM CHATFIELD FAMILY. Papers, 1838–1871, 1908. 2 boxes. MS 2367.

General and personal letters from various members of the family of William Chatfield, who emigrated from New York and settled in Sharon Center, Medina County, Ohio, in 1834. The letters, the diaries of Coy B. Chatfield, 1852–1863, and the diaries of Guy C. Chatfield reflect primarily the conditions and events in the local community.

501 BEZALEEL WELLS FAMILY. Papers, 1796–1803, 1814, 1849. 8 items. Gifts of Mrs. Lee Rodman, 1954; and others. MS 2372.

List and descriptions of lots sold by Bezaleel Wells in Steubenville, Jefferson County, Ohio, 1796–1803; early surveys of land near or in Steubenville, 1814 and n.d.; two land contracts, 1799; and commissions of Bezaleel Wells, 1797, and Francis A. Wells, 1849.

502 HEMAN ELY (1775–1852). Papers, 1817–1849. 5 boxes. MS 2390.

Account books, financial receipts, and business and personal letters addressed to Heman Ely, operator of a sawmill, gristmill, and iron furnace in Elyria, Ohio, and son of Justin Ely, the founder of that city. Included are nine ledgers and daybooks pertaining to the Lorain Iron Company, 1825–1848; gristmill and sawmill accounts, 1826–1831; Justin and Heman Ely's tax lists (Lorain County), 1826–1836; and assorted financial accounts and tax payment receipts, 1827–1845.

Also included is Heman Ely's journal, 1809–1810, kept while on a trip to Paris, France, and two typescript copies of this journal. (Gift of Arthur P. Williamson, 1969.)

503 JEROME B. BURROWS FAMILY. Papers, 1858–1900. 1½ boxes. MS 2394.

Primarily letters addressed to various members of this family, including Jerome B. Burrows, who served as a captain in the 14th

Independent Battery, Ohio Volunteer Light Artillery, as mayor of Painesville, Ohio (ca. 1866), and as judge of the Seventh Circuit Court of Ohio; and Jerome S. Burrows, student at Western Reserve College, late 1870's, and then proprietor of the *Painesville Telegraph*. The letters deal with personal and legal matters, the operation of the newspaper, and Republican Party politics in Lake County. Some letters from relatives deal with political and economic affairs in Kansas and Iowa during the mid 1850's. Correspondents include various U.S. Representatives, judges, and lawyers, including Julius C. Burrows, Ezra B. Taylor, and S. H. Tolles.

504 OHIO MILITIA. 2ND REGIMENT. Records, 1809–1819. ½ box. Purchased, 1924. MS 2396.

Including election returns, minutes of officers' meetings, financial accounts, court-of-inquiry reports, returns, and muster rolls for this regiment, the headquarters of which were in Coshocton, Ohio.

505 TUSCARAWAS COUNTY HORTICULTURAL SOCIETY AND FARMER'S CLUB. NEW PHILADELPHIA, O. Records, 1862–1863. 1 volume. Purchased, 1924. MS 2399.

Constitution and minutes of meetings of this society organized in December, 1862, "for the improvement of Agriculture, Horticulture, Stock & Wool growing, etc."

Also included in this volume is an extensive list of diseases, their symptoms and remedies, ca. 1865.

506 OHIO VOLUNTEER INFANTRY. 105TH REGIMENT. Records, 1862–1865, 1919–1924. 1 volume, 1 folder. Gift of Charles S. Maynard, 1928. MS 2400.

One volume containing enlistment records, 1862–1865; and one folder of letters received by Charles S. Maynard relating to reunion meetings of this regiment, 1919–1924.

507 ALFRED THOMAS GOODMAN (1845–1871).* Papers, ca. 1860–1871. 3 boxes. MS 2401.

Primarily copies of letters, journals, and other documents and research notes used by Goodman, secretary of the Western Reserve Historical Society (1867–1871), in preparing numerous biographical sketches and other publications. Included is a copy of the journal of Captain William Trent (1715–ca. 1787) kept while on a trip from Logstown to Pickawillany (in Pennsylvania) to visit a village of Miami Indians and other papers relating to the publication of this journal, 1871 †; copy of the journal of Captain Jonathan Heart (1748–1791), October 13–November 7, 1785 ‡; copies of correspondence between Captain Heart and Major William Judd, 1786–1791; copies of letters, military orders, reports, court testimony, and other papers relating to General Josiah Harmar (1753–1813) and his expedition against the Miami Indians of the Maumee Valley in 1790; biographical sketches (some newspaper clippings) of each Ohio governor, 1803–1868, and each justice of the Ohio Supreme Court, 1803–1852 §; and biographical sketches of John Armstrong, Salmon P. Chase, Colonel William Crawford, John Dunlap, General John Gibson, Colonel George Gibson, Josiah Harmar, Jonathan Heart, William Irvine, Arthur St. Clair, Winthrop Sargent, John Smith, Thruston Buckner, and J. P. Wyllys. Also included are copies of other articles by Goodman, as well as a few personal papers.

* Goodman's correspondence can be found in the archives of the Western Reserve Historical Society.

† See *Journal of Captain William Trent from Logstown to Pickawillany, A.D. 1752 . . . together with letters of Governor Robert Dinwiddie an Historical Notice of the Miami Confederacy of Indians . . . with a Short Biography of Captain William Trent*, ed. Alfred T. Goodman (Cincinnati: Printed by Robert Clarke & Company for William Dodge, 1871).

‡ See Consul Willshire Butterfield, *Journal of Captain Jonathan Heart . . .* (Albany, 1885).

§ See WRHS *Tract* No. 2 (September, 1870).

[144]

508 DEVEREUX FAMILY. Papers, ca. 1808-1932. 54 boxes, 28 volumes. Gifts of the Devereux Family, ca. 1932; Mrs. Edwin M. Ashcraft and Mrs. A. Winslow Powell, 1952; combined for ease of access, 1963. MS 2415.

Correspondence, business and legal documents, letter books, diaries, volumes of financial data, ships' logs, scrapbooks, newspaper clippings, genealogical data, daguerreotypes, engravings, and other material relating to the activities of various members of this prominent family, most of whom resided in Cleveland, Ohio. The three principal figures in this collection are John Devereux (1802-1881), sea captain of Marblehead, Massachusetts; John Henry Devereux (1832-1886), Civil War general, engineer, railroad industrialist, and philanthropist, of Cleveland; and Henry Kelsey Devereux (1860-1932), industrialist, philanthropist, and harness-horse fancier, of Cleveland. The comparatively small number of papers (2 boxes) relating to John Devereux includes seven ships' logs, 1818-1864, and six volumes of financial records, 1831-1862. A much larger quantity of material (32 boxes) relates to John Henry Devereux and his activities as a construction engineer on the Cleveland, Painesville & Ashtabula Railroad, 1851-1852; division and resident engineer of the Tennessee and Alabama Railroad and civil engineer for Nashville, Tennessee, 1852-1860; superintendent of Virginia railroads, 1862-1864; and officer of several railroads, including the Cleveland and Pittsburgh, the Lake Shore, the Cleveland, Columbus, Cincinnati, and Indianapolis, and the Atlantic & Great Western Railroad, 1873-1886. The papers of Henry K. Devereux (11 boxes) touch upon his activities as an engineer and real estate agent and official of several companies, including the Winslow Car Roofing Company, Paige Car Wheel Company, and the Forest City Live Stock and Fair Company, but deal in more detail with his efforts in behalf of harness racing and in the area of breeding and racing trotting horses. Specifically included are a broken series of diaries, 1876-1930; letter books, 1907-1912; stallion service records, pedigrees, photographs, and other memorabilia relating to horses which belonged to Devereux, 1905-1927. Also included in this collection

are 17 volumes of records of the Gentlemen's Driving Club of Cleveland, Ohio, with which Henry K. Devereux was associated from the time of its inception in 1895 until interest in it waned during World War I, 1895–1916.
Unpublished 27-page register available in the Society.

509 EPHRAIM GEORGE SQUIER (1821–1888). Papers, ca. 1845–1870. 2 boxes. MS 2446.

Address book, pocket diaries, memoranda books, and other bound and unbound notes (some in Spanish) kept by Squier, archaeologist and diplomat, and a collection of printed diagrams (some of which are attributed to Squier) of Indian earthworks in various Ohio counties and in Indiana, Kentucky, South Carolina, and Wisconsin. Also included are some of Squier's writings, such as a proof copy of an article on "Notices of the Minor of Aboriginal Art," 45 pages of notes on the Inca Empire, and a 283-page manuscript copy of "A Trip in Salvador," which describes a journey from La Union in San Salvador to San Vicente.

510 BALDWIN UNIVERSITY. SISTERHOOD OF THE HUNGRY SEVEN. BEREA, O. Records, 1884–1890. 1 volume. Gift of Elisha S. Loomis, 1939. MS 2492.

Constitution, bylaws, and minutes of meetings of this organization dedicated to "the development of our social, moral and intellectual natures" with membership limited to Philozetians who were students at Baldwin University.

511 BEREA LAW AND ORDER LEAGUE. BEREA, O. Records, 1887–1893. 1 folder. Gift of Elisha S. Loomis. MS 2493.

Constitution, minutes of meetings, vouchers, a treasurer's book and bank book, and several letters of this organization the purpose of which "shall be the maintenance of Law and Order generally in our village and especially the closing of Saloons."

512 ELISHA SCOTT LOOMIS (1852–1940). Papers, 1908–1939. 7 boxes. MS 2500.

Genealogical data, speeches, scrapbooks, and an assortment of letters received by Loomis, who served as head of the mathematics department of Cleveland's West High School, and as professor emeritus of mathematics, Baldwin Wallace College. Included are copies of compiled genealogies of the Oberholtzer family, of Michael Shire, and of Clara Byrde Loomis; and of speeches and papers prepared by Loomis on topics such as education, geometry, mathematics, Sunday schools in Ohio, and pioneer ancestors, 1876–1935. Also present are obituary and cemetery records, Berea, Ohio, 1904; a 198-page biographical account of the life of Dr. Aaron Schuyler, president (1875–1885) of Baldwin University; a 79-page autobiographical account, 1931, and one volume of "Recollections," 1939; and genealogical data on the following families: Beall, Benedict, Lawrence, Leete, LeFevre, Loomis (Lumas), Rhoades, Taylor, Trowbridge, and Wright.

513 DAUGHTERS OF THE AMERICAN REVOLUTION. LAKEWOOD CHAPTER. LAKEWOOD, O. Letters, 1937–1938. 1 loose-leaf binder. MS 2504.

Letters written to Mrs. Elatus G. Loomis, regent, by members of the Northwest Territory caravan while reenacting the trek of pioneers from Peabody, Massachusetts, to Steubenville, Ohio, 150 years earlier.

514 HANNA FAMILY. Papers, ca. 1830–1900. 4 boxes, 7 volumes (some copies). Gift of the Hanna Family, ca. 1938. MS 2510.

Originals, typescript or photostatic copies of legal documents, charts, letters, deeds, notes, wills, photographs, and magazine and newspaper clippings containing genealogical data relating primarily to members of the Hanna family in Cleveland and Ohio. Much of this was used in preparing *The Book of Benjamin Hanna: His Children, and Their Descendants* (1938). Emphasis is on Robert Hanna (1753–1837), Benjamin Hanna (1779–1853), and Leonard Hanna (1806–1862). Also included are seven volumes of congratulatory messages sent to Marcus A. Hanna after the following successful campaigns of the Republican Party in which Hanna played a major role: presidential, 1896; senatorial, 1898; Ohio State, 1899; and presidential, 1900.

Unpublished 14-page register available in the Society.

515 MARY A. R. PARSONS. Papers, 1899–1935. 2½ boxes. Gift of Mrs. Florence R. Bush, 1939. MS 2517.

Letters, charts, notes, newspaper clippings, and other papers relating to genealogical research conducted by Mrs. (Henry E.) Parsons of Avon Lake, Ohio, on several families including Crandall, Murdock, Reed, Schuyler, and Walker.

516 CONVERSATIONAL CLUB. CLEVELAND, O. Records, 1898–1964. 1 box. Gift of the Conversational Club, 1939, 1947, and 1965. MS 2521.

Minutes of meetings, membership rolls, financial accounts, reports of the 50-, 60-, and 70-year anniversary celebrations, and other documents pertaining to this women's literary club which was founded in 1878 and disbanded in 1964.

517 CUYAHOGA STEAM FURNACE COMPANY. CLEVELAND, O. Records, 1834–1900. 5 boxes, 15 volumes. Gift of the Family of David Z. Norton and Mary Castle Norton, 1933. MS 2525.

Primarily commercial and legal documents and record books of this company, Ohio's first steam-powered manufacturing concern formed under a state charter (1834), which produced furnace engines, hydraulic presses, boilers, mill gearing, castings, railroad-construction equipment, locomotives, plows, screw propellers, and cannons for the U.S. government. Other papers include newspaper clippings, abstracts of titles, stock certificates, promissory notes, legal briefs, contracts, land deeds, tax forms, letters patent, receipts, bills of sale, insurance policies, memoranda, and some business correspondence. Major shareholders at the time of the organization of this company were Josiah Barber, Richard Lord, Charles Hoyt, and Lake Risley. Elisha Sterling, William Bainbridge, and J. F. Holloway served in the capacity of president during the period from 1859 to 1887, when the Cuyahoga Steam Furnace Company was bought by the Cleveland Shipbuilding Company.

Unpublished 6-page register available in the Society.

518   MATTOON MONROE CURTIS (b. 1858). Papers, early 20th c. 2 boxes. MS 2529.

Letters, original essays, magazine articles, notes, newspaper clippings, photographs, and other papers of Professor Curtis (Department of Philosophy, Western Reserve University), most of which concern tobacco, snuff, snuffers, and snuff boxes.

519   JAMES McMAHON. Papers, 1863–1888. 14 items. Gift of Daisy A. McMahon. MS 2531.

Letters, commissions, and a pocket diary for 1864 kept by McMahon, who served in the 41st Regiment, Ohio Volunteer Infantry, during the Civil War. McMahon recorded his activities and accounts of battles, including the siege of Atlanta, in which he participated from April to September, 1864.

520   MAPLE LEAF LAND COMPANY. CLEVELAND, O. Records, 1900–1918. 3 boxes. MS 2538.

Articles of incorporation, contracts, deeds, leases, financial statements, reports, lists of stockholders, stock certificates, and correspondence pertaining to this real estate enterprise which developed and sold land in Mayfield and Gates Mills, Ohio. Also included are some papers dealing with the organizing of the Chagrin Valley Country Sports Club (now the Chagrin Valley Hunt Club), 1909.

521   RODNEY SEAVER. Diary, 1863–1865, 1871. 1 volume. Gift of Goodspeed's Book Shop, 1928. MS 2568.

Pocket diary containing an account of the activities of Seaver, of Company K, 2nd Regiment, Wisconsin Cavalry, and including descriptions of several battles in which he participated, primarily in 1864.

522   JAMES M. NASH (d. 1866). Papers, 1861–1866. 8 items. MS 2571.

Letters, muster-out roll, notices of promotions, and part of a diary for the fall of 1863 kept by Nash, an officer in Company B, 19th Regiment, Ohio Volunteer Infantry, from 1861 to 1865.

523   JOHN WILSON. Papers, 1833–1845. 1 folder. MS 2573.

Primarily land contracts and deeds of John Wilson of Canfield, Trumbull County, Ohio.

524   GRAND ARMY OF THE REPUBLIC. DEPARTMENT OF OHIO. Records, 1901. 1 box. MS 2611.

An invitation to the 35th National Encampment of the G.A.R. and many letters of reply from dignitaries throughout the country.

525   JOHN T. SHRYOCK. Papers, 1861–1865. 1 folder. MS 2615.

Primarily letters received by Shryock while he was the proprietor of the Zanesville (Ohio) *Currier and Gazette*. Among his correspondents, several of whom comment on various military campaigns during the Civil War, are Edward Ball and General Mortimer Dormer Leggett (1821–1896).

526   FIRST WARD CIVIC ASSOCIATION. CLEVELAND, O. Records, 1921–1924. 1 folder. MS 2629.

Constitution and bylaws, correspondence, resolutions, minutes of meetings, lists of members, and other papers relating to this association, whose object was "to create interest in municipal matters among private citizens." Members were active in municipal affairs and attempted to influence local government.

527 CHAUNCEY WARNER. Papers, 1790–1848. 1 folder. MS 2643.

Primarily deeds and contracts relating to tracts of land in Hartford County, Connecticut, and Lorain and Portage counties, Ohio.

528 ALEXANDER STEWART. Papers, 1806–1844. 1 folder. MS 2647.

Agreements, apprenticeship indentures, land surveys, receipts, and other financial papers of this farmer who resided in Franklin, Portage County, Ohio.

529 S. S. WARNER. Papers, 1863–1865. 1 folder. MS 2648.

Letters, enrollment lists, receipts, and other financial papers relating to Warner's activities as treasurer of the Huntington (Lorain County, Ohio) Bounty Fund.

530 OHIO VOLUNTEER INFANTRY. 51ST REGIMENT. Records, 1861–1864. 1 volume. Gift of Charles D. Gentsch, 1939. MS 2650.

Morning reports of Company K.

531 ALBERT GAILLARD HART (1821–1907). Papers, 1830–1907. 4 boxes. Gift of Albert Bushnell Hart. MS 2659.

Correspondence, land contracts and deeds, lectures, articles (published and unpublished), certificates, newspaper clippings, and other papers relating primarily to the military career of Dr. Albert G. Hart, who served as surgeon for the 41st Regiment, Ohio Volunteer Infantry, and later practiced medicine in Cleveland. The largest part of the collection consists of letters, 1861–

1864, written by Dr. Hart to his family describing his activities as a surgeon for the 41st, which saw action primarily in Tennessee; and of affidavits, certificates, and correspondence, 1880–1900, between Dr. Hart and veterans of the 41st concerning their pension claims. Also relating to the Civil War is a diary kept by Dr. Hart from the time his unit left Cleveland on March 8 until November 9, 1864; reports of sick, killed, wounded, discharged, and promoted, records of recruits examined, and field and special orders, 1861–1864; and copies of published articles on the role of the surgeon and the army hospital during the Civil War. Also included are school papers from Western Reserve College, 1830's; papers relating to land matters in Clarksville, Mercer County, Pennsylvania, 1838–1861; personal correspondence between Dr. Hart and his wife, 1840–1859; papers relating to reunions of the Bushnell family, 1880's, and of the 41st Regiment, 1882–1889; and some biographical and genealogical information, as well as copies of various essays, lectures, and reminiscences on medicine and other subjects.

532   U.S. ARMY. CAVALRY. MISSOURI. Muster Roll, 1861. 1 item. Gift of C. S. Marshall, 1920. MS 2667.

List of officers and privates mustered into the U.S. Cavalry from Missouri.

533   PRESBYTERY OF CLEVELAND, O. WOMAN'S MISSIONARY SOCIETY. Records, 1886–1935. 2 boxes. Gift of Carrie B. Smith, 1940. MS 2685.

Organizational record, constitution, bylaws, annual reports, minutes of meetings, and correspondence relating to this society which was concerned with both home and foreign missionary work.

534   JACOB S. SHRIVER. Letters, July–August, 1840. 28 items. MS 2700.

Replies of leading Whig politicians who were invited by Shriver and other members of the invitation committee to attend a convention sponsored by the Whigs of Virginia, Pennsylvania, and Ohio, and to be held on September 3, 1840, in Wheeling, for the purpose of aiding "the cause of Harrison, Tyler and Reform."

535   JAMES BARNETT (1821–1911). Papers, 1861–1906. 4 boxes. Gifts of Alexander C. Brown, 1946; N. F. Lukens; and others. MS 2702.

Correspondence, notes, and other papers relating to the activities of General Barnett of Cleveland, commander of the 1st Ohio Light Artillery and chief of artillery on the staff of General William S. Rosecrans, and later public official and civic leader. The 1st Ohio Light Artillery, which saw action primarily in Tennessee, was organized under Colonel Barnett in the spring of 1861. Papers include letters and orders pertaining to Barnett's regiment during the Civil War, 1861–1865; letters and reminiscences written by members of the regiment at Barnett's request, 1880–1890; correspondence concerning the G.A.R.'s Department of Ohio, 1880–1900; and a manuscript copy of a history of the 1st Ohio Light Artillery prepared by General Barnett. Also relating to this regiment are pocket diaries kept by three of its members, including three diaries of Philander B. Gardner (Battery E) of Berea, Ohio, 1862–1865; four diaries of Addison F. Stockham of Hambden, Ohio, 1862–1865; and three diaries of Newton G. Strong (Battery G) of Strongsville, Ohio, 1862–1864. Also included are letters to General Barnett, Director of Charities and Correction Warden in Cleveland, Ohio, and other papers concerning Bethel Associated Charities, in particular, the Bethel Union Relief Department, 1878–1899; and correspondence, statements, and annual reports of the Cleveland, Cincinnati, Chicago & St. Louis Railway Company, 1890–1895.

536   MRS. GOUVERNEUR MORRIS. Miscellany, ca. 1910–1920. 2 volumes. Gift of Mrs. Gouverneur Morris, 1922. MS 2704.

Including a typescript copy of a journal kept on a canoe trip along the north shore of Lake Superior, ca. 1910.

537   DUDLEY BALDWIN. Account Book, 1844–1845. 1 volume. Gift of Mrs. Gouverneur Morris, 1922. MS 2708.

Baldwin's account with P. M. Weddell & Company and Baldwin & Spangler of Cleveland, Ohio. Four pages of this volume contain diary-like entries made while on a voyage from San Francisco to New York on the *Golden Eagle,* undated.

538   JOHN FRANKLIN RUST (1835–1899). Papers, 1849–1889. 25 boxes. Gift of the Rust Family, 1944. MS 2710.

Correspondence, commercial and legal documents, and other papers relating to the activities of John F. Rust, Sr., who was active in the lumber and shipping businesses on the Great Lakes during the last half of the 19th century, while residing principally in Saginaw, Michigan, and Cleveland, Ohio; and to the activities of the companies with which he was associated. Included are invoices, receipts, trip accounts for lake vessels, tax records, insurance policies, agreements, deeds, contracts, bills of sale, mortgages, patents, redemption certificates, wills, land plots, township and range charts, circulars, and bound volumes of financial and statistical data. Rust's lumber firm in Cleveland was known as Rust, King & Company and later became Rust, King & Clint. Some of the financial records pertain to the C. G. King Company, J. F. Rust and Company, and George Rust and Company. The bulk of this collection consists of accounts of the many trips made by the companies' vessels and bound volumes of receipts and disbursements for each vessel, 1866–1884.

Unpublished 10-page register available in the Society.

539   ROLLIN C. HURD (1815–1874) AND FRANK H. HURD (1840–1896). Papers, 1839–1874. 2 boxes. MS 2711.

Correspondence, legal briefs, and other business papers relating to the activities of Rollin C. Hurd, attorney at law and judge of the Court of Common Pleas in Mount Vernon, Ohio; and of his son, Frank H. Hurd, attorney in Mount Vernon and Toledo, Ohio, who was elected as a Democrat to the Ohio State Senate in 1866 and to the U.S. Congress for three terms between 1875 and 1885. The papers of Rollin C. Hurd deal with a number of legal matters, but primarily with the case of Amasa Bunnell et al. v. Henry Stoddard contesting the disposition of the estate of Major Amos Stoddard (d. 1813), 1839–1874. The papers of Frank H. Hurd consist of letters addressed to him dealing primarily with state politics, 1857–1874 (1866–1868).

Also included here are some business papers of Messrs. Warden and Burr, also of Mount Vernon.

540 BENJAMIN F. SELLS (b. 1824). Papers, ca. 1860–1875. 1 folder. MS 2712.

Letters, ordnance returns, military orders, an autobiographical sketch, and papers relating to the court martial of Captain Benjamin F. Sells of Coshocton, Ohio, who served in the 122nd Regiment, Ohio Volunteer Infantry. Captain Sells was dismissed from the service for criticizing the war and the President and for vigorously supporting the candidacy of Clement L. Vallandigham for governor of Ohio in 1863. Also included is a 5-page essay on the Mexican War.

541 GEORGE H. HILDT. Papers, 1861–1864. 1 folder. MS 2714.

Among these Civil War papers are letters, military orders, muster rolls, and other papers concerning the activities of the 30th Regiment, Ohio Volunteer Infantry, of which Lieutenant Colonel Hildt was commanding officer. Included are some letters addressed to Benjamin F. Sells.

542 ANNE F. BROWN. Papers, 1836–1843. 11 items. MS 2719.

Composition, copy, day, and arithmetic books. Also included is a bookkeeping notebook of Marvin H. Brown of Pittsburgh, Pennsylvania, 1837.

543 ELIJAH WADSWORTH FAMILY. Papers, 1792–1868. 2 boxes. MS 2729.

Correspondence, agreements, and deeds relating to land (especially in Wadsworth Tract, Medina County, Ohio) owned by Elijah Wadsworth (1747–1817) of Durham, Connecticut, and James Wadsworth of New Haven, Connecticut. Also included are election returns, military receipts, morning reports, and provision returns for the several regiments in the 4th Division, Ohio Militia, commanded by Elijah Wadsworth, 1804–1813; and lists of lands belonging to Benjamin Tallmadge, 1801–1810, Elijah Wadsworth, 1802–1815, and Frederick Wolcott, 1804–1810. Correspondents of General Elijah Wadsworth, his son Frederick, and his cousin Wedworth Wadsworth of Durham, Connecticut, include shareholders in the Connecticut Land Company and other landowners and settlers in the Western Reserve such as Eliphalet Austin, Elijah Boardman, Abraham Bradley, Jr., Gideon Granger, Judson Guitteau, Uriel Holmes, Jr., Samuel Huntington (1765–1817), John W. Johnston, Ephraim Kirby, Jared P. Kirtland, Roger Skinner, John Sloane, Benjamin Tappan, Edward Tiffin, Frederick Wadsworth, James Wadsworth (from Geneseo), and Wedworth Wadsworth, Jr.

Unpublished 7-page register available in the Society.

544 FREEMASONS. ROYAL ARCH MASONS OF CLEVELAND, O. Records, 1842–1878. 1 volume. MS 2741.

List of members of Webb Chapter No. 14 of this organization which was founded in 1826, chartered in 1827, and revived in 1842.

545 GEORGE W. BROWN. Papers, 1834–1837. 1 folder. MS 2747.

Correspondence, circular letters, and accounts concerning the operation of the post office in North Bloomfield, Ohio. Brown served as postmaster in that township from 1834 to 1837.

546   BEEMAN CHEMICAL COMPANY. CLEVELAND, O. Records, 1891–1899. 1 volume. Gift of Alvin Good, 1941. MS 2752.

Articles of incorporation, bylaws, minutes of meetings, treasurer's reports, and other documents relating to this company which manufactured and sold pepsin, pepsin gum, and other confections.

547   PIONEERS MEMORIAL ASSOCIATION. CLEVELAND, O. Records, 1916–1936. 1 folder. MS 2753.

Minutes of meetings of this association founded in 1914 to preserve Cleveland's historic Erie Street Cemetery.

548   WILLIAM COX COCHRAN (d. 1936). Unpublished Manuscript. 2 volumes (typescript). MS 2757.

This ribbon copy of William C. Cochran's unfinished biography of his stepfather, General Jacob D. Cox, was prepared in 1940, after Cochran's death.

549   GRAND ARMY OF THE REPUBLIC. DEPARTMENT OF OHIO. ARMY & NAVY POST NO. 187. Records, 1861–1865, 1913–1920. 4 volumes. Gift of George Cogswell, ca. 1941. MS 2758.

List of members who served in the Civil War with information concerning their births, deaths, and military service; minutes of meetings of Post 187, 1913–1920; and a memorial volume to Louis Black, Company A, 150th Ohio Infantry.

550   KING'S DAUGHTERS SOCIETY OF BEREA, OHIO. Records, 1894–1900. 1 volume. Gift of E. S. Loomis, 1941. MS 2761.

Constitution, bylaws, and minutes of meetings of this society the object of which was "to develop spiritual life and to stimulate Christian activity," particularly through "the monthly study of the Bible."

551 WILLIAM DAVID EVANS. Papers, 1861–1865. 1 folder, 7 volumes. Gift of Mrs. G. Griswold. MS 2766.
William D. Evans, of Cleveland, Ohio, enlisted in the "Creighton Zouaves" on July 14, 1861, and subsequently was appointed principal musician, Company G, 27th Regiment, Ohio Volunteer Infantry. He served with this regiment for four years and saw action in many campaigns, including those in South Carolina and Georgia, both of which he describes in the seven pocket diaries which span the Civil War years.

552 GRAND ARMY OF THE REPUBLIC. DEPARTMENT OF OHIO. ARMY & NAVY POST NO. 187. Records, ca. 1899. 1 volume. Gift of George Cogswell. MS 2769.
"Personal War Sketches Presented to Army and Navy Post No. 187, Cleveland, Department of Ohio, by William Bingham, 1899."

553 ANNE SCARR. Diary, 1849–1850. 1 volume. Gift of Frank W. Bowler. MS 2781.
Diary kept by Anne Scarr while on a voyage from Cleveland, Ohio, to San Francisco, California, and including three letters she wrote to members of her family.

554 EUCLID AVENUE OPERA HOUSE. CLEVELAND, O. Records, 1869–1878. Gift of Miss Virginia Ellsler, 1941. MS 2784.
A list of plays produced at the opera house with an enumeration of the props needed for each act.

555 STEPHEN BASSETT FAMILY. Papers, 1805–1915. 2 boxes. Gift of Miss D. M. Lynn, 1941. MS 2788.
Personal and general correspondence of members of this family, including Stephen H. Bassett, who settled in Chester, Ohio, and May Louise Bassett (1863–1941) of Cleveland, 1805–1915; land deeds, tax payment receipts, and other financial papers, 1827–

1880; account books and pocket diaries (mostly meteorological information) of Mr. and Mrs. S. H. Bassett of Chester, 1846–1896; letters, memoranda, biographical sketches, and other papers containing genealogical information relating to members of the Bassett family which were collected by May L. Bassett, ca. 1890–1920; two sketches of the Bassett home and papers relating to its repair, 1893–1894; a list of principals of Cleveland's public schools, 1913–1914; and a few items pertaining to the Cleveland Woman's Club, 1914–1915.

556 LINCOLN COUNTY, ME. Record, 1808–1812. 1 volume. Gift of the Library of Western Reserve University, 1941. MS 2794.

Common Pleas Court docket giving the names of litigants in 978 cases and some miscellaneous accounts between the county and Nathaniel Thwing.

557 HORATIO FORD, *collector*. Railroad Records, 1897–1926. 2 boxes, 1 volume. Gift of Horatio Ford. MS 2797.

Records, including minutes of meetings, articles of incorporation, agreements, deeds, reports and resolutions, and franchises of the Cleveland and Eastern Railway Company, the Cleveland and Eastern Traction Company, the Eastern Ohio Traction Company, the Cleveland and Chagrin Falls Railway Company, and the Cleveland, Youngstown & Eastern Railway Company.

558 GEORGE WORTHINGTON COMPANY. CLEVELAND, O. Records, 1849–1870. 21 volumes. MS 2799.

Record books of this hardware company which was organized by George Worthington in 1849 to sell the products of the Cleveland Iron Company. Now one of the country's largest wholesale hardware dealers, the George Worthington Company is Cleveland's oldest business which exists under its original name. Specifically included are cashbooks, journals, sales books, and invoice books.

559   JAMES B. AND JOHN D. CAMPBELL. Papers, 1779–1914. 1 folder. Gift of John D. Campbell, 1942. MS 2800.

Primarily certificates of membership of James B. and John D. Campbell in various fraternal organizations. Also included is a supply, clothing, and pay record book for the 4th Pennsylvania Regiment kept by Lieutenant Thomas Campbell, 1779–1780.

560   CHARLES ASA POST (1848–1943). Papers, 1917–1941. 6 boxes. MS 2803.

Research notes, correspondence (1927–1941), and preliminary and final copies of an unpublished manuscript on social clubs in Cleveland, prepared by Post, a businessman and author of three works on local history: *Doans Corners and the City Four Miles West* (Cleveland: The Caxton Company, 1930); a pamphlet, "The Cuyahoga, the Crooked River that made a City Great," 1941; and *Those Were the Days* (Cleveland: The Caxton Company, 1935). Also included are some of Post's personal papers, including correspondence, 1917–1918; a private journal, 1930–1935; and a bound volume of letters received by Post from recipients of his book on Doans Corners, 1930–1931.

561   ELIJAH BOARDMAN. Letters, 1804–1820. 11 items. Gift of Mrs. E. H. Kresge, 1942. MS 2804.

Letters received by Boardman of New Milford, Connecticut, an original shareholder in the Connecticut Land Company, most of which are from Eli Baldwin, one of the first settlers in Boardman, Ohio.

562   MARIA D. COFFINBERRY FAMILY. Papers, 1767–1930. 3 boxes. Gift of Maria D. Coffinberry, 1947. MS 2805.

Correspondence, journals, newspaper clippings, broadsides, pamphlets, biographical and genealogical data, engravings, photographs, and other memorabilia touching upon the careers of various ancestors of Maria D. Coffinberry (1879–1952) of Cleveland.

These include Henry D. Coffinberry (1841-1912), Union naval officer and Cleveland shipbuilder; Gordius A. Hall (1794-1873), pioneer merchant in Zanesville, Ohio; James Hampson (1776-1843), Ohio soldier and legislator; James Morris Morgan (1845-1928), Confederate naval officer and diplomat; George Morgan (1743-1810), Revolutionary War soldier; John Morgan (1735-1789), physician in the American Revolutionary Army; and George W. Morgan (1820-1893), soldier, lawyer, congressman, and diplomat. Specifically included are letters of Ensign Henry D. Coffinberry while serving in the Union Navy on the Mississippi, 1862-1867; letters and business and legal documents of Gordius A. Hall, 1815-1872, and an account of his journey from New London, Connecticut, to Zanesville, May-June, 1817; letters and other documents (including a collection of early 19th-century broadsides) relating to Captain James Hampson and to other members of the Hampson family of Zanesville, 1807-1853; letters of James Morris Morgan, 1900-1909; and copies and originals of letters and other items relating to the careers of Colonel George Morgan and Dr. John Morgan, 1779-1791. Best represented in this collection is General George W. Morgan, whose papers include his sketch of the Mexican Wars with Texas and with the United States; calling cards and personal and diplomatic correspondence, 1858-1872; items relating to Morgan's activities (particularly those during the Civil War) in the Cumberland Gap and during the Vicksburg campaign, 1862-1901; and speeches, cartoons, broadsides, and political campaign materials, 1864-1916. Also included here are several letters addressed to Elijah Wadsworth (1747-1817), general in the Ohio Militia during the War of 1812, 1802-1815; and an assortment of pamphlets, photographs, and engravings relating to various members of the Morgan and Coffinberry families, 1846-1893.

Unpublished 27-page register available in the Society.
NUCMC 62-4435

563 GEORGE WASHINGTON CRILE (1864–1943). Papers, 1864–1943. 88 boxes. Gift of the Crile Family, 1948. MS 2806.

Correspondence, telegrams, diaries and journals, memoranda books, copies of articles and speeches, financial papers, charts and blueprints, biographical data, photographs, newspaper clippings, and other papers relating primarily to the life and varied career of Cleveland's Dr. George W. Crile, internationally known surgeon, scientist, explorer, author, and hospital administrator. To a lesser extent this collection reflects the activities of Dr. Crile's wife, Grace McBride Crile (d. 1948), and of other members of his immediate family. These papers cover the following general topics: training, practice, administration, and experimentation in the fields of medical science and modern medicine, the Spanish-American War and World Wars I and II, the Great Depression, the planning and implementation of research expeditions in the Western Hemisphere and elsewhere, and the establishment of the Cleveland Clinic, which Dr. Crile co-founded with Drs. William E. Lower, Frank E. Bunts, and John Phillips in 1921. Of special interest are Dr. Crile's writings and research notes and correspondence relating to the areas of medicine in which he was particularly interested (e.g., surgical shock and physiology, blood pressure in surgery, military surgery, and the thyroid gland) and which date from the 1890's when he was professor of histology, and later physiology and surgery, at the Western Reserve University School of Medicine; diaries, volumes of personal memorabilia, and journals containing accounts of his many trips and expeditions, including those to Europe (1892–1895), Mexico (1895), Cuba (1898), England and other European countries (1923), Scandinavia (1924), Africa (1927, 1935–1936), Key West, Florida (1936–1937), the Subarctic (1937), Mexico and Guatemala (1938–1939), and Honolulu (1939); correspondence and diaries relating to Dr. Crile's service as surgical director for the American Ambulance Service Hospital in Neuilly, France, and as organizer and director in chief of the United States Army Base Hospital No. 4 (Lakeside Unit) during World War I, 1914–1919; and correspondence, reports, financial and statistical data, and other material relating to the Cleveland Clinic and particularly to the Clinic disaster of May 15, 1929.

Unpublished 26-page register available in the Society.
NUCMC 67-968

564 ASHTABULA COUNTY SOCIETY OF CLEVELAND. Record Book, ca. 1908. 1 volume. Gift of Mrs. Herman J. Nord, 1942. MS 2812.

Roll-call book with names and addresses of this society's members, all former residents of Ashtabula County living in Cleveland.

565 WOMEN'S CHRISTIAN TEMPERANCE UNION. LAKEWOOD, O. Records, 1909–1934. 3 volumes. Gift of the Estate of Mrs. E. S. Loomis, 1942. MS 2813.

Lists of members, minutes of meetings, 1909–1921, and financial accounts, 1925–1934.

566 METHODIST-EPISCOPAL CHURCH. CANTON DISTRICT. ELKTON CIRCUIT. OHIO. Records, 1864–1940. 4 volumes. Gift of Mrs. Ruth Sloan, 1942. MS 2822.

Probationer and class records, lists of members, baptisms and marriages, and pastoral and statistical lists.

567 ORLANDO JOHN HODGE (1828–1912). Papers, 1822–1913. 16 boxes. MS 2823.

Correspondence, journals, copies of articles, speeches, and poems, certificates and commissions, land deeds and agreements, financial receipts, genealogical notes, and other papers pertaining to the activities of Orlando J. Hodge and several of his relatives.

Hodge, a soldier, politician, newspaperman, and author, was a U.S. Volunteer during the Mexican War (1847–1848), a member of the Ohio legislature and the Cleveland City Council, and owner and editor of the Cleveland *Sun and Voice* (1878–1888). Among these papers are his business, general, personal, and political correspondence, 1838–1912; a journal kept during the Mexican War, April 24, 1847–July 26, 1848; a series of daily pocket diaries and journals, 1850–1905; a journal containing "Incidents in War, Politics, Travels and Business During More than Seventy Years," compiled in 1899; a journal describing trips to Mexico (1885), Alaska (1888), Hawaii (1891), and Europe and Africa (1892); copies of speeches delivered by Hodge, 1903–1907; and several undated volumes of notes and writings on the genealogy of the Hodge, Doan, and other related families (see Orlando J. Hodge, *Hodge Geneaology*, 1900, and *Reminiscences*, 2 vols., 1902 and 1910). Correspondents include Theodore E. Burton, Charles F. W. Dick, Joseph Foraker, Charles Foster, Marcus A. Hanna, Tom L. Johnson, E. E. Shedd, and John Sherman.

Alfred A. Hodge (1825–1896), Orlando's brother, served in the U.S. Navy during the 1840's and saw action in the Mexican War. He lived on the Pacific Coast, ca. 1848–1860, before settling near Cleveland. Included here are his correspondence, 1840–1866; a journal describing his participation in the Mexican War, as well as his visits to Brazil and other South American countries, 1840's; and a journal containing accounts of gold mining in California, 1848, and prospecting for silver in Nevada, 1860.

David L. Wood, a brother-in-law, was quartermaster general of Ohio (1859–1861) and served in the 18th U.S. Regular Infantry (1861–1864). Included here are his correspondence, 1854–1880; an account book, 1859–1860; special and general orders, supply lists and invoices, financial receipts, and the like, 1860–1864; and the personal correspondence of Mrs. David L. Wood (Mandana S. Hodge), 1839–1858.

Also included are two volumes of memoirs of Velorus Hodge (b. 1800) written in 1883; correspondence of Mrs. Orlando J. Hodge, most of which concerns the D.A.R., 1887–1913; and a Cleveland Centennial Commission treasurer's book, 1895–1896.

568   ALBION M. DYER (1858–1912). Papers, 1909–1912. 1 box. MS 2830.

Research notes and copies of documents relating to the early history of the Western Reserve (primarily the Connecticut Land Company) accumulated by Dyer, curator of the Western Reserve Historical Society.

569   JOSEPH RICKEY. Plat, ca. 1879. 1 item. Gift of Mary L. Tolle, through William B. Stewart, 1943. MS 2833.

"Plat of Ohio and Pennsylvania State Boundary Line Resurveyed 1879" made by Rickey, a surveyor from Steubenville, Ohio.

570   PRESBYTERIAN CHURCH. SPRINGFIELD TOWNSHIP, O. Records, 1809–1938. 3 volumes. Gift of Minnie Ellet, 1943. MS 2835.

Two volumes containing both originals and copies of minutes of session meetings, annual reports, and lists of members; and one scrapbook, compiled by Miss Minnie Ellet, containing copies of deeds and abstracts of titles, broadsides, and newspaper clippings pertaining to the Presbyterian Church.

571   PAINE FAMILY. Papers, 1835–1861. 1 folder. Gift of Tracy H. Paine, 1940. MS 2842.

Stock certificates, reports, and other papers relating primarily to the Painesville and Fairport Railroad Company (incorporated in 1835) with which members of this family from Painesville, Ohio, were involved.

572   CHURCH OF CHRIST. GARRETTSVILLE, O. Records, 1889–1902. 1 volume. Gift of Mrs. Elsie Hunt Everett, 1943. MS 2843.

Minutes of meetings and membership roll kept until this church was united with the Baptist and Congregational churches to form the United Church.

573   MRS. CAROLINE P. HERRICK (d. 1918). Diary, January 29–May 9, 1900. 1 volume. MS 2848.

This diary was kept by Mrs. Herrick, the wife of Ambassador Myron T. Herrick, while on a cruise on the Mediterranean Sea in the company of her husband and several friends. In addition to comments on her daily activities, the diary includes photographs of persons on the trip and of places visited.

574   MYRON TIMOTHY HERRICK (1854–1929). Scrapbook, 1892–1904. 1 volume. Gift of Robert Lindsay, 1943. MS 2849.

Pencil sketches executed by Herrick while serving as a director of the Cleveland Electric Illuminating Company, which were collected by Robert Lindsay.

575   CHARLES S. COTTER. Papers, 1859–1864. 1 volume. Gift of Mrs. Mabel E. (Cotter) Hecker, 1943. MS 2857.

Orderly book, containing copies of special and general orders, 1861–1862, and several certificates and commissions of Colonel Cotter, 1st Regiment, Ohio Volunteer Light Artillery.

576   CHARLES HENRY SMITH (1837–1912). Papers, 1861–1865, 1880–1914. 6 boxes. Gifts of Mrs. C. H. Smith, 1918, 1943; Mrs. Frank E. Taplin, 1958–1962. MS 2860.

Commissions, muster rolls, supply lists, special orders, and other papers pertaining to the activities of Charles H. Smith, an officer in the 27th Regiment, Ohio Volunteer Infantry, 1861–1865; correspondence, programs, and badges relating to the Society of the Army of the Tennessee, 1880–1912; reports and minutes of reunion meetings of Fuller's Ohio Brigade (27th, 39th, 43rd, and 63rd Ohio regiments of infantry under the command of John W. Fuller), 1890–1910, and notes used by Smith for his book *The History of Fuller's Ohio Brigade, 1861–1865* (Cleveland: Press of A. J. Watt, 1909); and correspondence and affidavits relating to the Centennial Celebration of Perry's Victory, 1912–1914.

Also included are some papers concerning Mrs. Lucinda (Johnson) Smith's activities with various patriotic organizations.

577   JAMES A. BRIGGS. Papers, 1842–1849. 1 folder. Gift of the Estate of Mr. James A. Briggs, 1890. MS 2861.

Letters received by Briggs, a Cleveland lawyer and banker, primarily from Joshua R. Giddings (1795–1864), concerning personal and political matters.

578   BEN B. WICKHAM, *collector*. Van Sweringen Miscellany, 1918–1929. 3 boxes, 2 volumes. Gift of Ben B. Wickham through Raymond Blosser, 1943. MS 2865.

A collection of documents pertaining to the activities of Mantis J. and Oris P. Van Sweringen of Cleveland, including Exhibits 1–155 (in 2 volumes) entered in the case of the Pittsburgh & West Virginia Railway Company v. the United States of America et al., October term, 1929; typescript copies of proceedings of the city council concerning the Cleveland Union Terminal, 1918–1919; copies of ordinances authorizing construction of the Cleveland & Youngstown Railroad in Cleveland, with notes; a copy of Cleveland's proposed charter, 1913; and a copy of Cleveland's charter, 1923.

579   CHARLES AUGUSTUS OTIS (1868–1953). Papers, ca. 1920–1953. 2 boxes, 6 volumes. Gifts of Laurence H. Norton, 1943; Harold T. Clark, 1957. MS 2867.

General and personal correspondence (primarily 1948–1953), newspaper clippings, biographical sketches, and photographs of Otis, a Cleveland industrialist, banker, and civic leader. Six scrapbooks, ca. 1920–1950, contain newspaper clippings, letters, telegrams, and some printed materials. Correspondents include Robert A. Taft and many of Cleveland's prominent citizens.

580 **LEONARD CASE FAMILY. Papers, ca. 1795–1903.
4 boxes, 2 oversize volumes. Gifts of Leonard Case, Jr.,
1875, 1876; Eckstein Case, 1943; Karl O. Thompson,
1951, 1952. MS 2871.**

Basically the papers of Leonard Case (1786–1864), Cleveland lawyer, landowner, and first cashier and later president of the Commercial Bank of Lake Erie, who played an active role in the economic development of Cleveland and the Western Reserve; and of Leonard Case, Jr. (1820–1880), Cleveland philanthropist and civic leader. Included are approximately 300 maps, plats, surveys, and deeds (bound in two volumes) to tracts of land in the Western Reserve, but particularly in Cuyahoga County, ca. 1795–1881; deeds to tracts of land in Cleveland belonging to Leonard, Leonard, Jr., or William Case, 1844–1877; three account books relating to the Connecticut School Fund, 1849–1852; a volume containing the memoirs of Leonard Case, begun in 1853 and covering the period from 1778 to 1863, with genealogical data on the Case and Eckstein families; approximately 200 federal land grants awarding land in Michigan to veterans of the War of 1812, the Seminole War, and the War with Mexico issued between 1853 and 1854 when Leonard Case was a land commissioner for the state of Ohio; Case's manuscripts on the "Early Settlement of Warren, Trumbull County," (see W.R.H.S. *Tract* No. 30), and another manuscript on the history and settlement of the Western Reserve, 1863; and a copy of a newspaper account of the reminiscences of Benjamin Lane, who settled in Warren in 1799, to which are appended Case's comments and notes, 1863. Also included is a diary of William Case (1818–1862), son of Leonard Case and mayor of Cleveland from 1850 to 1851, railroad executive, and civic leader, covering the years from 1840 to 1855, and correspondence concerning politics and business and the sinking of the steamship *Griffith* in Lake Erie in 1850, 1844–1861; a field book belonging to Zophar Case (d. 1884), brother of Leonard Case, a lawyer and political leader who settled in Clinton County, Illinois, 1867–1868; and letters from various Cleveland businessmen to Eckstein Case, secretary-treasurer of Case School of Applied Science, 1887–1913.

581 CHARLES WHITTLESEY (1808-1886). Papers, 1831-1886. 7 boxes, 5 volumes. MS 2872.

Correspondence, memoranda, geological reports, charts, surveys and field notes, letters, and other documents relating to various activities of Colonel Charles Whittlesey. Included are surveys, sketches, and outline reports concerning iron and copper mining in the Lake Superior region, 1850-1875, and geological reports on Ohio, Wisconsin, and other areas; one volume containing real estate entries for Ohio City lots, Lake Superior lands, etc., 1852-ca. 1880; plats and abstracts of conveyances regarding silver mining in Humboldt County, Nevada Territory, 1860's; meteorological data charts compiled in Cleveland, the Lake Superior region, and elsewhere, 1860's; reports on petroleum exploration in Liverpool, Medina County, Ohio, 1860-1861; correspondence with Pierre Margry, 1872-1874, 1880-1886; catalogues of minerals, water registers for the Great Lakes, photographs and engravings of Indian artifacts, and copies of published and unpublished articles and lectures on genealogy, Indians, and other historical topics.

582 IRVING C. BOLTON (1888-1953). Papers, 1917-1919. 2 boxes. MS 2873.

Copies of bulletins, circulars, general and special orders, and memoranda issued by the 37th Division, Camp Sheridan, Alabama, and duty rosters and equipment records for the 135th Field Artillery, American Expeditionary Force, of which Bolton, a native Clevelander, was captain. Also included are copies of brigade orders for the 62nd Field Artillery Brigade, A.E.F., 1918.

583 JOHN A. ELLSLER (1822-1903). Papers, 1852-1877, ca. 1886. Gifts of Virginia Ellsler, 1943; Effie E. Weston, 1945. ½ box. MS 2875.

Typescript copy of *The Stage Memories of John A. Ellsler,* ed. Effie Ellsler Weston (Cleveland: Rowfant Club, 1950); and 11 letters addressed to Ellsler from other actors, including Edwin Booth and John Wilkes Booth.

584   ATLANTIC & GREAT WESTERN RAILROAD COMPANY. Records, 1869–1873. 20 volumes. MS 2877.

Record books of this railroad in receivership with Reuben Hitchcock, including account books, auditor's letter book, cashbook, journal, letter and receipt books, register of creditors, and transportation receipts.

585   FREDERICK A. BACON. Journal, 1835–1836. 1 volume. MS 2883.

Journal kept by Bacon, who was appointed midshipman in the U.S. Navy in 1832, while serving on board the frigates *Constitution* and *Shark*. Bacon recorded various incidents which occurred aboard ship as well as his observations on places he toured and museums and historic buildings he visited in Gibraltar, Lisbon, Genoa, Florence, Rome, Naples, and Athens.

586   NORTHERN OHIO DENTAL ASSOCIATION. Records, 1872–1942. 9 volumes, 1 box. Deposited by the Association, 1921, 1943, 1945. MS 2885.

Constitution and bylaws, minutes of meetings, membership lists, annual meeting programs, financial accounts, and some correspondence (1935) of this association, organized in 1857 to foster the "advancement and cultivation of dental science and art." Also included are copies of various dental society journals and other memorabilia of this association, which disbanded in 1943.

587   WILLIAM B. BRITTON. Letters, 1861–1864. 1 folder (typescript copies). Gift of Mrs. George R. Lamb, 1943. MS 2886.

Copies of letters written by Captain Britton, Janesville Fire Zouaves, 8th Regiment, Wisconsin Volunteer Infantry, to the editors of the *Janesville Gazette,* Janesville, Wisconsin, concerning the participation of his regiment in the Civil War.

588   OHIO VOLUNTEER LIGHT ARTILLERY. 1ST REGIMENT. Records, 1861–1862. 1 volume. Gift of William P. Palmer, 1922. MS 2894.

Abstracts of provisions issued to this regiment at Camp Dennison under Colonel James Barnett.

589   ALEXANDER BOURNE. Plats, 1813. 3 items. MS 2895.

Plat of a meridian line from the mouth of Eagle Creek to the Little Miami River, and a plat of a meridian line from the mouth of Brush Creek to the Indian boundary line, surveyed by Bourne in 1813. Also included is a survey of Ohio's Brush Creek.

590   HENRY B. CURTIS (b. 1799). Papers, 1824, 1829, 1833–1837, 1847. 1 folder. Gift of Mrs. Henry C. Devin, 1944. MS 2896.

Specifications, contracts, bills, orders, receipts, and other memoranda relating to the construction of the Curtis home in Mount Vernon, Ohio.* Actual construction of this building, now known as the Curtis-Devin home, was begun in 1834 by Westley Irvin and Eliphalet Armstrong, who followed a design published in Edward Shaw's *Civil Architecture* (1831).

* Some of these papers were published in the Appendix of I. T. Frary's *Early Homes of Ohio* (Richmond: Garrett and Massie, 1936).

591   EZRA WILLIAM HICKOK (1798–1869). Papers, 1811–1867. 1 folder. MS 2899.

Diary kept by Ezra W. Hickok of Jefferson, Ohio, and notes on the history of that community's Baptist Church, 1811–1867.

592   WARNER M. BATEMAN (1827–1897). Papers, 1837–1897. 24 boxes. Gift of Warner M. Bateman, Jr., 1952. MS 2900.

Correspondence, ledgers, account books, court records, notebooks, newspaper clippings, and other papers relating to the

[171]

business and political careers and personal life of Warner M. Bateman, attorney at law in Cincinnati, Ohio, who served as U.S. Attorney for the Southern District of Ohio, 1869–1877, and who had charge of John Sherman's campaign to obtain the presidential nomination at the National Republican Convention in 1880. In addition, these papers reflect Bateman's activities in breaking up the notorious "Whiskey Ring," organizing state railways, arranging the purchase of land for government buildings in Cincinnati, serving in the Ohio Senate (1865–1868), and lecturing in behalf of the Republican Party. Correspondents include Edwin Baltzley, Arthur E. Bateman, Elwood Bateman, Benjamin Butterworth, W. S. Cappeller, S. S. Carpenter, Ross A. Chamberlin, J. B. Chapman, N. H. Chapman, C. S. Dyer, Olive J. Ennis, B. D. Fearing, Charles Foster, James A. Garfield, John Goddard, Richard B. Gordon, S. S. Haines, N. Halstead, J. E. Hamilton, J. C. Harper, R. B. Hayes, Elizabeth Hedrick, J. W. Johnson, M. B. H. Johnson, Lincoln Club of Cincinnati, George J. Low, D. F. Lowe, D. W. McClung, Milton A. McRae, C. W. Moulton, George K. Nash, Thomas M. Nichol, William Penn Nixon, J. S. Robinson, W. K. Rogers, F. O. Romaine, John Sherman, Robert Smith, William Henry Smith, Wilber Stonex, William H. Taft, Josie C. Teetor, Charles T. Thompson, F. E. Trowbridge, Orrin Trowbridge, B. C. Williams, S. Williamson, and Jesse Wright.

Unpublished 40-page register available in the Society.
NUCMC 67-967

593   THOMAS J. HYATT FAMILY. Papers, 1863–1864. 1 folder. Gift of Elbert J. Benton. MS 2901.

Primarily letters * of Captain Thomas Jefferson Hyatt (1830–1864) to his wife, Mary, of Marlboro, Ohio. Hyatt served in the 126th Regiment, Ohio Volunteer Infantry, and participated in the battles of Cold Harbor, Petersburg, Monocacy, and Winchester, before being killed on September 19, 1864.

* See Hudson Hyatt, ed., "Captain Hyatt; being the letters written during the years 1863–1864 to his wife, Mary," *Ohio State Archaeological and Historical Quarterly*, 53: 166–183.

594 WILLIAM H. HUNT. Papers, 1910. 1 box. Gift of William H. Hunt, 1943. MS 2909.

Correspondence, financial reports, newspaper clippings, programs, and other materials relating to the Cuyahoga County Centennial Celebration, October 10–15, 1910, and to the International Congress of Aviation held at that time. Hunt was chairman of the executive committee for the Centennial.

595 BENJAMIN D. FORSYTHE. Papers, 1856–1859. 1 folder. MS 2919.

Circulars, letters, orders, and reports received by Lieutenant Forsythe, Recruiting Service, 4th Infantry, U.S. Army, Chicago, Illinois, from recruiting stations in New York, Pennsylvania, Michigan, Illinois, and Kentucky.

596 MYRON TIMOTHY HERRICK (1854–1929). Papers, ca. 1880–1935. 46 boxes, 1 package. Gift of Mrs. Parmely Webb Herrick and Parmely Herrick, Jr., 1942–1957. MS 2925.

Correspondence, speeches, articles, interviews, certificates, legal documents, programs, drawings, biographical and genealogical data, pamphlets and newspaper clippings, photographs, and family and personal papers of Myron T. Herrick, Cleveland financier, political leader, industrialist, and diplomat, who served as Governor of Ohio (1903–1906) and as U.S. ambassador to France (1912–1914 and 1921–1929). Also included in this collection are papers (primarily correspondence of Herrick's wife, Carolyn Parmely Herrick (d. 1918); his son, Parmely Webb Herrick (1881–1937); and his grandson, Parmely Webb Herrick, Jr. (1910–1957). Herrick's papers reflect his wide range of business, financial, political, and diplomatic interests from 1889 until the time of his death. A relatively small number of papers exist for his gubernatorial and first ambassadorial periods in comparison with the extensive amount of material relating to the 1920's, when he served a second time as ambassador to France. The files of correspondence and speeches for this period reflect upon a number of events and subjects, including postwar readjustment and German reparations, interallied debt, Franco-American relations, French politics, Russia and its new Bolshevik government, the American Food Relief Project, and the transatlantic flight of Charles A. Lindbergh. The following domestic issues are referred to here: the presidential election campaigns of 1924 and 1928, soldiers' bonus legislation, the League of Nations, the Sacco-Vanzetti trial, the Teapot Dome scandal, the Washington Armament Conference of 1921-1922, the Kellogg-Briand Pact, and rural credits for farmers. Also touched upon are the American Ambulance Hospital and the War Relief Clearing House during World War I.

The following are the main series of papers in this collection: letters of President and Mrs. William McKinley, 1889-1906; five letter books while Herrick was Governor of Ohio, 1904-1905; six boxes of speeches and materials used in their preparation, 1904-1929; guest registers, engagement books, inventories of furnishings, and other records of the U.S. Embassy in Paris, 1912-1914 and 1921-1929; sixteen boxes of correspondence during Herrick's second ambassadorial period, 1921-1929; and a series * of letters from Charles A. Lindbergh and his family to the Herrick family, 1927-1931, including letters carried by Lindbergh on his transatlantic flight in 1927. Notable correspondents include General Henry T. Allen, Calvin Coolidge, Herbert Hoover, Charles A. Lindbergh, Ida McKinley, William McKinley, Theodore Roosevelt, William Howard Taft, and Woodrow Wilson.

Unpublished 34-page register available in the Society.
NUCMC 62-4689

* Unpublished 13-page calendar of this series available in the Society.

597   JAMES E. BISHOP. Miscellany, 1939, 1940. 1 folder. Gift of Rev. James E. Bishop, 1944. MS 2926.
Includes two "Sketches" of the city of Steubenville, Ohio, prepared by Bishop while working for the W.P.A. Federal Writers' Project, 1939-1940; and some notes on Mormonism.

598   ROBERT C. LAMBERTON. Diary, 1862–1866. 61 pages (typescript copy made in 1944 of the original in private possession). MS 2934.

Diary kept by Lamberton while serving with the 84th and, after 1864, the 57th Pennsylvania Volunteers, containing statements on the weather and troop movements.

599   JAMES JOHN HAGERMAN (b. 1838). Memoirs, 1908. 65 pages (typescript copy made in 1943 of the original in private possession). MS 2935.

Hagerman, resident of Newport, Michigan, rose from a steamboat clerk to an officer in the Milwaukee Iron Company, and describes primarily his activities in the iron industry of the Great Lakes region between 1860 and 1890.

600   GEORGE CAMP CURTIS (1817–1894). Papers, 1886–1894. 1 folder. MS 2936.

Autobiographical sketch (prepared in 1886) of Rev. George C. Curtis, in which he discusses his years at Lane Theological Seminary, his services as minister to communities in Ohio, Michigan, and New York, and various trips to Europe after his retirement. Also included are some letters concerning the Curtis family genealogy.

601   DAVID AND JOHN McKINLEY. Papers, 1748–1794. 14 items (2 photostats). Gift of Hudson Hyatt, 1943. MS 2943.

Primarily surveys of land situated in Chanceford, York County, [Pennsylvania], belonging to the McKinley family.

602   JOHN HAYSLIP. Papers, 1801–1832. 2 folders. MS 2944.

Petitions, affidavits, and other legal papers relating to the proceedings of Ohio Militia regimental courts and Common Pleas courts, held in Hayslip's home in West Union, Adams County, Ohio. Also included are rosters, muster rolls, and election poll books for various brigades of the Ohio Militia during the War of 1812, and letters and other papers concerning pension matters, particularly those of Captain William Faulkner.

603 GRAND ARMY OF THE REPUBLIC. DEPARTMENT OF OHIO. CLEVELAND POSTS. Papers, 1907–1941. 1 box. MS 2947.

Letters, programs, and mayoral proclamations regarding the celebration of Memorial Day in Cleveland, and newspaper clippings, 1904–1935.

604 SAMUEL WILLIAMSON, JR. (1808–1866). Papers, 1820–1880. 2½ boxes. MS 2950.

Correspondence, land deeds, leases and agreements, financial papers, and appointments and certificates of Samuel Williamson, Jr., a lawyer, Ohio State Senator, and railroad executive from Cleveland. Most of the correspondence pertains to business, legal, or political matters, 1850–1866, during which period Williamson was the law partner of Albert Gallatin Riddle. Also included are land agreements and deeds of Samuel Williamson (d. 1834) and Matthew Williamson (d. 1832), brothers who settled in Cleveland in 1810, and letters of George T. Williamson, Dr. James D. Williamson, and other members of this prominent Cleveland family; and a journal of the activities of the commissioners appointed by the Ohio legislature to subscribe to the capital stock of the Cleveland, Columbus, & Cincinnati Railroad Company, 1848–1876. Other correspondents include Warner M. Bateman, R. G. Parsons, Rufus P. Spalding, E. B. Starkweather, J. P. Walworth, and other politicians, lawyers, railroad executives, and businessmen from cities throughout the Midwest and northeastern United States.

605 LANE AND WHEELER FAMILIES. Papers, 1821–1905. 5 boxes. MS 2951.

Personal and general correspondence, account and memoranda books, land deeds, financial receipts, and other papers relating to various members of these two families residing in Strongsville, Cleveland, and Berea in Cuyahoga County; Columbia and Copapa in Lorain County; and Brunswick in Medina County, Ohio. Included are letters of Thomas B. Boughton, Company H, 49th Regiment, Ohio Volunteer Infantry, 1862–1865, and some papers of Charles F. Lane, member of the Ohio legislature and mayor of Berea, Ohio, in the 1890's and early 1900's.

606   CLEVELAND ARTS CLUB. CLEVELAND, O. Record Book, 1913–1917. 1 volume. Gift of Charles A. Post, ca. 1940. MS 2967.

Minutes of meetings and treasurer's reports of this club which sought to "organize Cleveland Artists into a body for the betterment of Art Conditions in Cleveland."

607   REPUBLICAN PARTY. NATIONAL COMMITTEE. Report, June 6, 1924. 189 typescript pages. Gift of the Federal Reserve Bank Library in Cleveland, 1942. MS 2969.

"Hearings on Contests by the Republican National Committee for the Purpose of Making up Temporary Roll for the 1924 Convention," which was held in Cleveland. Involved in these contests were Arkansas, Mississippi, and Texas and the 3rd District of Georgia.

608   C. R. McLEAN AND WILBUR C. AMMON. Unpublished Manuscript, ca. 1938. 453 typescript pages. MS 2970.

Original and revised copy of notes on the early history of Akron and Summit County compiled by C. R. McLean, supervisor, and Wilbur C. Ammon, editor, District No. 5 (Akron and Summit County) of the W.P.A. Federal Writers' Project.

609   ADELLA PRENTISS HUGHES FAMILY. Papers, 1801–1904. 9 boxes, 1 volume. Gift of the Estate of Adella Prentiss Hughes, 1950. MS 2980.

Correspondence, land deeds, genealogical data, poems, calling cards and social invitations, music programs, religious tracts, circulars, broadsides, newspaper clippings, photographs, and other papers relating to the activities of Mrs. Adella Prentiss Hughes (1870?–1950), Cleveland musical impresario and founder and manager of the Cleveland Orchestra, and, more significantly, to the activities of her maternal grandparents and parents. These include Benjamin Rouse (1795–1871), Cleveland agent for the American Sunday School Union and organizer of various Cleveland charitable institutions; Mrs. Benjamin (Rebecca C.) Rouse (1799–1887), president of the Cleveland branch of the U.S. Sanitary Commission during the Civil War; Loren Prentiss (1822–1900), Cleveland attorney and public servant; and Ellen Rouse Prentiss (1830–1908). The papers of Benjamin and Rebecca C. Rouse include assorted correspondence, 1809–1884; land deeds and other legal documents, 1827–1863; a journal, account book, daybook, diary, letter book, and other manuscript and printed items relating to the American Sunday School Union and other religious and charitable institutions, 1830–1864; a record book, including the constitution and minutes, of the Cleveland Female Baptist Sewing Society, 1834–1836; and an account of the life of Benjamin Rouse and of the First Baptist Church, Cleveland, covering the years 1801 to 1837. Other major series include general and personal correspondence of Ellen R. Prentiss, 1843–1899; letters of Adella Prentiss, while a student at Vassar College, to her mother, 1886–1890; and correspondence and other memorabilia of Ellen R. Prentiss and her daughter, Adella, while on a visit to Europe, 1890–1891.

Unpublished 15-page register available in the Society.

610   MANX STREET SCHOOL. CLEVELAND, O. Reunion Records, 1893–1923. 2 volumes. Gift of Mrs. Frank E. Taplin and Mrs. Robert J. Dawson, 1944. MS 2990.

Scrapbook containing reunion programs, newspaper articles, badges, pictures, reunion minutes, and treasurers' reports.

611 CLARENCE H. HUTCHINSON. Papers, 1930's. 4 boxes (mostly copies). MS 2996.

Copies of records, notes, and other papers relating to the history of road construction throughout the Western Reserve accumulated by Hutchinson, an assistant engineer in the Cuyahoga County Surveyor's Office. The bulk of this collection consists of typescript copies of extracts from the published laws of Ohio, photocopies of township and county records, and copies of surveys, deeds, and contracts. Also included are notes, photographs, and other data regarding taverns and hotels in Cleveland. Most of these materials were apparently gathered under the auspices of the Ohio Historic Records Survey of the Works Progress Administration.

612 CLEVELAND MILITARY UNITS. Papers, 1877–1962. Gifts of Laurence H. Norton, 1942; Robert H. Jamison, 1964. 20 boxes, 1 package. MS 3000.

Primarily the papers of the First Cleveland Cavalry, 107th Regiment, Ohio National Guard, and of the Cleveland Gatling Gun Battery. The 16 boxes of papers relating to the First Cleveland Cavalry include minutes of meetings, correspondence, invoices and vouchers, financial statements and reports, ledger sheets, legal documents and briefs, blueprints, maps, photographs, newspaper clippings, and other materials relating to the activities of the unit from the date of its inception in 1877 until 1962. These activities include participating in ceremonial and commemorative functions, escorting prominent civil and military leaders (including U.S. Presidents), quelling riots and disorders in Cleveland and elsewhere in Ohio, and participating in the 1916–1917 punitive expedition to the Mexican border area and in World Wars I and II. Also included here are records of the Troop A Armory Company, 1922–1962; the Cavalry Riding Academy, 1928–1947; and the Cavalry Veteran Association, 1961–1962.

The four boxes of papers relating to the Cleveland Gatling Gun Battery include its constitution, bylaws, minutes of meetings, financial accounts, battery rosters, booklets of memoranda and statistical information, and other materials, 1878–1924. This battery was organized in response to the railroad strikes and recurring labor violence during the 1870's. It was disbanded in 1905, although a committee continued to manage its property until the mid-1920's.

Unpublished 13-page register available in the Society.

613   E. C. BLACKMAN & COMPANY. SOLON, O. Records, ca. 1858–1900. 6 boxes, 53 volumes. Gifts of Mrs. Charlotte B. Poulton, 1944; I. T. Frary, 1945; Mrs. Roger Alling, 1949. MS 3003.

Letter books, daybooks, ledgers, journals, invoice books, cashbooks, and correspondence of this cheese factory and warehouse, organized originally in 1861 under the name of Robbins & Blackman Company by Edwin C. Blackman and A. D. Robbins. Also included are newspaper clippings (mounted and unmounted) from the *New York Bulletin* containing the dairy-products market quotations, 1868–1887; a score book of "The Republic" baseball club of Solon, August, 1867; two record books of the Solon Presbyterian Church, 1876–1900; a daily record book for Solon's primary school, 1875–1878; and a daily record book for Solon High School, 1880–1886.

614   MARCUS F. ROBERTS. Diaries, 1859–1860, 1864, 1865. 3 volumes. Gift of the Cleveland Public Library, 1944. MS 3005.

Diaries, apparently kept by Roberts, who worked and lived in Wayne County, Indiana, 1859–1860, and who served (probably in the Indiana Volunteer Infantry) during the Civil War, spending most of 1864 in Alabama. He was mustered out as a first lieutenant on June 16, 1865.

615   CONGREGATIONAL CHURCH. NORTH RIDGEVILLE, O. Records, 1822–1957. 3 boxes. Deposited by the Trustees of the Church, 1945, and later. MS 3006.

Covenant and constitution, minutes of meetings, financial accounts, and other records of this church organized in 1822 in

Ridgeville. In addition to copies of annual reports, 1951–1957, and "The Ridgeville Register," 1953–1956, also included are records of the following church-related activities: the Ladies Benevolent Society, 1886–1917; the Plus Ultra Class, 1909–1915; and the North Ridgeville Christian Endeavor, 1909–1917.

616 PLINY PORTER FAMILY. Papers, 1812–1834, 1853. 2 folders. Gift of Winifred Wolcott, 1945. MS 3008.

General and personal correspondence of several members of this family, but primarily that of Pliny Porter (1787–1840) of Pompey, Onondaga County, New York, and his father, David Porter (1757–1815) of Williamsburg, Massachusetts.

Also included are typescript notes on the genealogy of the Porter family, compiled by Winifred Wolcott, ca. 1940.

617 JARED FARRAND FAMILY. Genealogical Papers, ca. 1925–1962. 10 boxes, 1 package (some copies). Gift of Harry M. Farrand, 1963. MS 3010.

Correspondence, notebooks, newspaper clippings, photographs, and printed items containing information relating to the history of the Farrand family. These materials were accumulated by Harry M. Farrand. This branch of the Farrand family includes those persons who were ancestors or descendants of Jared Farrand (1758–1862) of Norwich, Connecticut, who lived in Bennington, Vermont, and Dover, Ohio, before settling in Middleburgh Township, Ohio, where he died.

Unpublished 6-page register available in the Society.

618 BUTLER IVES. Diaries, 1850–1853, 1855, 1860. 7 volumes. Gift of Miss Helen Gilchrist, 1945. MS 3011.

Diaries containing meteorological observations, financial accounts, surveying notes, and other data relating to Butler's activities primarily as a surveyor in and around Oregon City and Portland, Oregon. In 1850, Ives left Detroit, Michigan, for California and Oregon, but by 1855 was back in Michigan. In 1860, he traveled extensively throughout the United States and records his observations in one of these volumes.

619 MARTIN E. GRAY. Papers, ca. 1835–1900. 13 boxes. MS 3012.

Correspondence, pocket diaries, account books, financial receipts, and land deeds and agreements of Martin E. Gray, a farmer who resided in Willoughby, Ohio, and was active in the Baptist Church. A deacon and member of the board of trustees of the Baptist Convention of the State of Ohio and of the missionary board of the Cleveland Baptist Association, most of Gray's correspondence is with members and officers of various local, state, or national Baptist organizations, such as the Ohio Baptist Education Society, the American Baptist Publication Society, the American Baptist Missionary Union, and Denison University. Correspondents include A. H. Adams, George E. Allen, Thomas Allen, Lena Brennan, Edward Bright, Louise A. Collacott, Ziba Crawford, Thomas K. Cree, J. M. Criswell, Julia Elwin, T. M. Fitch, F. C. Gibbs, Elizabeth M. Gill, Robert G. Gill, H. N. Gray, B. Griffith, George J. Kyle, J. E. Leonard, E. C. Long, R. B. McVeigh, H. L. Morehouse, S. B. Page, Charles Rhoads, Thomas Richmond, D. Shepardson, J. G. Snelling, H. H. Tuttle, J. B. Tuttle, Lavelle Vallette, and William Whitney.

620 EDWARD ALEXANDER SCOVILL (1819–1890). Papers, 1862–1871. 1 folder. MS 3015.

Letters addressed to Scovill, an officer in Hoffman's Battalion, Ohio Volunteer Infantry, and an administrator of the Union Prison on Johnson's Island, Sandusky, Ohio. Relating primarily to life in the prison, the letters include several from former inmates, as well as theater programs, tickets, and lists of prisoners.

621 HENRY N. JOHNSON. Papers, ca. 1892. 1 folder. Gift of H. N. Johnson, 1892. MS 3018.

Notes, memoranda, drawings, and diagrams of Kelley's Island, Erie County, Ohio.

622 JOHN HARMON FAMILY. Papers, ca. 1800–1872. 2 boxes. MS 3022.

Primarily the correspondence, diaries (1807–1819), autobiographical writings, speeches, financial accounts, and land papers of John Harmon (b. 1789), who settled in Portage County, Ohio, in 1806, and of other members of his family. The papers, which relate primarily to the early settlement of the county, also include election poll books for various townships in Portage County, 1808; a docket book, 1818–1824; a list of subscribers to the *Ohio Watchman*, 1835; and abstracts of Connecticut Land Company records as compiled by Orrin Harmon.

623 ASAHEL PORTER AND LEVERETT JOHNSON. Papers, 1809–1865. 2 folders. Gift of Mary Ligett, 1945. MS 3030.

Land deeds and contracts, financial accounts, and miscellaneous notes of Asahel Porter and of his nephew, Leverett Johnson, who settled in Cleveland (Westlake) in 1810. Included are inventories and accounts of the estate of Asahel Porter, 1820's, and subpoenas and other legal documents of Johnson, justice of the peace, 1821–1824. Also included here are a series of Cuyahoga County tax payment receipts issued to various members of the Foot(e) family, 1813–1865.

624 ABRAHAM LINCOLN (1809–1865). Collection of Papers, 1841–1870. 237 items. MS 3031.

Letters and documents (18 items) written or signed by Lincoln, 1841, 1850, 1860–1864; numerous petitions, primarily concerning patronage, addressed to President Lincoln and arranged by state; and 50 letters in which Lincoln is mentioned or discussed. This latter group includes letters to or from Edward Bates, Andrew Boyd, Salmon P. Chase, William Pitt Fessenden, President Andrew Johnson, and Edwin M. Stanton.

625   EMMA BOUTELLE HAWLEY (1880–1967). Genealogical Data, ca. 1940–1956. 25 boxes. Gift of Mrs. Emma B. Hawley, 1956. MS 3033.

Random correspondence, genealogical charts, memoranda, and photostatic copies of records relating to families researched by Mrs. Hawley, a professional genealogist, who also served as head genealogist for the Western Reserve Historical Society from 1942 until 1956. These papers represent her efforts at tracing family histories for persons in New York, Ohio, and other states.

Unpublished alphabetical card-file index is available in the Society.

626   MRS. CHARLES H. SMITH. Papers, 1912–1914. 2 boxes. Gift of Mrs. Mildred Smith Coulton, 1946. MS 3036.

Letters, invitations, programs, and newspaper clippings concerning the centennial celebration of Perry's victory on Lake Erie.

627   GRAND ARMY OF THE REPUBLIC. DEPARTMENT OF OHIO. MEMORIAL POST NO. 141. Records, 1891. 2 volumes. Gift of George Cogswell. MS 3037.

A descriptive book and a volume of "personal war sketches," 1891.

628   JENNIE M. AMES, *compiler*. Genealogical Data, 1927–1940. 4 boxes. Gift of Orsan B. and Fred B. Ames, 1946. MS 3040.

Typescript notes (some in loose-leaf binders) and some correspondence, 1927–1940, concerning the Bearce (var. Bearse, Bierce), Ames, and Reed families.

629 FRANK N. WILCOX (1887–1964). Maps, 1940's. ½ box. Gift of Frank N. Wilcox, 1948. MS 3041.

Topographical perspective maps of various areas in the Western Reserve as drawn by Wilcox and pertaining to his research on Indian trails.

630 MOORE FAMILY. Papers, 1732–1824. 1 folder. Gift of Edward Y. Moore, 1946. MS 3042.

Indentures, receipts, agreements, and documents relating to the probate cases of several inhabitants of Queens County, Nassau Island, New York, in which members of the Moore family (David, Joseph, Nathaniel, or William) were executors.

631 TRINITY CONGREGATIONAL CHURCH. PEPPER PIKE, O. Records, 1894–1954. 7 boxes, 1 oversize package. Deposited by the Church, 1947, 1969. MS 3046.

Minutes of meetings, treasurers' accounts, annual reports, pamphlets, and some correspondence relating to the church and to the activities of various church-related organizations, including the Christian Endeavor Society, the Ladies Aid Society, the Young Women's Missionary Society, the Pastoral Committee, the Founder's Circle, and the Junior Fellowship. Also included are church bulletins, 1896–1909, 1918; and plans and accounts relating to the construction of a new building, 1927–1930.

632 JAMES ABRAM GARFIELD (1831–1881). Papers, 1857–1936. 9 boxes, 1 package, 1 volume. Collected from 14 sources. MS 3049.

Correspondence between Garfield, teacher, soldier, U.S. Representative, and President, and various relatives, friends, and political acquaintances, 1866–1880; correspondence of Lucretia R. Garfield, 1874–1900; photocopies and typescript copies of correspondence between Garfield and Burke A. Hinsdale (1857–1900), 1857–1881; * letters and newspaper clippings (in scrapbooks) relating to President Garfield's assassination, illness, death, and burial, and to the erection of the Garfield Monument in Cleveland's Lakeview Cemetery, 1881–1890; an unbound diary of James A. Garfield, August, 1873; and papers concerning the opening of Lawnfield, Garfield's home in Mentor, Ohio, as a memorial museum, August, 1936. Garfield's correspondents include N. L. Chaffee, Frederick Kinsman, and Charles Whittlesey.

Unpublished 6-page register available in the Society.

* Gift of the Estate of Mary L. Hinsdale (see Mary L. Hinsdale, ed., *Garfield-Hinsdale Letters* [Ann Arbor: University of Michigan Press, 1949]).

633   VIRGINIA MILITARY DISTRICT. OHIO. Records, ca. 1787–1839. 10 boxes, 3 bound volumes. Purchased, 1914, 1950. MS 3050.

Primarily surveys (approx. 4,500) of land in the Virginia Military District (the area between Ohio's Scioto and Little Miami rivers) which was granted to Virginia by Congress in 1784 to be used to satisfy the claims of that state's Revolutionary War veterans. These surveys were made under the direction of Colonel Richard C. Anderson (1750–1826) and, later, Allen Latham and William Marshall Anderson. Also included are copies of warrants, miscellaneous papers of Allen Latham, and some personal papers of Dr. R. G. Lewis of Madisonville, Ohio, from whom this collection was purchased.

Unpublished 4-page register available in the Society.
NUCMC 62-4134

634   GEORGE LORD CHAPMAN. Papers, 1795–1893. 1 folder, 2 volumes. Gift of Marguerite Chapman, 1947. MS 3055.

Chapman, a native of East Haddam, Connecticut, moved to Brooklyn Township before 1820. In 1835 he was appointed coroner for Cuyahoga County and in 1836 was elected marshal of Ohio City. These papers include correspondence, receipts, inventories, and agreements relating to the estate of Selden Chapman of East Haddam, Connecticut, 1795–1807; land deeds and agreements which frequently involved Richard and Samuel Lord and Josiah Barber, realtors in Brooklyn Township, 1820–1850; record book of the Wayne, Medina & Cuyahoga Turnpike Road Company (of which Chapman was a director), 1824–1854; and a record book of the New Harbour Company, a joint-stock company dealing in the sale of land which was organized in Ohio City, 1835–1840.

Also included are several letters of John Hay (1882), William McKinley (1887, 1893), and John Sherman (1883).

635 CHARLES S. HOWE. Papers, 1909–1911. 1 folder. Gift of Karl O. Thompson, 1951. MS 3059.

Correspondence, leaflets, diagrams, and other papers concerning the activities of Dr. Howe, president of Case School of Applied Science (1902–1929), representing the Cleveland Chamber of Commerce, and of the other members of a special committee appointed by Cleveland Mayor Herman Baehr to consider plans for the construction of a bridge over the Cuyahoga River. This led to the construction of the Superior-Detroit High Level Bridge.

636 MARY P. BALLARD. Letters, 1845–1861. 1 folder. Gift of Mrs. William G. Hazel, 1951. MS 3060.

Primarily general and personal letters to Mary Ballard (later Mrs. William Ross of Pittsfield, Illinois) from her father (Rev. John Ballard of Griggsville and Perry, Illinois) and her sisters and brothers (one of whom served in the Illinois Volunteer Militia). During the years 1857–1858, Mary Ballard was a student at the Western Female Seminary, Oxford, Ohio.

637 BERTELLE M. LYTTLE. Papers, 1915–1959. 1 volume. Gift of Miss Bertelle M. Lyttle, 1950, 1959. MS 3061.

Bulletins, reports, correspondence, and newspaper clippings relating to the activities of the Cleveland Cinema Club and of the national "better films" movement in general. Also included are radio scripts for a series of programs on "Movies, Art, and Problems" directed by Miss Lyttle and broadcast over Cleveland stations WHK and WCLE, 1936–1938.

638 HURON AND LORAIN BAPTIST ASSOCIATIONS. OHIO. Records, 1938–1947. 1 folder. MS 3064.

Programs and typescript minutes of the joint annual meetings of these associations, and a copy of "The Huron Baptist Association Annual," 1946.

639 ST. JOHN'S EPISCOPAL CHURCH. CLEVELAND, O. Records, 1835–1871. ½ box (photostatic copies). Gift of Laurence H. Norton, 1952. MS 3066.

Articles of association (1836) and lists of communicants, burials, baptisms, and marriages.

640 EUCLID AVENUE NATIONAL BANK. CLEVELAND, O. Record, ca. 1886. 1 volume. Gift of E. G. Tillotson, 1945. MS 3068.

Original subscription list to stock in this bank which was incorporated in 1886. Among its first officers were John L. Woods, Charles F. Brush, and Solon L. Severance. After several mergers, this bank developed into the First National Bank of Cleveland.

641 DANIEL EDGAR MORGAN (1877–1949). Papers, 1929–1949. 35 boxes, 15 volumes.* Gift of Mrs. Arnaud Leavelle, 1955. MS 3069.

Correspondence, speeches, court opinions and other legal documents, newspaper clippings, pamphlets and other printed materials, official and unofficial reports and memoranda on civic, municipal, and national affairs which relate to Morgan's activities as an Ohio state senator (1929–1930), Cleveland's city manager (1930–1932), and judge of the Cuyahoga County Court of Appeals (1939–1949). In addition to these, the papers also touch upon Morgan's unsuccessful primary campaign for governor of

Ohio in 1934; Harold H. Burton's successful campaigns for mayor of Cleveland in 1935 and 1937; Morgan's wartime activities as a member of the National War Labor Board (Cleveland) in 1943 and 1944, and as chairman of the Cleveland Post-War Planning Council from 1943 to 1945; and, in general, to Republican Party politics in Cleveland and Ohio between 1929 and 1949. References are also made to the following persons: William E. Borah, John W. Bricker, Arthur H. Day, Sarah Bush Lincoln, Robert A. Taft, and Wendell Willkie; and to the following organizations: Citizens League of Cleveland, City Club of Cleveland, Cleveland Chamber of Commerce, Jackson Iron & Steel Company, National Conference on Christians and Jews, War Production Board, and the Welfare Federation of Cleveland.

Unpublished 6-page register available in the Society.
NUCMC 62-4391.

* This entry does not include a description of the unprocessed contents of 15 of these boxes which were discovered after the initial register was prepared.

642   WILLIAM SULLIVAN. Papers, 1851–1869, 1890–1891.
4 folders. Gift of Mrs. H. W. Sullivan, 1950. MS 3073.
Correspondence, circular letters, reports, and other papers relating to the activities of the Irish Emigrant Aid Society of Ohio and to the Fenian Brotherhood, for which Sullivan was centre of the Tiffin (Ohio) circle. Included are an 11-page biographical sketch of Thomas Davis (1814–1845) prepared in 1851; a subscription list "for Irish purposes," Tiffin, 1859; minutes of meetings of the Central Council, reports of the Central Corresponding Secretary, and official monthly reports and circulars of the Fenian Brotherhood, 1865; and letters and other papers of Dr. E. W. Sullivan concerning various Irish groups, including the Irish Parliamentary Party and the Irish-American Club Company of Cleveland, 1890–1891. Correspondents include Michael Cavenagh, James W. Fitzgerald, H. O'C. MacCarthy, Edward O'Flaherty, John O'Mahony, and William R. Roberts.

643   GLEASON F. LEWIS. Record Books, ca. 1853–1867.
          5 volumes. Gift of the Case Western Reserve University
          Library; purchased, 1892. MS 3074.
Record of work done in securing pensions and land grants for veterans of all United States wars prior to the Civil War by Gleason F. Lewis of Cleveland, Ohio. One volume consists of a general alphabetical index of all the volunteers who served in the Ohio Militia during the War of 1812.

644   MARY L. MATTHEWS. Papers, 1897–1950. 2 boxes.
          Gift of Roger Green, 1952. MS 3075.
Personal and general correspondence, 1938–1950, and genealogical data collected by Miss Matthews and others before her on the Matthews family of New York State and of allied families. Miss Matthews resided in Lancaster, Wisconsin, and Oberlin, Ohio.

645   WILLIAM GRINNELL FAMILY. Papers, 1860–1952.
          1 box. Gift of William P. Grinnell, 1952. MS 3076.
Letters, diaries, photographs, and other papers of members of this family from Ravenna, Ohio. Primarily relating to the Civil War, they include the service records and diary (1863) of Captain William Grinnell, 104th Regiment, Ohio Volunteer Infantry, 1863–1898; two volumes of records of ordnance and ordnance stores kept by Captain David D. Bard, 104th Regiment, Ohio Volunteer Infantry, 1862–1864; and two pocket diaries of John Hamilton Furry, also of the 104th, 1863–1864.

646   GEORGE SPENCER FRARY. Diary, 1864. 1 volume.
          Gift of Ihna T. Frary, 1950. MS 3079.
Frary served in the 171st Ohio National Guard and for a while was stationed at Johnson's Island in Lake Erie during the Civil War.

647 PROCTOR THAYER. Papers, 1841–1847, 1890. 10 items. Gift of Ihna T. Frary, 1950. MS 3080.

Letters addressed to Proctor Thayer, a student at Western Reserve College, from his brother Lyman G. Thayer, who was studying law in North Adams, Massachusetts, 1841–1847. Also included are five letters addressed to Joseph Masury of Beverly, Massachusetts, from a missionary couple named Batchelder, 1840–1844.

648 WILSON TRANSIT COMPANY. CLEVELAND, O. Records, 1881–1890. 3 volumes. Gift of Captain Joseph S. Wood, 1944. MS 3082.

Record books of three ships (*Charlemagne Tower, Jr.*, *Wadena*, and *Wallula*) from the freight-transportation fleet of this company, which was founded in 1872.

649 LADIES' LITERARY CIRCLE. BLOOMINGTON, O. Records, 1849–1850. 1 volume. Gift of Mrs. Gertrude F. Dautel, 1946. MS 3083.

Constitution, bylaws, lists of members, and minutes of meetings of this society which sought to cultivate the "pure morals" and improve the minds of its members.

650 CHARLES H. MERRICK. Papers, 1861–1866. 4 volumes. Gift of Dr. Eliza J. Merrick, 1947. MS 3088.

Letters (mounted in three scrapbooks) written by C. H. Merrick of North Eaton, Ohio, while serving first as principal musician and then as hospital steward in Company H, 8th Regiment, Ohio Volunteer Infantry, 1861–1864; and a pocket diary for 1862. The letters, addressed to his wife, present a detailed account of Merrick's activities and those of his regiment, which saw much military action in Virginia. One of the volumes contains medical notes, financial accounts, and lists of office furniture, medicines, and books of Dr. Charles H. Merrick, 1864–1866.

Also included is some personal correspondence (1 folder) of

R. L. Merrick, of Cleveland, 1885–1901; and obituary notices for Dr. Myra K. Merrick (1824–1899).

651 CLEVELAND COUNCIL OF SOCIOLOGY. CLEVELAND, O. Records, 1893–1914. 1 box. Gift of George Bellamy, 1947. MS 3090.

Correspondence, annual reports of the secretary and treasurer, lists of lecture topics, speakers, and members, and other records of this council which was organized in 1893 at the suggestion of Professors Richard T. Ely and John R. Commons and which was patterned after the Chautauqua Literary and Scientific Circles. During its existence the council was composed of many of Cleveland's leading public officials and civic leaders, including Newton D. Baker, George A. Bellamy, Starr Cadwallader, Harris R. Cooley, Rabbi Moses J. Gries, Charles S. Howe, Tom L. Johnson, M. A. Marks, G. K. Shurtleff, D. C. Westenhaven, and Peter Witt.

652 PETER TURNER. Papers, 1823–1873. 1 folder, 3 volumes. Gift of Willis Thornton, 1951. MS 3092.

Logbook kept by Midshipman Peter Turner on board the U.S.S. *Nonsuch*, commanded by his uncle, Daniel Turner, during an expedition under Colonel Oliver H. Perry, which sought to end piracy on the waters near Venezuela, May 20, 1823–September 7, 1824; logbook kept by Turner on board the U.S.S. *Cyane* off the coast of Brazil, December 27, 1825–June 4, 1827; letter book of Lieutenant Peter Turner, 1850–1861, 1870–1872, during which time he commanded various navy vessels; and correspondence regarding naval matters, 1861–1873.

653 NATIONAL SOCIETY OF THE COLONIAL DAMES OF AMERICA IN THE STATE OF OHIO. CLEVELAND, O. Records, ca. 1891–1952. 2 boxes. Deposited by Mrs. David N. Burruss, Jr., 1954. MS 3094.

Minutes of meetings of the Cleveland Circle, 1910–1923, and some correspondence, but mostly printed material relating to the national organization, including directories, yearbooks, pamphlets, copies of *The Messenger,* and reports of meetings.

654   PETER NEFF (1827–1903). Papers, 1884–1888. 3 folders. MS 3096.

Legal briefs, arguments, testimonies, and affidavits relating to the case of Sarah Neff et al. v. the Theologial Seminary of the Protestant Episcopal Church of Ohio at Gambier held in the Court of Common Pleas, Knox County, Ohio, and concerning the ringing of church bells. Neff, clergyman and inventor, served as librarian of the Western Reserve Historical Society from 1888 until his death in Cleveland in 1903.

655   WILLIAM GREY ROSE (1829–1899). Papers, 1852–1916. 1 folder. Gift of Hudson Hyatt, 1953. MS 3099.

Letters received by Rose, 1852–1878; copies of speeches, newspaper clippings, and data on the genealogy of the Rose family. A newspaper publisher and legislator in Pennsylvania, Rose came to Cleveland in 1865, served as mayor (1877–1879 and 1891–1893), and was Republican candidate for Lieutenant Governor of Ohio in 1883.

656   MARY LUKENS GILBERT. Papers, 1824–1843. 17 items. Gift of Harriet E. Leitch, 1951. MS 3101.

Personal and general correspondence of Mary L. Gilbert, an abolitionist and teacher in a Negro school, who resided in Wilmington, and later, Smithfield, Ohio. Her primary correspondent, Barclay Gilbert, her brother, lived in La Porte, Indiana. Also included are the proceedings of a meeting of anti-slavery advocates held in Boston, January 9, 1843, which concerned the *Liberator.*

657   PORTO RICO. Government Records, 1900–1901. 2 volumes (typescript copies). Gift of William H. Hunt. MS 3102.

Journal of the Executive Council of Porto Rico for the first Legislative Assembly, December 3, 1900–January 31, 1901; and journal of the House of Delegates for the first session, December 3, 1900–January 31, 1901, as certified by William H. Hunt, Secretary of Porto Rico.

658   MRS. T. ELLIS MINSHALL, *collector*. Russian Documents, 1724, 1793, undated. 4 items. Gift of Mrs. T. Ellis Minshall, 1948. MS 3104.

Document signed by Catherine II, Empress of Russia, December 31, 1793; document signed by Peter the Great, Emperor of Russia, December 28, 1724; illuminated document signed with the seal of Alexander II; and a writing album of Alexander II.

659   JAMES WILLIAM SELLERS. Letters, 1863–1867. 19 items. Gift of Mrs. Ellen Sellers Fletcher, 1954. MS 3108.

General and personal letters written by Sellers of the 49th Regiment, New York State Volunteers, to his parents while he was at Camp Pratt, Virginia, and the U.S. General Hospital, York, Pennsylvania.

660   INDEPENDENCE AND PARMA PLANK ROAD COMPANY, PARMA, O. Records, 1878–1908. 1 volume. Gift of Edward T. Buhl, 1954. MS 3109.

Minutes of meetings, copies of bonds and notices, and lists of stockholders.

661   *CHARLES CARROLL*. Logbook, 1835–1837. 1 volume. Gift of Allen J. Robinson, 1954. MS 3110.

Logbook of the ship *Charles Carroll* of Dorchester while on a whaling voyage in the South Pacific Ocean.

662   TAYLOR HAMPTON, *collector*. Material on the Nickel Plate Road, 1869–1960. 7 boxes (mostly photostatic copies). Gift of Taylor Hampton, 1966. MS 3114.

Manuscript notes and copies or originals of magazine and newspaper articles, pamphlets, blueprints and maps, annual reports and financial statements, stock certificates, timetables, photographs and charts, and some letters used by Taylor Hampton in the preparation of *The Nickel Plate Road: The History of a Great Railroad* (Cleveland: The World Publishing Company, 1947). Referred to in the collection are the New York, Chicago, and St. Louis Railroad; the Toledo, St. Louis and Western Railroad; the Chesapeake & Ohio Railway Company; the Erie and Western Railroad; the Van Sweringen Railway System; and the Cleveland Union Terminal Company.

Unpublished 8-page register available in the Society.

663 JONATHAN HALE FAMILY. Papers, 1810–1940. 10 boxes, 2 volumes. Gift of the Estate of Clara Belle Ritchie, 1957; purchased, 1960. MS 3115.

Letters, diaries, account books, biographical sketches, and recollections, newspaper clippings, household and estate papers, photographs, and daguerreotypes relating to Jonathan Hale and his family, who resided in Bath Township, Summit County, Ohio. Referred to in these papers are Jonathan Hale (1772–1854), who emigrated from Glastonbury, Connecticut, in 1810 and built the family homestead,* 1826–1827; Jonathan's son, Andrew Hale (1811–1884), and grandson, Charles Oviatt Hale (1850–1938), each of whom in turn maintained the homestead. These papers deal almost exclusively with Jonathan Hale's migration from Connecticut, the settlement and development of the farm in the Cuyahoga Valley, and the life led on the homestead during the 19th and early 20th centuries. Included here is the diary kept by Jonathan Hale on his first journey from Connecticut to Ohio in 1810.

Unpublished 5-page register available in the Society.
NUCMC 62-4392

* The Jonathan Hale Homestead has been operated as a museum by the Western Reserve Historical Society since 1958.

664   CHARLOTTE U. CLEVELAND (b. 1820). Papers, 1840–1851, 1896, 1914. Gift of Elizabeth G. Woodward. MS 3116.

General and personal letters from relatives addressed to Charlotte U. Cleveland, niece of Moses Cleaveland, who resided in Paw Paw Grove, Illinois, 1840–1851; and other assorted papers, including a tablet of genealogical data on the Cleveland family.

665   SIMON PERKINS (1771–1844). Papers, 1801–1919 (1805–1855). 103 boxes, 5 volumes, 5 packages. MS 3122.

Correspondence, land deeds and agreements, surveys, financial accounts and receipts, ledgers, daybooks, and other papers relating to the career of Simon Perkins, who played a major role in the early growth and development of the Western Reserve while acting in the capacity of surveyor, land agent, postmaster, soldier, and banker. Specifically included are materials dating from the periods during which Perkins was surveyor and land agent for the Erie Land Company, 1797–1830; postmaster of Warren, Ohio, 1801–1829; general in the 4th Division, Ohio Militia, during the War of 1812; co-founder and president of the Western Reserve Bank, 1813–1838; and member of the Board of Canal Fund Commissioners, 1826–1838. A large segment of this collection consists of deeds, powers of attorney, promissory notes, and field books relating to land transactions in counties throughout the Western Reserve of which Perkins was a party. Persons with whom he was associated in these matters include Eli Baldwin, Charles W. Brown, Daniel L. Coit, Ralph Cowles, Joshua Henshaw, Martin Kellogg, John Kinsman, Daniel Lathrop, Caleb Palmer, George E. White, and Alfred Wolcott.

Also included are account books and other business papers of relatives of Simon Perkins, many of whom also played important roles in the economic life of the Western Reserve, including Joseph, Jacob, Jacob Bishop, and Henry Bishop Perkins, 1840–1872.

Over one-half of this collection consists of letters addressed to Simon Perkins and date from the time of his arrival in the Western Reserve until his death. Although they deal with a variety of topics, emphasis is on land transactions.

Unpublished 9-page register available in the Society.

666   FRANZ SIGEL (1824–1902). Papers, 1861–1902. 13 boxes, 4 volumes. Gift of William Pendleton Palmer, 1922. MS 3123.

Papers dealing primarily with Sigel's activities as brigadier general and major general in the Union Army, 1861–1864, including letters, telegrams, dispatches, orders, reports, maps, newspaper clippings, and Sigel's notes, memoranda, and writings, and an autobiographical account. In either German or English, specifically included are military papers concerning Sigel's recruiting of German volunteers and his command of the Mountain Department of West Virginia and the Department of the Susquehanna, Harrisburg, Pennsylvania, 1861–1864; letters, statistics, research notes, and writings on the Battle of Cedar Mountain, the Manassas campaign (including the battles of Groveton, Second Bull Run, and Chantilly), the Shenandoah campaign, and the Battle of New Market; orders or dispatches from, or notes relating to, Generals Nathaniel P. Banks, Ambrose E. Burnside, John C. Fremont, Ulysses S. Grant, Samuel P. Heintzelman, Philip Kearney, B. F. Kelley, George B. McClellan, Irvin McDowell, John Pope, Fitz-John Porter, and Earl Van Dorn; recollection of President and Mrs. Abraham Lincoln; and scrapbooks containing clippings from German and English newspapers concerning Sigel's various commands, his relations with his superiors, and politics.

Unpublished 6-page register available in the Society.
NUCMC 62-4178

667   ALFRED MEWETT (1895–1955). Papers, 1736–1955. 19 boxes (some photostats and transcripts).* Gift of the Estate of Alfred Mewett, 1955. MS 3124.

Papers of, or collected by, Alfred Mewett, registrar of the Cleveland School of Art (1925–1943) and dean of the John Huntington

Polytechnic Institute of Cleveland (1930–1953), relating primarily to the 19th-century history of Mayfield Township (especially Gates Mills), Ohio, and of its environs (especially Chagrin Falls, Chardon, and South Euclid). Types of materials include correspondence, ledgers, daybooks, diaries, account books, census reports, cemetery-inscription lists, court-docket books, land agreements and deeds, genealogical and biographical data, interviews, reminiscences, newspaper clippings, maps, photographs, and an extensive amount of articles and other writings of Mewett. Specifically, Mewett accumulated letters, diaries, and other family papers of early residents of Mayfield and surrounding cities and towns; a physician's daybook, 1834–1839; records of St. John's Episcopal Church of Cleveland, 1835–1929, and of the Presbyterian Church of Mayfield, 1839–1860; records of several cultural groups, including the Mayfield Lyceum, 1845; school district records, 1847–1893; several diaries of men from this area who served in the Civil War, 1862–1865; letters of Jared Potter Kirtland, 1866–1873; and records of several business enterprises of the early 20th century, including the Gates Mills Milling Company and the Maple Leaf Land Company. Several folders of correspondence and receipts relate to Mewett's activities as registrar for the Cleveland School of Art, 1920's and 1930's. Families represented here include the following: Allen, Gates, Greenwalt, Lockemer, Rudd, Sharpe, Sorter, and Talbot.

Unpublished 11-page register available in the Society.
NUCMC 62-4390

* This entry does not include a description of the unprocessed contents of four of these boxes, which were discovered after the initial register was prepared.

668 AARON HUBBARD. Papers, 1791–1869. 1 box. Gift of Mrs. Calvin A. Dennison. MS 3125.

Personal and general correspondence, land agreements and deeds, receipts, surveys, and other family papers of Aaron Hubbard of Schoharie County, New York, and Cleveland, Ohio. Included are two volumes of records of court cases of Aaron Hubbard, justice of the peace, Schoharie County, and ledger and subscription list of the Cleveland-Twinsburg Plank Road, 1849–1862.

669   EDWARD A. WEBB. Papers, 1861–1865, 1891. 1 box. MS 3126.

Civil War papers of Lieutenant E. A. Webb, 27th Regiment, Ohio Volunteer Infantry, including letters written to his sister, Libbie Webb of Pecatonia, Illinois; muster rolls, supply lists and returns, and quartermaster reports; and certificates of appointment and pension papers.

670   JAMES HUMPHREY HOYT (1852–1917). Correspondence, 1894–1896. 1 box. Gift of Mrs. Elton Hoyt, 1956. MS 3127.

Primarily the political correspondence of Hoyt, Cleveland attorney and Ohio Republican politician, with several U.S. Senators and Representatives, Ohio Governors, and officers of various county Republican organizations. Correspondents include Theodore E. Burton, Asa S. Bushnell, Charles L. Kurtz, William McKinley, John Sherman, and Caleb B. Wick.

671   GUSTAVUS A. HYDE (1826–1912). Papers, 1843–1912. ½ box, 1 oversize package. Gift of G. A. Hyde, 1948. MS 3128.

Meteorological data recorded by Hyde while residing in Framingham, Massachusetts, and in Norwalk and Cleveland, Ohio. Also included are newspaper clippings regarding weather in Cleveland collected by Hyde, an engineer for the Cleveland Gaslight and Coke Company and volunteer for the United States Weather Bureau.

672   JAMES HOTCHKISS ROGERS (1857–1940). Music, 1900–1920. 2 folders. Gift of Mrs. James H. Rogers. MS 3131.

Music (mostly printed) written by James H. Rogers, music editor of the *Cleveland News* and the Cleveland *Plain Dealer* (1913–1932), who composed over 130 songs and over 350 works in all.

673 GEORGE MAGOFFIN HUMPHREY (1890–1970).
Papers, 1912–1963 (1953–1957). 25 boxes, 7 volumes.
Gift of George M. Humphrey, 1962. MS 3132.

Correspondence, typescript and printed speeches, official documents and reports, newspaper clippings, appointment records, photographs, and other materials relating primarily to George M. Humphrey's activities while serving as Secretary of the Treasury (1953–1957) during the administrations of President Dwight D. Eisenhower. This collection consists of Humphrey's personal and public papers as opposed to the official papers of the Treasury Department. Comprising manuscript, typescript, and printed materials, it presents a complete record of Humphrey's public life as Secretary of the Treasury.* The major series are of congratulatory messages sent to Humphrey at the time of his joining President Eisenhower's cabinet, 1952–1953; correspondence and other materials relating to his numerous official and political trips and speeches, 1953–1957; correspondence, programs, photographs, and other items relating to awards, academic degrees, and other honors bestowed on Humphrey, 1947–1963; mounted and unmounted newspaper clippings and magazine articles by or about Humphrey, 1949–1961; and printed reference materials including various congressional hearings containing testimony by Humphrey, and annual reports of the U.S. Treasury, 1953–1957. Also included is a lesser amount of correspondence relating to Republican Party affairs, 1953–1957; and to the Republican National Convention of 1956.

Unpublished 20-page register available in the Society.

* Selections from this collection were published in *The Basic Papers of George M. Humphrey as Secretary of the Treasury, 1953–1957*, ed. Nathaniel R. Howard, W.R.H.S. Publication No. 119 (Cleveland: The Western Reserve Historical Society, 1965).

674   GEORGE MAGOFFIN HUMPHREY (1890–1970).
Papers, 1922, 1929, 1948, 1950–1970. 5 boxes, 1 oversize package. Gift of Mrs. George M. Humphrey, 1970. MS 3132a.

Additional correspondence, newspaper clippings, publications, photographs, and other papers relating to the business and political career of George M. Humphrey. This material consists primarily of more than 1,700 pieces of correspondence between Mr. Humphrey and numerous national and foreign statesmen and businessmen with whom he had been associated, 1950–1969. Most of these date from the period Mr. Humphrey served as Secretary of the Treasury (1953–1957). The 74 letters from Dwight D. Eisenhower reflect the close relationship which continued to exist between the two men after both had left public office. Other notable correspondents include Bernard Baruch, Ezra T. Benson, Richard E. Byrd, John Foster Dulles, Oveta Culp Hobby, Herbert Hoover, John L. Lewis, Henry Cabot Lodge, and Richard M. Nixon.

Of a more routine nature is the following correspondence: letters congratulating Mr. Humphrey on becoming a partner, 1922, and then president of M. A. Hanna & Company, 1929; congratulatory messages addressed to Mr. and Mrs. Humphrey, 1952–1953; letters concerning the publication of *The Basic Papers of George M. Humphrey as Secretary of the Treasury, 1953–1957*, ed. Nathaniel R. Howard (Cleveland: The Western Reserve Historical Society, 1965), 1965; and letters of sympathy addressed to Mrs. Humphrey following the death of her husband, 1970. Noteworthy are two folders of correspondence, minutes of meetings, memoranda, and reports concerning the Economic Cooperation Administration's Industrial Advisory Committee, of which Mr. Humphrey served as chairman, 1948–1949. This committee was concerned with German reparations and the postwar development of Germany's steel industry. Also included is a 6-page autobiographical account prepared by Mr. Humphrey in 1963, and a copy of a 22-page oral-history interview with Mr. Humphrey, 1969.

675 WAR OF 1812. Collection of Papers, 1810–1820. 1 box. Accumulated from several sources by the Society, late 19th c. MS 3133.

Correspondence relating to various military and political aspects of the War of 1812, and records of the 4th Division, Ohio Militia, commanded by Major General Elijah Wadsworth, including payroll lists, petitions, court-martial proceedings, surgeon's inventories, and quartermaster reports. Correspondents include Ensign Church, David Clendenin, W. W. Colgreave, Peter Hitchcock, Return J. Meigs, and Simon Perkins.

676 CLEVELAND IRON MINING COMPANY. CLEVELAND. O. Correspondence, 1860–1864, 1883–1886. 1½ boxes. Gift of S. Livingston Mather, 1958. MS 3136.

Correspondence between various officers of this company, including Samuel L. Mather, with mine superintendents in Marquette (1860–1864) and Ishpeming (1883–1886), Michigan, relating to mining operations in the Lake Superior region.

677 LAURA E. CLEMENS. Genealogical data, 1900–1934. 2 boxes. Gift of Mrs. Raymond C. Smith, 1958. MS 3137.

Notes, memoranda, charts, and some letters relating to the descendants of Thomas Adgate (d. 1707) of Norwich, England, and Saybrook, Connecticut.

678 DUDLEY J. HARD (b. 1872). Papers, 1864–1939. 8 boxes, 1 package. Gift of Lyle Thoburn, 1958. MS 3138.

Papers relating primarily to the military activities of Colonel Dudley J. Hard, 107th Regiment, Cavalry, Ohio National Guard, 1894–1910, and later, 135th Field Artillery, 37th Division, A.E.F., 1918–1919. Included are accounts of the actions of the 8th Regiment, Infantry, Ohio National Guard, during the Spanish-American War and during the punitive expedition into Mexico, 1916–1917; a file of orders, bulletins, memoranda, letters, rosters, payrolls, and maps issued from the 62nd Field Artillery command to the 135th Field Artillery, 1917–1919; Colonel Hard's diary kept while in France during the autumn of 1918; photographs, souvenir volumes and programs, and pamphlets concerning various Cleveland military units and officers; and commissions and other certificates of Curtis V. Hard (1845–1917), commander of the 8th Regiment, Infantry, Ohio National Guard, and father of Major General Dudley J. Hard.

679   ALEXANDER VARIAN, JR. (d. 1864). Letters, 1861–1864. 1 volume (copies of original letters, made by Elizabeth Varian, 1861–1864). Gift of Mrs. Frank B. Steele, 1960. MS 3141.

Alexander Varian served in the 1st Regiment, Ohio Volunteer Infantry, from September, 1861, until he was wounded and died on June 2, 1864, in Resaca, Georgia. Varian comments on various battles in which he saw action in Kentucky, Tennessee, and Georgia, as well as on personal and family matters.

680   JUSTUS L. COZAD (1833–1910). Autobiographical Account, 1902–1904.* 1 volume. Gift of Gertrude Cozad, 1941. MS 3142.

The "Life and Times of Justus L. Cozad" was written by a native Clevelander who had been engaged in surveying, railroading, and the land-title business. In the 1850's Cozad worked in Kansas, Missouri, and Nebraska. His autobiography for this period contains comments on Indians and their reservations, descriptions of various towns, and details concerning travel in both pro- and anti-slavery territories. In the 1860's and 1870's he was associated with the Indianapolis, Pittsburgh and Cleveland Railroad, the Indianapolis and St. Louis Railroad, and the Bellefontaine Railway. After 1871 he was partner with Jay Odell in a land-title company in Cleveland.

Unpublished 5-page register available in the Society.

* Published in part in Gertrude Cozad, comp., *The Life and Times of Justus Lafayette Cozad* (Claremont, California, 1941).

681   EVELINE BOSWORTH COOK. "Recollections," 1905–1906. 50 typescript pages. MS 3143.

"Recollections of Eveline Bosworth Cook relating to the Hale-Hammond Pioneers of Bath, Ohio, and their associates—their privations, characters, homes, home lives, peculiarities and especially their religious habits and the Old Center Church."

682   IHNA THAYER FRARY (1873–1965). Papers, 1933–1936. 1 box. Gift of I. T. Frary, 1943, 1962. MS 3144.

Correspondence and bulletins concerning the Federal Art Project and the Historic American Buildings Survey in which Mr. Frary participated. Also included are two of Frary's manuscripts, one on Cleveland's Doans Corners * area on the east side, where Frary was raised, and one on owning and driving an automobile during World War I.

* See also Charles Asa Post, *Doans Corners and the City Four Miles West* (Cleveland: The Caxton Company, 1930).

683   SAMUEL J. RITCHIE (1838–1908). Papers, 1870–1920. 40 boxes, 11 volumes. Gift of Clara Belle Ritchie, 1956. MS 3145.

Correspondence, memoranda, legal documents, account books, biographical data, photographs, receipts, and other papers of Samuel J. Ritchie, who was active in the lumber, railroad, and iron industries. During the last two decades of the 20th century, Ritchie served as president of the Central Ontario Railroad, Canadian Copper Company, and Anglo-American Iron Company of Cleveland, all of which merged in 1902 and formed the International Nickel Company. Ritchie discovered copper and nickel mines in Sudbury, Ontario, and owned large coal properties in West Virginia. The bulk of this collection consists of Ritchie's business correspondence, 1870–1910. Also included are papers relating to Ritchie's trip to England and the Continent promoting the use of nickel, 1889; and papers relating to the construction of Ritchie's house in Akron, Ohio, 1904–1905. Notable correspondents include Stevenson Burke, Benjamin Butterworth, Elbert H. Gary, Thomas W. Cornell, Myron T. Herrick, Sir John Alexander McDonald, Henry P. McIntosh, William McKinley, James McLaren, George W. McMullen, Ambrose Monell, Sir Oliver Mowatt, Henry B. Payne, Charles M. Schwab, Benjamin F. Tracy, and Sir Charles Tupper.

Unpublished 6-page register available in the Society.
NUCMC 62-4337

684 JAMES FREDERICK JACKSON (d. 1927). Papers, 1904–1923. 1 box. MS 3146.

Copies of speeches delivered between 1904 and 1923 by Jackson, superintendent of the Cleveland Associated Charities, on various aspects of charity, social work, philanthropy, family life, and social welfare.

685 PHILOMATHIAN SOCIETY. ORANGE, O. Records, 1849–1852. 1 volume. MS 3147.

Constitution, bylaws, and minutes of meetings of this debating society, of which James A. Garfield was an officer.

686 FAYETTE BROWN (1823–1910). Papers, 1841–1891. 4 boxes. MS 3150.

Primarily general and personal correspondence between Mrs. Cornelia Curtiss Brown and her husband, Fayette Brown, Cleveland industrialist, designer, and manufacturer of hoisting machinery, and other members of their family. Also included are letters received by Cornelia Curtiss while residing in Allegheny City, Pennsylvania, and copies of several poems composed by Miss Curtiss.

687 FERDINAND V. HAYDEN. Papers, 1846–1865. 1 box. MS 3154.

Letters received by Hayden, a teacher in Oberlin, Ohio, and many deposit slips with various private banks.

688 HENRY B. BOYNTON (b. 1829). Papers, 1854–1887. ½ box. Gifts of William Rathbun, 1960; Mrs. Howard K. Preston, 1968. MS 3160.

Including a journal of William A. Boynton, student at the Hiram Eclectic Institute and traveling bookseller, 1854–1856, and continued by his brother, Henry B. Boynton, a farmer in Orange, Ohio, 1858–1864. James A. Garfield, cousin to these brothers, is frequently mentioned in this journal, as are other of his friends and relatives. Also included are several letters from Garfield to Henry B. Boynton, 1856–1880; and newspaper clippings concerning Garfield.

689 BRECKSVILLE CONGREGATIONAL CHURCH. BRECKSVILLE, O. Records, 1816–1947. 8 volumes. Deposited by the Brecksville Congregational Church, 1961. MS 3168.

Confession of faith, covenant, minutes of church committee and trustee meetings, and registers of members of this church and of its predecessors, the Church of Christ (organized in 1816) and the First Congregational Society of Brecksville.

690 JOHN EVELYN DENISON (1800–1873). Diaries, 1824–1825. 6 volumes (268-page typescript copy, prepared in 1927). MS 3172.

Copies of diaries and of several letters (written to his mother) of John E. Denison of Ossington Hall, Nottinghamshire, England, a member of the House of Commons from 1823 until 1872, when he was created Viscount Ossington. These items were written while Denison was on a tour of Canada and the United States in the company of Edward (Smith-Stanley), 13th Earl of Derby; James Archibald Stuart-Wortley-Mackenzie, Lord Wharncliffe; and Mr. Peter Caesar Labouchere. Visiting throughout the eastern United States, Denison comments on terrain, political habits, labor (slaves), and local customs.

691   JOEL BLAKESLEE (1787–1863). Papers, ca. 1820–1860. 1½ boxes. MS 3173.

Personal and general correspondence and copies of speeches delivered by Blakeslee, who resided in Colebrook and New Lyme, Ashtabula County, Ohio. Blakeslee, who was connected with the Ashtabula Historical Society in the 1850's, collected information and spoke on topics such as the early history of Ashtabula County, United States independence, and slavery. One paper on the history of Madison, Lake County, Ohio, refers to early settlers, such as Electra Tappan, Asa Turney, Abraham Tappan, and Cyrus Cunningham. Also included is an account book, 1820–1827, and papers of Samuel Hendry, clerk in the Ashtabula Court of Common Pleas, ca. 1826–1860. The latter include bail bonds, Jefferson Township tax records (1858), case depositions, and correspondence concerning business or legal matters. Correspondents include Quintus F. Atkins, Rev. Joseph Badger, Joshua R. Giddings, Rice Harper, P. R. Spencer, David Tod, and Benjamin F. Wade.

692   MARGARET VAN HORN DWIGHT (1790–1834). Journal, Fall, 1810. 1 volume. MS 3174.

Original manuscript journal of a trip by wagon from New Haven, Connecticut, to Warren, Ohio, published as *A Journey to Ohio in 1810*, ed. Max Farrand (New Haven: Yale University Press, 1913).

693   JOHN SEWARD (b. 1784). Papers, 1803–1846. 8 items. MS 3176.

Diary kept while John Seward was a student and teacher in Granville, Ohio, 1803–1806; copy of a sermon he delivered; and several letters addressed to him and his wife in Aurora, Ohio.

694   RUFUS PERCIVAL RANNEY (1813–1891). Docket Book, 1836–1853. 1 volume. Gift of Mrs. R. C. Rudolph, 1960. MS 3180.

Docket book belonging to Ranney, an attorney at law in Warren, Ohio. Included are entries for cases contested in Portage, Trumbull, and Ashtabula counties; a synopsis of the law of real property taken principally from James Kent's *Commentaries on American Law* (1826–1830); and some financial records.

695   WILLIAM L. FOOTE. Papers, 1819–1856. 2 folders. MS 3181.

Land contracts and deeds and personal and general correspondence of William L. Foote of Ohio City (which was annexed to Cleveland in 1854). Most of Foote's correspondents were members of his family still residing in Connecticut.

696   ABIGAIL REID FAMILY. Correspondence, 1823–1844. 1 folder. Gift of Mrs. Florence R. Bush, 1960. MS 3182.

General and personal correspondence between members of this family, primarily from Jerousha Whipple of Nelson, New York, to his sister, Abigail Reid of Lorain County (mouth of the Black River), Ohio.

697   HENRY H. HOSFORD. Genealogical Papers, ca. 1930–1961. 2 folders. Gift of Mrs. C. A. Rogers, 1962. MS 3184.

Correspondence, notes, charts, and memoranda books concerning the genealogy of the Hosford family and of other related families, including Field, Knowlton, Marshall, Nutting, Plant, Rogers, and Woods.

698   GEORGE HURLBUT. Diary, 1862. 1 volume. MS 3185.

Kept during the year Hurlbut enlisted in the 14th Battery, Ohio Volunteer Light Artillery, and saw action during several engagements in Mississippi. This volume contains accounts of camp life as well as of Hurlbut's activities while on leave.

699 HENRY L. BURNHAM. Diary, June 5–September 7, 1862. 1 volume. Gift of Mrs. V. J. Torok, 1951. MS 3186.

Kept while Burnham, of Kinsman, Ohio, served in Company K, 84th Regiment, Ohio Volunteer Infantry, which was stationed at Camp Chase (Ohio) and in Cumberland, Maryland.

700 SYLVANUS C. BOYNTON (d. 1912). Papers, 1852–1916. 2 folders (some copies). MS 3188.

Originals and copies of letters, agreements, deeds, and other documents relating to the "Chiriqui Grants" (Panama) and the formation and activities of the Isthmus Pacific Railway Company of New York, of which Boynton was elected president in 1897. This company was organized in order to build and operate railroads within New Granada, Costa Rica, and the United States of Colombia. The papers after 1912 deal primarily with the settlement of Boynton's estate in Elyria, Ohio.

701 WILLIAM B. CASTLE. Account Book, 1853–1854. Gift of Laurence H. Norton. MS 3189.

Financial accounts of Castle during the time he served as mayor of Ohio City (which merged with Cleveland in 1854). Also included are some entries regarding appointments in the police department.

702 CONGREGATIONAL CHURCH. STREETSBORO, O. Records, 1833–1881. 2 volumes. MS 3190.

Articles and confession of faith, minutes of meetings, lists of members, and other records of this congregation which in 1874 became the First Presbyterian Church of Streetsboro.

703 JONES FAMILY. Papers, 1857–1878. 1 box. MS 3191.

Primarily letters received by Andrew B. and Charles M. Jones of North Washington, Hardin County, Ohio, from various relatives, and including some which touch upon the Civil War.

704 ASHLAND AND WAYNE COUNTIES, O. Deeds, 1833–1893. 1 folder. MS 3193.

Assorted deeds to land in Ashland County, 1853–1893, and in Wayne County, 1833–1841.

705 WILLIAM PENDLETON PALMER (1861–1927), *collector.* Civil War Miscellany, 1832–1910 (1860–1866). 7 boxes, 2 packages, 6 volumes. Gift of William P. Palmer, 1927. MS 3194.

Letters, telegrams, commissions and discharge papers, general and special orders, circulars, broadsides, maps, drawings, naval papers, and scrapbooks relating to both the Union and Confederate forces. Included are letters sent or received by Pierre G. T. Beauregard, Judah P. Benjamin, Ulysses S. Grant, Robert E. Lee, Abraham Lincoln, Henry H. Lockwood, John S. Mosby, Gideon J. Pillow, Gideon Welles, and other military and political leaders; papers relating to the Confederate medical services and hospitals, and to the armies and veterans' organizations of both the Union and the Confederacy; newspaper clippings (2 boxes) accumulated by Thomas C. Reynolds, Governor of Missouri, primarily from Missouri and Louisiana newspapers and dealing with politics and the Civil War, 1845–1886; scrapbook including several speeches of George C. Richardson, mayor of Cambridge, Massachusetts, 1856–1865; registers of three Confederate ships, 1861–1862; and various items relating to the 6th Ohio Volunteer Cavalry, the 127th New York Volunteers, the Department of the Trans-Mississippi, and the battles of Chickamauga and Missionary Ridge.

Unpublished 6-page register available in the Society.

706 CIVIL WAR. Miscellany, 1860–1875. 5 boxes. Collected from various sources by the Society, 1890–1930. MS 3195.

Letters, notes, memoranda, circulars, orders, broadsides, cartoons, maps, newspaper clippings, muster rolls, and patriotic cards relating to both the Union and Confederacy. Included are letters sent or received by Samuel Cooper, Jefferson Davis, Josiah Gorgas, Joseph E. Johnston, Robert E. Lee, Gideon Pillow, Leonidas Polk, and Carter L. Stevenson; papers relating to Union naval affairs, 1861–1865, to the Army of Mississippi, 1861–1862, and to the Army of Tennessee, 1863; records of both Union and Confederate quartermaster and medical departments, 1861–1865; records of the Gambier Council of the National Union League, College Township, Knox County, Ohio, 1862–1867; correspondence and other papers of Ohio state officials, 1862–1867; and correspondence received by Mary C. Brayton from the National Home for Disabled Volunteer Soldiers, Dayton, Ohio, 1873–1874.

Unpublished 6-page register available in the Society.

707 CHARLES WHITTLESEY (1808–1886). Papers, 1806–1889. 18 boxes, 1 oversize package. Combined from various sources for ease of access in 1962. MS 3196.

Papers relating to every aspect of the career of Charles Whittlesey, soldier, lawyer, geologist, historian, and co-founder of the Western Reserve Historical Society, who lived in Cleveland from 1832 until his death. Included are his personal, business, and military correspondence, 1806–1886; insurance, legal, and financial papers and account books, 1807–1885; diaries and memoranda books, 1857, 1867, 1870–1885; letters, memoranda, reports, invoices, orders, and other papers relating to Whittlesey's service as colonel of the 20th Regiment, Ohio Volunteer Infantry, during which time he saw action in the battles of Fort Donelson and Shiloh, 1861–1862; manuscript notes and writings and letters concerning a variety of historical and scientific subjects, including prehistoric Indians, Lieutenant Colonel John Bradstreet's expeditions, Chippewa Indians, and John Fitch (1743–1798); and notes and writings on moral and religious topics. A large segment of this collection relates to Whittlesey's activities as a geologist and includes field notes and memoranda books kept while investigating the geology and mineralogy of Ohio, Wisconsin, Michigan, and the Lake Superior and Upper Mississippi regions, 1838–1884; and papers concerning his activities as agent for the Humboldt and Eagle River mining companies, 1853–1859. Correspondents include Edward Adams, E. B. Andrews, Horatio Bigelow, and Clinton French.

Unpublished 11-page register available in the Society.

708   ALEXANDER B. McFARLAN. Papers, 1819–1866. 4 boxes. MS 3197.

Correspondence, legal papers, diaries, and notebooks relating to McFarlan's activities as superintendent of masonry and inspector of cement during the construction of the Chesapeake and Ohio Canal.

Unpublished 1-page register available in the Society.

709   JOSEPH REMENYI (1892–1956). Letters, 1922–1948. 1 folder. Gift of Mrs. Joseph Remenyi, 1962. MS 3198.

Letters from 27 well-known literary figures addressed to Joseph Remenyi, Hungarian-born author, educator, and newspaper editor who served as professor of comparative literature at Western Reserve University (1929–1956). Correspondents include James Branch Cabell, Willa S. Cather, Waldo Frank, Langston Hughes, Robert Nathan, Allan Tate, and Mark Van Doren.

710   WILLIAM McKINLEY (1843–1901). Papers, 1850–1912. 16 boxes, 1 package. Received from seven sources and combined for ease of access in 1962. MS 3201.

Letters, copies of speeches, financial papers, magazine and newspaper clippings, and photographs relating primarily to the life and activities of McKinley, U.S. Representative, Governor of Ohio, and U.S. President. A small number of papers relate to other members of his family. Specifically included are quartermaster papers of First Lieutenant William McKinley, Jr., 23rd Regiment, Ohio Volunteer Infantry, 1863–1864; financial papers concerning the Walker-McKinley Fund, 1893–1899; telegrams, newspaper clippings, and other material regarding the death and funeral of President McKinley, 1901; ten large bound volumes containing letters of condolence received by Mrs. McKinley; and several letters and a diary relating to the Civil War service of Andrew J. Duncan, McKinley's brother-in-law, who served in the 23rd Regiment, Ohio Volunteer Infantry, 1861–1864.

Unpublished 6-page register available in the Society.

711   AUGUSTUS AND RODERICK SKINNER. Papers, 1824–1872. 2 folders. MS 3202.

Financial receipts, land agreements and deeds, and letters concerning the business and legal activities of Roderick W. Skinner, attorney at law in Painesville, Ohio, 1824–1870; and financial receipts, land deeds, and letters concerning the business activities of Augustus Skinner, also of Painesville, 1826–1872.

712   GEORGE TOD (1773–1841). Papers, 1783–1834 (1800–1829).* 4 boxes. Gift of the heirs of George Tod, 1871. MS 3203.

General, military, and political correspondence,† notebooks, reports, petitions, accounts, judicial and legal papers, and financial papers relating to the varied career of George Tod, Ohio State Senator, State Supreme Court justice, and judge of the Third District Circuit Court of Appeals. All aspects of his life are touched upon in this collection, which includes notebooks on moral and theological questions kept at Yale, 1794–1795; three volumes of notes on lectures given at Litchfield Law School by Tapping Reeve, 1796–1797; papers concerning Tod's activities as tax appraiser, road supervisor, and State Senator from Trumbull County (Youngstown), Ohio, 1802–1812; minutes of the Ohio Supreme Court, summonses, and other legal papers, 1801–1809; correspondence, military reports, receipts, invoices, and returns concerning Tod's military participation as an officer in the army during the War of 1812; and dockets and proceedings of the Third District Circuit Court of Appeals, 1812–1829. Correspondents include Ethan A. Brown, Leonard Case, David Clendenin, Isaac Cowles, Gideon Granger, John Harmon, Homer Hine, Samuel Huntington, Turhand Kirtland, Calvin Pease, Elisha Whittlesey, and William Woodbridge.

Unpublished 5-page register available in the Society.

* A portion of this collection is on microfilm which is available in the Library. Selections from the microfilm have been published in Richard C. Knopf, *Document Transcriptions of the War of 1812 in the Northwest*, Vol. 10 (Columbus, Ohio: The Ohio Historical Society, 1962).

† Letters from this collection concerning the War of 1812 were printed in the W.R.H.S. *Tracts* Nos. 15 (1873), 17 (1873), 19 (1873), and 28 (1875).

713 OHIO MILITIA. 4TH DIVISION. Records, 1812–1815.* ½ box. MS 3203a.

Receipts, returns, accounts, contractors' certificates, and some letters relating to the military activities of this division primarily during the War of 1812 in and around Lower Sandusky. Also included is a record book of Ensign Church, a U.S. contractor, 1812. Most frequently referred to are David Clendenin, Peter Hitchcock, Simon Perkins, and Elijah Wadsworth.

* Some of this collection was at one time part of the George Tod Papers (item 712).

714 SAMUEL HOLDEN PARSONS (1735–1789). Papers, 1760–1830 (1770–1790). 1 box. MS 3204.

Personal and business correspondence,* and military and legal papers relating to the activities of General Parsons, a member of the Connecticut General Assembly, commander of the Connecticut Division of the Continental Army, and a director of the Ohio Company of Associates. Specifically referred to are matters such as the recruiting, supplying, organizing, and disciplining of troops, the handling of prisoners of war, and the interests of Parsons in lands in the Western Reserve area of Ohio. Also included are some papers concerning the personal and civil affairs of the Parsons family and an orderly book, 1778–1779. The Revolutionary War generals and officers who corresponded with Parsons include John Bigelow, Nathanael Greene, William Heath, Henry Knox, Alexander McDougall, Jonathan Trumbull, and George Washington.

Unpublished 5-page register available in the Society.

* Some correspondence has been published in Charles S. Hall, *Life and Letters of Samuel Holden Parsons* (Binghamton, New York: Otsenigo Publishing Company, 1905).

715   ALLEN TRIMBLE (1783–1870). Papers, 1793–1868.*
       4 boxes. MS 3205.

Personal and business correspondence, land deeds, surveys, financial papers, and other personal papers of Trimble, Ohio State Representative, Senator, and Governor, and of other members of his family, including William Allen Trimble (1786–1821), soldier and U.S. Senator, and William Henry Trimble (1811–?), Ohio State Representative and soldier. These papers relate to a wide range of political and military subjects, including the War of 1812; the activities and interests of the Whig, Democrat, Republican, and American (or Know-Nothing) parties; the construction of roads, the Ohio Canal, and other "internal improvements"; the tariff issue and the United States Bank; and slavery, the Missouri Compromise, and the annexation of Texas. Also included are papers pertaining to land development in the Virginia Military District and land transactions in Highland County, Ohio. Correspondents include Samuel C. Andrews, Caleb Atwater, Carter Beverley, A. Buford, John W. Campbell, George Clark, William Creighton, James Heaton, Homer Hine, Alfred Kelley, Joseph G. King, Isaac Meason, Ralph Osborn, William Russell, John L. Taylor, and several other Trimbles.

Unpublished 25-page register available in the Society.

* Part of this collection has been published in "Autobiography and Correspondence of Allen Trimble, Governor of Ohio; with Genealogy of the Family" (reprinted from the old Northwest Genealogical Society, Columbus, Ohio, 1909).

716 JONES, DAY, COCKLEY & REAVIS. CLEVELAND, O. Records, 1917–1959. 72 volumes. Gift of Jones, Day, Cockley & Reavis, 1967. MS 3206.

Records relating to various legal or financial transactions engaged in by different Cleveland businesses or industries for which the firm of Jones, Day, Cockley & Reavis, or one of its predecessors, served as legal counsel. After the activity (e.g., reorganization, refinancing, dissolution, etc.) the relevant documents were bound into these "legal bibles." They usually include letters, memoranda, deeds, indentures, contracts, and stock certificates. Included among the 44 companies represented by this firm are the Chesapeake and Ohio Railway Company, 1928–1930, 1936; Cleveland Terminals Building, 1931; Goodyear Tire and Rubber Company, 1921, 1927; Lake Erie Chemical Company, 1933; Otis Steel Company, 1936, 1937, 1942; Pere Marquette Railway Company, 1930–1932; Republic Steel Corporation, 1930, 1934–1936, 1941; Van Sweringen Company, 1928, 1930; and White Motor Company, 1934.

Unpublished 6-page register available in the Society.
RESTRICTED: Details available in the Society.

717 JOSEPH WILLIAM BRIGGS (1813/4–1872). Papers, 1852–1872, 1921. ½ box. MS 3207.

Correspondence, diaries, certificates, and newspaper clippings relating to Briggs' activities as developer of the free mail delivery system and as special agent to the U.S. Post Office Department, Cleveland, Ohio, 1863–1872. Specifically included are letters from Briggs to members of his family, 1852–1872; letters to Briggs concerning the postal service, mostly from C. Cochran, Jr., 1861–1872; and diaries kept while Briggs visited cities throughout the United States and directed the installation of city free delivery service.

718 FIRST CONGREGATIONAL CHURCH. CANFIELD, O. Records, 1809–1859. 1 folder. MS 3208.

Subscription lists, minutes of meetings, and several other documents concerning the activities of the members of this church, including their efforts to construct a meeting house (ca. 1809). Comfort S. Mygatt, Elijah Wadsworth, and Elisha Whittlesey were active in these affairs. Whittlesey having served as secretary.

719 FIRST CALVINISTIC CONGREGATIONAL SOCIETY. STREETSBORO, O. Records, 1836–1875. 1 folder. Gift of R. M. Sperry, 1959. MS 3209.

Constitution, subscription lists, minutes of meetings, and other documents relating to this society which was incorporated under Ohio law in 1837.

720 PRESBYTERIAN CHURCH. WOMAN'S HOME AND FOREIGN MISSIONARY SOCIETY. STREETSBORO, O. Records, 1896–1905. 1 volume. MS 3210.

Constitution (adopted 1896), minutes of meetings, a list of members, and financial accounts of this society whose members sought to aid the missionary program of the Presbyterian Church by prayer and contribution.

721 HARRIET M. MACDONALD. Letters, 1918–1920. 1 folder. MS 3211.

Letters written by Miss MacDonald while serving as a Red Cross nurse in France during World War I.

722 ALPHONSO HOLLY FAMILY. Papers, 1802–1956. 3 folders. MS 3216.

Deeds, contracts, and financial papers of Alphonso Holly of Cleveland and of other members of this family.

723 KATHLEEN B. SEAMAN TOZIER (1865–1968). Papers, 1899–1931. 1 box, 1 oversize package. Gift of Mrs. Charles B. Tozier, 1963. MS 3217.

Correspondence, charts, certificates, and memoranda tracing the lineage of Mrs. Tozier, a leader in Cleveland patriotic and civic endeavors. Also included is a 20-page copy of the roster of officers and enlisted men of the 1st and 2nd Battalions, 2nd Regiment, Ohio Militia, during the War of 1812, and a collection of lapel emblems and insignias of various patriotic and historical societies.

724   W. F. HARRADENCE. Diaries, 1889–1909. 18 volumes. MS 3219.

Daily diaries kept by Mr. Harradence, drama critic for the *Illustrated London News*, proprietor of *The Drama*, and contributor to other literary journals, such as *Topical Times*. These contain comments about literary periodicals, plays and dramas given in London, and authors and performers.

725   JOEL SMITH FAMILY. Papers, 1781–1851. 1 folder. MS 3221.

Primarily land deeds and agreements of Joel Smith of Litchfield County, Connecticut, and of his descendants who settled in Berlin Centre, Trumbull County, Ohio.

726   ALFRED COLLINS MARKLEY. Commissions, 1864–1901. 12 items. Gift of Mary L. Hildebrand, 1962. MS 3222.

U.S. Army commissions, including Markley's appointment to first lieutenant, 127th U.S. Colored Troops, 1865. Markley lived in Philadelphia, Pennsylvania.

727   RALPH A. HARMAN FAMILY. Papers, 1903, 1908–1909, 1915–1919, 1932, 1936. 5 boxes. MS 3225.

Newspaper clippings and other printed material in various foreign languages, but primarily the correspondence between Ralph Augustus Harman, Cleveland financier and businessman, and various friends and relatives during World War I. Commented on are subjects pertaining to wartime France, American intervention, the Versailles Peace Conference, President Woodrow Wilson's peacemaking efforts, and the situation in Cleveland during this period. Correspondents besides Ralph A. Harman include his wife, Grace Fleming Harman; his daughter, Sue Wade Harman, who served as a nurse for the American Red Cross Tuberculosis Commission for Italy, 1918–1919; and his sister, Mrs. Edouard Charpentier of Paris, France.

Unpublished 4-page register available in the Society.

728 JAMES WICKES TAYLOR (1819–1893). Papers, 1846, 1851–1893. ½ box. MS 3226.
Personal and family letters and other assorted papers of Taylor, lawyer and government official, who served as a U.S. Treasury agent (1859–1869) and as U.S. consul to Winnipeg (1870–1893). Specifically included are letters addressed to his sister and brother-in-law, Mr. and Mrs. C. B. Brace, 1851–1893; a few letters addressed to his mother, 1860–1878; several other letters and copies of speeches, undated; and newspaper clippings containing obituary notices for James W. Taylor, 1893.

729 PERKINS FAMILY. Certificates. 29 items (1 oversize package). Gift of Mrs. Ralph Perkins, 1964. MS 3228.
Military commissions, diplomas, and other documents relating to Jacob Bishop, Frances, and Ralph Perkins.

730 ORLANDO CHARLES RISDON. Papers, 1861–1872. 3 boxes. Gift of Jeanette Risdon, 1939, 1942. MS 3229.
Official and personal correspondence, military orders and reports, vouchers and other financial papers, maps, photographs, and newspaper clippings relating primarily to Brigadier General Risdon's activities during the Civil War. Risdon, who helped to organize the 53rd U.S. Colored Infantry, saw action in the battles of Rich Mountain (West Virginia), Middle Creek (Kentucky), Tazewell (Tennessee), Arkansas Post (Arkansas), and Chickasaw, Port Gibson, Champion Hill, and Vicksburg (Mississippi).

Unpublished 4-page register available in the Society.

731   ALEXANDER C. BROWN. Resolution, 1960. 1 item (bound). Gift of Mrs. Mary Brown Garfield. MS 3230.
This resolution honoring Brown and presented to him on his retirement is an excerpt from the minutes of a meeting of the board of directors of the Ohio Bell Telephone Company, Cleveland.

732   ALEXANDER HARPER FAMILY. Papers, 1814–1904. 3 boxes, 12 volumes. Gift of Laurence Harper Norton. MS 3231.
Primarily daybooks, ledgers, and other household papers relating to members of this family which resided in Unionville, Ashtabula County, Ohio. Captain Alexander Harper and his wife, who settled in Ashtabula County in 1798, were among the earliest permanent settlers in the Western Reserve. These papers relate to Captain Harper's descendants who remained on the family homestead.*

Unpublished 4-page register available in the Society.

* The Harper homestead, Shandy Hall, is operated as a museum by the Western Reserve Historical Society.

733   MARY JANE BLAIR. Letters, 1866–1867. 1 folder. MS 3232.
Letters written while on a tour of several European countries, including Ireland, England, Switzerland, and Italy.

734   MOSES CLEAVELAND (1754–1806). Papers, 1796–1805. ½ box (95 items). Obtained from Samuel C. Morgan and Colonel David Young in 1868. MS 3233.
Correspondence, expense accounts, memoranda regarding land sales in Western Reserve, and other papers relating to Cleaveland's activities as a director and agent of the Connecticut Land Company, trustee of the Erie Land Company, and founder of the city of Cleveland in 1796. Dealt with are the negotiations for land titles, including those with the Indians, and the surveying and settling of the land. Correspondents include Henry Cham-

pion, Daniel Coit, Samuel Huntington, Turhand Kirtland, Seth Pease, Simon Perkins, Lemuel Storrs, and Joshua Stow.

Unpublished 3-page register available in the Society.

735   SETH PEASE (1764–1819). Papers, 1792–1807 (1795–1797). 1 box. Obtained from Horace Pease, 1869–1871. MS 3234.

Correspondence, land surveys and maps, memoranda, notebooks, and financial papers relating to Pease's activities as surveyor for the Connecticut Land Company. Of special interest are the documents relating to Pease's early map of the Western Reserve area. Also included are some items concerning surveys made by Pease in Connecticut and in Penobscot, Maine, and throughout the Holland Purchase in New York State.

Unpublished 3-page register available in the Society.

736   EPHRAIM ROOT (1762–1825). Papers, 1769–1837 (1790–1813). 3 boxes. Obtained from Buel Sedgewick in 1869. MS 3235.

Correspondence, financial papers, and legal documents primarily concerning Root's activities as a shareholder and as clerk of the Connecticut Land Company. Specifically included is a set of draft slips and a volume concerning the drawings held to parcel the company's land in 1798 and 1807. Correspondents include Elijah Boardman, Jonathan Brace, Judson Canfield, Henry Champion, Daniel Coit, Gideon Granger, Uriel Holmes, James Kingsbury, Turhand Kirtland, Samuel Mather, Jr., Simon Perkins, Oliver Phelps, Elijah Wadsworth, and John Young.

Unpublished 9-page register available in the Society.

737   OLIVER PHELPS FAMILY. Papers, 1792–1879 (1794–1810, 1830–1870). 5 boxes. MS 3236.

Correspondence, land papers, memoranda, financial papers, and other materials relating primarily to the land interests of Oliver

Phelps (1749–1809), jurist and New York State Representative; Oliver Leicester Phelps (1775–1813), of Canandaigua, New York; and Oliver Phelps (1796–1877), lawyer of Canandaigua, New York, and Washington, D.C. Represented in this collection are all aspects of the purchase, development, and sale of land in Ohio, 1792–1879; New York, 1826–1865; and Michigan, 1838–1871. Most voluminous are the papers concerning transactions in Ohio, including frequent references to the work of Calvin Austin and of Aaron, Ahaz, and C. C. Merchant. Also referred to are the Connecticut Land Company, 1795–1805; the Firelands, 1801–1879; the American Land Company, 1849–1869; and the Phelps-Gorham Purchase (New York), 1826–1865. Among the land agents who acted in behalf of members of the Phelps family are Heman Ely, Orrin Harmon, and Charles C. Paine.

Unpublished 6-page register available in the Society.

738   TURHAND KIRTLAND (1755–1844). Papers, 1794–1868 (1795–1840). 13 boxes. Gifts of Mary L. W. Morse; C. B. Newell; J. P. Kirtland, 1870–1912. MS 3237.

Correspondence, surveys, land contracts, financial and tax records, and other papers relating to Kirtland's activities as agent for the Connecticut Land Company, the Big Beaver Land Company, and the Union Land Company, and as founder of Poland, Ohio. Although dealing primarily with land speculation and development in the Western Reserve, some of these papers refer to local matters in Poland, including civil offices, mill operations, the mails, and the Reading Room and Literary Society, 1794–1868; several Ohio schools, including the Burton Academy, 1804–1845; the Episcopal Society of Canfield, Boardman, and Poland, 1804–1838; and the Maryland Lotteries, 1824–1827. Of interest is a journal of William Law, Jr., kept while on a trip to the Western Reserve, ca. 1799. Correspondents include Caleb Atwater, Joshua Atwater, Samuel Bellamy, Thaddeus Betts, Thomas Bull, Leonard Case, Henry Champion, Esther Cleaveland, Isaac Cowles, Solomon Cowles, Martin Ellsworth, William Ely, Caleb

Goodwin, Levi Goodwin, Daniel Holbrook, Edward Hooker, Samuel Huntington, Phinehas Johnson, William Law, Charles Marvin, Isaac Mills, Seth Overton, Lemuel Punderson, Charles R. Sherman, George W. Stanley, Lemuel Storrs, Titus Street, Elisha Whittlesey, Ezekiel Williams, and John Young.

Unpublished 17-page register available in the Society.

739 EDWARD TIFFIN (1766–1829). Papers, 1785–1853. 3 boxes. MS 3238.

General correspondence, commercial and legal documents, maps, and surveys relating to Tiffin's activities as surveyor general of the Northwest Territory, first Governor of Ohio, and U.S. senator. In addition to other personal and family papers, also included are sermons and booklets of medical-prescription data dealing respectively with Tiffin's endeavors as a lay preacher and as a physician. Correspondents include Joseph Anderson, Lewis Cass, George Graham, Josiah Meigs, Thomas T. Tucker, and William Woodbridge.

Unpublished 11-page register available in the Society.

740 LAURENS W. WOLCOTT. Diaries, 1863–1865. 2 volumes. Gift of Mrs. Luther Miller, 1963. MS 3240.

These Civil War diaries contain Wolcott's brief comments on troop movements, skirmishes, and other activities of his regiment, the 52nd Illinois Militia.

741 CHARITY SCHOOL FOR BOYS. WOLVERHAMPTON, ENG. Record Book, 1716–1798. 1 volume (photostatic copy). Gift of Robert C. Norton. MS 3241.

Minute book which contains three signatures of Button Gwinett.

742 GEAL GROVER NORRIS (b. 1822). Autobiographical Account, 1855. 1 volume. Gift of Elton R. Norris, 1965. MS 3243.

Account of the life of a schoolteacher in Ashtabula County, Ohio.

743 U.S. ARMY. INFANTRY. 2ND REGIMENT. Roster, 1791. 14 pages (photostatic copies from the National Archives Record Group N. 94). Gift of W. R. Branthoover, 1965. MS 3244.

Roster of troops engaged in the Battle of the Maumee of the Lakes, November 9, 1791.

744 DAVID SHRIVER, JR. Papers, 1811–1852. 2 folders. MS 3245.

Letters and contracts concerning the construction of roads, particularly the Cumberland Road. Correspondents of Shriver, who was superintendent of the Cumberland Road, include William Harris Crawford, Alexander James Dallas, and Andrew Stewart.

745 WOMAN'S CHRISTIAN TEMPERANCE UNION. CLEVELAND, O. Records, 1874–1951. 2 boxes. MS 3247.

Constitution, articles of incorporation, minutes of board and committee meetings, letters, and financial records of this organization, which was founded in 1874 and incorporated in 1880 as the Woman's Christian Temperance League, auxiliary to the Woman's Christian Temperance Union of Ohio. After 1886, these records relate to the Non-Partisan Woman's Christian Temperance Union, 1886–1932, and to the Woman's Philanthropic Union, 1933–1951. In addition to advocacy of temperance, these records touch upon social, civic, and charitable activities, such as the sponsorship of the Central Friendly Inn, which developed into a recognized social settlement. These temperance organizations attracted support from many notable Clevelanders, including Alva Bradley (1814–1885), Joseph Perkins, and John D. Rockefeller.

746 *CITY OF BUFFALO.* Logbook, 1923–1925. 1 volume. Gift of David F. Gottschalk, 1962. MS 3248.

Captain's log of the Cleveland and Buffalo Transit Company steamer *City of Buffalo,* which sailed between Cleveland and Buffalo, New York.

747 ROBBINS FAMILY. Papers, 1788–1903. 1 folder. MS 3249.

Land deeds and tax receipts relating to land owned by members of this family, including Josiah, Electa M., and Charles W. Robbins, in and around Weathersfield, Trumbull County, Ohio.

748 BARNEY J. YOUNG. Account Book, 1886–1923. 1 volume. MS 3250.

Financial accounts of Young, a dealer in manufactured tobacco in Millersburg, Ohio.

749 LOUIS A. MOSES FAMILY. Papers, 1907–1957. 1 box. Gift of Mrs. Marian Moses Kuhne, 1963. MS 3251.

Primarily correspondence, notes, and newspaper clippings containing data on the ancestry of Louis Augustus Moses (1876–1952), Cleveland realtor, and of his wife, Olive (Crane) Moses (d. 1957). Also included are memorial resolutions and letters of condolence addressed to Mrs. Moses upon the death of her husband; and one folder of notes, newspaper clippings, and letters of Howard R. Dille which relate to the genealogy of the Dille family.

750 WILLIAM WEISHEIMER FAMILY. Papers, 1874–1929. 1½ boxes. Gift of Mrs. John A. Lindsay, 1964. MS 3253.

This collection relates to various members of this family and includes the following: several certificates and letters from Germany addressed to William Weisheimer of Cleveland, Ohio, 1874–1915; autograph albums belonging to Marie Weisheimer, 1885, 1888; Marie Weisheimer's music, composition, and dressmaking school notebooks, ca. 1890's, and school-attendance registers for her classes at Cleveland's Normal School, 1895–1907; three diaries kept by Marie Weisheimer while on summer trips to Detroit and other cities in Michigan (1900), down and back on the St. Lawrence River (1904), and throughout the western United States (1905); a series of letters to Marie Weisheimer from John G. Eberhard, Company H, 20th U.S. Infantry, written while the latter was stationed in Manila, Philippine Islands, during the Spanish-American War and afterwards, 1898–1901; several letters addressed to Harry A. Spencer (who married Marie Weisheimer in 1907), primarily from his father, Dr. George Spencer, professor of dermatology at the Cleveland Homeopathic Medical College, 1902–1929; and a scrapbook containing copies of articles published by Dr. Spencer and an assortment of his notes on matters pertaining to chemistry, 1910's.

751   JAMES MASON FAMILY. Papers, 1832–1903. 2 boxes. Gift of Mrs. Lucretia Garfield Comer, 1963. MS 3254.
Land contracts and other legal papers of James Mason (1817–1885) and his wife, of Cleveland, Ohio; poems and other writings of Mary L. Mason (d. 1899); but primarily personal and family correspondence among members of the Garfield, Mason, Robinson, and Strong families.

752   GEORGE W. TODD. Genealogical Data, 1920's. 3 boxes. MS 3257.
Genealogical data concerning the Avery, Davis, Foote, Morse, Osborn, Spaulding, Stockwell, Todd, and Wilson families.

753   HEZEKIAH ELDREDGE (1795–1845). Papers, 1821–1876. 1 box, 14 bound volumes, 1 oversize package (some photocopies). Gift of Mrs. Rogers D. Rusk, 1965, 1969. MS 3259.
Agreements and receipts, statements for labor and building materials, pass and time books, and some correspondence (1821–1849) of Hezekiah Eldredge, architect, carpenter, and builder, and of his son, Alonzo. Eldredge, a builder of churches, residences, banks, warehouses, and stores, was active in the Rochester (New York) area (1825–1834) and in Cleveland, Ohio (1834–1845). Also included are 14 volumes of ledgers, journals, account books, and a ciphering book, 1830–1876; one oversize package of plans drawn by Eldredge; and "Hezekiah Eldredge (1795–

1845) Master Builder of Western New York State and the Western Reserve" by Sarah E. Rusk, 80 pages plus footnotes (photocopy of typescript), undated.

754   SAMUEL MATHER, JR. Record Book, 1825–1840. 1 volume. Gift of R. Henry Norweb, 1965. MS 3262.
"Division of Lands in the Western Reserve State of Ohio belonging to Samuel Mather Junior Esq. deceased among his heirs," including Thomas, Samuel, and James Mather, Anna Lord, Mehitable and Margaret Sill, Fanny Chapman, and Lydia Hubbard. The land consisted of tracts in Lafayette and York townships, Medina County, and in Sheffield, Ashtabula County.

755   DAVID G. SWAIM (d. 1897). Letters, 1861–1874. 2 volumes. Purchased by the Leonard C. Hanna Final Fund, 1965. MS 3263.
A collection of letters received by Swaim, an army officer who served as assistant adjutant general, Department of the Missouri, and later as judge advocate at Fort Leavenworth, Kansas. The letters, which relate to personal, business, and political matters, include approximately 140 from James A. Garfield (1831–1881) covering the period 1861–1874.

756   PERRY AUTOGRAPH COLLECTION. Letters and Documents, 1781–1952. 67 items. Gift of Mr. and Mrs. A. Dean Perry, 1964. MS 3264.
Letters and documents signed by notable American political, literary, and military figures, originally collected by Edward B. Greene of Cleveland, Ohio. The majority of these items relate to military figures of the Civil War and date from 1862 to 1870. Among the letters there are 24 addressed to General William T. Sherman. Of special interest are six Abraham Lincoln items, including three holograph letters. Also represented here are Henry Ward Beecher, Dwight D. Eisenhower, Ralph Waldo Emerson, Edward Everett, William Pitt Fessenden, Nathanael Greene, Ol-

iver Wendell Holmes (1809–1894), Washington Irving, Henry Wadsworth Longfellow, James Russell Lowell, Robert Morris (1734–1806), William Hickling Prescott, Daniel Webster, and John Greenleaf Whittier.

757   ST. PAUL'S EPISCOPAL CHURCH. CLEVELAND, O. Records, 1846–1862. 1 box. MS 3266.

Mortgage deeds, promissory notes, and receipts and disbursements, 1846–1861; treasurers' accounts, 1846–1858; and a building committee report, 1860–1862.

758   BENJAMIN WOOD. Papers, 1838–1896. 1 box. Gift of Mrs. John La Monte through Professor Roy F. Nichols, 1955. MS 3267.

Financial papers and five letter books of Benjamin Wood of Independence and, later, Cleveland, Ohio. The letters, addressed to various members of his family, include comments on a variety of local and national events and issues. Also included are papers relating to the construction of a church and a schoolhouse in Independence in the 1850's.

759   CHARLES ALBERT TURNER (1843–1863). Letters, 1862–1863. 1 folder. Gift of Charles C. Pinkerton, 1954. MS 3268.

Letters written while Turner was serving in Kentucky with the 101st Regiment, Ohio Volunteer Infantry, during 1862 and with the Mississippi Marine Brigade until his death soon after the Vicksburg campaign. Turner was born near Monroeville, Ohio, and most of these letters are addressed to his parents, Albert and Hannah (Covert) Turner. In the letters Turner comments on his battlefield experiences while in Kentucky, camp and hospital conditions, and his activities during the first half of 1863 while serving as a cavalryman on board the U.S.S. *Diana*, which patrolled the Mississippi and Tennessee rivers.

760   ROBERT CASTLE NORTON (1879–1959), *collector*. Autographed Documents of the Signers of the Declaration of Independence. 107 items. Gift of Robert C. Norton, 1959. MS 3269, 3269a.

Includes at least one letter or document, most of which are dated between 1775 and 1783, signed by each of the 56 signers of the Declaration of Independence. Several of the signers are represented by more than one item. These include Abraham Clark, John Hancock, Thomas Heyward, Samuel Huntington (1731–1796), Richard Henry Lee, Philip Livingston, Robert Morris (1734–1806), John Morton, Thomas Stone, Matthew Thornton, William Williams (1731–1811), and George Wythe.

761   ROBERT CASTLE NORTON (1879–1959), *collector*. Autograph Letters of U.S. Presidents. 37 items. Gift of Robert C. Norton, 1959. MS 3270.

Includes at least one letter signed by each U.S. President from George Washington through Dwight D. Eisenhower.

762   CHARLES F. SCHWEINFURTH. Plans, 1898. 35 pages. Gift of Schafer, Flynn & Van Dijk, 1966. MS 3272.

Architectural plans for the Cox-Prentiss house, 3411 Euclid Avenue, Cleveland, Ohio.

763   RAYMOND F. BLOSSER. Research Notes, 1940–1946. 2 folders. Deposited by Raymond F. Blosser, 1966. MS 3273.

Letters, newspaper clippings, and notes made during interviews with persons concerning Oris P. and Mantis J. Van Sweringen.

RESTRICTED: Details available in the Society.

764   ROBERT OWEN FRITZ (d. 1935). Letters, May–September, 1898. 1 folder. MS 3274.

Letters and postcards written by Fritz to members of his family in Cleveland, Ohio, while he was serving in Troop C, 1st Regiment, Ohio Cavalry, during the Spanish-American War. The letters contain comments about general camp routine and conditions, and the training program at Camp George H. Thomas, Chickamauga Park, Lytle, Georgia, and at a camp in Lakeland, Florida.

765   THOMAS CONOLLY. Journal, 1813–1815. 2 pieces of birch bark. Gift of R. Henry Norweb, 1958. MS 3275.

Accounts of three engagements during the War of 1812, including the Battle of Lundy's Lane, July 23, 1814.

766   WILLIAM ELEROY CURTIS (1850–1911). Papers, 1877–1912. 3 boxes. Gift of William E. Curtis II, 1966. MS 3276.

Correspondence, copies of speeches and magazine articles, newspaper clippings, and photographs relating to the activities of William E. Curtis, author, journalist for two Chicago newspapers, 1873–1911, and director of the Bureau of the American Republics, 1890–1893. Papers relate primarily to Pan-American relations and the World's Columbian Exposition (1893), with special emphasis on Curtis' articles on Christopher Columbus and on various European and Latin-American countries. Among his correspondents were national and international figures such as Albert J. Beveridge, William McKinley, Franklin MacVeagh, and the Duke of Veragua.

Unpublished 11-page register available in the Society.
NUCMC 67-969

767   W. BINGHAM COMPANY, CLEVELAND, O. Records, 1841–1849, 1854–1857. 3 boxes, 1 oversize volume. Deposited by the W. Bingham Company, 1962. MS 3280.

Ledgers, journals, and account book of this hardware company, founded by William Bingham in 1841, which supplied local shipbuilding, mining, and railroad industries. Also included is a journal, 1836–1839, of the Potter, Clark, and Murphey Company, from whom Bingham acquired his original inventory.

768   PETER WITT (1869–1948). Papers, 1895–1948. 6 boxes, 4 packages. Gift of Mrs. Stuart V. Cummins, 1967, 1968. MS 3281.

Correspondence, speeches, articles, reports, campaign literature, notes, scrapbooks, newspaper clippings, and photographs relating primarily to the political activities of Peter Witt, Cleveland city clerk under Mayor Tom L. Johnson (1903–1910), traction commissioner under Mayor Newton D. Baker (1912–1915), and unsuccessful candidate for mayor of Cleveland in 1915 and 1932 and for governor of Ohio in 1928. An outspoken and controversial public figure for over 50 years, Witt was recognized as an expert in the field of public transportation and served as a transit consultant for several other cities. These papers also touch on Witt's labor union sympathies, the single-tax issue, Alfred E. Smith's 1928 campaign, the Cleveland Railway Company, and the Cleveland Union Terminal. Also included are notes made by Louis Plost during interviews with Witt in the 1940's. Correspondents include a wide range of local and national political figures including Eugene V. Debs, Elizabeth J. Hauser, Tom L. Johnson, Brand Whitlock, and A. F. Whitney.

Unpublished 8-page register available in the Society.

769   NATHANIEL MASSIE (1763–1813). Papers, 1782–1852. 7 boxes. MS 3282.

Correspondence, legal briefs, court dockets, appeals, summonses, powers of attorney, land warrants, land surveys, and receipts accumulated during the conduct of Massie's activities as a surveyor and land speculator in Kentucky and Ohio, but primarily in the area known as the Virginia Military District in southern Ohio. Although he founded the city of Chillicothe and was active in territorial and, later, state politics, the bulk of Massie's papers deal solely with his land dealings. The few papers after 1813 relate to the settlement of Massie's estate and to various land transactions and legal affairs of his son, Henry Massie (1811-1862), a prominent Chillicothe lawyer and banker. These papers of Henry Massie touch upon Kentucky's Transylvania College, 1832; general economic conditions, 1834; and settlement in Illinois, 1836. Correspondents include Richard C. Anderson, Sam Ayres, Andrew Boyd, William Buchannon, Thomas Carneal, George Clark, William Creighton, Israel Donalson, William Ellsey, Charles Harris, Jessie Hunt, Joseph Kerr, Robert Means, John P. Pleasants, Robert Pollard, Nathaniel Pope, Bird Price, William Starling, John Sterrett, and W. Warfield.

Unpublished 12-page register available in the Society.
NUCMC 69-2089

770   DARIUS CADWELL (1821-1905). Papers, 1848-1902. 8 boxes. MS 3283.

General and business correspondence, speeches, letter books, legal briefs, deeds, and financial papers relating to Cadwell's activities as a lawyer and public official in Cleveland, Ohio, but primarily as provost marshal for the 19th District of Ohio during the latter years of the Civil War. The papers from these years, 1863-1866, include correspondence, quarterly returns, abstracts of requisitions, circulars, invoices, general orders, memoranda, and other printed forms relating to the responsibility of the provost marshal, which included military discharges, substitutes, deserters, prisoners, draft quotas, enlistments, induction physicals, and, in general, the administration of military justice. The remainder of the collection consists of receipts for goods, services, and money, 1849-1902; a broken series of 44 account books, 1853-1901; deeds and contracts relating to land dealings in Minnesota, Ohio, and Wisconsin, and correspondence with James D. Ray, who operated a real estate office in Duluth, Minnesota, during the land boom of the early 1870's, 1869-1878; and canceled checks from several Cleveland banks, 1875-1887.

Unpublished 10-page register available in the Society.
NUCMC 69-2088.

771 FRANK AUGUSTUS SCOTT (1873–1949). Papers, 1848, 1906–1935. 8 boxes. Gift of Mrs. Frank A. Scott, 1968. MS 3284.

Correspondence, speeches, articles, newspaper clippings, photographs, and scrapbooks relating to both the business and the personal life of Frank A. Scott, a prominent Cleveland businessman who served as President and Chairman of the Board of the Warner and Swasey Company from 1920 to 1928, and who was especially active in local civic, cultural, charitable, and educational institutions. The correspondence reflects Scott's wide range of activity and interest in organizations such as the American Society of Mechanical Engineers, 1923–1928; Case School of Applied Science, 1920, 1925–1928; Cleveland's Central Armory, 1919–1928; Cleveland Engineering Society, 1923–1927; Cleveland Insurance Company, 1923–1924; Cleveland Trust Company, 1913–1929; Hydraulic Steel Company, 1923–1924; Municipal Traction Company, 1908–1909; St. Martin's Episcopal Church and St. Paul's Episcopal Church, 1922–1927; Standard Parts Company, 1920–1924; University Hospitals (Cleveland), 1913–1928; Warner and Swasey Company, 1915–1929; Western Reserve University, 1918–1928; and White Sewing Machine Company, 1919–1926. Between 1907 and 1935, Scott frequently delivered speeches and published articles on subjects such as the metal-working industries, the war effort, industrial management, the iron and steel industry, patent law, and European postwar recovery. His articles appeared in *Iron Age, Machinery,* the *New York Evening Post,* and other local papers and journals.

Among the scrapbooks are several containing "The Newspaper History of the Liquidation of the Properties of the Cleveland Railroad Company, Including the Story of the Receivership of the Municipal Traction Company," 1908–1909; and one containing newspaper clippings and correspondence relating to Newton D. Baker, 1931–1935. In addition to his correspondence with businessmen, Scott also expressed his opinions on pending federal legislation to congressmen. Correspondents include Elroy McKendree Avery, Newton D. Baker, Frances P. Bolton, Theodore E. Burton, Harry L. Davis, Simeon D. Fess, Frederick H.

Goff, Ambrose Swasey, Charles F. Thwing, Robert E. Vinson, Worcester R. Warner, and William Porter White.

Unpublished 13-page register available in the Society. NUCMC 69-2090

772   CORREL SMITH. Diary, 1861–1862. 1 volume. Purchased, 1968. MS 3285.

Civil War diary kept by Captain Smith, Company G, 19th Regiment, Ohio Volunteer Infantry, containing his comments on supplies, camp routine, and distances marched.

773   EPHRAIM BROWN FAMILY. Papers, ca. 1800–1900. 1 box. Gift of Alexander C. Brown, Jr., 1968. MS 3286.

Primarily personal and general correspondence of Ephraim Brown and his wife, Mary, of North Bloomfield, Ohio, and of their children. Most of Ephraim's letters were written while he was either traveling or residing in distant cities while fulfilling his duties as Ohio State Representative, Senator, and road commissioner during the 1830's and 1840's.

774   GEORGE H. BENDER (1896–1961). Papers, 1912–1960. 5 boxes. Gift of Mrs. George H. Bender, 1967. MS 3288.

Correspondence, speeches, biographical accounts, newsletters, campaign and election literature, certificates and testimonials, souvenir programs, newspaper clippings, and articles by or about Bender, who served as Ohio State Senator (1921–1931), chairman of Cuyahoga County Republican Central Committee (1938–1954), and U.S. Representative (1939–1949, 1951–1954) and Senator (1954–1957). The papers touch on several aspects of Bender's career, including his stand against police raids during Prohibition, his sponsorship of pension-bill amendments and civil service laws for Ohio police, and his support of schoolteachers, while in the Ohio Senate; and his sponsorship of an anti-poll tax bill and the Full Employment Bill, while in the House of

Representatives. The correspondence, while primarily from constituents, also includes letters from both local and national political figures.

775 DANIEL L. COIT FAMILY. Papers, ca. 1800–1905. 1 box. Gift of Mr. and Mrs. Robert W. Lindsay, 1967. MS 3289.

Personal and general correspondence, land deeds, maps, and surveys of tracts of land in Cleveland and in Liverpool, Ohio, belonging to Daniel L. Coit, an original shareholder in the Connecticut Land Company; Henry H. Coit, who settled in Cleveland in the early 1800's and then moved to Liverpool; and William H. Coit, who resided for most of his life on Cleveland's east side, including Euclid, until his death in the 1890's. Also included are various commission certificates of Henry H. Coit and a combined recipe book and garden journal, ca. 1837.

776 E. G. WOOD FAMILY. Papers, 1862–1865. 125 items. Purchased, 1967. MS 3290.

Primarily letters addressed to Rev. and Mrs. E. G. Wood of Chesterville, Ohio, from their two sons, Julius V. Wood of Company C, 96th Regiment, Ohio Volunteer Infantry, and Lucius V. Wood of Company E, 121st Regiment, Ohio Volunteer Infantry. Julius participated in several battles, including Arkansas Post, saw action in the Vicksburg campaign, and lost an arm during an expedition through Louisiana (November, 1863). Lucius did not see much combat but was close to camp matters and politics. His comments include references to the Copperheads. Also included is Julius' 23-page diary, August 8–October 31, 1862; and a partial diary and scrapbook, undated.

777 STEPHEN MARCH FAMILY. Papers, 1636–1862 (1770–1828). 1½ boxes. Gift of Mrs. Margaret G. March, 1963. MS 3291.

Correspondence, financial receipts, land deeds, legal papers, and certificates relating to several members of this family, most of whom resided for a time in Worcester County, Massachusetts. Specifically included are contemporary copies of Indian deeds to land in Dorchester, Massachusetts, 1636, 1684; scattered legal papers, deeds, and certificates, 1674–1811, mostly relating to Stephen March (d. 1821) and including several items concerning the accusation that Daniel and Stephen March of Sutton, Massachusetts, were Tories, 1777–1779; letters, financial accounts, and memoranda relating to the activities of George March and Oliver March as co-executors of the estate of Stephen March of Worcester, Massachusetts, 1807–1828; general and personal correspondence between George March, a mechanic and machine operator in various woolen factories in Massachusetts, and his relatives, including Oliver March and George and Hannah Robinson, 1816–1831; and an account book of George March while he was involved in weaving and clock repairing, 1849–1858.

778   JEPTHA HOMER WADE (1811–1890). Papers, 1845–1888. 2 boxes. Gift of George Garretson Wade. MS 3292.

Correspondence, letter book, circulars, pamphlets, business and legal documents, and newspaper clippings relating primarily to the business interests of Jeptha H. Wade, painter, Cleveland businessman, and developer of the telegraph, These materials concern Wade's role in the expansion and consolidation of telegraph lines and companies in the Midwest between 1845 and 1858. They also reflect upon his relations with the Cleveland and Cincinnati Telegraph Company, the Western Union Telegraph Company, and the Pacific Telegraph Company. Of interest is a volume of letters from San Francisco concerning the consolidation of telegraph lines in the Far West, 1860–1861; and letters from or about persons who had financial interests in the telegraph, including Amos Kendall, Ezra Cornell, and Samuel F. B. Morse.

Unpublished 7-page register available in the Society.

779 YOUNDT FAMILY. Land Papers, 1753–1829. 15 items. Gift of Bertha Witwer, 1968. MS 3293.

Deeds, indentures, and draughts of land in Earl and Ephrata townships, Lancaster County, Pennsylvania, belonging to members of the Youndt (also Yund and Yount) family.

780 FREDERICK L. TAFT (d. 1913). Papers, 1899–1908. 3 volumes. Gift of Frederick L. Taft, 1957. MS 3294.

Two scrapbooks of newspaper clippings, 1899–1908, and one volume of letters addressed to Governor Myron T. Herrick endorsing Taft for appointment as Probate Judge in Cuyahoga County, January, 1905.

781 JOSEPH MENNING (1874–1967). Papers, 1895–1921, 1940–1945. 1½ boxes. Gift of Mrs. Carl T. Howe, 1967. MS 3295.

Some correspondence, financial receipts, newspaper clippings, certificates, and other papers touching on Menning's activities as a member of the Knights of Labor (late 1890's), a Cleveland City Councilman (1909–1911), and a Cuyahoga County Commissioner (1911–1919).

782 SAUL S. DANACEAU (1896–1965). Papers, 1929–1958. ½ box, 3 volumes. Gift of Mrs. Saul S. Danaceau, 1967. MS 3296.

Some correspondence, campaign literature, and three scrapbooks of newspaper clippings relating to Danaceau's career as Cuyahoga County assistant prosecutor (1936–1958) and Common Pleas Court judge (1958–1965), but particularly to his opposition of Cleveland's city-manager plan between 1929 and 1931.

783 MARTIN L. SWEENEY (1885–1960). Papers, 1931–1939. ½ box, 1 volume. Gift of Robert E. Sweeney, 1967. MS 3297.

Copies of speeches, 1931–1939; campaign literature and a scrapbook of newspaper clippings, 1934–1937, relating to the political activities of Sweeney, who served as U.S. Representative from Ohio's 20th District (Cleveland) from 1931 to 1943. This material touches on Sweeney's campaign for mayor of Cleveland in 1933, his relations with Rev. Charles E. Coughlin and the National Union for Social Justice, and his support of William Lemke for President of the United States in 1936.

784 WILLIAM G. TORRANCE. Papers, 1821–1836. ½ box. Gift of Mr. and Mrs. Homer C. Bunting, 1968. MS 3299.

An account book kept by William G. Torrance, a schoolmaster in the Long Run Settlement (Pennsylvania?), and a journal kept on a trip from Greensborough, Westmoreland County, Pennsylvania, to New Lisbon, Ohio, August 8–25, 1831. Also included are a scattering of family letters dating to 1901.

785 ARNOLD C. SAUNDERS FAMILY. Papers, 1881–1904. 4 boxes. Gift of Arnold C. Saunders, Jr., 1967. MS 3300.

Primarily letters, reports, abstracts, charts, memoranda, and copies of legal documents relating to the genealogy of the Saunders family compiled for Arnold C. Saunders, Cleveland businessman, by Elizabeth C. Neff, 1900–1904. Also included are several business letters and legal documents, dated between 1881 and 1904.

786 GEORGE W. HODGES (1827–1918). Letters, 1861–1865. ½ box. Gift of Mrs. Harry A. DuBroy, 1968. MS 3303.

Letters of George W. Hodges while serving in Company G, 41st Regiment, Ohio Volunteer Infantry, during the Civil War. Hodge rose to the rank of sergeant before being mustered out in November, 1865. The letters, addressed to his wife, Marana, contain many personal, family, and general comments in addition to remarks on the activities of his regiment, which was stationed in Tennessee, Georgia, Alabama, and Texas.

787   JOSEPH A. PEPOON (1797–1874). Papers, 1820's. 1 box. Gift of Mrs. Harry A. DuBroy, 1968. MS 3303a.
Several letters and some genealogical notes, but primarily copies of sermons and lectures delivered before congregations throughout the Western Reserve. Rev. Joseph Pepoon's family settled in Painesville, Ohio, in 1804, and in 1826 he was ordained an evangelist in the Presbyterian Church.

788   RALPH LEETE (1823–1905). Papers, ca. 1840–1903. 1½ boxes. Gift of Mrs. Helen J. Crawley, 1968. MS 3304.
Primarily correspondence of Ralph Leete, an attorney at law in Ironton, Ohio. Many of the letters touch upon Ohio political issues, since Leete was active in the Democratic Party in the 1840's 1850's, and 1860's. The bulk of the correspondence is between Leete and his relatives, particularly his son, William H. Leete.

789   ROBERT CASTLE NORTON (1879–1959), *collector*. Autographs of Generals and Patriots of the American Revolution. 250 items. Gift of the Estate of Robert C. Norton. MS 3305.
This collection includes many holograph letters and documents dating between 1776 and 1783. One hundred and three generals in the Continental Army are represented, including George Washington, Nathanael Greene, Benjamin Lincoln, Horatio Gates, Baron von Steuben, Tadeusz Kosciuszko, Francis Marion, Casimir Pulaski, and Ethan Allen. In addition to other patriot leaders, such as Silas Deane, Henry Dearborn, John Dickinson, John Paul Jones, Henry Laurens, Paul Revere, and Jonathan Trumbull, 12 British and several French officers are also represented here.

790   RAY T. MILLER (1893–1966). Papers, 1906–1966. 59 boxes, 9 oversize volumes, 1 package. Gift of the Miller Family, 1968. MS 3308.
Correspondence, speeches, certificates, diaries, daybooks, news-

paper clippings, photographs, miscellaneous printed material, and personal memorabilia relating primarily to the political career and personal life of Ray T. Miller, Cleveland lawyer and political leader. Specifically, Miller was a student at Notre Dame University (1911–1914), a lawyer in Cleveland from 1915, Mayor of Cleveland (1933–1934), and chairman of the Cuyahoga County Democratic Party (1938–1964).

The papers are divided into two series: correspondence (20 boxes) and non-correspondence (39 boxes, 9 oversize volumes, and 1 package). The correspondence, 1906–1966, and enclosures are arranged in chronological order. The non-correspondence is arranged chronologically under the following subdivisions: Knights of Columbus, speeches, lists, financial records, diaries, daybooks and calendars, photographs, scrapbooks, account books, and oversize items.

These papers relate to Miller's college career at Notre Dame University; his service during World War I with the 135th Machine Gun Battalion, 37th Division, which served in France; his legal and political career in Cleveland, 1924–1935; and his activities as chairman of the Cuyahoga County Democratic Party. Of special interest is the material relating to the Cleveland mayoral campaigns of 1933 and 1935; the struggle between Miller and W. Burr Gongwer for control of the Democratic Party, 1938–1940; the Cuyahoga County Charter Commission, 1950; Adlai E. Stevenson, 1952, 1956; John F. Kennedy, 1960; and Frank Lausche and Dean Clarence Manion. A considerable amount of material concerns World War I, the Knights of Columbus, radio station WERE, the annual Cuyahoga County Democratic conventions, and Notre Dame University and its football teams. Correspondents include Frank M. Barry, Robert J. Bulkley, Paul E. Butler, Frank T. Cullitan, James A. Farley, W. Burr Gongwer, Luke E. Hart, Francis J. Heazel, Alvanley Johnston, Patrick J. Kirwin, Frank J. Lausche, Clarence Manion, John H. Nolan, Al Sutphin, Charles A. Vanik, Alexander F. Whitney, and Stephen M. Young.

Unpublished 22-page register available in the Society.

791 ROBERT JOHNS BULKLEY (1880–1965). Papers, 1886–1967. 44 boxes, 5 packages. Gift of Mrs. Robert J. Bulkley, 1966, 1967. MS 3310.

Correspondence, speeches, memoranda, reports, campaign literature, certificates, personal memorabilia, newspaper clippings, photographs, and other papers relating to Robert J. Bulkley's career as a Cleveland lawyer, banker, and civic leader, but particularly as a Democratic U.S. Representative from Ohio's 21st District (1911–1915) and as U.S. Senator from Ohio (1930–1939). The bulk of the correspondence, which comprises over one-half of this collection, is concentrated in the periods 1910–1915 and 1930–1965. While in the House, Bulkley was an active member of the Banking and Currency Committee and of the Glass Subcommittee, which drafted the Federal Reserve Act, and chairman of the House Subcommittee on Rural Credits. Both the correspondence and non-correspondence for this period is arranged under such headings as political, constituent requests, business and personal, three-cent coin, banking and currency, the La Follette Seamen's Act, tariff, patents, patronage, rural credits, pension cases, and the Central Oregon Irrigation Company. In addition of these, other matters referred to include immigration problems, safety legislation for Great Lakes ships, Prohibition and the Hobson Amendment, workmen's compensation, parcel post, Cuyahoga River improvement, postal rates, South American trade, Colorado miners' strike, naval armament limitations, anti-Catholicism and *The Menace*, the Cleveland Immigration League, anti-miscegenation laws, a proposed federal children's bureau, the Kahn Law, the Oldfield Bill, war taxes, the Clayton Anti-Trust Act, the Federal Reserve System, and the Panama Canal Tolls controversy.

After being defeated in his bid for re-election to the House in 1914, Bulkley returned to Cleveland, where he helped organize the Morris Plan Bank for which he served as President and Chairman of the Board during the next 38 years. During World War I Bulkley was associated with the General Munitions Board (later the War Industries Board), the Council of National Defense, and the United States Shipping Board Emergency Fleet Corporation.

The collection touches upon these activities, but deals in more depth with the Northern Ohio Opera Association, 1927-1938; J. R. Edwards and Company, 1927-1964; and the Positype Corporation, 1928-1931.

Elected to the U.S. Senate in 1930 and again in 1932, Bulkley was active on the Banking and Currency Committee. Of special interest during this period are papers dealing with the Prohibition issue, 1930-1933; banking and currency reform and the Banking Acts of 1933 and 1935; President Roosevelt's proposed court reforms, 1937-1938; and materials relating to other New Deal reform measures which Bulkley generally supported, including the Federal Deposit Insurance Corporation and the Federal Securities Exchange Act.

After his defeat by Robert A. Taft in the 1938 election for U.S. Senator, Bulkley returned to banking and the practice of law, although he did remain in touch with national, state, and local politics, to the extent that he was Ohio's favorite-son candidate for the 1952 Democratic presidential nomination. Of interest during this period are the papers relating to the following: Cleveland City School District Sinking Fund, 1940-1951; United States Board of Immigration Appeals, 1941-1945; National Probation and Parole Association, 1948-1954; Cuyahoga County Charter Commission, 1950; the Kaiser-Frazer Corporation, 1951-1954; National Democratic Convention, 1952; and the Pugwash Conferences, 1956-1957.

Also included are biographical sketches and data on Bulkley and his father, Charles H. Bulkley, and an assortment of papers from Bulkley's school days at Cleveland's University School and at Harvard University, which he attended between 1898 and 1902 and where he edited the *Crimson*.

Notable correspondents from the period 1910-1918 include officers or representatives of banking firms, manufacturers, farmers' organizations, labor unions, transit companies, Great Lakes shippers, mills and foundries, motor-car companies, and textile industries, in addition to lawyers, congressmen, and other public officials. Among these are J. J. Adams, William A. Ashbrook, Elbert H. Baker, Newton D. Baker, Alfred Benesch, A. F. Biles,

S. P. Bush, James H. Cassidy, John H. Clarke, Thomas Coughlin, Robert Crosser, Frank X. Cull, Hayden Eames, Harry C. Gahn, Carter Glass, Frederick H. Goff, W. Burr Gongwer, Dudley N. Hartt, Robert H. Jamison, James T. Lloyd, Gilbert H. Montague, Herbert Myrick, Attlee Pomerene, Henry S. Sherman, Frederick N. Sinks, John N. Stockwell, Maurice Weidenthal, and Peter Witt.

Notable correspondents from the period 1930–1965 include Frederick Hobbes Allen, C. E. Althouse, Newton D. Baker, Bernard Baruch, Dudley S. Blossom, Jr., S. P. Bush, Martin L. Davey, Cyrus S. Eaton, Marriner S. Eccles, J. R. Edwards, James A. Farley, James Fusco, Leon Henderson, Howard P. Ingels, Joseph Laronge, Ray T. Miller, Gilbert H. Montague, Margaret A. Parsons, Herbert Pillen, Franklin D. Roosevelt, Charles Sawyer, James W. Shocknessy, John E. Sweeney, Harry S. Truman, Robert R. Young, Stephen M. Young, and Charles B. Zimmerman.

Unpublished 35-page register available in the Society.

792 CARL V. WEYGANDT (1880–1964). Papers, 1928–1964. 2 boxes. Gift of Mrs. Carl V. Weygandt, 1968. MS 3317.

Newspaper clippings, certificates, photographs, memorial resolutions, and some letters and speeches relating to Judge Weygandt, who served as Chief Justice of the Ohio Supreme Court (1933–1963). One folder of material concerns the Conference of Chief Justices held in Virginia in 1950.

793 HENRY PLATT CUSHING (1860–1921). Notebooks, 1898–1916. 15 volumes. Gift of Dr. Charles Bacon, 1966. MS 3320.

Geological field notes kept by Dr. Henry P. Cushing, geologist and member of the New York State Geological Survey from 1893. In one of these volumes (most of which relate to New York State) is an account of an expedition made in 1890 to Glacier

Bay, Alaska. The party, organized by Dr. H. F. Reid of the Case School of Applied Science, sought to explore and map the basin of Muir Glacier.

794   OGHEMA NIAGRA (1865–1950). Papers, 1908–1950. 1 box. Purchased, 1967. MS 3321.

Letters, affidavits, agreements, photographs, and other printed items relating to the activities of Oghema Niagra, better known as Chief Thunderwater, who resided in Cleveland, where he was active in cultural affairs. A member of the Osankee Tribe of the Algonquin Nation, Chief Thunderwater assisted in rehabilitating paroled Indians, especially by finding them jobs.

795   BETHANY PRESBYTERIAN CHURCH. CLEVELAND, O. Records, 1889–1917. 1 volume. Gift of Mrs. Edwin H. Bach, 1968. MS 3324.

Registers of communicants, baptisms, marriages, and deaths.

796   PETER HITCHCOCK FAMILY. Papers, 1787–1904. 48 boxes. Gift of the Hitchcock Family. MS 3325.

Correspondence, speeches, notebooks and diaries, account books, certificates, docket books, school papers, biographical data, financial receipts, legal documents, military papers, and other materials relating to various members of this family who played an active role in the development of the Western Reserve. This collection includes papers of Peter Hitchcock (1781–1853), lawyer, who settled in Burton, Ohio, in 1806; Reuben Hitchcock (1806–1883), lawyer, jurist, railroad executive, and receiver; Henry Lawrence Hitchcock (1813–1873), of Burton and Hudson, teacher, minister, and college president; Peter Hitchcock, Jr. (1818–1886), of Burton, justice of the peace, Ohio State Representative and Senator, and newspaper proprietor; and Peter Marshall Hitchcock (1839–1906), of Cleveland, soldier and businessman. Approximately one-half of this collection consists of correspondence which refers to business and legal matters, personal affairs, politics, education, religion, land dealings, and other aspects of 19th-century life in the Western Reserve. In addition to the correspondence, also of interest are the following: papers relating to local institutions in Burton, including the Temperance Society, Burton Institute, Erie Literary Society, Burton Academy, and Congregational Church, 1803-1861; papers concerning the 4th Division, Ohio Militia, 1815, 1820-1840; an account of a trip by Seabury Ford and Reuben Hitchcock, both students at Yale, from New Haven, Connecticut, to Burton in 1824; docket books of Peter Hitchcock, Jr., 1843-1860; correspondence, legal papers, reports, insurance papers, and other materials of Reuben Hitchcock relating to his railroad interests, with emphasis on his being receiver of the Atlantic & Great Western Railway, 1860-1879; and a variety of official and personal Civil War papers, including a series of letters of Peter H. Hitchcock while serving as an officer in the 20th Regiment, Ohio Volunteer Infantry, including descriptions of the battles of Pittsburgh Landing, Vicksburg, and Atlanta (Sherman's campaign in Georgia), 1861-1864. Other institutions touched upon are Western Reserve College and the Lake Erie Female Seminary.

Unpublished 15-page register available in the Society.

797   MILTON SUTLIFF. Letters, 1838-1867. 87 items. Gift of Mrs. Caroline Macnaughton, Mrs. Robert I. Gale, Jr., and Fred R. White, Jr., 1968. MS 3326.

Two series of letters addressed to Milton Sutliff, an attorney at law in Warren, Ohio, concerning Ohio and national politics, including the slavery issue. One series consists of 37 letters from Joshua R. Giddings and spans the years 1838-1863; the second series consists of 50 letters from Benjamin F. Wade covering the period 1838-1867.

798   CHARLES HERBERT GARVIN (1890-1968). Papers, 1928-1965. 2½ boxes. Gift of Mrs. Charles H. Garvin, 1968. MS 3328.

Letters, speeches, magazine articles, newspaper clippings, and research notes relating to the activities of Charles H. Garvin, physician and surgeon, civic leader, and author. After his arrival in Cleveland in 1916, Dr. Garvin practiced medicine, delivered speeches and wrote many articles on the position of the Negro physician in medicine, and worked for the advancement of Negroes within his profession and within the social structure of this city. Specifically included are several letters, 1928–1965; copies of speeches, notes, and published articles on topics such as the Negro physician in Cleveland and in the United States as well as on a variety of medical subjects; and research notes and an unpublished manuscript, "Africa's Contribution to Medicine."

799 U.S. CONGRESS. HOUSE OF REPRESENTATIVES. COMMITTEE ON RECONSTRUCTION. Journal, 1868–1869. Purchased, 1968. MS 3329.

Minutes of committee meetings held between January 11, 1868, and March 3, 1869. This committee was at first concerned with the impeachment of President Andrew Johnson and, after Johnson's acquittal, with reviewing the new constitutions of the southern states seeking restoration with the Union. Committee members included Thaddeus Stevens (chairman), John A. Bingham, George S. Boutwell, John F. Farnsworth, Calvin T. Hulburd, Halbert E. Paine, and James Brooks.

800 UNITED SPANISH WAR VETERANS. MAJOR ALBERT D. ALCORN'S CAMP NO. 110. Records, 1923, 1952–1961. ½ box. Gift of Harry O. Gray, 1968. MS 3330.

Charter, 1923, and minute book, 1952–1961, of this camp located in Lakewood, Ohio.

801 JAMES H. EASTBURN. Diary, 1862–1865. 1 volume. Gift of A. C. Watkins, 1968. MS 3331.

James H. Eastburn of Sheldon, Illinois, served in Company E, 76th Regiment, Illinois Volunteer Infantry, as did his brothers,

Isaac H. and Thomas F. Eastburn. Eastburn recorded comments on his daily activities, the weather, camp life and routine, marches, and a few military engagements in which he participated. Also included in this volume are 33 photographs of members of this regiment.

802   JAMES PATTERSON HENDERSON. Papers, ca. 1820–1845. 3 boxes (some copies). Gift of Mrs. Frederick Lamb and Edward S. Claflin, 1968. MS 3332.

Correspondence, essays and other school papers, speeches, financial receipts, and other writings of James P. Henderson, who, after graduating from Jefferson College (now Washington and Jefferson) in Washington, Pennsylvania, settled and practiced medicine in Newville, Richland County, Ohio. While a student of medicine, Henderson took voluminous lecture notes, was active in various scholastic societies, and delivered numerous addresses. He also kept drafts of the letters he sent to friends and relatives, including his father, Rev. Matthew Henderson (1762–1835) of Elizabethtown, Pennsylvania. In his letters during the 1830's, Dr. Henderson frequently comments on local business and political conditions in Newville and throughout the state. Also included here is a journal kept on a trip around Ohio during November and December, 1835.

803   ELIZA BALLOU GARFIELD (1801–1887). Diary, January 1–July 2, 1881. 1 volume. Gift of Mrs. Elizabeth C. Kraemer, 1968. MS 3334.

Diary kept by the mother of President James A. Garfield during the last year of his life. Mrs. Garfield comments on a variety of incidents relating to herself and to other members of her family which occurred at Lawnfield, the President's home in Mentor, Ohio, and at the White House, where she resided from March until June, 1881.

804 ROSEMARY HUGHES. Letters, 1939–1941. 1 folder. Gift of Rocena L. Stockwell, 1968. MS 3336.

Addressed to Winifred Brooker of Cleveland, these letters contain Miss Hughes' observations on military and political events in England and on the Continent as well as in the United States during the outbreak and early months of World War II. Miss Hughes, a music student at the University of London, worked as a clerk for a government bureau and was secretary of the English Speaking Union at Dartmouth House in London.

805 E. SWIFT NEWTON. Letters, 1942–1944. 1 folder (mimeographed copies). Gift of Martha W. White, 1968. MS 3336a.

Letters containing a diary-like account of Newton's activities as an overseas club director for the American Red Cross during World War II. Mimeographed for distribution to his friends and relatives, these letters contain comments on the war effort, anecdotes relating to the Red Cross club, and much personal and general commentary.

806 WILLIAM HERMAN KNAPP (1801–1888). Papers, ca. 1850–1901. 11 boxes. MS 3338.

Surveys, notes, memoranda, field notes, and papers relating to surveys of land made throughout Cuyahoga County by William H. Knapp, who apparently was associated with C. C. and Aaron Merchant, since their names appear on many of the papers, especially those which date from the period after Knapp's death. Many of the papers are arranged in folders and filed in alphabetical order by the name of the township; others are arranged by job number.

807 GOODWIN AND MILLARD FAMILIES. Papers, 1818–1880. 1 folder. Gift of Mrs. Perry Cragg, 1968. MS 3339.

A miscellaneous assortment of letters, memoranda, recipes, poetry, and teaching certificates relating to various members of these two families who resided in or near Huntsburg, Geauga County, Ohio. Of interest is a short journal kept by Emery Goodwin while traveling from New Hartford, Connecticut, to the Western Reserve, April 22–April 30, 1818, and while doing carpentry work in Warren, Ohio, June 15–November 21, 1818.

808 OLIVER H. PERRY MONUMENT COMMITTEE. CLEVELAND, O. Records, 1857–1860. ½ box. Gift of Mr. and Mrs. John F. Shepard, 1968. MS 3340.

Letters, resolutions, agreements, and other documents relating to the activities of this committee which resulted in the erection of a monument to Commodore Oliver H. Perry on September 10, 1860. The statue was located on Cleveland's Public Square. The letters, which are primarily replies from persons who were invited to attend the ceremonies, include several from survivors of the Battle of Lake Erie. Harvey Rice (chairman) and Alfred T. Goodman were active members of the committee.

809 HARVEY HUNTINGTON BROWN (1848–1923). Papers, 1879–1905. 4 boxes. MS 3342.

Letters addressed to Harvey H. Brown, Cleveland shipper, manufacturer, and financier, who was involved in the Lake Superior iron-ore business and in lake-vessel transportation. Brown and his father, Fayette Brown, organized Harvey H. Brown & Company, which until 1901 represented the Lake Superior Iron Ore Company and the Champion Iron Company. Brown's correspondents include numerous shippers, bankers, and manufacturers throughout the Midwest. Some of the letters also pertain to Brown's civic, charitable, and club activities.

810 ASA A. LAWRENCE (1835–1916). Papers, ca. 1855–1916. 2 boxes. MS 3343.

Correspondence, cashbooks, diaries, financial receipts, land surveys and deeds, and photographs relating to the activities of Asa A. Lawrence, soldier, merchant, and politician. While residing in Hannibal, Missouri, Lawrence enlisted in the 3rd Regiment, Missouri Cavalry, in 1861 and subsequently rose to the rank of captain in the 32nd Regiment, Missouri Volunteer Infantry. He also served in the 4th Regiment, Veterans Reserve Corps, and, after the war, was an officer in the Bureau of Refugees, Freedmen, and Abandoned Lands. Settling in St. Mary's County, Maryland, Lawrence was active in Republican politics during the 1870's and 1880's. These papers touch briefly on the aforementioned activities, but most of the material has to do with Lawrence's service during and immediately after the Civil War, including letters from Lawrence to his wife while in action with the 32nd Missouri.

811 ECHLIN P. GAYER. Genealogical Papers, ca. 1910–1950. 4 boxes, 1 package. MS 3344.

Primarily manuscript or typescript memoranda, letters, photocopies of documents, notebooks, and some printed material relating to the genealogy of the Gayer family and of related families such as Gorham and Phelps.

812 MAIL-STAGE WAY BILLS, ca. 1820–1839. 3 boxes. MS 3345.

Relating to various stagecoach stations in northeastern Ohio, including those in Fairport, Poland, and Warren.

813 HARRY C. OBERHOLSER (1870–1963). Papers, 1890–1960. 5 boxes. Gift of the Cleveland Zoo, 1968. MS 3346.

Correspondence, financial statements, research notes, biographical sketches, photographs, and other scattered papers touching upon the activities of Dr. Oberholser, ornithologist, who served in the Fish and Wildlife Service of the United States Department of the Interior (1895–1941) and was curator of ornithology at the Cleveland Museum of Natural History (1941–1947). The bulk of this collection consists of printed material relating to ornithology or to Dr. Oberholser, including copies of his published articles.

814 WILLIAM VAN SITTERT (d. 1930). Papers, 1910–1916. 3 boxes. MS 3347.

A corrected typescript copy (about 400 pages) of Van Sittert's unpublished "Bibliography of the Battle of Lake Erie and of the Principal Officers in the Action." Van Sittert, a salesman at Cleveland's Burrows Brothers Company bookstore, prepared several maps of the battle illustrating Commodore Oliver H. Perry's victory on September 10, 1813. Also included are several letters relating to the compilation of Van Sittert's bibliography, and one box of newspaper clippings containing reports on the centennial celebration of Perry's victory in 1913.

815 JOHN P. AGENBROAD (1822–1912). Papers, 1849–1904. 3 boxes. MS 3348.

The bulk of this collection consists of copies of sermons preached by Rev. John P. Agenbroad, who graduated from Granville College (1850) and Newton Theological Seminary (1853) and was ordained in Marietta, Ohio, in 1853. He subsequently served in Urbana, Troy, Akron, and Mount Washington, Ohio, and in Wisconsin, Illinois, and Indiana, before retiring in Dayton, Ohio, in 1884. Also included are several letters and commissions, 1849–1891.

816 C. G. KING COMPANY. CLEVELAND, O. Records, 1880's. 2 boxes. MS 3349.

Primarily correspondence and receipts relating to the supplying of building materials to firms within the city.

817 PARSONS FAMILY. Papers, 1860–1910. 2 boxes. MS 3351.

Personal and family papers of members of this family relating primarily to their activities as students at the Burton Academy during the 1860's and at Hiram College in the 1880's and 1890's. Specifically included are copybooks, report cards, tuition receipts, examination papers, compositions, booklets of poetry and autographs, and other mementos. Those represented here include Willie L., Emma, and Myrta Parsons. Of interest is a series of letters from Adelaide Gail Frost (b. 1868), a graduate of Hiram College, to Myrta Parsons, 1894–1900. During this period Miss Frost served as a missionary in Mahoba, N.W.P., India, where she supervised a girls' orphanage.

818   ADELAIDE RUDOLPH (1858–1953). Papers, 1885–1950. 2 boxes. Gift of the Cleveland Public Library. MS 3353.

Primarily personal and general letters addressed to Miss Adelaide Rudolph, a teacher and, for most of her career, librarian at Columbia University. After her retirement she worked on a history of Hiram, Ohio, at the Cleveland Public Library. Miss Rudolph, a niece of President and Mrs. James A. Garfield, corresponded with her cousins, including Abram, Harry A., Irvin McD., James R., and Mary Garfield. Also included are several letters from Joseph Rudolph (father of Adelaide) while serving with Company A, 23rd Regiment, Ohio Volunteer Infantry, during the Civil War, 1861; journal of Adelaide Rudolph, 1900–1907, 1928–1937; and genealogical data and an assortment of newspaper clippings relating to the Garfields and Rudolphs.

819   REUBEN F. SMITH. Papers, ca. 1900–1910. 1 box. MS 3354.

Correspondence, reports and minutes of meetings, speeches, newspaper clippings, and other papers relating to the Presbyterian Church in the United States. Smith, a Clevelander, was very active in the Presbytery of Cleveland, serving as chairman of the Committee on Systematic Beneficences for the Synod of Ohio. Correspondents include officers of the Board of Foreign Missions and the General Assembly and various Presbyterian ministers. Also included is an account of the history of Presbyterianism in the Western Reserve.

820   A. A. McCASLIN. Papers, 1900–1915. 1 box. MS 3355. Primarily financial receipts from Cleveland businesses.

821 KATHERINE B. JUDSON. Papers, ca. 1920's. 3 boxes. MS 3356.

Drafts of articles, notes, and copies of letters and documents used in her research on topics such as the Pacific Northwest and the exploration and settlement of America.

822 FIRST METHODIST-EPISCOPAL CHURCH. CLEVELAND, O. Records, 1900–1942. 4 boxes, 1 package. MS 3362.

Letters, pamphlets, photographs, memorials, addresses, resolutions, receipts, newspaper clippings, and other materials arranged in such a manner as to depict the "History of the First Methodist-Episcopal Church." Although most of this arrangement was undertaken by W. C. Talmadge in the first quarter of this century, much of the material deals with Methodism in Cleveland as far back as 1827, the date this church was organized. Also included are several periodicals containing articles about this church, a Methodist Hymnal, and other memorabilia.

823 BRITISH WAR RELIEF SOCIETY. CLEVELAND REGIONAL COMMITTEE. CLEVELAND, O. Scrapbooks, 1940–1942. 13 volumes, 1 package. Gift of Mrs. Harold T. Clark, 1949. MS 3363.

Primarily newspaper clippings relating to the activities of this committee which raised funds to aid refugee civilians in Britain and which supported the American Hospital (Oxford), the American Ambulance Service, and children's nursery homes in England. Also included are several leaflets, letters, and news bulletins of the local committee as well as of the national society.

824 CHARLES CANDEE BALDWIN (1834–1895). Papers, 1848–1912. 8 boxes. Gifts of Charles C. Baldwin; S. Prentiss Baldwin, 1919, 1930; Mrs. S. P. Baldwin, 1942. MS 3367.

Primarily letters, charts, memoranda, and other papers (relating to the histories of the Baldwin, Candee, and Kellogg families) collected by Baldwin, a prominent Cleveland lawyer, banker, and circuit judge, who served as President of the Western Reserve Historical Society (1886–1895). Also included are the following: a volume of records of land transactions in Ashtabula, Ohio, 1848–1855; two volumes concerning real estate holdings of Judge Baldwin in Cuyahoga County, but particularly in Cleveland, 1850–1900; speeches and writings on various topics relating to Ohio history, and notes on maps of North America and navigation in Lake Erie, 1890's; and some letters to Baldwin from persons such as Florence Harkness, Rutherford B. Hayes, Albert A. Wright, and G. Frederick Wright, 1892.

825 HENRY HOLCOMB (1830–1919). Papers, 1864–1919. 8 boxes. Gift of Henry Holcomb, 1910–1919. MS 3368. Primarily several series of autobiographical scrapbooks compiled by Holcomb after his retirement as a manufacturer of furnaces in Painesville, Ohio. The scrapbooks, compiled ca. 1895–1919, include newspaper clippings, letters and records and copies thereof, and photographs, as well as Holcomb's comments and revisions. Subjects referred to in these volumes include the history of the First Church (Congregational) of Painesville, 1810–1910; events relating to Holcomb's personal and family history, 1830–1864; and his experiences as a band musician in the 2nd Brigade, 3rd Division, 23rd Army Corps, 1864–1865, compiled from a series of pocket diaries and letters written by Holcomb during the Civil War.

Other scrapbooks deal with financial, economic, and political matters, such as the currency question and the trusts, 1896–1912; the campaign and election of 1896; state, national, and municipal reform, ca. 1900–1910; and Painesville city politics, 1900's.

826 ELEANOR (PAINTER) STRONG. Miscellany, ca. 1941. ½ box. Gift of the Rowfant Club, 1969. MS 3369. Typescript copy and galley proofs of *Spring Symphony* (New York and London: Harper and Brothers, 1941), a novel by Eleanor Painter.

827 CHARLES WADDELL CHESNUTT (1858–1932). Papers, 1891–1932. 2 boxes. Gift of the Rowfant Club, 1969. MS 3370.

Personal and business correspondence, typescript and manuscript copies of several speeches and short writings, newspaper clippings, invitations and programs, photographs, and other papers relating to Chesnutt's activities in Cleveland as a court reporter and as a novelist and short-story writer. The bulk of this collection consists of Chesnutt's correspondence with magazine and book publishers and editors, local and state political and civic leaders, representatives of various Negro welfare organizations (including the National Association for the Advancement of Colored People), and with business associates, 1921–1932. Chesnutt had extensive dealings during this period with the Houghton Mifflin Company and the Micheaux Film Corporation in regard to the publishing and to the securing of the motion-picture rights to his writings. Correspondents include Ernest Angell, Harry E. Davis, W. E. B. DuBois, and Walter White.

828 GEORGE P. METCALF (b. 1844). Unpublished Reminiscences, 1886. 235 pages (typescript copy). MS 3372.

These reminiscences include accounts of Metcalf's childhood on a farm in Liverpool, Medina County, Ohio, and of his student days in Oberlin, but primarily of his activities as a soldier in Company D, 136th Regiment, New York Volunteer Infantry, 1862–1865. A lawyer in Mississippi during part of 1869, Metcalf had a strong interest in the attitudes and actions of the residents of this state toward Reconstruction.

829 COMMERCIAL BANK OF LAKE ERIE. CLEVELAND, O. Records, 1816–1840. 6 volumes. Gifts of Truman P. Handy, 1877; Case Western Reserve University Archives, 1969. MS 3373.

Discount ledgers, daybooks, and letter book of Cleveland's first bank, organized in 1816, reorganized in 1832, and dissolved in

1845. It was incorporated by Seth Doan, Alfred Kelley, David Long, Erastus Miles, John H. Strong, Philo Taylor, George Wallace, and Samuel Williamson, with Alfred Kelley as president and Leonard Case as cashier.

830   GEORGE C. ENTRICAN. Account Books, 1824–1842. 3 volumes. MS 3377.

Entrican was a blacksmith in Geneva and Benton, New York, before moving to the Western Reserve and settling in Brecksville, Ohio, where he continued blacksmithing.

831   HARRY CONRAD GAHN (1880–1962). Scrapbooks, 1908–1930. 3 volumes. Gift of Mrs. Harry C. Gahn, 1969. MS 3380.

Primarily newspaper clippings relating to the political career of Gahn, a Republican who served as a Cleveland city councilman (1910–1921) and as a U.S. Representative from the 21st Ohio District (1921–1923), during which time he authored the Anti-Lynching Bill. Also included are some certificates and campaign literature.

832   DAVID OVIATT HUDSON (1814–1839). Notebook, 1834, 1836. 1 volume. Purchased, 1968. MS 3381.

Primarily copies of compositions on matters pertaining to philosophy prepared by Hudson while attending Western Reserve College in Hudson, Ohio, 1834. Also included are the comments of Hudson's teacher, Professor Clement Long.

833   GEORGE R. NOTT FAMILY. Papers, ca. 1870–1911. ½ box. Gift of Mrs. Pierre de Reeder, 1967. MS 3383.

Includes three notebooks and several letters of George R. Nott of New Haven, Connecticut, containing genealogical data on the Nott family, 1870's and 1880's; two unidentified notebooks of genealogical data, undated; and a journal kept irregularly by

Mrs. James W. Whitney (née Nott), 1894–1904, but primarily while on a visit to England, France, Germany, and other European countries, 1895–1896.

834 CYRUS H. STOCKWELL (d. 1864). Papers, 1862–1864. ½ box. Gift of Miss Rocena L. Stockwell, 1963. MS 3384.

Thirteen letters and three diaries kept by Stockwell from the time he enlisted in Company G, 77th Regiment, Illinois Volunteer Infantry, on September 1, 1862, until he was wounded during battle near New Orleans, Louisiana, in April, 1864. Stockwell spent some time on patrol boats in and around Louisiana and Texas.

835 CITIZENS LEAGUE OF GREATER CLEVELAND, O. Records, 1896–1968. 23 boxes. Deposited by the Citizens League of Greater Cleveland, 1969. MS 3385.

Some correspondence and several reports and pamphlets, but primarily candidate information questionnaires. The latter were filled out by individuals seeking public office (in municipal and county government) in Cleveland. Frequently included with the questionnaires are letters, memoranda, and newspaper clippings. The Municipal Association, organized in 1896, sought to encourage citizen interest in municipal affairs, disseminate information, promote honest and efficient government, and elect competent public officials. Known as the Civic League for a short time, the association was reorganized in 1923 as the Citizens League.

836 KEIM FAMILY. Papers, 1890–1918. ½ box. Gift of Evelyn O. Keim, 1969. MS 3386.

Assorted certificates and school books belonging to members of this Cleveland family.

837   SARAH MUMFORD GREGORY (1855–1950). Scrapbooks, ca. 1920–1950. 2 volumes. Gift of William R. Gregory, 1962. MS 3387.

Several letters, photographs, and newspaper clippings, including the "Memoirs" of Mrs. Gregory, which appeared in *The Independent* (Jonesville, Michigan) in 1949. She was the wife of Edgar B. Gregory, publisher and editor of *The Independent*, 1890–1930.

838   BERYL PEPPERCORN (1892–1969). Papers, 1924–1942, 1957–1958, 1969. 1 box, 1 package. Gift of Mrs. Beryl Peppercorn, 1969. MS 3388.

Some loose papers and pamphlets and a series of scrapbooks containing mostly printed materials relating to the activities of the Amalgamated Clothing Workers Union. Peppercorn was a Cleveland labor leader and served as manager of the Cleveland Joint Board, Amalgamated Clothing Workers Union (1922–1958). Included in these volumes are broadsides, pamphlets, programs, letters, newspaper clippings, and telegrams relative to organizing unions in various businesses in Cleveland and in several other cities in Ohio. The bulk of this material focuses on the period 1933–1940.

839   CARLOS PARSONS LYMAN (b. 1838). Papers, 1795–1915 (1861–1865). 1 box. Deposited, 1969. MS 3389.

Primarily letters and diaries of Carlos P. Lyman, written while he was serving as a private in the 6th Regiment, Ohio Volunteer Cavalry, and later as a captain in the 100th Regiment, U.S. Colored Infantry. The letters, addressed to various members of his family, 1861–1865, and the diaries, 1862–1865, provide a detailed record of his activities while at Camp Dennison and Camp Chase in Ohio (1861–1862), in Virginia and Washington, D.C. (1862–1864), and in Tennessee and Missouri (1864–1865). Also included in these writings are comments on camp conditions, marching and troop movements, and battles. Additional papers include an autobiographical sketch of Lyman, ca. 1905; a diary for 1859; and an assortment of agreement and land deeds, certificates, financial receipts, and newspaper clippings relating to Lyman or members of his family who resided in Mesopotamia, Ohio, 1795–1915.

840 *ASHTABULA SENTINEL.* ASHTABULA, O. Records, 1832–1833. 3 volumes. MS 3390.

Mail book, list of subscribers, and minutes of meetings of stockholders who organized the *Ashtabula Sentinel* as a weekly newspaper with Orramel H. Fitch as its first editor.

841 GILCHRIST TRANSPORTATION COMPANY. CLEVELAND, O. Records, 1892–1914. 1 box. Gift of Mrs. Richard E. Barnes, 1969. MS 3392.

Daily reports, agreements, account records, and miscellaneous reports and papers of the Gilchrist Transportation Company, a Cleveland-based shipping firm dealing primarily with the transportation of coal and ore on the Great Lakes during the early 1900's. Included are an account book relating primarily to banking and insurance matters, 1892–1901; three agreements involving the cities of Detroit and Cleveland and the Lake Carriers' Association of West Virginia, 1905–1906; and daily reports on all the vessels of the company, June–November, 1908.

842 CLEVELAND METROPOLITAN SERVICES COMMISSION. CLEVELAND, O. Records, 1957–1962. 8 boxes. Gift of the Citizens League of Greater Cleveland, 1969. MS 3395.

This fact-finding agency, organized in 1955, was a private institution formed through the cooperative efforts of political, business, labor, and civic leaders. METRO focused its attention on the services of local government and published the results of its studies.

843 WILLIAM WALLACE WHITTLESEY (1820–1890). Papers, 1830–1869. 3½ boxes. MS 3396.

Primarily letters addressed to William W. Whittlesey of Canfield, Ohio, from his parents, Elisha and Polly Whittlesey, and from his many brothers, sisters, and cousins. While most of the letters are of a personal or general nature, some do touch upon his activities as Eben Newton's law partner (1843–1847) and clerk of the Mahoning County Court of Common Pleas (1848–1868). In addition to much fatherly advice, the letters from Elisha Whittlesey (1783–1863) contain instructions relative to the handling of local business matters for most of this period during which Elisha and his wife resided in Washington, D.C.

844 W. BURR GONGWER (1873–1948). Papers, 1901–1948. 25 items. Gift of Mrs. William R. Barney, 1967. MS 3397.

Several letters, newspaper clippings, and a diary of W. Burr Gongwer, Cleveland Democratic leader who served as secretary to Tom L. Johnson, was an ally of Newton D. Baker, and became chairman of the Cuyahoga County Democratic Central Committee in 1924. The diary was kept by Gongwer while on a trip to Europe in the company of Newton D. Baker and Joseph C. Hostetler during May and June, 1914.

845 HERMON ALFRED KELLEY (1859–1925). Papers, ca. 1892–1921. 1 box. MS 3400.

Two scrapbooks containing memoranda, letters (some copies), newspaper clippings, and other material used by Kelley, a Cleveland attorney and businessman, in compiling *A Genealogical History of the Kelley Family Descended from Joseph Kelley of Norwich, Connecticut* (Cleveland, 1897). Also included are 40 letters from prominent people, saved by Kelley for their autographs.

846 ALTA SOCIAL SETTLEMENT. CLEVELAND, O. Records, 1895–1963. 7 boxes, 1 volume. Deposited by Alta Social Settlement, 1969. MS 3401.

Correspondence, treasurers' accounts, minutes, reports, photographs, and newspaper clippings relating to Alta Social Settlement, which grew out of the Cleveland Day Nursery and Free Kindergarten Association. This settlement was named after Alta Rockefeller when its building in the Italian neighborhood on Murray Hill was dedicated in 1900. John D. Rockefeller provided the financial support for Alta House until the Welfare Federation of Cleveland took it over in 1922. Specifically included here are files of correspondence and other business papers, 1895–1959; lists of objectives and statements of philosophy, 1930's; minutes of meetings of the board of trustees, frequently including annual reports of the headworker, 1937–1963; records pertaining to anniversary celebrations held in 1940, 1950, and 1960; and annual directors' reports, 1947–1959. This collection reflects a wide range of settlement-house activities as they changed over the years to meet the changing needs of the community it served. It also reflects the activities of a large number of Clevelanders who supported Alta House, in addition to members of the Rockefeller family who maintained an active interest in the settlement until 1954. Also touched upon are Alta House's relations with other settlements in Cleveland, as well as with various national settlement organizations.

847 CHARLES HEGINS (1766–1820). Papers, 1814–1822. ½ box. Gift of Mrs. Mina H. Gibson, 1969. MS 3402.

Letters, accounts, and receipts relating primarily to Hegins' activities as an army contractor during the War of 1812. Between 1814 and 1816 Hegins purchased food and other goods for regiments of the U.S. Army stationed in Pennsylvania, Ohio, and Michigan. During some of this period he was in partnership with E. Pentland and William Steele. A resident of Sunbury, Pennsylvania, Hegins spent much of his time in Pittsburgh, Erie, Detroit, and Washington, D.C. After June, 1816, Hegins continued to purchase supplies for troops in Pennsylvania. Deeply in debt by October, 1818, he had to have his personal property auctioned to settle his accounts. Many of the letters are from Hegins to his wife, Amelia Drum Hegins (1781–1825), and several papers dating after 1820 relate to the settling of his estate.

Also included here is an undated 16-page (typescript) sketch prepared by Mina S. Gibson of Charles Hegins and his family.

848   FRANCES ESMOND DURDIN LEWIS (1760–1834). Papers, 1763–1841. 2½ boxes. Gift of Mrs. Mina S. Gibson, 1969. MS 3403.

Letters, land deeds and agreements, financial receipts, estate papers, and other personal and family materials relating to Mrs. Frances E. D. Lewis, who resided in or near Philadelphia, Pennsylvania. Much of this collection deals with the relatives of Mrs. Lewis, who, for the most part, also resided in Pennsylvania.

849   SARAH LANMAN SMYTH (b. 1842). Diary, 1842–1857. 1 volume. Gift of the Rowfant Club, 1968. MS 3407.

This "diary" was kept for Sarah L. Smyth by her parents during the first 15 years of her life. During these years this family resided in New Haven and Milford, Connecticut, while Sarah's father, an ordained Baptist minister, traveled a great deal in New York, Ohio, and Michigan.

850   VIRGIL C. TAYLOR (b. 1838). Record Books, 1865, 1873–1905. 8 volumes, 1 folder. Gift of Dr. Alexander T. Bunts, 1967. MS 3408.

Account books containing a record of the financial activity of Virgil C. Taylor, Cleveland realtor, banker, and proprietor of V. C. Taylor & Son, a leading Cleveland real estate firm organized in 1872. Also included are financial statements, 1884–1891, and a record book of the Cherry Run Security Oil Company of Cleveland, which invested in land in Venango County, Pennsylvania, 1865.

851 BENJAMIN SUMMERS (b. 1801). Papers, 1838–1875. 6 volumes. MS 3409.

Including a journal kept by Summers, a farmer in Vermilion Township, Ohio, 1838–1867. Summers, who was active in Erie County politics, recorded in some detail his farming, business, and political activities, as well as the status of his farm and other land holdings, and his travels throughout the state. Also included are memoranda relating to his activities as a guardian, executor, or trustee of various estates, 1850–1870, and a journal for the year 1875.

852 MARION D. WARD. Letters, 1862–1865. 1 box. MS 3410.

Letters written by Ward while serving as sergeant in Company D, 102nd Regiment, Ohio Volunteer Infantry, and addressed to various friends, including Miss Artie M. Dickson of Olivesburgh, Richland County, Ohio. In the letters Ward, an anti-abolitionist, describes his general duties, drills, marches, and the lack of food and other aspects of camp life, as well as his own feelings about the war and its causes and the competence of the military leadership. Ward apparently saw little battle action with this regiment while stationed in Kentucky, Tennessee, and Alabama.

853 HUBERT HERRICK WARD. Papers, 1918–1944. 1 box. Gift of Annette P. Ward, 1946. MS 3411.

Scattered letters (some photostats), proposals, photographs, and newspaper clippings relating primarily to Ward's promotion of various business interests during the 1920's and 1930's. Most of this concerns the financing and development of the Portland Vegetable Oil Mills Company of Portland, Oregon, 1920–1921; plans for a proposed flax and linen industry in Oregon; and the Pacific Northwest, 1934–1936.

854 THOMAS, WHEELER, AND WHITE FAMILIES. Papers, 1832–1872. ½ box. MS 3412.

Several series of personal and general correspondence between members of these widely scattered families between 1832 and 1850. The correspondents, including Mary A. Roys, Isabella A. Thomas, Mary A. Thomas, Susan A. Thomas, Homer Wheeler, Maro Wheeler, Austin H. White, and Susan White, resided in Bristol, Indiana; Utica, New York; and Chagrin Falls and Willoughby, Ohio. Of this group, Susan A. Thomas was a student at Mount Holyoke Female Seminary during the early 1840's, and Homer Wheeler attended Indiana University, 1844–1845. Also included are Susan A. Thomas' notes on sermons preached at the seminary, 1841–1842; and two booklets containing an account of the wages paid farmhands in Fairfield, Ohio, 1862–1872.

855 DANIEL D. HOPPER. Papers, 1853–1883 (1861–1865). ½ box. MS 3413.

Primarily personal letters addressed to Lieutenant Daniel D. Hopper, Company F, 10th Regiment, Ohio Volunteer Cavalry, from his wife, Delina (Woodrow) Hopper, and from other relatives residing in Youngstown, Ohio.

856 ASA DEARBORN LORD (1816–1874). Papers, ca. 1840–1860. 1 folder. MS 3414.

Consisting of speeches and letters addressed to Dr. Lord, who served as principal of the Western Reserve Teachers' Seminary at Kirtland, Ohio (1839–1847), Superintendent of Public Schools in Columbus, Ohio (1848–1856), and director of the Institution for the Blind in Columbus (1856–1868). The papers touch on all of these activities as well as on Dr. Lord's editorship of various educational journals and his efforts in establishing teachers' institutes in Ohio. Correspondents include Ira Mayhew, John D. Philbrick, and Albert Picket, Sr.

857 DARIUS F. HUNSBERGER. Papers, 1864. 1 folder. MS 3415.
Mostly ordnance and quartermaster reports, circulars, general orders, letters, muster and payrolls, and other papers relating to the military activities of Captain Hunsberger and his unit, Company H, 164th Regiment, Ohio Volunteer Infantry.

858 EMMANUEL PROTESTANT EPISCOPAL CHURCH. CLEVELAND, O. Records, 1876–1889. 1 volume (copied from original, 1889). Purchased, 1969. MS 3417.
Articles of association (1876) and minutes of meetings, which include results of vestry elections, treasurers' reports, and resolutions.

859 HENRY E. PARSONS. Tax Book, 1824–1858. 1 volume. Gift of E. H. Fitch, 1965. MS 3418.
Record of the taxes paid by Parsons on land owned by Elijah and Nehemiah Hubbard and Samuel Mather in Ashtabula County, Ohio.

860 ELIJAH WHITTLESEY. Notebook, ca. 1853. 1 volume. Gift of Wallace H. Cathcart, 1892. MS 3419.
Containing biographical sketches of John Heckewelder, Eliphalet Austin, and Elijah Wadsworth, and some financial records, March 24–April 27, 1853.

861 LYMAN LITTLE. Papers, 1864. 1 folder. MS 3421.
Primarily correspondence concerning gold and silver mining in the Sierra Mining District, Humboldt County, Nevada Territory, between A. P. K. Safford and his attorney, Lyman Little of Cleveland, Ohio.

862   ERIE LAND COMPANY. Records, 1801. 33 items. MS 3422.

Lists of lands in the Western Reserve sold to various persons, including James Allyn, David S. Boardman, Peter C. Brooks, Moses Cleaveland, Daniel L. Coit, Solomon Griswold, William Hubbard, David Hudson, Daniel Lathrop, Samuel P. Lord, Roger Newberry, Ephraim Root, Ephraim Starr, and Frederick Wolcott.

863   MRS. M. S. FERGUSON. Correspondence, 1846–1861. 1 folder. Gift of Mrs. Julia P. Bailey. MS 3424.

Primarily letters received by Mrs. Ferguson of Ways Station, Bryan County, Georgia. Some are from her son, C. W. Ferguson, who served in the 8th Regiment, Georgia Volunteer Infantry, and was stationed at Manassas Junction, Virginia, in 1861.

864   R. F. HUMISTON. Scrapbook, 1866–1868. 1 volume. Gift of Clara J. Craft, 1915. MS 3426.

Primarily accounts of and newspaper clippings concerning the post-Civil War South, the American Missionary Association, and the Freedmen's Bureau.

865   GEORGE W. STANLEY. Docket Book, 1819–1841. 1 volume. Gift of Robert E. Mix. MS 3427.

Containing Middlesex County [Connecticut?] court dockets, 1819–1837; and Lucas, Cuyahoga, Ashtabula, and Lorain County (Ohio) dockets for Common Pleas courts, 1837–1841.

866   CLEVELAND HOSPITAL AID SOCIETY. CLEVELAND, O. Record Book, 1868–1878. 1 volume. MS 3428.

Constitution, minutes, and lists of members of this society-auxiliary (headed by Mrs. H. B. Tuttle) which sought to solicit funds and then purchase materials needed by the Cleveland City (Protestant) Hospital.

867   JAMES BACKUS. Field Notes, June–July, 1789. 3 volumes (106 [2] pp.). MS 3429.

Made while surveying in the 16th and 17th ranges located northwest of the Ohio River (part of the Northwest Territory).

868   IRA WRIGHT. Field Notes, 1804, 1806. 6 items. MS 3430.

Made while surveying land adjacent to the Portage Path, an Indian trail between the Cuyahoga and Tuscarawas rivers in Ohio. These booklets are signed and dated by Abraham Tappan.

869   EDWARD R. BLACKWELL. Field Notes, ca. 1807. 1 folder. MS 3431.

Made while surveying lots in Cleveland (township 6, range 12) and in other townships in the Western Reserve.

870   FREDERICK JOHN ROBINSON (1782–1859). Correspondence, 1832–1833. 7 items. MS 3432.

Correspondence between William IV of England and Frederick J. Robinson, Secretary of State for War and the Colonies, concerning disturbances in Jamaica relative to the proposed emancipation of slaves on that island.

871   JOSEPH BUELL. Papers, 1806–1811, 1836. 1 folder. MS 3433.

Correspondence concerning the Aaron Burr conspiracy and the seizure and confiscation of Burr's ships and property. Included are letters of General Buell, General Henry Dearborn, J. G. Jackson, Thomas Kirker, C. A. Rodney, and Edward Tiffin; a list of property taken from Harman Blennerhassett and names of men who carried the load, December 13, 1806; summons, June 27, 1807; "Interrogatories" concerning Aaron Burr, 1807; and miscellaneous undated notes on Aaron Burr's life, including pension records and a copy of a decree in the case of Eliza B. Burr v. Aaron Burr, July 8, 1836.

872   EAST END BAPTIST CHURCH. CLEVELAND, O. Records, 1902–1919. 1 folder. MS 3434.

Reports of the pastor, board of deacons, and treasurer, and specifications and contracts with the architectural firm of Maurer & Mills of Cleveland for the construction of a new building (1919).

873   FRANCIS M. LEONARD (b. 1816). Papers, 1831–1836, 1839, 1869. 6 items. MS 3435.

Journal recounting Leonard's experiences while attending religious meetings and social gatherings in towns throughout northeastern Ohio, especially in Geauga County, 1831–1836; copies of two speeches, 1833, 1839; and Leonard's appointment as postmaster of Thompson, Ohio, 1869.

874   WILLIAM HINZMANN. School Book, ca. 1860. 1 volume. Gift of J. A. Robinson, 1911. MS 3436.

Lessons copied by William Hinzmann while attending school in Germany. Hinzmann was residing in Cleveland at the time of his death.

875   HENRY E. BOURNE (1862–1946). Papers, 1896–1919, 1946. 1 folder. Gift of Henry E. Bourne, 1946. MS 3437.

Papers relating to the founding and activities of the Municipal Association of Cleveland (now the Citizens League of Greater Cleveland), for which Bourne, professor of history at Western Reserve University, acted as secretary during its first year, 1896. Included are letters from various board members, 1896–1917; reports and newspaper clippings, 1896–1919; and a 10-page autobiographical account, 1946.

876   SALTSPRING SUGAR ESTATE. HANOVER PARISH. COLONY OF JAMAICA. Records, 1832–1835. 13 items. MS 3438.

Counterclaims, rules, and other papers pertaining to the treatment of slaves on this plantation.

877   MATTHEW BIRCHARD FAMILY. Papers, 1761–1879. 1 folder. Gift of the Estate of Matthew Birchard, 1918. MS 3439.

Land contracts, deeds, and other papers relating to the Matthew Birchard family of Becket, Massachusetts Bay Colony, 1761–1776; will of Matthew Birchard, 1783; receipts from W. A. Birchard, Warren, Ohio, dealer in Mineral Ridge and Brier Hill Coal and Slack, 1866–1867; and notes on the genealogy of the Birchard family.

878   BENJAMIN F. STICKNEY. Papers, 1788, 1798–1830. 1 folder. Gift of Charles E. Bliven, 1892. MS 3450.

Primarily correspondence of Stickney, who was at various times a resident of New Hampshire; Fort Wayne, Indiana; and then Toledo, Ohio. He served as postmaster and agent for Indian affairs northwest of the Ohio River, Port Lawrence, Michigan Territory. Papers include a copy of the proceedings of the Fourth of July (1788) celebration in Marietta, Ohio; and a copy of a declaration by William Henry Harrison, Governor of the Indiana Territory, addressed to members of the Delaware Tribe, May 4, 1812. Correspondents include Lewis Bond, J. L. Comstock, Paul Hamilton (Secretary of the Navy), Henry Hart, Samuel Mitchell, Thomas Paine, Anthony Shane, Amos Spafford, Caleb Stark, and Two Stickney.

879   MORTIMER D. LEGGETT (1821–1896). Papers, 1887. 1 folder. MS 3451.

Some correspondence with Captain W. R. Hodges and General George F. McGinnis concerning events at Vicksburg and Shiloh, 1887; typed articles "General Lewis Wallace's Division at Shiloh" (18 pages), "Lessons of the War" (19 pages), and "The Siege of Vicksburg" (3 pages).

880   WILLIAM H. DOAN. Papers, 1815–1897. 1 folder. Gift of I. T. Frary. MS 3452.

Estate agreement, 1815; deeds to land in Cleveland, 1820, 1831; and assorted business and financial papers of William H. Doan, in partnership with George N. Chase in refining carbon oil, naphtha, and gasoline in Cleveland, 1868–1897. These papers include leases to Doan and Chase from Standard Oil of Ohio and receipts from John D. Rockefeller, 1872–1876.

881 J. T. JOHNSTON. Papers, 1841–1881. 1 folder. MS 3453.

Johnston, a resident of Gustavus, Ohio, accumulated material concerning the murder of Frances M. Buel by her stepfather, Ira W. Gardner. Included is a copy of the sermon delivered at Frances Buel's funeral, newspaper clippings, poems and eulogies, and notes on the lineage of Ira W. Gardner.

882 AURELIA HAYDEN. Correspondence, 1832–1841. 1 folder. MS 3454.

Letters from her brother, C. Hayden, of Dayton, Ohio, who was a teacher and whiskey inspector for Madison County. Hayden writes about local politics, architecture, business, Universalism, and Harwinton, Connecticut, the home of Aurelia Hayden.

883 OHIO MILITIA. 20TH DIVISION. Records, 1841–1848. 1 folder. Gift of Mr. Crane, 1920. MS 3455.

Receipts, invoices, contracts, and letters from various officers of this division, primarily concerning the cost and repair of public arms. Major General John Crowell was commander of this division stationed in Warren, Ohio.

884 OHIO VOLUNTEER INFANTRY. 187TH REGIMENT. Records, 1865–1866. 14 items. MS 3456.

Volunteer description lists of and accounts of pay and clothing of Company A.

885   HENRY J. FAUDEL. Papers, 1896–1899, 1910, 1916. 1 folder. Gift of Henry J. Faudel, ca. 1917. MS 3457.

Letters, telegrams, statements, bids, and drawings pertaining to the Brecksville Road Improvement, 1897–1899. Also included is a 9-page (typescript) history of Cuyahoga County Road Improvement from 1889 to 1910 written by Faudel, who resided in Independence, Ohio.

886   ANONYMOUS. Notebook, ca. 1797. 1 volume. Gift of John Andrews, 1951. MS 3458.

An Indian vocabulary list, dated: Sandusky, April 19, 1797.

887   ENOCH GREGORY FAMILY. Papers, 1806–1948. 1 folder. Gift of William M. Gregory. MS 3459.

Primarily land deeds, agreements, letters, and financial receipts of Enoch Gregory of Queensbury, Warren County, New York, 1806–1860.

888   ELIJAH WARD. Papers, 1792–1832. 18 items. MS 3460.

Deeds to tracts of land in Hampshire County, Massachusetts, 1792–1808; in Chagrin Township, Cuyahoga County, Ohio, 1823; and in Mentor Township, Geauga County, Ohio, 1830; and appointments and certificates of Elijah Ward, an elder and deacon in the Methodist-Episcopal Church in Steubenville, Ohio.

889   PARMELEE FAMILY. Papers, 1831–1915. 1 folder. MS 3461.

Receipts and lists of taxes paid by this family from Twinsburg, Ohio.

890   MORRIS I. HOLLY. Letters, 1861–1862. 1 folder. MS 3462.

Letters written by Sergeant Holly to his family while he was serving in Company A, 7th Regiment, Ohio Volunteer Infantry.

891 CLEVELAND JUNTO. CLEVELAND, O. Records, 1858–1861. 1 volume. MS 3463.

Constitution, bylaws, and minutes of meetings of this society, whose members sought to improve themselves "in the arts of reasoning, composition and oratory and also to acquire a Knowledge of the proper manner of conducting deliberative assemblies."

892 HEZEKIAH HINE. Papers, 1817–1869. 1 folder. MS 3464.

Land deeds and agreements, post office account, and other papers of Hine, resident of Shalersville, Portage County, Ohio.

893 RENSELEAR RUSSELL HALL. Papers, 1909, 1917–1918. 1 folder. MS 3465.

Mostly concerning Hall's service in the U.S. Army during World War I.

894 MESSRS. CHARLES H. SEYMOUR & COMPANY. NEW YORK, N.Y. Letters, 1856–1857. 1 folder. MS 3466.

Business letters received by this importing firm, including letters from Winslow Bros., J. R. & W. P. Lee, P. & J. P. Hawes & Company, and Hirsch & Andrews, all of Boston, Massachusetts.

895 GEORGE WASHINGTON BOWEN (1838–1908). Notebook, 1851–1852. 1 volume. Gift of Michigan Historical Collections, 1949. MS 3467.

Bowen, who kept this notebook while attending the Cleveland Institute of Homeopathy, served in the 5th U.S. Colored Cavalry, 1864, and later practiced medicine in Fort Wayne, Indiana.

896   NEW YORK, CHICAGO AND ST. LOUIS RAILROAD COMPANY. McCOMB, O. Records, 1894–1895. 1 volume. MS 3468.
Train register maintained by an agent at McComb.

897   THEODORE ELIJAH BURTON (1851–1929). Papers (Series I), * 1876–1928. 39 boxes. MS 3469.
Personal and political correspondence, speeches and articles, interview notes, biographical data, campaign material, and other papers relating to Theodore E. Burton's wide range of interests and activities as a Cleveland lawyer, U.S. Representative (1889–1891, 1895–1909, 1921–1928), U.S. Senator (1909–1915, 1928–1929), author, lecturer, world traveler, banker, and member of various national and international commissions. In addition to being chairman of the House Rivers and Harbors Committee, 1898–1909, Burton was also active in the Interparliamentary Union, 1904–1927; Republican National Conventions, 1904–1924; Inland Waterways Commission, 1907–1908; National Monetary Commission, 1908–1912; National Waterways Commission, 1908–1912; American Peace Society, 1911–1928; and World War Debt Funding Commission, 1922–1927. This collection contains much material relating to most of this country's foreign and domestic problems, especially those relating to economics, monetary and banking matters, the development of harbors and waterways, immigration policy, tariffs, and the world peace and disarmament movements. Burton's correspondence, dating between 1896 and 1916 and comprising over two-thirds of this collection, relates to the following domestic issues: judicial reform, veterans' pension claims, patent legislation, anti-trust legislation, shipping subsidies, labor laws, postal savings and one-cent postage, naval appropriations, Indian policy, railroad legislation, prohibition, disarmament, and pure-food legislation; and to U.S. policy toward Cuba, Nicaragua (canal), Panama (canal), Puerto Rico, and the Philippines. A substantial amount of material relates to Ohio and Cleveland politics, specifically to local patronage and election campaigns; construction of Cleveland's Federal Build-

ing, 1904; the 1907 mayoral campaign, which resulted in Burton's defeat by Tom L. Johnson; and the Ohio flood disaster, 1913. Also included are research notes used by Burton in preparing *Financial Crises and Periods of Industrial and Commercial Depression* (New York: D. Appleton and Company, 1902) and his biography, *John Sherman* (Boston and New York: Houghton Mifflin Company, 1906); papers reflecting his lifelong association with Oberlin College, from which he graduated in 1873. Notable correspondents include Charles F. Adams, Nelson W. Aldrich, Newton D. Baker, Richard Bartholdt, Samuel F. Bemis, Albert J. Beveridge, Charles J. Bonaparte, Charles F. Brush, Nicholas M. Butler, Joseph G. Cannon, Andrew Carnegie, Fred W. Carpenter, George B. Cortelyou, James M. Cox, Harry M. Daugherty, Charles G. Dawes, George Dewey, Charles Dick, William A. Dunning, Stuyvesant Fish, Joseph B. Foraker, John W. Foster, Felix Frankfurter, James R. Garfield, Lindley M. Garrison, Elbert H. Gary, Washington Gladden, Samuel Gompers, William C. Gorgas, Marcus A. Hanna, Andrew L. Harris, John Hay, Myron T. Herrick, Frank H. Hitchcock, Hamilton Holt, L. Paul Howland, Charles E. Hughes, Tom L. Johnson, Frank B. Kellogg, Henry C. King, Philander Knox, Robert Lansing, Henry C. Lodge, William Loeb, Jr., John D. Long, Nicholas Longworth, Maurice Maschke, Samuel Mather, Medill McCormick, Robert E. McKisson, William H. Moody, George K. Nash, Thomas N. Page, Gifford Pinchot, James F. Rhodes, Cecil S. Rice, Theodore Roosevelt, Elihu Root, Edward W. Scripps, Leslie M. Shaw, James S. Sherman, Henry L. Stimson, Willard D. Straight, Mark Sullivan, William H. Taft, Henry M. Teller, Charles F. Thwing, Benjamin F. Trueblood, Joseph P. Tumulty, John W. Weeks, George W. Wickersham, Frank B. Willis, and Leonard Wood.

Unpublished 46-page register available in the Society.
NUCMC 62-4384

* See also the following Series II and III.

898   THEODORE ELIJAH BURTON (1851-1929). Papers (Series II),* 1870-1916. 84 boxes, 41 volumes. MS 3469a.

Additional papers of Theodore E. Burton including correspondence, letter books, notebooks, speeches and articles, campaign material, and newspaper clippings relating to Burton's political and congressional activities as well as to his personal life. Burton's correspondence comprises two-thirds of this collection and parallels the subject matter of Series I. Among the non-correspondence is much material relating to two of Burton's books, *Financial Crises and Periods of Industrial and Commercial Depression* and *John Sherman;* and 23 boxes and 41 volumes of newspaper clippings, 1875-1916.

Unpublished 21-page register available in the Society.

* This collection was discovered after Series I had been arranged and catalogued.

899   THEODORE ELIJAH BURTON (1851-1929). Papers (Series III),* 1870-1958. 32 boxes, 3 oversize packages. Gift of the Oberlin College Library, 1968. MS 3469b.

Additional papers of Theodore E. Burton, including correspondence, speeches and articles, diaries and journals, biographical data, land deeds and business papers, and scrapbooks primarily of newspaper clippings relating to his activities. Specifically included are a broken series of daily diaries and travel journals, 1875-1929; correspondence, 1885-1929; 22 scrapbooks dealing with subjects such as congressional campaigns, general political matters, the Republican National Convention (1924), Burton's speeches, the Ohio primary election of 1928, American Peace Society (1928), and letters and obituaries relating to Burton's death, 1929; and non-correspondence including material relating to the peace movement and background material used by Burton in preparing the several books he authored. Also part of this collection is a quantity of manuscript writings and galley proofs of Forrest Crissey (d. 1943), author of *Theodore E. Bur-*

ton: American Statesman (1956), and correspondence of Grace Burton, niece and lifelong confidante of Theodore E. Burton, 1903–1958.

* This collection was received after Series I and II had been arranged and catalogued.

900 JONATHAN GOLDSMITH. Papers, 1804–1858. 2 volumes (typescript copies of originals in the possession of Carl H. Johnson). Gift of Elizabeth G. Hitchcock, 1963. MS 3472.

Deeds, letters, and agreements, 1804–1858, and an account book, 1836–1838, of Jonathan Goldsmith of Painesville, Ohio, a master architect and builder of homes in the Western Reserve.

901 U.S. ARMY. AMERICAN EXPEDITIONARY FORCES. BASE HOSPITAL NO. 4. Reunion Records, 1919–1961. 2 volumes. Gift of H. D. Piercy, 1947, 1964. MS 3473.

A history and roster of Base Hospital No. 4 (the Lakeside Unit) by George W. Crile, letters, copies of speeches delivered at anniversary celebrations, minutes of the officers' meetings, and other records accumulated by Dr . H. D. Piercy, keeper of the archives of the Lakeside Unit of Cleveland, Ohio.

902 EARLY SETTLERS' ASSOCIATION OF THE WESTERN RESERVE. CLEVELAND, O. Records, 1960–1966. 2 loose-leaf notebooks. Gift of the Early Settlers' Association, 1962 and later. MS 3474.

Primarily biographical and genealogical information relating to members of this association.

903 ADAM M. BEERS (1840–1912). Papers, 1863–1865. ½ box. Gift of Bernard B. Bowling, 1970. MS 3476.

Primarily official papers relating to the activities of Dr. Adam M. Beers, who served as assistant surgeon in the 9th and 92nd Regiments, Ohio Volunteer Infantry, during the period from 1863 to 1865. Specifically included are military orders, circulars and letters, requisitions, receipts, lists of camp and garrison equipment, monthly reports of sick and wounded, and returns of medical and hospital property.

904   CHARLES P. SALEN (1860–1924). Papers, ca. 1890–1920. ½ box, 2 volumes. Gift of Mrs. David Lowensohn, 1969. MS 3478.

Primarily newspaper clippings, campaign and election material, and photographs relating to Charles P. Salen and to other members of his family. Salen, an associate of Mayor Tom L. Johnson, held several positions in both municipal and county government, including Secretary of the Board of Elections, Director of Public Works, and County Clerk. Also included here is a copy of an unpublished record of the branch of the Salen family which was founded by Peter Salen (1810–1895).

905   ROBERT A. MANRY (1918–1971). Papers, June 1–August 17, 1965. ½ box. Gift of Robert A. Manry, 1967. MS 3479.

Logbook, notebook of sextant sightings, charts, several letters, and notes relating to Manry's 78-day crossing of the Atlantic Ocean from Falmouth, Massachusetts, to Falmouth, England, in the *Tinkerbelle*, a 13½-foot sloop.

906   WILLIAM J. RADDATZ (1880–1940). Scrapbooks, 1904–1940. 4 volumes. Gift of Leslie Raddatz, 1970. MS 3480.

Newspaper clippings, pamphlets, magazine articles, photographs, programs, and some letters touching upon the career of William J. Raddatz, a Cleveland advertising and printing executive. President of the Cleveland Advertising Club (1916–1917) and of the Stratford Press, Raddatz was active in many civic and charitable enterprises. In addition he was author of several works on William Shakespeare.

907 FRANK B. STEARNS (1879–1955). Diary, 1915. 1 volume. Gift of John C. Lanphear, 1970. MS 3481.

Scattered and generally brief comments relating to the designing, testing, manufacturing, and selling of Stearns-Knight automobiles. Stearns, a pioneering automobile manufacturer in Cleveland, headed the F. B. Stearns Company, which produced the gasoline-powered Stearns-Knight until 1925, when the company was taken over by the Willys Company of Toledo.

908 AMERICAN PEACE SOCIETY. CLEVELAND (O.) BRANCH. Records, 1913–1919. 1 folder. Gift of the Case Western Reserve University Archives, 1970. MS 3482.

Letters, financial receipts and reports, lists of members, and other scattered records kept by the secretary of this branch, Emma M. Perkins. Members included Newton D. Baker, Theodore E. Burton, and Charles F. Thwing.

909 WADE PARK COMMITTEE. CLEVELAND, O. Records, 1926–1927. 1 folder. Gift of the Case Western Reserve University Archives, 1970. MS 3483.

Correspondence, proposals, minutes of meetings, copies of agreements, and other records relating to residential restrictions in the Wade Park Allotment on Cleveland's east side. In general this material concerns the efforts of local residents to prevent non-Caucasians from buying, occupying, or using any property in this area, which included Bellflower and East Boulevards and Hazel, Magnolia, and Mistletoe Drives.

910 EUCLID INNERBELT ASSOCIATION. CLEVELAND, D. Records, 1961–1968. 5½ boxes. Gift of Thomas J. Miller, 1970. MS 3484.

Code of regulations, minutes of meetings, correspondence, progress reports, bills and invoices, budgets, financial statements, photographs, maps, newspaper clippings, pamphlets, and other records of this association, which was incorporated in 1966 for the purpose of assisting charitable, religious, or educational institutions in acquiring property located in or near the Euclid Innerbelt area and preparing reports and recommendations for the development of this area. This collection consists of the files of Thomas J. Miller, who served as executive director of this association. Specifically included are minutes of member meetings, 1961–1966, and minutes of trustee meetings, 1966–1968; correspondence files of the executive director, 1961–1968; reports on collecting basic inventory data, 1961, and on the evaluation of real estate tax, 1964; and lists of the property and property owners in the area, including the names of owner and tenant and tax valuation. Among the institutions involved with this association were Cleveland State University, Young Men's Christian Association of Cleveland, Episcopal Diocese of Ohio, Cleveland Automobile Club, and Young Women's Christian Association of Cleveland. This collection reflects the Association's special concern with the development of Fenn College (now Cleveland State University).

911 EUCLID INNERBELT ASSOCIATION. CLEVELAND, O. Records, 1960–1966. 1½ boxes. Gift of Edward Bartlett, 1970. MS 3484a.

This collection consists of the files of Edward Bartlett, chairman of the Euclid Innerbelt Association. Included are copies of articles of association, 1960; minutes of trustee meetings and correspondence, 1960–1966; financial reports, 1961, 1963, 1965; and an assortment of reports, memoranda, news releases, and public statements.

Also included here is one folder of papers relating to the Near West Side Development Association.

912 QUINCY A. CASE FAMILY. Diaries, 1864–1871, 1903. 9 volumes. Gift of Mrs. Robert R. Eastman, 1964. MS 3485.

Diaries kept by Quincy A. Case and several unidentified members of the Case family of Kingsville, Ashtabula County, Ohio.

The diaries in general contain only random notes on daily activities and some genealogical data. The three diaries of Quincy A. Case (b. 1848) cover the period from 1868 to 1871 and contain references to his work in a planing mill.

913   GEORGE ARMSTRONG GARRETSON (1844–1916). Papers, ca. 1897–1916. 3 boxes. Gift of the Estate of George E. Garretson, 1970. MS 3486.

Correspondence, military orders, speeches, newspaper clippings, and other materials relating primarily to the military activities of George A. Garretson during the Spanish-American War. Garretson was appointed Brigadier General of Volunteers in May, 1898, then served as commander of the 2nd Brigade, 1st Division, 2nd Army Corps, until being relieved of duty on November 30, 1898. General Garretson also commanded the 1st Brigade, Provisional Division, which participated in the engagements at Guanica and Yauco, Porto Rico, during July and August, 1898. The military papers include letters, telegrams, special and general orders, a scrapbook of newspaper clippings, and several accounts of the military service of General Garretson, 1897–1903 (May 25–December 17, 1898).

General Garretson served as president of Cleveland's National Bank of Commerce (1890–1916). The papers relating to his business and personal activities include subscription lists and letters concerning the reorganization of Cleveland's Union Club in 1901, and three letter books, 1910–1916.

914   CHARLOTTE S. LEWIS. Diaries, 1870–1891. 16 volumes. Gift of Bessie Lewis. MS 3487.

These diaries contain daily entries reflecting Miss Lewis' household activities while residing in Hudson, Ohio. Most of the volumes contain some financial accounts as well as dates of births, marriages, and deaths of relatives and friends living in or near Hudson.

Also included here is one diary of Wilbert W. Lewis of Hudson for the year 1875, during which Mr. Lewis was employed as a farmhand.

915 WILLIAM ROBERTSON & SONS. UTICA, LICKING COUNTY, O. Records, 1831–1833, 1838–1840, 1845–1849. 5 volumes. MS 3488.

William Robertson (1786–1840) was a wool carder and mill owner in Utica. These ledgers relate primarily to the operation of his business, which was continued by his sons after his death.

Also included here is an account book of Salathiel Chapman (a relative of William Robertson) of Simsbury, Connecticut, 1810–1812.

916 WHEELOCK & OSBORN. BEDFORD, O. Records, 1857–1862. 4 volumes. Gift of H. W. Van Patter, 1967. MS 3489.

Journal, 1857–1859; daybooks, 1859–1860; and one volume of mounted receipts of Wheelock & Osborn, merchants located in Bedford. After 1861, the company operated under the name of Osborn & Hammond.

917 U.S. WAR DEPARTMENT. Intelligence Reports, 1917–1921. 18 volumes. Gift of the Estate of Newton D. Baker, 1960. MS 3490.

The first series of volumes (I–VIII) contains weekly intelligence summaries prepared by Captain W. K. Wallace. The summaries consist of dispatches relating to the progress of World War I and were prepared for the information of the Secretary of War (Newton D. Baker) and Chief of Staff. According to the foreword in the first volume, "The chief sources of information are the Commander-in-Chief, American Expeditionary Forces, our Military Attachés, Liaison Officers with Foreign Armies, State and Navy Department, Allied Governments, Persons on Special Mission, and Confidential Agents." These volumes cover the period from June 2, 1917, to October 5, 1918.

The second series of volumes (VI–XV) is entitled *The European War, Weekly Intelligence Summary,* [by] Military Intelligence Division, General Staff, War Department (Washington, D.C.: Government Printing Office, 1919–1921). These ten volumes contain the summaries prepared from October 12, 1918 until February 26, 1921.

918   NEWTON DIEHL BAKER (1871–1937). Letters, 1891, 1897, 1902–1904, 1906, 1915–1937. 2½ boxes (some copies). Deposited by Hazel P. Hostetler, 1970. MS 3491.

Primarily letters and, in some cases, typescript copies of letters from Newton D. Baker to his relatives. The main series consist of 211 letters from Baker to his wife, Elizabeth L. Baker, 1902–1937 (scattered); 44 letters from Baker to his brother, Frank H. Baker, and the latter's wife, Harriet Lamon Baker, 1915–1936; and typescript copies (bound in three volumes) of Baker's letters to his children, Elizabeth, Margaret, and Newton D. Baker III, 1918–1937. Also included are 32 items of correspondence with notable political figures, 1891–1937. Although these letters are largely personal in nature, they do contain Baker's comments on his political and business activities, particularly while he was a public official for the City of Cleveland and Secretary of War. They also contain references to people (e.g., Tom L. Johnson and Woodrow Wilson) with whom he came in contact and events (e.g., World War I) with which he was involved. Subjects referred to include the League of Nations, woman suffrage, Prohibition, the New Deal, presidential elections, and, in general, most of the major political issues of Baker's time.

919   HENDRICK E. PAINE FAMILY. Papers, 1788–1941 (1806–1890). 8 boxes, 7 oversize volumes. Gift of Mrs. Karen Henderson, 1970. MS 3492.

Account books, financial papers, land deeds and agreements, estate papers and other legal documents, letters, a diary, newspaper clippings, and genealogical data relating to various mem–

bers of the Paine family of Lake County, Ohio. The bulk of this collection focuses on the activities of Hendrick E. Paine (1789–1881), whose family settled in Painesville in 1803. In 1818 Hendrick E. Paine moved to Leroy Township, where he served in the capacity of township trustee and justice of the peace. Also referred to are Eleazar Paine (d. 1804), Charles C. Paine (d. 1838), and Henry Paine (1810–1868). This material consists largely of general, business, and personal papers, with emphasis on land ownership and development and farming. The following are the main series of papers: deeds to land in Connecticut as well as in the Western Reserve, 1788–1854; an account book of Eleazar Paine and Hendrick E. Paine, 1788–1812, and 33 account books, booklets, and indexes of Hendrick E. Paine, 1815–1869; numerous financial accounts, statements and receipts, mostly of Hendrick E. Paine, 1829–1854; tax receipts, 1830–1870; two docket books, summonses and writs of Henry Paine as justice of the peace, ca. 1840–1865; eight volumes of Leroy Township school-district record books and school registers, 1876–1897; and letters, documents, and memoranda of Mary D. Kewish containing genealogical data on the following families: Barnes, Clague, Ellsworth, Hobart, Loomis, Mills, Paine, Phelps, and Tuttle, ca. 1880–1941.

920   INDEPENDENT ORDER OF GOOD TEMPLARS. COLLINWOOD LODGE NO. 13. CLEVELAND, O. Records, 1880–1889. 3 volumes. Gift of Dr. William H. Harrison, 1950. MS 3493.

Constitution, bylaws, lists of members, minutes of meetings, and financial accounts of this lodge whose members united in the cause of temperance.

921   LAKE SHORE CRUDE OIL TRANSPORTATION COMPANY. CLEVELAND, O. Records, 1870–1871. 1 volume. Gift of Douglas Schofield, 1945. MS 3494.

A statistical account of the number of railroad cars and the number of gallons of oil transported by this company for its customers, including Standard Oil Company, Critchley, Fawcett & Company, Hussey, Payne & Company, and Joseph Stanley.

922 PARKS FOSTER. Vessel Book, 1899. 1 volume. Gift of the Cleveland Natural Science Museum, 1949. MS 3495.

Names of crew members and their job titles and wages, as well as a record of the receipts and disbursements of this steamer, which worked on the Great Lakes under the command of Captain E. J. Burke. Its cargoes consisted of coal and ore.

923 IRA H. OWEN. Vessel Book, 1899. 1 volume. Gift of the Cleveland Natural Science Museum, 1949. MS 3496.

Names of crew members and their job titles and wages, as well as a record of the receipts and disbursements of this steamer which worked on the Great Lakes under the command of Captain D. J. Duncanson. Its cargoes consisted of cord, wheat, coal, and ore.

924 SAMUEL HUNTINGTON (1765–1817). Letters, 1801–1817. 148 items. MS 3497.

Letters addressed to Huntington, who lived in the Western Reserve from 1800 until his death. These letters date during the periods that Huntington served as Ohio State Senator, Supreme Court Justice, Governor (1808–1810), and Representative. Subjects touched upon include state politics and elections, land transactions, and the War of 1812. Correspondents, many of whom are connected with the early settlement and development of the Western Reserve, as well as of the state of Ohio, include Henry Champion, Moses Cleaveland, Gideon Granger, Stanley Griswold, Return J. Meigs, Jeremiah Morrow, Calvin Pease, John Smith, Amos Spafford, Edward Tiffin, George Tod, Elisha Tracy, Elijah Wadsworth, and Thomas Worthington.

925 WISCONSIN MILITIA. MINERAL POINT GUARDS. Records, 1846–1848. 1 volume. Purchased, 1927. MS 3498.

Proceedings of organization, constitution, bylaws, minutes, and roll-call reports of this volunteer company of light artillery made up of citizens of Iowa County in the Wisconsin Territory. The Mineral Point Guards were organized on March 23, 1846. This volume deals primarily with their organizational scheme, regulations, drills, elections of officers, and resignations.

926 AMBROSE SWASEY (1846–1939). Letters, 1931. 157 items (bound in one volume). Gift of Mrs. Warren J. Henderson, 1944. MS 3499.

Letters of congratulation addressed to Swasey, Cleveland engineer and business leader, on the 85th anniversary of his birth. Included are messages from leading business and political leaders throughout the United States.

927 U.S. ARMY. 18TH CORPS. Order Book, April 22–December 1, 1864. 1 volume. MS 3500.

Copies of general and special brigade orders issued for the 2nd Brigade, 1st Division, 18th Army Corps, while under the commands of Brigadier General Hiram Burnham, Colonel E. M. Cullen, Colonel William L. Schley, Lieutenant Colonel S. Moffitt, and others. The 18th Corps was deactivated on December 3, 1864.

Also included in this volume are copies of several general and special orders issued by the commanding officers of the 2nd Brigade, 3rd Division, 24th Army Corps, January 1–April 19, 1865.

928 MARYLAND ARTILLERY. BALTIMORE BATTERY. Records, 1862–1863. 1 volume. MS 3501.

Post-guard reports from various Confederate prison camps in Maryland and Virginia which were under the jurisdiction of the Baltimore Battery of Light Artillery. These daily reports consist of names of guards and lists of prisoners, their charges, sentences, and other remarks.

929 JOHN S. ELLEN. Journal, 1861–1864. 1 volume. Gift of Mrs. Bert Crawford, 1952. MS 3502.

Ellen, a resident of Painesville, Ohio, served in the 23rd Regiment, Ohio Volunteer Infantry, from 1861 until he was discharged with the rank of first lieutenant on November 30, 1864. The intermittent entries, though generally brief, do include occasional comments on marches and troop movements, battles and skirmishes with Confederate forces, and the Union's military and political leadership. Also included in this volume are Ellen's notes relating to the study of law.

930 GOODRICH SOCIAL SETTLEMENT. CLEVELAND, O. Records, 1897–1960. 10 boxes. Gift of the Goodrich Social Settlement, 1970. MS 3505.

Correspondence, minutes of meetings, annual reports, pamphlets, news sheets, manuals, anniversary publications, registration forms and financial records, and unpublished histories of this settlement house which was organized on Cleveland's east side in 1897. It was founded by Flora Stone Mather (1852–1909), who was largely responsible for the Settlement's finances until it began to receive support from the Community Chest in 1920. During its early history Goodrich House worked with the Consumers League, the Legal Aid Society, the Music Settlement, the Society for the Blind, Sunbeam School, and the Home Gardening Association. The records reflect these relationships, as well as those with the various people it served, including the German and Irish residents, who were replaced by eastern Europan immigrants and, more recently, by Appalachian whites and southern Negroes. Goodrich House's activities included social clubs, crafts program, adult education, day nurseries, and camps. Among those associated with Goodrich House were Newton D. Baker, Henry E. Bourne, Starr Cadwallader, Alice P. Gannett, and Frederick C. Howe. Of special interest are the letters of

Flora Stone Mather, 1893–1909; the comprehensive minutes of the board of trustees and the executive committee, 1903–1959; "The Goodrich Herald," 1951–1959; and the material relating to the Settlement's camp program, 1947–1960.

Unpublished 7-page register available in the Society.

931   INDIANA. MORGAN RAID COMMISSION. Journal, April 4–October 22, 1867. 1 volume. Purchased, 1918. MS 3506.

This journal contains the proceedings of this commission which was created by Governor O. P. Morton to investigate the losses or damages incurred by Indiana residents as a result of the Confederate raid led by General John H. Morgan in July, 1863. Citizens from 19 counties filed claims totaling over $497,000 before this commission, which was in session from April 4 to December 18, 1867. The entries in this volume record the specific details of each claim and indicate whether or not the commissioners approved it.

932   SAMUEL FINDLEY (1786–1870). Notebooks, ca. 1813. 2 volumes. Purchased, 1970. MS 3507.

Containing biblical exercises and Findley's writings on topics relating to religion and theology. After his ordination, the Reverend Mr. Findley settled in Guernsey County, Ohio, in 1818; served as pastor for Presbyterian churches in the communities of Fairview, Washington, and Antrim, 1824–1850; and in Antrim founded Madison College, which was incorporated in 1839. He was also editor (1827–1834) of *The Religious Examiner,* the organ of the Associate Reformed Church.

933   RYAN GOWDY & COMPANY. XENIA, O. Daybook, 1836–1837. 1 volume. Purchased, 1970. MS 3508.

Ryan Gowdy settled in Xenia, Guernsey County, Ohio, in the 1810's and was the town's first merchant.

934   FORTNIGHTLY MUSICAL CLUB. CLEVELAND, O. Records, 1896–1967. 4 boxes, 18 volumes. Deposited by the Fortnightly Musical Club, 1970, 1971. MS 3509.

Minutes of meetings, newspaper clippings, concert programs and notices, and other miscellaneous papers and volumes relating to the activities of this club. Founded in 1894, its objective was to "advance the interests of music in Cleveland." The club presented programs of chamber music, seasonal concerts, and recitals and sponsored lecture classes and scholarships in the field of music. In 1912, it contributed to the establishment of the Cleveland Music School Settlement. Specifically included are yearbooks, 1896–1960 (incomplete); three guest books, 1910–1918, 1949–1956; fifteen scrapbooks, 1910–1956; and papers concerning anniversary celebrations in 1936, 1946, 1956, and 1966.

935   BOOK AND THIMBLE CLUB. CLEVELAND, O. Records, 1890–1957. 4½ boxes. Gift of Mrs. J. H. Bond, 1970. MS 3510.

Constitution and bylaws, record books, programs, letters, leaflets, newspaper clippings, photographs, and other materials relating to the activities of this women's club which was organized in 1890 and which became inactive after 1957. Its members (limited to 25) were primarily concerned with literary pursuits but did occasionally engage in civic and charitable activities. This club was instrumental in organizing the Consumers League of Ohio in 1900. Specifically included are the following: secretaries' books, 1890–1897, 1906–1957; treasurers' books, 1891–1923; annual printed programs, 1894–1957; an attendance book, 1905–1947; and several brief accounts of the history of the club prepared by Mrs. D. H. Maloney (1937), Miss Milly E. Brown (1940), Mrs. Seth Hayes (1942), and Mrs. Charles B. Ewing (1954).

    Also included are several letters addressed to the club from Mrs. D. H. Maloney, who was living in Amsterdam, Holland, 1938–1939; and from Mrs. Louise (Maloney) Bruin, 1945–1946. The latter series contains Mrs. Bruin's comments on life in Amsterdam during the Nazi occupation of World War II.

936 ABEL W. FAIRBANKS (1817–1894). Sketchbook, August 15, 1878. 1 volume. Gift of Mrs. Francis R. Bolles, 1970. MS 3511.
This volume, "Respectfully dedicated to Mr. & Mrs. A. W. Fairbanks by the Delineators," contains pen, pencil, and watercolor sketches by several Cleveland artists, including Otto Bacher and Herman Herkomer, members of the Cleveland Art Club. These sketches are of scenes at the Fairbanks home on the shore of Lake Erie in the Bratenahl section of Cleveland.

937 NEAR WEST SIDE DEVELOPMENT ASSOCIATION. CLEVELAND, O. Records, 1963–1966. 2½ boxes. Gift of Thomas J. Miller, 1970. MS 3512.
Articles of association, minutes of trustee meetings, correspondence, treasurer's reports and invoices, membership lists, director's reports, newspaper clippings, and several photographs relating to this association during the period in which Thomas J. Miller served as its executive director. This association was organized in 1963 to coordinate the activities of the residents and institutions of the near west side with Cleveland's Urban Renewal Department in order to facilitate the development of this section of the city; as well as to prepare reports, make recommendations, and assist in planning urban development. Representatives of over 20 business, banking, educational, religious, charitable, and medical organizations participated in the founding of the Near West Side Development Association. These records reflect the Association's interest in land use, schools, traffic problems and street relocations, and housing.

938 GEORGE PRICHARD. Account Book, 1832–1867. 1 volume. Gift of Warren Skidmore, 1970. MS 3513.
Prichard, a blacksmith, resided in Hiram, Portage County, Ohio, in the early 1830's.

939 CLEVELAND DEVELOPMENT FOUNDATION. CLEVELAND, O. Records, 1954–1969. 64 boxes, 54 volumes, 2 packages. Gift of the Cleveland Development Foundation, 1970. MS 3514.

Correspondence, minutes of meetings, reports, ledgers, photographs, and newspaper clippings relating to the activities of this foundation which was incorporated in June, 1954, "to furnish assistance to projects and undertakings for the improvement of the public peace, health, and safety, civic development, and public welfare in the Cleveland metropolitan area of northeast Ohio and to participate in programs for the elimination of slum conditions and in urban redevelopment and other projects conducive to the progress of the community. . . ." This foundation has been instrumental in coordinating technical, governmental, and financial institutions in attempting to find solutions to urban redevelopment problems. The projects in which it has been active include Kerruish Park Housing, East Woodland Slum Clearance, St. Vincent Slum Clearance, Cuyahoga Community College, Cleveland State University, University-Euclid Urban Renewal, Erieview, University Circle Research Center, and the Hough Housing Corporation.

RESTRICTED: Details available in the Society.

940 WILLIAM ELLISON (d. 1864). Letters, 1861–1864. 44 items. Gift of Mrs. Wilbur D. Prescott, 1970. MS 3515.

Ellison wrote these letters while serving during the Civil War with Battery D, 1st Illinois Artillery. Most of these are addressed to his sister, Ann Ellison of Iroquois County, Illinois. Ellison's letters contain comments on the following: his family and his duties, his health and his attitudes concerning other soldiers, the problems associated with obtaining food and other supplies, and occasionally on military encounters in which his battery was engaged.

941 YOUNG WOMEN'S CHRISTIAN ASSOCIATION. CLEVELAND, O. Records, 1878–1960. 12 boxes. Gift of the Young Women's Christian Association, 1970. MS 3516.

Correspondence, rosters, attendance records, reports, histories, bulletins, broadsides, scrapbooks, and minutes of the Association, its advisory board, and its board of trustees. The Young Women's Christian Association (Y.W.C.A.) of Cleveland was founded in 1869 as the Women's Christian Association of Cleveland. Its purpose was to promote the temporal and spiritual welfare of women residing in the city. It provided instruction in women's trades and domestic and office work, as well as recreational facilities. By the turn of the century, the Association helped women to find employment and maintained a residence, retreats, and rest homes for the aged or incurably ill. The records touch on these activities as well as on the Association's involvement after World War I with the movement to outlaw war and with race relations, immigrant problems, and aid to the unemployed during the economic depression of the 1930's.

Unpublished 4-page register available in the Society.

942 HIRAM P. OVIATT (1821–1872). Papers, 1816–1897. ½ box. Gift of Mrs. Lin A. Hamilton, 1970. MS 3518.

Diaries, letters, land deeds, military papers, and photographs relating to Hiram P. Oviatt and his wife, Lucy Ann (Bullard) Oviatt. One diary was kept by Hiram P. Oviatt while he was prospecting for gold in California in 1850. Two letters contain references to political conditions in Canada, 1827–1828. The remaining papers concern members of the Bullard, Hamilton, and Oviatt families of Euclid, Ohio. Other correspondents include Hanna Bullard and Tyler Parker.

943   TRW, INC. CLEVELAND, O., AND DETROIT, MICH. Records, 1900–1969. 80 linear feet. Gift of TRW, Inc., 1971.

Financial and business records, correspondence, union literature, proceedings of labor negotiations, company publications, newspaper clippings, photographs, and a wide range of additional files of TRW (formerly Thompson Ramo Wooldridge, Inc.), one of the world's largest manufacturers of products for the automotive, aerospace, electronic, and related industries. This collection reflects the corporate development of TRW, especially that of its immediate predecessor, Thompson Products, Inc., with heavy emphasis on labor relations during the period from 1933 to 1956. These records are divided into five series: Early Records, History, National Air Races, Labor Relations, and Publications and Public Relations.

The Early Records series consists of 46 bound volumes and one folder of records of TRW's predecessors, both in Cleveland and in Detroit, and other companies acquired before 1926. These include ledgers, journals, trial balance and payroll books, and proceedings and minutes of the Cleveland Cap Screw Company (1900–1908), Electric Welding Products Company (1908–1915), Steel Products Company (1915–1926), and Thompson Products Company (1926–1958), 1900–1929. Original incorporators of the Cleveland Cap Screw Company were David J. Kurtz, Frederick E. Bright, H. V. Bright, J. E. Morley, and W. F. Carr. Alexander Winton acquired control of the company in 1905 when Charles E. Thompson (later president of Thompson Products) became general manager. During this period, the company, which originally manufactured cap screws, bolts, and studs, moved into new fields with the production of automobile valves (1904) and aircraft valves (1915). In 1916, the company acquired its first plant outside Cleveland, the Michigan Welding Products Company in Detroit; and Frederick C. Crawford, who became president in 1933 and served as chairman of the executive committee (1953–1967), joined the company.*

The History series consists primarily of various accumulations of data compiled by the company's Historical Records Division between 1947 and 1954. These include the following: labor-relations case summaries, 1934–1954; files concerning TRW's labor history, 1935–1967; exhibits of literature and other documents relating to labor relations, 1944–1947; exhibits concerning National Labor Relations Board elections, 1945 and 1947; unpublished typescript copy of "Thompson Products: A Study in New Deal Legislation," in five parts; and files used in preparing the January, 1951, issue of *Friendly Forum* commemorating Thompson Products' 50th anniversary. Additional materials consist of biographies of company executives; files on the history of aviation, automobiles, and the Ford Motor Company; and financial and economic history files and indexes,** including documents relating to the merger of Thompson Products, Inc., with the Ramo-Wooldridge Company in 1958. Also included here is a chronological account of the history and development of the Crawford Door Company, 1927–1953, and several folders of material on labor relations, 1953.

The National Air Races series consists of folders filed chronologically which deal with the annual National Air Race and the National Aircraft Show. The company was instrumental in developing the National Air Races, the first of which was held in 1929, and one year later established the Thompson Trophy. The files consist of correspondence, printed programs, memoranda, invitations, and other literature, 1929–1967.

The Labor Relations series, comprising nearly one-half of this collection, consists of files which relate to the implementation of the company's philosophy that management and labor could deal effectively with one another without the involvement of labor leaders and unions outside the company or of governmental agencies which attempted to regulate labor relations. Management acted upon the premise that productivity would be increased if the workers were kept informed of the company's progress as well as problems, and teamwork was the key word in management-labor relations. This was manifested in an unusual series of publications and shop meetings. These files are particularly significant since TRW, a company which now employs over 80,000 people, has never had a strike or work stoppage.

This series is divided into five sub-series: Master File, Free File, Type File, Legal File, and Subsidiaries File. These files, all of which overlap to a certain extent, are in the same order in which they were arranged by the company's Labor History Division. The Master File, 1918, 1923, 1927, 1929, 1933–1935, and 1937–1956, is arranged chronologically and contains correspondence, reports, minutes of meetings, inter-office memoranda and letters, miscellaneous company and worker publications, and other similar materials. The Free File, 1933–1951, is arranged chronologically and contains originals and copies of newsletters, news releases, newspaper clippings, bulletins, reports, and other materials of a quasi-public nature which were distributed both within the company and to the public. The Type File is arranged alphabetically and consists of various categories of material, mostly published, relating to the company's labor relations. The following are among the headings listed in the index to the Type File: Addresses, A.F.L. Publications, Aircraft Workers Alliance, Books (including booklets, pamphlets, and other company publications), C.I.O. Publications, Company Bulletins, Employment Reports, Forms, Grievances, History, Labor Relations, Letters, Magazine Articles, Manuals, Newspaper Articles, News—*Friendly Forum*, Old Guard Minutes, Organization Charts, Personnel Administration, Posters, Reports—Annual and Financial, Surveys, Training, Vacations, and WPDC (War Production Drive Committee). The Legal File consists of proceedings of cases involving Thompson Products held before the National Labor Relations Board, National War Labor Board, U.S. Circuit Courts of Appeals, and other federal and local courts, 1937–1947. Also included here, and filed in chronological order, are correspondence, memoranda, affidavits, petitions, statements, briefs, and other papers relating to matters arising out of legal proceedings, 1935–1947. The Subsidiaries File consists primarily of labor-relations documents concerning company plants outside Cleveland. The largest part of this file deals with the plant in Detroit, 1920–1950. Also referred to here are conditions at the Toledo Steel Products Company, 1936–1945; and at Thompson Products' West Coast plant, 1937–1953.

The last series, Publications and Public Relations, consists of runs of company publications, and newspaper clippings relating to company activities and interests. Among the publications are annual reports (stockholders), 1932–1968, and annual reports (employees), 1940–1952, 1955; the *Friendly Forum,* 1934–1969; manuals, handbooks, and guides, 1940–1951; newsletters to supervisors, 1945–1957; and labor turnover reports, Old Guard bulletins, and memos to managers, 1956–1958. A file of loose newspaper clippings, 1943–1955, includes photographs, brochures, and magazine articles; five scrapbooks contain mounted clippings, 1939–1944.

RESTRICTED: Details available in the Society.

* For background on the early history of TRW see the special issue of *Friendly Forum* (Cleveland: Thompson Products, Inc., January, 1951); and F. K. Dossett's unpublished account, "Physical and Economic History: A Chronological Record of the Physical and Economic Development of Thompson Products, Inc.," May, 1949.

** Includes indexes to documents and records and copies thereof deposited in the Baker Library of the Graduate School of Business Administration, Harvard University, between 1949 and 1954.

944   TIFFIN MANUFACTURING COMPANY. TIFFIN, O. Records, 1875–1959. 168 volumes and 2,000 items. Gift of Mr. and Mrs. Harold Musgrave, 1966, 1967.

A nearly complete collection of business records of this company, organized in 1875 by Jacob Scheiber, which manufactured various types of wood products, including house, office, and church furniture. Between 1900 and its closing in 1966, the company specialized in church furniture, especially altars and altar rails, baptismal fonts, confessionals, pews, pulpits, station frames, and vestment cases. Although it served institutions from coast to coast, most of its activities were concentrated in the northeastern United States, in cities such as Cincinnati, Cleveland, Columbus, Detroit, New York, Philadelphia, and Toledo. These records reflect the changes in the design of church interiors and furniture as well as the growth and development of the company.

Specifically included are daybooks, 1875–1949; journals, 1875–1955; ledgers, 1875–1900; cashbooks, 1880–1941; order books, 1881–1930; time books, 1889–1959; invoice books, 1890–1915; letter books, 1900–1940; and an assortment of other records, catalogues, letters, and receipts. Of special interest are 628 blueprints and drawings and nearly 900 photographs of church interiors and furniture.

945   WORKS PROGRESS ADMINISTRATION. OHIO HISTORIC RECORDS SURVEY: HISTORIC SITES OF CLEVELAND. Records, 1930's. 508 boxes.

Data, compiled by the personnel on this project, relating to boarding houses, bridges, buildings, canals, cemeteries, churches, civic and social institutions, dwellings, educational institutions, hospitals, hotels, military sites, manufacturing and commercial agents, public buildings, railroads, restaurants and saloons, roads, streets, street railways, and theaters and halls. Also included are copies of real estate transfer records for Cleveland (1800–1885) and for other political subdivisions in Cuyahoga County.

Unpublished 16-page register available in the Society.

PART I: MANUSCRIPTS

SECTION B:
Special Collections

946 WILLIAM PENDLETON PALMER (1861-1927), *collector*. Papers relating to the Civil War. 46 boxes, 1 oversize volume. Gift of William P. Palmer, 1927.

This collection includes a wide range of papers and records relating to both the Union and the Confederacy before, during, and after the Civil War.*

Accounts, reminiscences, and recollections include those of Joe Atkinson on the Confederate cavalry; anonymous soldier on the battles of South Mountain and Antietam; anonymous Union soldier on the Battle of Missionary Ridge; Levi F. Bauder on the rescue of the 5th Connecticut Volunteer Infantry flag during the Battle of Cedar Mountain; Henry Harrison Bingham on General Winfield Scott Hancock; Stephen F. Blanding on the cruise of the U.S. gunboat *Louisiana* from 1862 to 1864; John P. Brogan on the Army of the Shenandoah under General Philip Sheridan at Cedar Creek, Virginia; Emile Bourlier on spying for the Union and escaping from a rebel prison; D. Cleveland on the Battle of Nueces; Weston Ferris on life in prison; Ulysses S. Grant on troop operations; N. W. Greenman on the Battle of Resaca; Paul Leland Haworth on "Reconstruction and the Union, 1865-1912"; Richard E. Hopkins on Mosby's cavalry in Wheeling, West Virginia; Horatio C. King on the execution of a deserter at Bolivar Heights, Virginia; William Kohler on the Confederate post office at Austinville, Virginia, 1864-1865; Edward S. Lathrop on his war experiences; R. S. Matthews on his services during the war; Joseph E. Moody on his capture and imprisonment in Libby, Andersonville, and other Confederate prisons; Edward

Palmer, M.D., on hospital services in the 2nd Colorado Regiment; James Pollard on Colonel Ulric Dahlgren's raid into Virginia; Isaac D. Seabrook on the war on the coast of South Carolina; Mary E. W. Sherwood on her experiences with the Sanitary Commission in New York City; John Lorimer Worden on his imprisonment by the Confederates in 1861; H. E. Young on the fight at Pocataligo; and Pedro de Zea on "Apuntes Historicos Sobre La America Del Norte."

Among the autobiographical and biographical accounts are those for Daniel Ammen, Frank Crawford Armstrong, Turner Ashby, John Brown Baldwin, Milledge Luke Bonham, P. D. Bowles, Eli Metcalfe Bruce, James Stone Chrisman, Philip S. Crooke, Neal Dow, R. C. Gatlin, William Glenny, Henry Gray, John Brooks Henderson, Oliver Otis Howard, Andrew Atkinson Humphreys, James D. Imboden, Thomas Jonathan (Stonewall) Jackson, William H. Jackson, Robert M. Jones, James Lawson Kemper, Joseph Brevard Kershaw, Robert Klotz, James Henry Lane, Evander McIvor Law, Robert E. Lee, John McCausland, Henry E. McCulloch, Lafayette McLaws, William Miller, Gideon Johnson Pillow, Henry E. Reed, William Starke Rosecrans, Grandison Dulaney Royston, Franklin Barlow Sexton, William Tecumseh Sherman, Isaac Ruth Sherwood, Francis Asbury Shoup, Thomas Kirby Smith, John J. Thomas, George W. Triplett, Adoniram Judson Warner, Daniel Price White, William C. Wickham, and John Lorimer Worden.

Autographs include those of the U.S. Naval Academy class of 1861; N. A. Flournoy's book of autographs of prisoners confined on Johnson's Island, July 26, 1862; Union officers in 1861; Charles Pomeroy Stone's autograph letter book, 1863; and two volumes containing autographs of 2,400 Union officers.

A series of official documents, most of which contain signatures of major Union or Confederate political and military leaders, includes a variety of appointments, certificates, commissions, discharges, ordinances, pardons, summonses, and writs. A series of general and special orders include those signed by Thomas Antisell, Pierre G. T. Beauregard, Theodore S. Bowers, Braxton Bragg, Edward S. Bragg, Jefferson Davis, Thomas Jonathan

(Stonewall) Jackson, Andrew Johnson, Joseph Eggleston Johnston, Abraham Lincoln, George W. Morgan, Gideon J. Pillow, Leonidas Polk, and William Tecumseh Sherman.

Essays, sermons, speeches, and addresses include the following: Pierre G. T. Beauregard on giving marching orders to the Army of Department No. 2 at Chattanooga, Jefferson Davis on slavery, George P. Goodwin on the Confederate cause, Winfield Scott Hancock on recruiting for the 2nd Army Corps, Isaac P. Langworthy on slavery and national fast day, Mary K. Maule on the Order of American Knights and Sons of Liberty, W. J. Randolph on the mortal wounding of Stonewall Jackson, James Mattach Scovel on Thaddeus Stevens, Isaac D. Seabrook on the Southern policy of negation and social ideas of the South, Charles Sumner on slavery and the war, and Thomas Hart Taylor's farewell to his brigade.

Journals and diaries exist for the following: A. Eneas Armstrong covering the outbreak of the war, 1858–1861; John M. Butler while acting master on board the U.S.S. *New Ironsides* out of Hampton Roads, Virginia, 1863; Alexander Robert Chisolm before and during the bombardment of Fort Sumter, 1861; Chester W. Coff while a soldier in camp near Suffolk, Virginia, 1863; D. R. Hundley while a prisoner on Johnson's Island, 1864; Sidney S. Lyon regarding ground surveys of Chickasaw Bayou, 1863; C. H. McLellan while a ship owner in Bath, Maine, 1858–1860, 1863, 1865–1867, 1869, and 1872–1877; W. H. Paine, 1863–1878, including correspondence with Major General J. Watts dePeyster; Henry A. Richardson while serving as assistant surgeon for the U.S. Navy on board the U.S.S. *Cambridge*, 1861–1862; John Simpson while a crewman on board the U.S.S. *Brooklyn*, U.S.S. *Richmond*, and U.S.S. *Metacomet*, 1861–1865; Robert K. Smith while acting assistant surgeon, U.S. Army, and surgeon, U.S. Volunteers, 1862; Joseph A. Waddell while a resident of Staunton, Virginia, 1860–1865; and John H. Wheeler, a state official of North Carolina and colonel during the war.

The bulk of this collection consists of letters, reports, telegrams, and dispatches relating to the activities of many leading figures, including the following: John Adams, Edward P. Alexander, John J. Almy, Jacob Ammen, James P. Anderson, Robert Anderson, John A. Andrew, Frank C. Armstrong, Turner Ashby, Adam Badeau, Nathaniel P. Banks, John G. Barnard, James Barnes, Henry A. Barnum, George L. Beal, Pierre G. T. Beauregard, Henry W. Benham, Judah P. Benjamin, John L. Beveridge, Henry H. Bingham, Louis Blenker, Emile Bourlier, Jeremiah T. Boyle, Braxton Bragg, Samuel Breck, John C. Breckinridge, Joseph E. Brown, William H. Browne, George P. Buell, Stephen G. Burbridge, William W. Burns, Ambrose E. Burnside, Benjamin F. Butler, Daniel Butterfield, James H. Carleton, John C. Carter, Silas Casey, Robert F. Catterson, James R. Chalmers, Salmon P. Chase, Benjamin F. Cheatham, Jonathan P. Cilley, Robert E. Clary, Patrick R. Cleburne, Gustave P. Cluseret, Howell Cobb, John Cochrane, Philip St. George Cooke, Samuel Cooper, Michael Corcoran, Jacob D. Cox, Andrew G. Curtin, Samuel R. Curtis, Lysander Cutler, John A. B. Dahlgren, Ulric Dahlgren, Charles A. Dana, Jefferson Davis, Varina H. Davis, Zachariah C. Deas, John A. Dix, Grenville M. Dodge, Daniel S. Donelson, Abner Doubleday, Samuel F. DuPont, Jubal A. Early, Washington L. Elliott, John England, Lucius Fairchild, John B. Floyd, Gustavus V. Fox, Samuel G. French, Samuel A. Gilbert, Quincy A. Gillmore, States Rights Gist, Ulysses S. Grant, Wade Hampton, William J. Hardee, Isham G. Harris, William B. Hazen, Daniel H. Hill, Thomas C. Hindman, Theophilus H. Holmes, Joseph Holt, John B. Hood, Alvin P. Hovey, Oliver O. Howard, John K. Jackson, Joseph E. Johnston, Thomas Jordan, James L. Kemper, Erasmus D. Keys, William S. King, Evander McIvor Law, Alexander R. Lawton, Robert E. Lee, John Letcher, Abraham Lincoln, Henry H. Lockwood, James Longstreet, Mark P. Lowrey, William W. Mackall, Stephen R. Mallory, Arthur M. Manigault, Joseph K. F. Mansfield, George B. McClellan, John A. McClernand, Lafayette McLaws, George G. Meade, Montgomery C. Meigs, Christopher G. Memminger, Jonathan B. Moore, Oliver P. Morton, John S. Mosby, Francis R. Nicholls, Lucius B. Northrop, Ely S. Parker, John J. Peck, John Pegram, William N. Pendleton, Henry W. Perkins, Gideon J. Pillow, Leonidas Polk, John Pope, David D. Porter, Fitz-John Porter, George W. Randolph, John R. Rawlins, Felix H. Robertson, Daniel Ruggles, Isaac M. St. John, James A. Seddon, William H. Seward, Philip H. Sheridan, William T. Sherman, Edmund K. Smith, Gustavus W. Smith, James Y. Smith, Preston Smith, James Speed, Edwin M. Stanton, Alexander H. Stephens, Edwin H. Stoughton, Abraham E. Strickle, James E. B. Stewart, Edward D. Tracy, William H. T. Walker, Lewis Wallace, Adoniram J. Warner, Gideon Welles, John A. Wharton, Joseph Wheeler, William H. C. Whiting, Henry A. Wise, Ambrose R. Wright, Marcus J. Wright, and William L. Yancey.

In addition, an assortment of miscellaneous items includes certificates, cipher codes, circulars, deeds and other slave documents, depositions, financial records, invoices, lists, memoranda, muster rolls, newspaper clippings, passes, payrolls, petitions, poems, record books, requisitions, returns, rolls, rules and regulations, scrapbooks, service records, ships' papers, statistical tables, subscription lists, tax receipts and returns, and vouchers.

* Other Civil War papers collected by Mr. Palmer are described elsewhere in this volume (items 451, 462, 465, 466, 474, 666, and 705).

947   SHAKER COLLECTION.* Papers and Records, ca. 1782–1940 (1800–1870). 75 linear feet. Gift of Wallace H. Cathcart, 1942.

Letters, journals and diaries, ledgers and account books, daybooks, hymnals and music, legal documents, inspirational writings and drawings, testimonies, sermons, speeches, covenants, directives, contracts, wills, financial receipts, surveys and land deeds, newspaper clippings, broadsides, and photographs relating to each of 20 Shaker communities located in 10 eastern states. This material was collected by Wallace H. Cathcart (1865–1942) from 1907 until his death, during which time he served as President (1907–1913) and Director (1913–1942) of the Western Reserve Historical Society. The major communities represented and the life span of each include the following: Enfield (1790–1917), Connecticut; Kissimmee, Florida; Pleasant Hill (1806–1910) and South Union (1807–1922), Kentucky; West Union (1810–1827),

Indiana; Alfred (1793–1932) and Sabbathday Lake (1794–?), Maine; Hancock (1790–?), Harvard (1793–1918), Shirley (1793–1908), and Tyringham (1792–1875), Massachusetts; Canterbury (1792–?) and Enfield (1793–1923), New Hampshire; Sodus and Groveland (1826–1895), Mount Lebanon (1787–1947), and Watervliet (1787–1938), New York; North Union (1822–1889), Union Village (1806–1912), Watervliet (1806–1910), and Whitewater (1824–1907), Ohio. In addition to presenting a detailed account of the activities of the members of this utopian sect, the collection also touches upon several general subjects of historical interest including architecture, art, education, industry, social and intellectual life, music, religion, transportation, and travel, as well as the War of 1812 and the Civil War. Much of the correspondence after 1900 relates to Cathcart's attempts to acquire Shaker manuscripts and to accumulate data on the various Shaker communities.

* Because this collection is being reorganized and recatalogued in conjunction with the preparation of a separate "Guide," this descriptive entry is general and brief.

948 MANUSCRIPTS VERTICAL FILE. 3 file cabinets. Single items or very small collections (fewer than 10 items or less than 20 pages) are generally filed here in either of two alphabetical series for ease of storage and access. The types of items found here include agreements, autobiographical and biographical accounts, certificates, constitutions and bylaws, contracts, deeds, depositions, diaries, financial accounts and receipts, field notes, indentures, letters, maps, memoranda, minutes of meetings, petitions, reminiscences, speeches, subscription lists, surveys, and wills.

In Series I, items are arranged in alphabetical order by personal names; in Series II, items are arranged in alphabetical order by organizational names.

Series I: Squire Abbott, J. M. Ackley, Ashael Adams, Jr., John Adams (1735–1826), Christian Amis, E. B. Andrews, Mrs. S. G. Andrews, James Applegate, James Armstrong, Benedict Arnold,

Edward Atkinson, Elroy M. Avery, Henry W. Avery, Thomas Avery, Asa Bacon, Jr., Leonard Bacon, John Willis Baer, James Bagg, Adams Bailey, Edward M. Bailey (Savannah, Ga.), William D. Bailey (Marietta, O.), Alvin V. Baird, Newton Diehl Baker, Samuel J. Baker, H. B. Banning, Dudley Baldwin (Cleveland, O.), H. H. Baldwin, James Baldwin (Litchfield, Conn.), Norman C. Baldwin (Cleveland, O.), George Bancroft (1800–1891), George H. Barber, William Barnett (Westmoreland Co., Pa.), Phineas T. Barnum, John Barr, Mordecai Bartley, Clara Harlowe Barton, Elisha Bates (1780–1861), Frances Courtenay Baylor, D. W. Bearsley (Cleveland, O.), Thomas Hart Benton, Sir William Berkeley (1606–1677), Emmanuel Bierstedt, Grace Bedell Billings, Nathan Birdsey (Bainhill), Margaret P. Birney, James G. Blaine, Henry Blatchford, Harman Blennerhassett, Arthur H. Blower, Major Lewis Bond, Rufus L. Bonney, Thomas C. Boone, Noadiah Potter Bowler, William O. Bowler, Jonathan Brace, Joseph Brant (1742–1807), Emma Sanford Brayton, Sarah A. Brewer, Dwight Briggs, Daniel Brodhead (1736–1809), Elliott B. Bronson, Rev. C. A. Brooks, Eustus Brooks, Israel Brown, John Brown (1736–1803), Joseph Emerson Brown (1821–1894), Minnie M. Brown, William Cullen Bryant, Franklin Buchanan (1800–1874), Ezekiel Wells Buell, Charles C. Burleigh (1810–1878), Aaron Burr (1756–1836), Harold Hitz Burton, Theodore Elijah Burton, Benjamin Franklin Butler, Colonel Thomas Butler, John Calfee, Alexander Campbell (1788–1866), Andrew Carnegie (1835–1919), Lorenzo Carter (1767–1814), Freeman Grant Cary, Lewis Cass (1782–1866), William W. Castle, Epaphroditus Champion, Philander Chase (1775–1852), Salmon P. Chase (1808–1873), James S. Clarke (Cleveland, O.), Henry Clay (1777–1852), David Clendenin, Oren L. Cleveland, De Witt Clinton, Oliver W. Cobb, William Frederick Cody, Andrew J. Coe, Stephen Coffin, William Cogswell, John W. Coleman, Daniel Lewis Collier, Dudley Colman, John P. Converse, Charles Cornwallis, Ralph Cowles (Leroy, O.), Jacob Dolson Cox, William Cumback (1829–1905), Eleroy Curtis, George Darrow, Jefferson Davis (1808–1889), Lewis Day (d. 1812), Joseph A. DeBoes, Stephen Decatur (1779–1820), Alexander L. DeMaioribus,

[305]

Moses Deming, Lemuel T. Denison, Harold D. Dennis, Charles W. F. Dick, John Dodge (Beverly, Mass.), Daniel A. Dorsey, Abner Doubleday, Lyman C. Draper, Henry T. Drowne, Solomon Drowne, Homer Earle, William Eaton (Fort Washington), Lewis B. Edwards, Marion Hall Elliot, Justin Ely, I. S. Emery, James Emmitt (1806–1895), William C. Endicott (1826–1900), Estwick Evans (1787–1866), Thomas Ewing (1789–1871), John H. Farley (1845–1922), Allan Shepard Felch, Cyrus West Field, Howard N. Findley, Thomas W. Fleming (1874–1948), Ferdinand Foch, Nelson Foos, Herschel Foote, Seabury Ford (1801–1855), John Wien Forney, Thomas Forster, Benjamin Franklin (1706–1790), John Charles Fremont, B. B. French, Isaac Galland, Albert Gallatin (1761–1849), P. C. Gallegher, James Galloway, Samuel Galloway (1720–1785), J. B. Gardiner, Eliza Ballou Garfield, James A. Garfield (1831–1881), James R. Garfield, Lucretia (Rudolph) Garfield, Ebenezer L. Gibbs, General W. H. Gibson, Joshua R. Giddings, Benjamin Ives Gilman, John M. Godfrey, Peter Goldrick, Jonathan Goldsmith (1783–1847), Lucia A. Goldsmith, Julia W. Goodrich, William H. Goodrich (1823–1874), Hannah Flagg Gould, Jesse R. Grant (1858–1934), Ulysses S. Grant, Horace Greeley, Nathanael Greene, Benjamin Henry Grierson, Alexander Gunn (1837–1901), Gideon Hale, Marcus A. Hanna, Seville Hanna, Florence K. Harding, Warren G. Harding, James Harlan (1820–1899), George Harrington, George B. Harris (Cleveland, O.), Benjamin Harrison (1833–1901), William Henry Harrison, Jonathan Haskell, Clara Louise (Stone) Hay, John Hay (1838–1905), Amos Sutton Hayden, Hiram Collins Haydn, Ralph A. Hayes, Rutherford B. Hayes, Arthur Perroneau Hayne, William Heald (b. 1766), Jonathan Heart, Elise A. Herrick, Elbert Herring, John Heth, Eri Hickox (1790–1864), Thomas Wentworth Higginson, Samuel P. Hildreth (1783–1863), Ethan A. Hitchcock (1798–1870), William Hollaway, Oliver O. Howard (1830–1909), Ezekiel Hover, Henry Howe (1816–1893), William D. Howells (1837–1920), William Hull (1753–1825), Samuel Huntington (1731–1796), Samuel Huntington (1765–1817), Thomas Jefferson (1743–1826), Tom L. Johnson (1854–1911), Amos Kendall (1789–1869), Byron Kilbourne, John Kirkpatrick (1819-1869), Jared Potter Kirtland, Henry Knox (1750-1806), Louis Kossuth (1802-1894), Daniel Lathrop, Peter A. Laubie, Richard Henry Lee (1732-1794), Abraham Lincoln (1809-1865), Samuel Phillips Lord, Daniel Loring, Arthur Clyde Ludlow, D. B. Lyman, Duncan McArthur, John W. McClung, Alexander McDowell McCook, William Osborne McDowell, Robert P. McFarland, James Henry McGiffert, James McHenry, Helen McKinley, William McKinley (1843-1901), Robert Erastus McKisson, John McLean (1785-1861), Stanley L. McMichael, Joab Madison, William H. Malden, Daniel Wilbert Manchester, John Mathews (Marietta, O.), Thomas Maylin, George Gordon Meade, Thomas Francis Meagher, Return J. Meigs, Bryce Metcalf, Augustus Moore (Cincinnati, O.), Robert Morris (1734-1806), James Morrison (Northern Ireland), Samuel F. B. Morse, Elijah Murray, Eben Newton, Florence Nightingale, Horace Nye (Marietta, O.), Barney Oldfield, Anna Long Onstott, Robert Patterson (1792-1881); Simon Perkins (1771-1844), Oliver Phelps (1749-1809), Thomas Pownall (1722-1805), W. A. Reynolds, Frederick Sleigh Roberts, Elijah Robertson, John D. Rockefeller, Ralph R. Root (1828-1889), James Ross (Pittsburgh, Pa.), Benjamin Rush (1745-1813), Jacob Sharpe, William Tecumseh Sherman, Eliza R. Snow, John Steele (1764-1815), John Cleves Symmes, William H. Taft (1857-1930), Moses Thompson (1776-1858), Charles Franklin Thwing, Frederick Townsend (1825-1897), Jonathan Trumbull (1740-1809), Dwight D. Turner, Clement Laird Vallandigham, Benjamin Franklin Wade, John Walworth, George Washington (1732-1799), Anthony Wayne (1745-1796), Elisha Whittlesey, Woodrow Wilson, Henry Alexander Wise, Oliver Wolcott (1726-1797), and Elizur Wright.

Series II: Albany (O.) Manual Labor University, American Congressional Temperance Society, American Sunday School Union, Ashland County (O.) Female Anti-Slavery Society, Athens (O.) County Pioneer Association, Atlantic & Great Western Railway Company, Carroll County (O.) Railroad Company, Case Western Reserve University, Central Baptist Association (O.), Central Ohio Normal College, Chillicothe (O.) Mutual Insurance Company, Citizens Light Company (Cleveland), Cleveland

Academy, Cleveland and Mahoning Valley Railroad, Cleveland Bar Association, Cleveland, Columbus & Cincinnati Railroad, Cleveland Female Seminary, Cleveland Hospital for Women and Children, Cleveland Paper Company, Cleveland Philharmonic Orchestra, Cleveland Board of Park Commissioners, Cleveland City Auditor, Cleveland Department of Public Safety, Cleveland Firemen's Relief Association, Cuyahoga County Court of Common Pleas, Cuyahoga County Medical Society, Cuyahoga County War Service League, Dartmouth College, Eckhard & Steler Funeral Directors (Berea, O.), Erie Land Company, Euclid Avenue Opera House, Expedition Railroad Line (O.), Free Trade Club (Cleveland), Historic American Buildings Survey, Lake View Cemetery Association (Cleveland), Lane Theological Seminary, Leroy and Burton Plank Road Company (O.), Liberty Hall Academy (N.C.), Librarian Society of Cleveland, Marietta & Cincinnati Railroad Company (O.), Massachusetts Anti-Slavery Society, Massachusetts Historical Society, New York Homeopathic Physicians' Society, North Carolina Gold Mining Company, Northeastern Ohio Teachers' Association, Oberlin College, Ohio and Nashville Railroad, Ohio Baptist Education Society, Ohio Monument Association, Ohio River Land and Marble Company, Pennsylvania and Lake Erie Dock Company, Pennsylvania and Ohio Canal, Poland (O.) Library Society, Richmond Classical Institute, Ripley and Locust Grove Turnpike Company (O.), St. John's Methodist-Episcopal Church (Cleveland), Springfield Association for the Promotion of Temperance (O.), Standard Oil Company, U.S. Office of Internal Revenue, U.S. Post Office, Western Reserve Horse Breeders Association, Wheeling and Lake Erie Railway Company, and Whig Party.

949 OVERSIZE MANUSCRIPTS. 24 items. Accumulated from various sources, and filed here because of unusually large size.

Including the following: a papal bull granted by Pope Gregory XIII to the Church of Cuzco in Arequipa, Peru, 1578; first diploma granted by Western Reserve College, 1830; records of the Trinity Congregational Church of Cleveland, 1960-1969; C. K. Stellwagen's drawing of the Cabinet Room of the White House while Abraham Lincoln was President; John Heckewelder's map of northeastern Ohio and western Pennsylvania, 1796 *; documents relating to the Sterling Lindner Company of Cleveland; contract between John Livingston and the Connecticut Land Company, 1795; charter of the Ohio Society of the National Society of Dames of the Loyal Legion, 1915; logbook of the master brig *Blackwalnut*, undated; census schedules for Logan County, Kentucky, 1840; album of Sereno P. Fenn relating to the founding of the Young Men's Christian Association in Poland, 1924-1925; architectural drawings of Jonathan Goldsmith (1783-1847); and 22 *Fraktur* illustrations, including birth certificates and drawings, done by Pennsylvania Germans, 1783-1846.

* Published in *The Heckewelder Map, 1796,* facsimile reproduction accompanied by a 27-page illustrated booklet by Mildred Walmsley and Mary Lou Conlin, W.R.H.S. Publication No. 121 (Cleveland: The Western Reserve Historical Society, 1968).

PART I: MANUSCRIPTS

SECTION C:
Collections on Microfilm

950 CONNECTICUT LAND COMPANY. HARTFORD, CONN. Records, 1795–1828. Microfilm, 3 reels (negative and positive). Originals in the Connecticut State Library.

Register of transfers, register of certificates, mortgages of scrip, votes and proceedings, account of drafts, and a stock ledger of the Connecticut Land Company; letters, agreements, deeds, accounts, and receipts of this company's trustees and shareholders, as well as of early settlers in the Western Reserve, including Gideon Granger, Uriel Holmes, Jr., Oliver Phelps, and Ephraim Root, and several field books of early surveyors, including those of Moses Warren.

See NUCMC 60-909.

951 REBECCA (SHAW) EDMISTON. Journal, 1851–1883. 1 volume on microfilm, 1 reel (negative and positive), prepared in 1953. Original in private possession.

Miss Shaw graduated from the Willoughby (Ohio) Female Seminary in 1851. After residing in Ohio for a while, she married John Edmiston and moved to Crab Orchard, Kentucky. Entries are of a personal and family nature with references to her travels throughout Ohio and surrounding states.

952   ROBERT TODD LINCOLN COLLECTION OF THE PAPERS OF ABRAHAM LINCOLN (1809–1865), 1790–1916. 194 volumes on microfilm, 94 reels (positive), prepared in 1947. Originals in the Library of Congress.

Correspondence and other papers relating primarily to the presidency of Abraham Lincoln.

See NUCMC 59-183.

953   SHAKER MANUSCRIPTS COLLECTION. Microfilm, 9 reels (positive). Originals in the New York State Library.

Record and memoranda books, diaries, and other materials (some printed) relating to various Shaker families, but primarily those located in Colonie, Groveland, and Watervliet, New York.

954   SHAKER MANUSCRIPTS. Microfilm, 10 reels (positive), prepared in 1952. Originals in the Filson Club.

Journals, account books, lists of members, proceedings of church and union meetings, and other materials relating to the various Shaker communities, including that in Pleasantville, Kentucky, 1815–1917.

See NUCMC 62-3426.

955   OXFORD TOWNSHIP, DELAWARE COUNTY, O. Records, 1828–ca. 1843. 1 volume on microfilm (negative). Original in private possession.

Primarily results of township elections, minutes of trustee meetings, copies of indentures and agreements, accounts relating to the apportionment of school funds, and several surveys.

PART I: MANUSCRIPTS

SECTION D:
Recent Accessions and Other Collections in Preparation

956 PERLEY PEABODY PITKIN. Papers, 1862–1864. 13 boxes. MS 1668.

Invoices, lists of stores received, manifests, orders, payroll lists, reports of persons hired, and other papers pertaining to the activities of Captain Pitkin, assistant quartermaster, U.S. Army, stationed in Brady Junction, Virginia.

957 SIMON PERKINS FAMILY. Papers, 1834–1910. 46 boxes. MS 3107.

Personal, business, and political papers relating primarily to three descendants of Simon Perkins (1771–1844). These men, who spent most of their active lives in the Western Reserve, were Joseph Perkins (1819–1885), banker, railroad executive, and philanthropist; Jacob Perkins (1821–1859), politician, businessman and railroad executive; and Jacob Bishop Perkins (b. 1854), Cleveland real estate owner and businessman.

958 FLORENCE ELLINWOOD ALLEN (1884–1966). Papers, 1896–1966. 29 boxes, 1 package. Gift of the Estate of Florence E. Allen, 1967, 1970. MS 3287.

Correspondence, diaries, biographical and genealogical material, speeches, newspaper clippings and scrapbooks, certificates and awards, photographs, and articles by or about Florence E. Allen, journalist, attorney, suffragette, and jurist.

959   JEPTHA HOMER WADE FAMILY. Papers, 1837–1925. 16 boxes, 1 volume, 1 package. Gift of Jeptha H. Wade III, 1966. MS 3292a.

Letters, account books, estate papers, journals, land deeds, tax papers, certificates, notebooks, genealogical data, and photographs relating to members of this Cleveland family, especially Jeptha H. Wade (1811–1890), his son, Randall P. Wade, and his grandson, Jeptha H. Wade (1857–1926).

960   CLEVELAND MUNICIPAL LIGHT PLANT ASSOCIATION. CLEVELAND, O. Records, 1937–1952. 20 boxes. Gift of Paul W. Walter, 1967. MS 3298.

This association was founded in 1937 to protect the interests of the Cleveland Municipal Light Plant (opened in 1914) and to reestablish the plant as a factor in the setting of rates in Cleveland's light and power industry.

961   HARRY L. EASTMAN (1882–1963). Papers, 1926–1967. 13 boxes, 10 volumes, 1 package. Gift of Mrs. Harry L. Eastman, 1968. MS 3301.

Correspondence, legal briefs, speeches, scrapbooks, photographs and other papers relating to the career of Eastman, a Cuyahoga County Juvenile Court judge (1926–1959).

962   PAUL W. WALTER (b. 1907). Papers, 1932–1954. 110 boxes. Gift of Paul W. Walter, 1967. MS 3302.

Campaign manager for Harold H. Burton, 1936 (Mayor of Cleveland), and 1940 (U.S. Senator from Ohio), and for Robert A. Taft (U.S. Senator from Ohio and Republican presidential nominee), 1938, 1940, 1944, 1948, 1950, and 1952.

963   ZENAS BALL FAMILY. Papers, 1820–1951. 14 boxes. Gift of Mrs. C. Robert Hughes, 1968. MS 3306.

Zenas Ball (1792–1860) and Aaron T. Ball of Knox County, Ohio, and Webb C. Ball (d. 1922), a Cleveland jeweler.

964 CARL D. FRIEBOLIN (1878–1967). Papers, 1890–1967. 53 boxes. Gift of the Estate of Carl D. Friebolin, 1967. MS 3309.
Cleveland lawyer and civic leader and U.S. referee in bankruptcy, 1916–1967.

965 GRASSELLI FAMILY. Papers, ca. 1800–1920. 18 boxes. Gift of Caesar A. Grasselli II, 1965. MS 3311.
Relating to Eugene R. Grasselli (1810–1882), Caesar A. Grasselli (1850–1927), Thomas S. Grasselli (1874–1942), and E. Grasselli & Son and its successor, the Grasselli Chemical Company, which merged with E. I. du Pont de Nemours Company in 1928.

966 HOSEA PAUL. Papers, 1856–1923. 8 boxes. MS 3312.
Surveyor in Cuyahoga and Summit counties, Ohio.

967 PHILIP L. COBB (1870–1929). Genealogical Papers, 1905–1922. 7 boxes MS 3313.
Letters, memoranda, and charts relating to Cobb's genealogical research.

968 GARFIELD FAMILY. Genealogical Papers, 1920–1950. 4 boxes. MS 3314.
Correspondence of James R. Garfield and Helen Newell Garfield regarding the genealogy of the Garfield family.

969 PAUL BELLAMY (1884–1956). Papers, 1907–1967. 7 boxes, 4 volumes. Gift of Mrs. Paul Bellamy, 1967. MS 3315.
Editor of the Cleveland *Plain Dealer*, 1933–1954.

970 ADA WATTERSON YERKES FAMILY. Papers, 1850–1963. 8 boxes. Gift of Miss Roberta Yerkes, 1966, 1968. MS 3316.

Primarily family letters, diaries, and genealogical data relating to relatives of Ada Watterson Yerkes of New Haven, Connecticut. Among her ancestors were many of the Harpers and Nortons who resided in northeastern Ohio, including Colonel Alexander Harper (1744–1798), founder of Harpersfield Township, Ashtabula County.

971 JOSEPH C. ROOT. Genealogical Papers, 1905–1912, 1930's. 20 boxes. Gift of Joseph C. Root, 1967. MS 3318.

Concerning the genealogy of the Root family and Joseph C. Root's activities as proprietor of the Root Genealogy Company of Omaha, Nebraska.

972 HIRAM HOUSE. CLEVELAND, O. Records, 1893–1968. 61 boxes, 15 volumes. Gifts of Mrs. George A. Bellamy, 1967, 1969; Hiram House Camp, 1971. MS 3319.

Correspondence, minutes of meetings, financial statements and ledger books, scrapbooks, photographs, publications, and other records of this social settlement founded in 1896 by George A. Bellamy, who served as its director from 1896 to 1946.

973 DONALD F. LYBARGER FAMILY. Papers, 1865–1962. 23 volumes. Gift of Judge Donald F. Lybarger, 1968. MS 3322.

Includes 11 volumes of family letters and memorabilia, 1865–1962, and 10 scrapbooks, 1922–1962. The latter relate primarily to Lybarger's activities as Cuyahoga County Recorder (1933–1950) and as judge of the Cuyahoga Court of Common Pleas (1950–1969), as well as to his interests in philately and the history of Cleveland and the Western Reserve.

974 MARY EMMA (BETTS) STERLING (b. 1837). Diaries, 1872–1892. 19 volumes. Gift of Lawrence S. Robbins, Jr., 1968. MS 3323.
Wife of Frederick A. Sterling (b. 1831), Cleveland merchant and banker.

975 SAMUEL V. PERRY (1896–1968). Papers, ca. 1920–1968. 11 boxes, 5 volumes. Gift of Mrs. Samuel V. Perry, 1968. MS 3327.
Cleveland municipal court clerk, active in Negro organizations.

976 RALPH S. LOCHER. Papers, 1961–1967. 42 boxes. Gift of Ralph S. Locher, 1968. MS 3337.
Correspondence, speeches, and campaign and election literature relating to Locher's activities as Mayor of Cleveland.

977 FREDERICK J. AND SAMUEL B. PRENTISS. Papers, 1839–1865. 15 boxes. MS 3350.
Civil- and criminal-case papers of these two Cleveland law partners.

978 HISTORIC AMERICAN BUILDINGS SURVEY. NORTHERN DISTRICT OF OHIO. Records, 1933–1937. 11 boxes. MS 3352.
Correspondence, field notebooks, and photographs by Carl Waite relating to this survey which was conducted under the auspices of the Works Progress Administration.

979 CASTALIA SPORTING CLUB. CLEVELAND, O. Records, 1878–ca. 1950. 12 boxes, 2 volumes. MS 3358.
Correspondence, minutes of meetings, annual reports, land deeds and agreements, insurance policies, letter books, account books, registers, blueprints, and other records relating to this club, the purpose of which was to pursue lawful sporting activities such

as hunting and fishing and to protect fish and game. Founded in 1878 by residents of Cleveland, the club owned property in Margaretta Township, Erie County, Ohio.

980 LICKING COUNTY PAPERS, 1803–1899. 24 boxes. MS 3359.

Eight series of correspondence, speeches, writings, and financial records including records of the Licking County Pioneer, Historical, and Antiquarian Society and the Madison Farmers' Association; and papers of members of the Wilson, Seymour, and Buckingham families.

981 CHARLES ROSCOE HOWLAND (1871–1947). Papers, 1936–1945. 9 boxes, 7 volumes. MS 3360.

Journals, pocket diaries, and biographical and genealogical data concerning the Howland family.

982 FREDERICK C. WAITE. Papers, 1853–1954. 3 boxes. MS 3361.

Concerning Post and Devol family genealogies.

983 DARIUS LYMAN FAMILY. Papers, 1805–1890. 11 boxes. MS 3364.

Correspondence, land deeds and surveys, journals, and other papers of Darius Lyman (1789–1867) of Portage County, Ohio, lawyer and state legislator; John P. Converse (1792–1865) of Parkman, Geauga County, Ohio, businessman and state legislator (1841–1842); and Robert B. Parkman (1771–1832), lawyer, businessman, and jurist.

984 WILLIAM GANSON ROSE. Papers, ca. 1940–1950. 10 boxes. MS 3365.

Primarily newspaper clippings used in compiling *Cleveland, the Making of a City* (Cleveland and New York: The World Publishing Company, 1950).

985 LAURENCE HARPER NORTON (1888–1960). Papers, ca. 1760–1960. 85 boxes. Gift of the Estate of Laurence H. Norton. MS 3371.

Laurence H. Norton, soldier, banker, industrialist, Ohio state legislator, and Cleveland civic and cultural leader, served as private secretary to Ambassador Myron T. Herrick (1912–1914, 1921–1924), and as president of the Western Reserve Historical Society (1934–1960). Among the papers, which include many of those of his ancestors, are the following: correspondence, legal documents, financial records, newspaper clippings, and photographs relating to various members of the Norton, Castle, and Harper families, ca. 1760–1945; correspondence and financial papers of Robert Harper, 1820–1840; correspondence of Alexander J. Harper, 1855–1894; general, business, personal, and political correspondence of Rice Harper, including letters of Jay Cooke, 1862–1887; genealogical charts, correspondence, newspaper clippings, and other materials concerning the genealogy of the Norton and Harper families, ca. 1880–1948; correspondence, record books, newspaper clippings, certificates, and photographs relating to Troop A, Ohio National Guard, and the 135th Field Artillery, 37th Division, 1887–1923; and correspondence, newspaper clippings and other volumes relating to the social engagements of Ambassador Herrick, 1912–1913.

986 PAUL BROTHERS. AKRON, O. Records, 1839–1917. 85 boxes. Gift of Robert W. Bordner, 1968. MS 3376.

Field books, maps, and other survey records of this firm which did most of the land surveying in Summit County during the 19th century. Hosea Paul held the office of Summit County Surveyor.

987 JOHN P. GREEN (1845–1940). Papers, 1869–1910. 15 boxes (approx.). Purchase and gift, 1969. MS 3379.

Cleveland lawyer active in local and state politics (especially the presidential campaign of William McKinley in 1896) as well as a prominent leader of the Negro community.

988 PATRICK J. BURNS. Papers, 1923–1945. 6 boxes. Gift of Patrick J. Burns, 1969. MS 3382.
President, Cleveland Carpenter's Local 105.

989 MARVIN CLINTON HARRISON (1890–1954). Papers, ca. 1915–1952. 18 boxes. Gift of Allen Hull, 1969. MS 3391.
Cleveland attorney whose papers include primarily legal briefs and depositions and other papers concerning the Solanics case, which involved the United Automobile Workers and Thompson Products Company of Cleveland, Ohio, 1937–1942.

990 CONSERVATION ORGANIZATIONS. CLEVELAND, O. Records, 1939–1942. 3 boxes. Gift of the Case Western Reserve University Archives, 1969. MS 3394.
Relating to the National Wildlife Federation, Ohio Natural Resources Council, and Cuyahoga County Conservation Council.

991 SAMUEL HENDRY, ET AL. Papers, 19th c. 7 boxes. Gift of E. C. Lampson. MS 3399.
Papers relating to economic, legal, political, and military affairs in Ashtabula County.

992 MARIE R. WING. Papers, ca. 1920–1969. 4 boxes. Gift of Marie Wing, 1969. MS 3404.
Cleveland attorney and feminist.

993 CLEVELAND AREA CHURCH FEDERATION. CLEVELAND, O. Records, 1912–1961. 35 boxes, 6 volumes. Deposited by the Greater Cleveland Council of Churches, 1969. MS 3406.
Includes annual reports, minutes of committee and department meetings, publications, correspondence, newspaper clippings,

and other records of this organization, now known as the Greater Cleveland Council of Churches.

994 BARKER FAMILY. Papers, 1821–1923. 1½ boxes. Purchased, 1969. MS 3416.

Primarily personal correspondence of the Donaldson and Barker families, located predominantly in Huron County, Ohio.

995 A. DONALD GRAY (1891–1939). Papers, ca. 1920–1939. 40 boxes (approx.). MS 3470.

Correspondence, financial records, photographs, and plans relating to Gray's activities as a landscape architect in Cleveland.

996 GREATER CLEVELAND GROWTH ASSOCIATION. CLEVELAND, O. Records, 1881–1959. 150 boxes (approx.). Deposited by the Growth Association, 1969. MS 3471.

Includes annual reports (printed) of the Cleveland Chamber of Commerce, 1881–1930; minutes of chamber meetings, 1892–1959; and minutes of meetings of the executive committee of the Greater Cleveland Growth Board, 1962–1963, 1966–1967. The Chamber of Commerce and the Greater Cleveland Growth Board merged in 1968 to form the Greater Cleveland Growth Association.

997 MERCHANT FAMILY. Papers, 1820–1905. 32 boxes, 1 oversize package. MS 3477.

Papers relating to the activities of Ahaz Merchant (1794–1862), Cuyahoga County surveyor (1833–1835, 1845–1850); to those of his son, Aaron Merchant (1817–1875), Cuyahoga County surveyor (1854–1869); and also to the activities of Corwin C. Merchant, son of Aaron Merchant and also a surveyor. The papers include surveys, field notes, plats, account books, and ledgers.

998   CITY CLUB OF CLEVELAND. Records, 1917–1966. 38 boxes, 11 volumes. Gift of the City Club, 1970. MS 3517.

Correspondence, annual reports, minutes of board meetings, financial and membership records, and publications and newspaper clippings relating to this club which was organized in 1912 to provide a forum for the discussion of important local, national, and international issues.

999   FRANCES PAYNE BOLTON (b. 1885). Papers, ca. 1940–1969. 400 boxes (approx.). Gift of Mrs. Frances P. Bolton, 1963–1969.

Primarily papers relating to Mrs. Bolton's activities as U.S. representative from Ohio's 22nd District from 1940 to 1969.

1000   CONSUMERS LEAGUE OF OHIO. CLEVELAND, O. Records, 1909–1965. 70 boxes (approx.). Gift of the Consumers League, 1971.

Correspondence, reports, minutes of meetings, newspaper clippings, and other records of this organization founded in 1900 to improve the lot of the worker and to increase protection offered the consumer. This collection refers to such topics as child labor, women in industry, minimum-wage laws, social security, and unemployment insurance.

1001   SAMUEL MATHER FAMILY. Papers, ca. 1872–1945. 30 boxes (approx.). Gift of Mrs. Robert H. Bishop, Jr., 1969, 1970.

Correspondence, diaries, photographs, scrapbooks, genealogical data, and other papers relating to the activities and interests of members of this prominent Cleveland family, particularly Samuel Mather (1851–1931), iron merchant, financier, and philanthropist, and his wife, Flora Stone Mather (1852–1909). Other notable persons represented in this collection include John Hay (1838–1905), Amasa Stone (1818–1883), and Constance Fenimore Woolson (1840–1894).

1002 NATIONAL ASSOCIATION FOR THE ADVANCEMENT OF COLORED PEOPLE. CLEVELAND BRANCH. CLEVELAND, O. Records, ca. 1935–ca. 1963. 75 boxes.

Records include administrative reports, committee minutes and reports, financial records, general correspondence, membership records, convention materials, public relations materials, data concerning other organizations, general subject file, and records of chapter activities and concerns such as housing, labor, legislation, legal cases, youth programs, and education.

RESTRICTED: Details available in the Society.

1003 SAMUEL H. SILBERT (b. 1883). Papers, 1927–1968. 100 boxes (approx.). Gift of Samuel H. Silbert, 1969.

Correspondence, memoranda, court dockets, speeches, newspaper clippings, financial records, photographs, and other papers relating to Silbert's public and civic life in Cleveland during which he spent over 50 years as judge of the Cuyahoga County Court of Common Pleas.

1004 URBAN LEAGUE OF CLEVELAND. Records, 1917–1969. 57 boxes. Gift of the Urban League, 1970.

Includes minutes of meetings, correspondence, committee reports, financial records, pamphlets, and newspaper clippings.

1005 THE WESTERN RESERVE HISTORICAL SOCIETY. CLEVELAND, O. Records, 1867–1969. 250 boxes (approx.).

General administration records include: articles of incorporation, constitution, bylaws, certificates of existence and tax-exemption status, 1867–1965; director's annual and quarterly reports and general activity reports, 1867–1965; general correspondence, 1867–1963; donation records, 1867–1939; membership records, 1867–1905, 1939–1958; visitors' registers and attendance records for Museum and Library, 1869–1969; financial records, 1872–1960; and general subject files, 1910–1964.

Library records include the following: accession and acquisition books, 1866–1949; exchange records, 1870–1915; donation records and copies of gift acknowledgments, 1909–1959; and correspondence of the librarian, 1946–1967. Museum records include accession books, 1894–1939, and subject files of the curator, 1947–1969.

Among other records are scrapbooks, 1867–1968; a record file of the Society's publications, 1870–1969; and various awards, blueprints, and photographs.

PART II: OHIO GOVERNMENT ARCHIVES

ADAMS COUNTY

1006 BOARD OF SCHOOL EXAMINERS. Records, 1838–1847. 1 volume. Gift of Wallace H. Cathcart, 1910. MS 437.

Rules, proceedings, minutes of special meetings, and several letters attesting to the character and ability of prospective teachers.

1007 COMMISSIONERS OF INSOLVENTS. Records, 1824–1828, 1832–1842, 1866–1870, 1874–1875, 1888–1890. 1 volume. Gift of Wallace H. Cathcart, 1910. MS 435.

Proceedings of the Commissioners of Insolvents, who dealt with matters pertaining to debtors and bankruptcy. The records after 1832 consist of loose papers laid in this volume.

ASHLAND COUNTY

1008 GENERAL (COUNTY). Records, 1874–1880. 1 folder. MS 1345.

Poll sheets of school districts in Vermilion, 1878–1879; search warrants, quitclaim deeds, and other agreements, 1874–1880.

1009 SULLIVAN TOWNSHIP. COMMON SCHOOLS. DISTRICT NO. 1. Records, 1847–1854. 1 volume. Gift of George McConnell, 1927. MS 1208.

Daily and general registers, teachers' reports, and quarterly summaries.

ASHTABULA COUNTY

1010 CENSUS (COUNTY). Records, 1847–1875. 8 boxes. Gift of E. C. Lampson. MS 3398.

Schedules for each special quadriennial county census taken beginning in 1847.

1011 GENERAL (COUNTY). Records, 1811–1870. 7 boxes. MS 2065.

One volume containing census records for each of 32 townships within Ashtabula County, 1811–1835; a series of booklets containing census records for each of 28 townships, 1843; election poll books for various townships, 1811, 1816, 1858, 1862–1870, and an abstract of votes cast in the general election of 1844; one folder of wolf-scalp bounty payment certificates, 1811–1828; five boxes of subpoenas and warrants issued by various justices of the peace during the 1830's; one folder of marriage licenses, 1832–1840; and ten applications for tavern licenses filed in Ashtabula County, 1842.

1012 ASHTABULA TOWNSHIP. GENERAL. Records, ca. 1840–1889. ½ box. Gift of J. Frederick Waring and Edward H. Fitch, 1964. MS 3242.

A collection of surveys, maps, plats, powers of attorney, deeds, and indentures relating to land transactions in this township.

1013 CONNEAUT TOWNSHIP. JUSTICES OF THE PEACE. Records, 1830–1833. 1 folder. MS 2646.

Copies of subpoenas and warrants issued by Asa Jacobs, justice of the peace in Conneaut, which from 1804 to 1832 was known as Salem.

1014 JEFFERSON AND LENOX TOWNSHIPS. COMMON SCHOOLS. DISTRICT NO. 5. Records, 1834–1888. 1 volume. MS 1310.

Minutes of meetings of the school directors and accounts of the treasurers during this period.

1015 TRUMBULL TOWNSHIP. COMMON SCHOOLS. DISTRICT NO. 9. Records, 1849–1898. 1 volume. Gift of Mrs. Abbie Spafford Proctor, 1928. MS 1230.

Minutes of meetings and some financial records of this district.

1016 WINDSOR TOWNSHIP. BOARD OF EDUCATION. Records, 1853–1879. 1 volume. MS 3503.

Minutes of board meetings, school fund and contingent fund disbursement statements, treasurers' reports, and amendments and resolutions relating to the construction and operation of the public schools in this township.

1017 WINDSOR TOWNSHIP. COMMON SCHOOLS. DISTRICT NO. 1. Records, 1838–1886. 1 volume. Purchased, 1929. MS 1748.

Minutes of meetings, teachers' reports, and financial accounts.

1018 WINDSOR TOWNSHIP. GENERAL. Records, 1811–1867. 4 volumes. Gift of Elmo Martin, 1941. MS 2767.

Copies of contracts, deeds, subpoenas, and commissions, 1811–1867; book of earmarks, 1811–1850; list of taxable property in Windsor, 1823; and a record book for School District No. 5, 1833–1847.

CARROLL COUNTY

1019 GENERAL (COUNTY). Records, 1834–1869. 4 volumes. Gift of Edward F. Lawler. MS 1135.

Account book of a Carrollton Township newspaper, 1834–1838; record book of the Carroll County Clerk, 1836–1844; account book of Centre Township, 1837-1869; and record book of stray horses found, 1849-1864.

1020   WASHINGTON TOWNSHIP. COMMON SCHOOLS. DISTRICT NO. 4. Records, 1857-1887. 1 volume. Gift of the Prentiss Fund, 1925. MS 3420.

Minutes of meetings of qualified voters and directors, and some financial accounts.

CHAMPAIGN COUNTY

1021   URBANA TOWNSHIP. CLERK. Records, 1855-1892. 1 volume. MS 1427.

Records of estrays as recorded by township clerks.

CLERMONT COUNTY

1022   GENERAL (COUNTY). Records, 1801-1805, 1819, 1831, 1856-1857, 1863. 1 box. MS 1086.

Census records for townships within this county, 1801, 1802, 1819; county tax records, 1801-1802, and treasurers' receipts, 1801-1805; loose papers relating to the Court of Common Pleas, the Sheriff, and the justice of the peace, 1801-1805; lists of merchants and their capital for the year 1831; registers of births, deaths, and marriages for the year ending March 1, 1857; and poll books containing votes of the qualified voters of Clermont County who were in the military service of the United States, 1863.

COLUMBIANA COUNTY

1023   GENERAL (COUNTY). Records, 1803-1854. 5 volumes. MS 1134.

Court case records, copies of laws of the Ohio legislature, abstracts of votes by township, list of justices of the peace, 1803–

1832; record book of the clerk of the Court of Common Pleas, 1817–1839; minutes of meetings of the Board of County Commissioners, 1829–1838; Center Township records, including minutes of trustee meetings, treasurers' records, copies of agreements, and militia rolls, 1824–1854.

1024 BUTLER TOWNSHIP. COMMON SCHOOLS. DISTRICT NO. 5. Records, 1846–1861. 1 volume. MS 908.

Daily attendance register and teachers' reports and general registers.

1025 CENTER TOWNSHIP. JUSTICES OF THE PEACE. Records, 1818–1821. 1 volume. MS 566.

Docket book for various justices of the peace and constables from this township.

1026 NEW LISBON. GENERAL. Records, 1844–1851. 1 volume. MS 1255.

Lists of delinquent taxpayers.

1027 PERRY TOWNSHIP. COMMON SCHOOLS. DISTRICT NO. 5. Records, 1838–1852. 1 volume. MS 578.

Daily register, quarterly reports, and general register, including names of students and attendance records.

CRAWFORD COUNTY

1028 BUCYRUS. MAYOR'S COURT. Records, 1868–1876. 1 volume. Gift of the F. F. Prentiss Fund, 1922. MS 1122.

Records of court cases held before G. Donnenwirth and George McNeal, mayors of Bucyrus.

1029 BUCYRUS TOWNSHIP. TRUSTEES. Records, 1858–1877. 1 volume. MS 1120.

Minutes of trustee meetings, records of receipts and expenditures, poor fund and road reports, and a few surveys and land profiles in connection with land drainage, 1858–1877.

1030 HOLMES TOWNSHIP. GENERAL. Records, 1829–1849. 1 volume. Gift of the F. F. Prentiss Fund, 1922. MS 1124.

Election results, minutes of trustee meetings, records of indentures, treasurers' accounts and various other financial records, record of surveyor's plat, reports of school directors, and list of names of residents of Holmes who were subject to military call.

CUYAHOGA COUNTY

1031 AUDITOR. Records, 1819, 1823–1869. 115 volumes. Gift of the Cuyahoga County Records Commission, 1960, 1962.

These Auditor's tax duplicates contain the record of real estate taxes levied in Cleveland and other townships and villages in Cuyahoga County, and also certain information on individual companies or corporations enumerated for assessment including real and personal property valuations. The volumes for these years are complete, although the tax records from 1810—when the county was incorporated—until 1818 and from 1820 to 1822 have been lost.

Unpublished 19-page register available in the Society.

1032 AUDITOR. Records, 1899–1901. 3 volumes (reprint of typed copy). Gift of the Bank of Commerce. MS 37.

"Reference directory of all the taxpayers in Cuyahoga County who returned for taxation $500.00 or more in personal property, money, or credit; an accurate compilation from tax duplicates on file in the office of the County Auditor, Cleveland."

1033 COURT OF COMMON PLEAS. Records, 1810–1912. 51 volumes (disbound).* Deposited by the Cuyahoga County Court of Common Pleas, 1966.

These volumes contain a complete account of the trial proceedings held in the Cuyahoga County Court of Common Pleas between 1810 (the year the county was incorporated) and 1912.

* These records have been microfilmed by the Court of Common Pleas.

1034 GENERAL (COUNTY). Records, 1809–1896. 1 folder. MS 2062.

Accumulation of various documents relating to governmental activities, including election returns for grand and petit jurors in Euclid, 1812; Cuyahoga County census report, 1819; Strongsville Township census report, 1823; list of mercantile capital within the county, 1833; papers relating to the annexation of certain parts of Newburgh and Brooklyn townships to Cleveland, 1867–1896.

1035 GRAND JURY. Record, October 6, 1898. 469 pages. Gift of C. H. Grisson. MS 419.

Testimony taken before the grand jury of Cuyahoga County, concerning the investigation of the improvements of the Brecksville Road in Newburgh, Independence, and Brecksville townships.

1036 TREASURER. Records, 1810–1828. 1 volume. MS 379.

"Order Book" containing records of payments to individuals for various services and statements of orders drawn upon the treasury of Cuyahoga County.

1037 BROOKLYN TOWNSHIP. GENERAL. Records, 1855–1924. 6 boxes, 48 volumes. Gift of Brooklyn Village, 1950. MS 3130.

Including the minutes of meetings of township trustees, 1861–1922; township fund, school fund, and poor fund accounts, 1855–

1924; proceedings of the board of education, 1891–1911; criminal-case dockets, 1856–1905; civil-case dockets, 1867–1905; and two record books of the Cuyahoga Steam Furnace Company, 1832–1834, 1851–1871.

Unpublished 2-page register available in the Society.

1038   CLEVELAND. BOARD OF EDUCATION. Record, December 20, 1924. ½ box (typescript copies). Gift of Robert J. Kutak, 1926. MS 1192.

Copy of a teaching unit dealing with the Western Reserve.

1039   CLEVELAND. BOARD OF ELECTIONS. Records, 1896. 1 oversize package. Gift of Leonard F. Fuerst, 1947. MS 3100.

Poll books and tally sheets for Wards 24 and 25.

1040   CLEVELAND. BOARD OF ELECTIONS. Records, 1907, 1908. 52 boxes. MS 3475.

Men's registration records for every precinct in each of the city's 26 wards during the general registration in October and November, 1907, and during the special registration in September, 1908. There are two sets of records for each precinct, because electors were required to register in duplicate. In addition to name and address, the age, length of residence, country of birth, date of naturalization (where applicable), and marital status of each voter were also recorded.

1041   CLEVELAND. BOARD OF MANAGERS OF THE PUBLIC SCHOOLS. Records, 1846–1856. 1 volume. MS 393.

Minutes of meetings, 1848–1850; results of examinations of teachers at Rockwell Street School, August 15 and November 23, 1851; lists of books ordered and books received; and some computations.

1042   CLEVELAND. CHARTER COMMISSION. Records, 1913. 1 folder (typescript copies). Gift of Edward M. Williams. MS 2658.

Copies of letters, minutes of meetings, calendars, resolutions, recommendations, and speeches relating to the activities of the 15 commissioners who prepared a home-rule charter for the city of Cleveland which was approved by the voters in July, 1913, and went into effect on January 1, 1914.

1043   CLEVELAND. CHARTER COMMISSION. Records, 1913. 1 box (typescript copies). MS 885.

Amendments, calendars, proceedings, proposals, questionnaires, recommendations, and correspondence concerning the activities of the members of this commission, which included Mayor Newton D. Baker, Edward W. Doty, Mayo Fessler, and Earl H. Wells.

1044   CLEVELAND. CITY COUNCIL. Record, ca. 1892. ½ box. Gift of L. P. Beman. MS 1125.

Petition urging the Council "to at once take proper action to provide for the purchases of sufficient suitable land for park purposes" and signed by hundreds of Cleveland residents.

1045   CLEVELAND. CITY COUNCIL. Records, 1909. 5 boxes (typescript). Gift of Peter Witt. MS 896.

Papers dealing with railways and the Street Railway Ordinance, including minutes of meetings of the Council of the Whole, January 20 to October 14, 1909; addresses of Homer H. McKeehan, July 19 and 20, 1909; transcript of the proceedings before Hon. R. W. Taylor concerning differences between the Cleveland Council and the Cleveland Railway Company over the proposed Street Railway Ordinance, October 18 to December 1, 1909; and minutes of City Council meetings, October 25 to December 18, 1909.

1046 CLEVELAND. COMMON SCHOOLS. DISTRICT NO. 1. Records, 1836–1867. 1 volume. Gift of H. H. White, 1919. MS 10.

Minutes of annual meetings and school board election results for this district, which after 1845 became East Cleveland Township School District No. 1.

1047 CLEVELAND. FIRE DEPARTMENT. ENGINE COMPANY NO. 5. Records, 1885–1886. 1 volume. Gift of Edmund W. Geiger, 1969. MS 3378.

A journal containing daily roll call and monthly reports, and accounts of fires, including the extent of damage.

1048 CLEVELAND. MAYOR'S ADVISORY WAR COMMITTEE. Records, 1917–1920. 54 boxes, 2 packages. Gift of Harry L. Vail, 1920. MS 3374.

Correspondence, memoranda, committee reports, financial records and audit reports, and other materials relating to the activities of this committee which was organized by Mayor Harry L. Davis in April, 1917, for the purpose of handling "any extraordinary matters which might arise during the period of the war." This committee, which attempted to coordinate various institutions in the city with the national war effort, relied heavily on local organizations such as the Chamber of Commerce and the Red Cross. The committee functioned in areas such as rent control, Americanization programs, propaganda, and the surveillance of subversive elements. Specifically referred to are the Rent Adjustment Board, Four Minute Men, Committee on Patriotism, and Cleveland War Service Record.

The Cleveland War Service Record was an attempt to compile a record of the services rendered by local citizens during the war. The data compiled fill 330 cabinet drawers and occupy 495 linear feet of space. These cards contain names, addresses, and Selective Service numbers of servicemen, and often such information as place of birth, occupation, nationality, race, citizenship, division of service, languages spoken, wages, and education. The nine series of cards are arranged alphabetically by name of individual, employer, or military unit.

Unpublished 11-page register available in the Society.

1049   MAYFIELD TOWNSHIP. COMMON SCHOOLS. Records, 1842–1864. 2 volumes. Gift of Margaret Lapham, 1943; deposited by the Mayfield School District. MS 2853.

Surveys and minutes of meetings of the directors of various districts.

1050   NEWBURGH TOWNSHIP. GENERAL. Records, 1815–1915. 4 boxes, 7 volumes, 3 packages. Gift of Mrs. Carl Ruhe, 1948. MS 3058.

Town books (minutes of meetings of electors and trustees, election results, court dockets, copies of receipts and petitions), 1815–1903; school fund records, 1838–1889; treasurers' books, 1839–1890; election poll books and tally sheets, 1843–1866, 1893–1915; township clerks' records, and a miscellaneous assortment of petitions, mortgages, ordinances, resolutions, contracts, bonds, and receipts, ca. 1840–1910. Also included are several volumes of notes on the political history of Newburgh compiled by Henry H. Bohning, township clerk at the turn of the century.

1051   NEWBURGH TOWNSHIP. COMMON SCHOOLS. DISTRICT NO. 1. Records, 1827–1879. 1 volume. Gift of Jonathan Edwards, 1948. MS 2880.

Notices and minutes of meetings of qualified voters of this district.

1052   NEWBURGH TOWNSHIP. COMMON SCHOOLS. SUB-DISTRICT NO. 4. Records, 1854–1879. 1 volume. Gift of Dr. Ludlow, 1925. MS 2295.

Minutes of meetings of qualified voters and school directors and some financial accounts.

1053 OHIO CITY. GENERAL. Records, 1836–1851. 11 items. MS 3423.

Includes documents relating to a loan negotiated by Ohio City, 1837; amendment to the act which incorporated Ohio City, 1837; abstract of votes for and against the union of Ohio City and Cleveland, 1851; and a memorandum of agreement concerning the annexation of Ohio City to Cleveland, 1854.

1054 OLMSTED TOWNSHIP. CLERK. Records, 1827–1886. 1 volume. Gift of Mrs. H. J. Offenberg, 1952. MS 3077.

Lists of earmarks and strays. Also included is a 21-page historical sketch of "Olmstead" as "compiled by Crisfield Johnson, published by D. W. Ensign, David Stearns narrator."

1055 PARMA TOWNSHIP. JUSTICES OF THE PEACE. Records, 1835–1841. 1 volume. Gift of K. K. Hodgman, 1933. MS 1841.

Docket book of Oliver Emerson, who resided in Parma.

1056 ROCKPORT TOWNSHIP. JUSTICES OF THE PEACE. Records, 1843–1854. 1 volume. MS 1265.

Docket book of Royal Millard.

1057 ROYALTON TOWNSHIP. JUSTICES OF THE PEACE. Records, 1858–1876, 1899. 1 volume. Gift of Dr. and Mrs. Jerome R. Tousley, 1961. MS 3167.

Docket book containing entries of several justices of the peace, and including copies of warrants, subpoenas, and judgments rendered in civil cases.

1058 WARRENSVILLE TOWNSHIP. COMMON SCHOOLS. SUB-DISTRICT NO. 5. Records, 1884–1890. 1 volume. MS 11.

Proceedings of school directors' meetings, contracts between teachers and directors, certificates for pay, and the district clerk's account book.

1059 WILLEYVILLE. GENERAL. Records, 1835–1846. 1 folder. MS 1317.

Statement showing sale of lots in Willeyville (partitioned from Ohio City in 1837), 1835–1836; certificates of tax sales, 1838–1844; and notices of tax delinquency, 1843–1846.

ERIE COUNTY

1060 BIRMINGHAM TOWNSHIP. CEMETERY. Records, 1839–1890. 1 volume. MS 3192.

Articles of association, minutes of meetings, and copies of agreements and deeds of the Birmingham Cemetery Association.

1061 FLORENCE TOWNSHIP. GENERAL. Records, 1866–1880. 1 volume. MS 3192a.

Copies of bonds of township officers, including the treasurer, justice of the peace, constable, assessor, and road supervisor.

1062 KELLEY'S ISLAND TOWNSHIP. TRUSTEES. Records. 1840–1872. 1 volume. Gift of Norman Hills, 1927. MS 1201.

Copy of the act establishing the township of Kelley's Island, January 21, 1840; results of annual elections and minutes of trustee meetings as recorded by Datus Kelley, George C. Huntington, William S. Webb, and George P. Bristol, township clerks.

FAYETTE COUNTY

1063 ELECTIONS (COUNTY). Records, 1836–1873. 1 folder. MS 2324.

Poll books of elections held in various townships in Fayette County, including: Concord, 1866; Green, 1843, 1866; Jefferson, 1853; Marion, 1845, 1873; Paint, 1866; Union, 1836, 1843, 1864; and Wayne, 1836, 1866. Also included is an abstract of votes cast in Fayette County in October, 1873.

GALLIA COUNTY

1064 GALLIPOLIS TOWNSHIP. TRUSTEES. Records, 1828–1839. 1 volume. Gift of Judge W. R. White. MS 572.

Minutes of trustee meetings, resolutions, election results, and financial statements.

GEAUGA COUNTY

1065 BAINBRIDGE TOWNSHIP. GENERAL. Records, 1822–1931. 7½ boxes, 1 volume, 1 package. Deposited by the Bainbridge Township Trustees, 1969. MS 3405.

Including township trustee record book, 1822–1894; bonds of township officials, 1838–1924; teachers' quarterly reports, 1842–1875; justice dockets, 1847–1852, 1861–1901, 1886–1929; land and road tax lists, 1851–1871; township clerks' account book, 1862–1873; records of individual donations to aid in procuring substitutes to fill Bainbridge's quota under the draft laws of 1863 and 1864, 1865; copies of township records including poll books and minutes of trustee meetings, 1872–1903; tally sheets and poll books, 1874–1929; school board reports, 1894, 1901–1912; petitions, 1898-ca. 1918; reports of superintendent of schools, 1900–1909; treasurer's account book, 1905–1923; and minutes of trustee meetings, 1918, 1921, 1924.

1066 RUSSELL TOWNSHIP. TRUSTEES. Records, 1827–1850. 1 volume. Gift of Elwyn B. Robinson, 1952. MS 3106.

Copies of election poll books, indentures, and financial receipts, and minutes of trustee meetings.

GUERNSEY COUNTY

1067 CAMBRIDGE TOWNSHIP. TRUSTEES. Records, 1815–1845, 1872. 20 items. MS 2197.

Election poll books for 1815, 1820, 1823, 1829, 1832, 1834, 1835, 1836, 1839, 1840, 1841, 1844, and 1845, and specifications and other papers concerning the building of the Marietta & Pittsburgh Railroad in Cambridge, 1872.

LAKE COUNTY

1068 PERRY TOWNSHIP. TRUSTEES. Records, 1815–1848. 1 volume. Gift of Vaughn E. Wyman, 1935. MS 2026.

Organization of the township, minutes of meetings, lists of householders, and copies of indentures and other legal documents relating to Perry, which was part of Geauga County until 1840, when Lake County was organized.

1069 WILLOUGHBY TOWNSHIP. CEMETERY. Records, 1861, 1866, 1875, 1878, 1884–1888. 1 volume. Gift of the Estate of Martin E. Gray, 1910. MS 430.

Minutes of meetings held to consider the upkeep of the township's burying grounds.

1070 WILLOUGHBY TOWNSHIP. JUSTICES OF THE PEACE. Records, 1834–1866. 4 volumes. Gift of Sidney S. Wilson, 1916. MS 475.

Docket books containing numerous and detailed reports of legal proceedings held in Willoughby Township under John M. Henderson and O. H. Sharp.

1071 WILLOUGHBY TOWNSHIP. TRUSTEES. Records, 1815–1874. 2 volumes. Gift of Sidney S. Wilson, 1916. MS 91.

Minutes of trustee meetings, election results, school district records, indentures, and land records of the township, which until 1834 was named Chagrin.

LORAIN COUNTY

1072 BLACK RIVER TOWNSHIP. GENERAL. Records, 1817–1848. 2 volumes, Gift of Charles H. Gallup, 1911; and others. MS 1083.

Election results, financial reports, minutes of trustee meetings, and school district reports, 1817–1848; and a tax list extracted from the duplicate of 1823.

MAHONING COUNTY

1073 COURT OF COMMON PLEAS. Records, 1854–1864. 1 volume. Gift of Mrs. Charles E. Foster, 1931. MS 1570.

Docket book containing the proceedings of 73 civil cases which were contested in this court.

1074 INFIRMARY. Records, 1855–1859. 1 volume. MS 1298.

Book of entries kept by Superintendent James Shields which contains information about the inmates of the Mahoning County Infirmary.

1075 CANFIELD TOWNSHIP. GENERAL. Records, 1802–1809, 1909–1915. ½ box. MS 1250.

Quarterly reports of accounts with the general post office, 1802–1804; minutes of trustee and elector meetings, a record of earmarks (cattle), and some financial accounts, 1805–1809; tax lists, 1807–1809; and minutes of trustee meetings and copies of resolutions and agreements, 1909–1915.

1076 CANFIELD TOWNSHIP. COMMON SCHOOLS. DISTRICT NO. 3. Records, 1826–1853. 1 volume. MS 1243.

Plat of this school district, minutes of meetings, lists of householders, copies of deeds, and teacher reports.

1077 YOUNGSTOWN TOWNSHIP. COMMON SCHOOLS. DISTRICT NO. 5. Records, 1832–1858. 1 volume. Gift of Mrs. Charles E. Foster, 1931. MS 1569.

Account book kept by the treasurer of this school district.

MEDINA COUNTY

1078 AUDITOR. Records, 1826. 1 volume. Gift of William Everhard, 1943. MS 3097.

Duplicate of taxes levied on the property of residents of the various townships in Medina County.

PORTAGE COUNTY

1079 RAVENNA TOWNSHIP. COMMON SCHOOLS. DISTRICT NO. 6. Records, 1835–1885. 1 volume. MS 30.

Minutes of annual meetings, resolutions, and procedures relating to school matters in this district.

1080 SHALERSVILLE TOWNSHIP. GENERAL. Records, 1814–1876. 3 volumes. Gifts of Mrs. Mark Davis, 1946; Spray N. Hine, 1961. MS 3093.

Records of marks and brands, 1814–1857; and of civil actions contested in this township, 1854–1876.

ROSS COUNTY

1081 CHILLICOTHE. GENERAL. Records, 1846–1849. 1 folder. MS 3425.

Lists of the number of horses and other domestic animals sold at auction within the city, signed by various auctioneers and justices of the peace.

SUMMIT COUNTY

1082 STOW TOWNSHIP. MAGISTRATES COURT. Records, 1886–1919. Gift of Millard M. Thompson, 1965. 1 volume. MS 3255.

Magistrates docket for this township.

1083 TALLMADGE TOWNSHIP. JUSTICES OF THE PEACE. Records, 1852–1856. 1 volume. Gift of J. W. Walton. MS 1146.

Docket book of Lucius C. Walton.

TRUMBULL COUNTY

1084 ELECTIONS (COUNTY). Records, 1807–1832. 2 folders. MS 1297.

Poll books (many originally in the Elisha Whittlesey Papers) from these townships: Austin, Boardman, Bristol, Brookfield, Canfield, Coitsville, Deerfield, Ellsworth, Fowler, Franklin, Green, Hartford, Hiram, Hubbard, Hudson, Liberty, Newton, Poland, Troy, Vernon, Vienna, Warren, Weathersfield, and Youngstown.

1085   JUSTICES OF THE PEACE. Records, 1817–1820. 1 folder. Gift of Miss Elizabeth Hauser. MS 2550.

Copies of marriage certificates signed by various justices of the peace of this county.

1086   GREENE TOWNSHIP. COMMON SCHOOLS. DISTRICT NO. 2. Records, 1827–1892. MS 3504.

Minutes of annual and directors' meetings and copies of certificates and agreements relating to the operation of this district's public schools.

1087   SOUTHINGTON TOWNSHIP. COMMON SCHOOLS. DISTRICT NO. 3. Records, 1838–1889. 1 volume. MS 1573.

Minutes of meetings of the directors and of the qualified voters of this district (later Sub-district No. 2).

1088   WARREN TOWNSHIP. CLERK. Records, 1802–1822. 77 pages (typescript copy). Gift of K. O. Thompson, 1951. MS 3057.

True copy of "Warren Township Record Book A" as certified by George C. Braden, Warren Township clerk in 1902. Included are minutes of trustee meetings, election results, and financial accounts.

TUSCARAWAS COUNTY

1089   DOVER TOWNSHIP. COMMON SCHOOLS. DISTRICTS NO. 1 AND 5. Records, 1830–1870. 2 volumes. MS 1445.

Records of School District No. 1 include minutes of meetings, copies of teacher contracts, and some of the treasurers' accounts, 1830–1870; records of School District No. 5 consist of a teachers' register and report book.

Also included here is a 32-page religious address.

1090 ELK TOWNSHIP. COMMON SCHOOLS. DISTRICT NO. 4. Records, 1842–1885. Gift of P. B. Winters. MS 577.

Minutes of meetings of the school directors and qualified voters, and memoranda of agreements made in behalf of this school district.

1091 SALTCREEK TOWNSHIP. COMMON SCHOOLS. DISTRICT NO. 6. Records, 1844–1878. 1 volume. MS 1375.

Minutes of meetings of the school directors, copies of agreements, and financial accounts.

INDEX

LIST OF SUBJECT HEADINGS

Academies, institutes, and seminaries
Architecture and architects
Art and artists
Banking and banks
Bible
Cemeteries
Civil War
Colleges and universities
Communications
Confederate States of America
Conservation
Construction
Crime and punishment
Dairy products
Disaster relief
Economic life and conditions
Education
Engineering and engineers
Farming and farms
Fraternal and patriotic societies
Fur trade
Great Lakes
Horse racing and breeding
Hotels, inns, and taverns
Immigration
Indians
Industry and manufactures
Inventions and inventors
Journalists, editors, and publishers
Labor and unions
Land companies
Land deeds, surveys, and records
Law, lawyers, and jurists
Libraries and historical associations
Literary and debate societies

Livestock
Lotteries
Maps
Mathematics books
Medicine
Merchants
Mexican War
Milling and mills
Mining and mines
Monuments
Motion pictures
Music and music societies
Negroes
Northwest Territory
Oratory
Political parties
Politics
Public welfare
Reconstruction
Religion
Revolutionary War
Science and scientists
Slavery
Spanish-American War
Sports
Tariffs
Temperance
Tobacco
Transportation
Travels
War of 1812
Weather and meteorological data
Whaling
Woman suffrage
World War I
World War II
Writings and writers

The numbers after index entries refer to the item numbers. Names of individual churches have not been included, but are listed by denomination under Religion. Places, such as towns, cities, and counties, are listed alphabetically under the state name.

A. D. Anderson & Company, 132
Abbott, Benjamin W., 391
Abbott, Caroline Younglove, 213
Abbott, David (grandfather), 391
Abbott, David (grandson), 391
Abbott, Samuel, 55
Abbott, Squire, 948
Academies, institutes, and seminaries, 10, 16, 27, 31, 33, 39, 44, 54, 106, 114, 137, 160, 196, 216, 238, 243, 247, 249, 258, 307, 325, 365, 392, 406, 422, 492, 600, 612, 636, 667, 688, 738, 796, 815, 817, 854, 856, 895, 948, 951
Account books, collection of, 132
Ackerman, Solomon, 360
Ackley, J. M., 948
Ackley, John, 166
Adams, A. H., 619
Adams, Ashael, Jr., 948
Adams, Charles Francis, 178

Adams, Charles Francis, Jr., 897
Adams, Comfort A., 247
Adams, Edward, 707
Adams, J. J., 791
Adams, John (1735–1826), 203, 948
Adams, John, 946
Adams, John Quincy, 203
Adams, Roswell, 186
Adams Express Company, 132
Adgate, Thomas, 677
Africa, 563, 567, 798
Agenbroad, John P., 815
Aiken, William Martin, 82
Alabama, 188, 410, 508, 582, 614, 786, 852
Alabama Volunteer Infantry, 466
Alaska, 567, 793
Albany Manual Labor University, 948
Alcott, Seth R., 446
Aldrich, Nelson W., 897

Alexander, Edward P., 946
Alexander II (Emperor of Russia), 658
Alexandria Canal Company, 70
Allegheny College, 31
Allen, Ethan, 789
Allen, Florence Ellinwood, 958
Allen, Frederick Hobbes, 791
Allen, George E., 619
Allen, Henry T., 596
Allen, John W., 107, 114, 196, 247
Allen, Thomas, 619
Allen family, 667
Alling, Francis A., 319
Alling, George H., 319
Alling & Brother Company, 319
Allyn, James, 862
Almy, John J., 946
Alta Social Settlement, 846
Althouse, C. E., 791
Amalgamated Clothing Workers Union, 838
Ambler, Henry Lovejoy, 200
American Anti-Slavery Society, 365
American Baptist Home Mission Society, 325
American Baptist Missionary Union, 325, 619
American Baptist Publication Society, 619
American Bible Society, 20, 247, 392
American Colonization Society, 247, 365
American Congressional Temperance Society, 948
American Food Relief Project, 596
American Fur Company, 55
American Land Company, 737
American Library Association, 37
American Missionary Association, 864
American Peace Society, 897–899, 908
American Protective League, 372
American Revolution. *See* Revolutionary War
American Society of Mechanical Engineers, 771
American Sunday School Union, 609, 948
Ames, Jennie M., 628
Amis, Christian, 948
Ammen, Daniel, 946
Ammen, Jacob, 946
Ammon, Wilbur C., 608
Anderson, James P., 946
Anderson, Joseph, 739
Anderson, Paul, 247
Anderson, Richard C., 633, 769
Anderson, Robert, 946
Anderson, William Marshall, 633
Andrew, John A., 946
Andrews, E. B., 707, 948
Andrews, John, 473
Andrews, Mrs. S. G., 948
Andrews, Samuel C., 715
Andrews, Sherlock D., 196
Angell, Ernest, 827
Angell, James B., 387
Anglo-American Iron Company, 683
Anthony, Susan B., 400
Antisell, Thomas, 946
Anti-Slavery Bugle, 126, 365
Applegate, James, 948
Appleton, John, 462
Archer, Asa, 92

[354]

Architecture and architects, 82, 590, 753, 762, 872, 882, 900, 944–945, 947, 949, 995
Arkansas, 607, 730
Arkansas Volunteer Infantry, 466
Armstrong, A. Eneas, 946
Armstrong, Eliphalet, 590
Armstrong, Frank Crawford, 946
Armstrong, James, 948
Armstrong, John, 507
Armstrong, William, 299
Arnold, Benedict, 392, 948
Art and artists, 18, 39, 54, **177**, 333, 372, 466, 470, 574, 606, 629, 667, 705, 936, 947, 949
Ashbrook, William A., 791
Ashby, Turner, 946
Ashland County Female Anti-Slavery Society, 948
Ashtabula County Female Anti-Slavery Society, 61
Ashtabula County Society of Cleveland, 564
Ashtabula Historical Society, 691
Ashtabula Sentinel, 426, 840
Ashtabula, Warren & Liverpool Railroad, 412
Asmun, Thomas, 438
Associate Synod of North America, 57, 58
Athens County Pioneer Association, 948
Atkins, Quintus F., 1, 180, 247, 426, 691
Atkinson, Edward, 948
Atkinson, Joe, 946
Atlantic & Great Western Railroad, 396, 486, 508, 584, 796, 948
Atlantic Ocean, 905

Atwater, Amzi, 1, 46, 163, 166, 278, 375
Atwater, Caleb, 46, 247, 715, 738
Atwater, Joshua, 738
Austin, Calvin, 279, 737
Austin, Eliphalet, 1, 247, 279, 543, 860
Austin, Walter P., 466
Averill, Augustin, 247
Avery, Catherine Hitchcock, 49
Avery, Eben, 188
Avery, Elroy McKendree, 49, 771, 948
Avery, Hannah, 421
Avery, Thomas, 948
Avery, William S., 279
Avery family, 752
Axtell, Silas, 46
Ayres, Sam, 769

Babcock, Perry H., 268
Babcock, Mrs. Perry H., 268
Bacher, Otto, H., 177, 936
Backus, Isaac, 28
Backus, James, 339, 867
Bacon, Asa, Jr., 948
Bacon, Frederick A., 585
Bacon, Leonard, 948
Badeau, Adam, 946
Badger, Joseph, 1, 40, 338, **426**, 691
Baehr, Herman, 635
Baer, John Willis, 948
Bagg, James, 948
Bailey, Adams, 948
Bailey, Edward M., 948
Bailey, John R., 454
Bailey, William D., 948
Bainbridge, William, 517

[355]

Baird, Alvin V., 948
Baker, Elbert H., 791
Baker, Elizabeth, 918
Baker, Frank H., 918
Baker, Harriet Lamon, 918
Baker, Lyman, 425
Baker, Margaret, 918
Baker, Newton D., 168, 651, 768, 771, 791, 844, 897, 908, 917–918, 930, 948, 1043
Baker, Mrs. Newton D. (Elizabeth L.), 918
Baker, Newton D., III, 918
Baker, Samuel J., 948
Baldwin, Asa, 446
Baldwin, Charles Candee, 824
Baldwin, Dudley, 179, 537, 948
Baldwin, Edward, 132
Baldwin, Eli, 247, 446, 561, 665
Baldwin, George S., 446
Baldwin, H. H., 948
Baldwin, Henry, 446
Baldwin, Horace, 446
Baldwin, James, 948
Baldwin, Jesse, 272, 446
Baldwin, John, 425
Baldwin, John Brown, 946
Baldwin, Joseph L., 100
Baldwin, Mary, 446
Baldwin, N. A., 466, 476
Baldwin, Norman C., 948
Baldwin, Samuel S., 284
Baldwin, William, 446
Baldwin family, 824
Baldwin Institute, 392
Baldwin Wallace University, 425, 510, 512
Ball, Aaron T., 963
Ball, Edward, 525
Ball, Webb C., 963

Ball, Zenas, 963
Ballard, John, 636
Ballard, Mary P., 636
Baltic (Confederate barge), 323
Baltimore and Ohio Railroad, 465
Baltzley, Edwin, 592
Balyard, John, 132
Bancroft, George, 247, 948
Banking and banks, 31, 110, 139, 171, 180, 212, 230, 247, 366, 380, 408, 579–580, 640, 665, 687, 715, 769–770, 791, 829, 841, 897–899, 913, 957, 974, 985
Banks, Nathaniel P., 666, 946
Banning, H. B., 948
Baptist Board of Foreign Missions, 325
Baptist General Tract Society, 181
Barber, George H., 948
Barber, Josiah, 247, 517, 634
Barber, Noyes, 421
Barber, Ohio C., 355
Barber Match Company, 355
Barber's Benevolent Union, 35
Barclay, Thomas, 294
Bard, David D., 645
Barker, Phineas, 1
Barker family, 994
Barnaby, James, 210
Barnard, John G., 946
Barnard, Josiah, 70
Barnes, James, 946
Barnes family, 919
Barnett, James, 36, 466, 535, 588
Barnett, William, 948
Barnitz, Albert, 430
Barnum, Henry A., 946
Barnum, Phineas T., 948

Barr, John, 1, 166, 247, 948
Barry, Frank M., 790
Bartholdt, Richard, 897
Bartlett, Edward, 911
Bartlett family, 48
Bartley, Mordecai, 247, 948
Barton, Benjamin Smith, 67
Barton, Clara H., 485, 948
Baruch, Bernard, 674, 791
Basic Papers of George M. Humphrey as Secretary of the Treasury, 1953–1957, 674
Bassett, Henry D., 445
Bassett, Homer F., 445
Bassett, John M., 445
Bassett, May Louise, 555
Bassett, Stephen H., 555
Batchelder, Mr. and Mrs., 647
Bateman, Arthur E., 592
Bateman, Elwood, 592
Bateman, Warner M., 592, 604
Bates, Edward, 624
Bates, Elisha, 335, 948
Bates, Levi, 70
Battey, Robert, 451
Battles, E. D., 44
Bauder, Levi F., 946
Baylor, Frances Courtenay, 948
Beach, Moses, 247
Beal, George L., 946
Beall, Reasin, 123, 338
Beall family, 512
Bearce (Bearse, Bierce) family, 628
Beard, Jedediah, 154
Beardsley, David H., 1, 166
Bearsley, D. W., 948
Beattie, William D., 196
Beatty, C. P., 407
Beatty, Zaccheus A., 407

Beauregard, Pierre G. T., 423, 705, 946
Beckwith, Lemuel, 298
Bedford Female Benevolent Sewing Society, 63
Beebe, Joseph A., 223
Beebe, Oliver B., 223
Beecher, Henry Ward, 756
Beeman Chemical Company, 546
Beers, Adam M., 903
Beethoven Society and Seville Musical Association, 257
Belgium, 410, 497
Bell, James M., 407
Bellamy, George A., 651, 972
Bellamy, Paul, 969
Bellamy, Samuel, 738
Bellefontaine Railway, 680
Bemis, Samuel F., 897
Bender, George H., 774
Benedict family, 512
Benesch, Alfred, 791
Benevolent societies. *See* Public welfare
Benham, Henry W., 946
Benjamin, Judah P., 301, 423, 705, 946
Benson, Ezra T., 674
Benton, Elbert Jay, 22
Benton, Thomas Hart, 948
Bentzel, Balser, 132
Berea Law and Order League, 511
Berkeley, Sir William, 948
Bethany College, 434
Bethel Associated Charities, 535
Bethel Union Relief Department, 535
Betts, Thaddeus, 738
Beveridge, Albert J., 766, 897

Beveridge, John L., 946
Beverley, Carter, 715
Beynon, B. G., 269
Bible, 20, 30, 78, 181, 247, 386, 392, 550
Bickham, Maria, 33
Bickham, William D., 33
Bickham, William Strickle, 33
Bierce, Lucius V., 219, 247, 267
Bierstedt, Emanuel, 948
Big Beaver Land Company, 738
Bigelow, Horatio, 707
Bigelow, John, 178, 714
Bigelow, Timothy, 219
Biles, A. F., 791
Billings, Grace Bedell, 948
Billman family, 480
Bimel-Standish Company, 497
Bimeler, Joseph, 366
Bingham, Henry Harrison, 946
Bingham, John A., 799
Bingham, William, 552, 767
Birchard, Matthew, 877
Birchard, W. A., 877
Bird, Charles, 110
Bird, Henry, 110
Birdsey, Nathan, 948
Birney, Margaret P., 948
Bishop, James E., 597
Bissell, J. P., 1
Bissell, Robert, 32
Bissell, Samuel, 32
Bissell, Thankful, 32
Bissell, William, 425
Black, Louis, 549
Black River, 696
Blackman, Edwin C., 613
Blackwalnut (master brig), 949
Blackwell, Edward R., 869
Blaine, James G., 948

Blair, Mary Jane, 733
Blair, Thompson, 139
Blakeslee, Joel, 691
Blanding, Stephen F., 946
Blatchford, Henry, 948
Blenker, Louis, 946
Blennerhassett, Harman, 871, 948
Bloom, Sol, 401
Blosser, Raymond F., 763
Blossom, Dudley S., Jr., 791
Blower, Arthur H., 948
Boardman, Charles A., 154
Boardman, David L., 247
Boardman, David S., 446, 862
Boardman, Elijah, 446, 543, 561, 736
Boardman, William W., 446
Bobb, Emma C., 363
Bohning, Henry H., 1050
Bolton, Charles E., 478
Bolton, Charles Knowles, 411
Bolton, Frances P., 771, 999
Bolton, Irving C., 582
Bolton, Thomas, 297
Bonaparte, Charles J., 897
Bond, Lewis, 878, 948
Bond, William Key, 247
Bonham, Milledge Luke, 946
Bonney, Rufus L., 948
Bonsall, Sallie, 119
Book and Thimble Club, 935
Book of Benjamin Hanna: His Children, and Their Descendants, 514
Boone, Thomas C., 466, 948
Booth, Edwin, 583
Booth, John Wilkes, 583
"Boquet of the Social Band," 79
Borah, William E., 641
Boston Athenaeum, 411

Bostwick, E. B., 247
Boughton, George, 132
Boughton, Thomas B., 605
Bourlier, Emile, 946
Bourne, Alexander, 589
Bourne, Henry E., 875, 930
Boutwell, George S., 799
Bowditch, N. J., 70
Bowdoin, Elizabeth, 70
Bowdoin, James, 70
Bowen, George Washington, 895
Bowers, Theodore S., 946
Bowler, Noadiah Potter, 948
Bowler, William O., 948
Bowles, P. D., 946
Boyd, Andrew, 624, 769
Boyle, Homer C., 365
Boyle, Jeremiah T., 946
Boynton, Henry B., 688
Boynton, S. A., 498
Boynton, Sylvanus C., 700
Boynton, William A., 688
Brace, C. B., 728
Brace, Mrs. C. B., 728
Brace, Jonathan, 736, 948
Braden, George C., 1088
Bradley, Abraham, Jr., 543
Bradley, Alva, 745
Bradley, George P., 177
Bradstreet, John, 707
Brady, Samuel, 338
Bragg, Braxton, 423, 474, 946
Bragg, Edward S., 946
Branch Bible Society of Boardman, 386
Brannis, Chester, 59
Brant, Joseph, 948
Brayton, Mary Clark, 213, 706
Brayton, Emma Sanford, 948
Brazil, 567, 652

Breck, Samuel, 946
Breckenridge, J. C., 76
Breckinridge, John C., 423, 946
Brennan, Lena, 619
Brent, George William, 423
Brewer, Sarah A., 948
Bricker, John W., 641
Briggs, Dwight, 948
Briggs, James A., 192, 577
Briggs, Joseph William, 717
Bright, Edward, 619
Bright, Edward, Jr., 325
Bright, Frederick E., 943
Bright, H. V., 943
Brinkerhoff, R., 419
Brinkerhoff family, 363
Bristol, George P., 1062
Bristol, Simeon, 59
British War Relief Society, 823
Britton, William B., 587
Brodhead, Daniel, 948
Brogan, John P., 946
Bronson, Elliott B., 948
Bronson, Lenos, 59
Brooker, Winifred, 804
Brooks, C. A., 948
Brooks, Eustus, 948
Brooks, James, 799
Brooks, P. C., 412
Brooks, Peter C., 862
Brough, John, 132, 419
Brown, Alexander C., 731
Brown, Anne F., 542
Brown, Bartholomew, 345
Brown, Charles W., 665
Brown, Ephraim, 412, 773
Brown, Mrs. Ephraim (Mary), 412, 773
Brown, Ephraim A., 412
Brown, Ethan A., 712

Brown, Fayette, 686, 809
Brown, Mrs. Fayette (Cornelia Curtiss), 686
Brown, George W., 545
Brown, Harriett, 345
Brown, Harvey Huntington, 809
Brown, Israel, 948
Brown, John (abolitionist), 948
Brown, John (educator), 80
Brown, John (merchant), 948
Brown, John Weld, 53
Brown, Joseph Emerson, 946, 948
Brown, Lucinda White, 4
Brown, Marvin H., 542
Brown, Milly E., 935
Brown, Minnie M., 948
Brown, S. J., 4
Brown University, 160
Browne, William H., 946
Browning, Phebe (Mrs. Wesley Browning), 127
Browning, Wesley, 127
Bruce, Eli Metcalfe, 946
Bruin, Mrs. Louise (Maloney), 935
Brush, Charles F., 640, 897
Bryant, Gilman, 166
Bryant, William Cullen, 948
Bryson, Samuel, 468
Buchanan, Franklin, 948
Buchanan, James, 203
Buchannon, William, 769
Buchtel College, 434
Buckingham family, 980
Buckner, Thruston, 507
Buel, Frances M., 881
Buell, Ezekiel Wells, 948
Buell, George P., 946
Buell, Joseph, 871
Buford, A., 715

Bulkley, Charles H., 791
Bulkley, Robert Johns, 790–791
Bull, Thomas, 738
Bullard, Hanna, 942
Bulloch, James D., 178
Bungert, Lucy A. H., 450
Bunnell, Amasa, 539
Bunts, Frank E., 563
Bunts, Hermes, 132
Burbridge, Stephen G., 946
Burke, E. J., 922
Burke, Gaius, 1
Burke, Henry, 70
Burke, Stevenson, 683
Burleigh, Charles C., 948
Burnham, Henry L., 699
Burnham, Hiram, 927
Burns, Patrick J., 988
Burns, William W., 946
Burnside, Ambrose E., 465, 666, 946
Burr, Aaron, 871, 948
Burr, Eliza B., 871
Burrows, Charles W., 215
Burrows, Jerome B., 503
Burrows, Julius C., 503
Burrows Brothers Company, 814
Burton, Grace, 899
Burton, Harold Hitz, 401, 641, 948, 962
Burton, Theodore Elijah, 296, 567, 670, 771, 897–899, 908, 948
Burton Academy, 243, 738, 796, 817
Burton Institute, 796
Bush, S. P., 791
Bushnell, Asa S., 670
Bushnell family, 531
Butler, Benjamin, 363

Butler, Benjamin Franklin, 400, 946, 948
Butler, John, 129
Butler, John M., 946
Butler, Nicholas M., 897
Butler, Paul E., 790
Butler, Renley S., 451
Butler, Thomas, 948
Butterfield, Consul W., 24
Butterfield, Daniel, 946
Butterworth, Benjamin, 592, 683
Byington, Joel, 247
Byrd, Richard E., 674

C. G. King Company, 538, 816
C. H. Smith, Flour, Grain and Mill Feed, 395
C.S.S. *Alabama,* 178
Cabell, James Branch, 709
Cadwallader, Starr, 651, 930
Cadwell, Darius, 770
Calfee, John, 948
California, 24, 33, 53, 369, 497, 537, 553, 567, 618, 778, 942
Calhoun, John, 424
Calhoun, John C., 247
Cameron, Simon, 400
Camp, Ann O., 438
Camp, Henry C., 438
Campbell, Alexander, 948
Campbell, James B., 559
Campbell, John, 154, 428
Campbell, John D., 559
Campbell, John W., 715
Campbell, Thomas, 559
Canada, 30, 187, 215, 454, 497, 683, 728, 942
Canadian Copper Company, 683
Candee & Scribner, 44
Candee family, 824

Canfield, Harmon, 247
Canfield, Judson, 247, 736
Canfield, Norman, 154
Cannon, Joseph G., 897
Canteen Club, 205
Canton Ladies Anti-Slavery Society, 13
Cappeller, W. S., 592
Carey, J. B., 497
Carleton, James H., 946
Carneal, Thomas, 769
Carnegie, Andrew, 897, 948
Carpenter, Fred W., 897
Carpenter, S. S., 592
Carr, W. F., 943
Carter, John C., 946
Carter, Lorenzo, 1, 948
Cary, Freeman Grant, 948
Case, Esther, 363
Case, Leonard, Sr., 38, 223, 247, 580, 712, 738, 829
Case, Leonard, Jr., 580
Case, Quincy A., 912
Case, William, 196, 580
Case, Zophar, 580
Case School of Applied Science, 580, 635, 771, 793
Case Western Reserve University, 948. *See also* Western Reserve University
Casey, Silas, 946
Cass, Lewis, 166, 247, 739, 948
Cassels, J. Lang, 196, 242
Cassidy, James H., 791
Castalia Sporting Club, 979
Castle, William B., 701
Castle, William W., 948
Castle family, 985
Cathcart, Wallace H., 54, 172, 946

Cather, Willa S., 709
Catherine II (Empress of Russia), 658
Cattell, Jonas D., 362
Catterson, Robert F., 946
Cavalry Riding Academy, 612
Cavalry Veteran Association, 612
Cavenagh, Michael, 642
Cemeteries, 351, 512, 547, 632, 667, 948, 1060, 1069
Central Friendly Inn, 745
Central Ohio Normal College, 948
Central Ontario Railroad, 683
Central Oregon Irrigation Company, 791
Chaffee, N. L., 632
Chain Makers National Union, 497
Chalmers, James R., 946
Chamberlin, Ross A., 592
Champion, Epaphroditus, 948
Champion, Henry, 46, 223, 279, 734, 736, 738, 924
Champion Iron Company, 809
Chapin, Luther, 247
Chapman, Fanny, 754
Chapman, Frederick L., 450
Chapman, George Lord, 634
Chapman, J. B., 592
Chapman, N. H., 592
Chapman, Salathiel, 915
Chapman, Seldon, 634
Charity. *See* Public welfare
Charity School for Boys, 741
Charlemagne Tower, Jr. (freighter), 648
Charles Carroll (whaling vessel), 661
Charles H. Seymour & Company, 894

Charpentier, Mrs. Edouard, 727
Chase, George N., 880
Chase, Philander, 948
Chase, Salmon P., 181, 272, 400, 507, 624, 946, 948
Chatfield, Coy B., 500
Chatfield, Guy C., 500
Chatfield, William, 500
Chautauqua Literary and Scientific Circles, 651
Cheatham, Benjamin F., 946
Cherry Run Security Oil Company, 850
Chesapeake and Ohio Canal, 708
Chesapeake & Ohio Railroad Company, 221, 662, 716
Chesapeake Bay, 269, 465
Chesnutt, Charles Waddell, 827
Chidester, Royal, 455
Chidester, William, 455
Chillicothe Library, 52
Chillicothe Mutual Insurance Company, 948
Chillicothe Polemic Society, 52
Chilton, Robert H., 423
Chisolm, Alexander Robert, 946
Chittenden, R. L., 100
Chrisman, James Stone, 946
Church, A. E., 387
Church, Ensign, 154, 217, 675, 713
Church, James, 254
Church, Jerusha, 217
Church, Nathaniel, 217
Church, Samuel, 217
Cilley, Jonathan P., 946
Cincinnati Baptist Missionary Society, 325
Cincinnati Baptist Social Union, 324

Cincinnati Daily Commercial, 33
Citizens League of Greater Cleveland, 641, 835, 875
Citizens Light Company, 948
City Club of Cleveland, 641, 998
City of Buffalo (steamer), 746
City of Erie (steamer), 463
Civil War
  artists, 18, 466
  battles, 90, 121, 124, 132, 296, 457, 519, 521, 525, 551, 587, 593, 598, 666, 679, 698, 705, 730, 740, 759, 776, 796, 801, 834, 839, 929, 940, 946
  camp life, 121, 659, 698–699, 759, 772, 801, 839, 852, 946
  courts martial, 440, 540
  draft, 129, 529, 770, 946, 1022, 1065
  general, 127, 192, 210, 218, 247, 312, 338, 382, 400, 429, 434, 448, 454, 456, 462, 485, 488, 503, 508, 522, 605, 614, 624, 636, 645, 667, 703, 710, 726, 755–756, 786, 810, 818, 828, 852, 855, 863, 890, 931, 947, 948, 952, 985
  medical, 213, 451, 474, 531, 609, 650, 659, 705–706, 759, 903, 946
  music, 457, 551, 650, 825
  naval affairs, 178, 562, 706, 834, 946
  pensions, 643, 669
  prisons, 90, 252, 620, 646, 928, 946
  regimental records, 134, 144, 170, 181, 236, 239, 248, 251, 270, 296, 300, 310–311, 314, 342, 351, 358, 370, 372, 430, 453, 466, 475–476, 506, 530–531, 535, 540–541, 575–576, 588, 730, 857, 884, 927
  supplies, 465, 567, 645, 669, 706, 710, 770, 772, 857, 940, 946, 956
  telegraph, 447, 778, 959
  writings about, 22, 33, 213, 236, 314, 453, 466, 531, 535, 576, 666, 879, 946
  See also Confederate States of America; Grand Army of the Republic; *military regiments by state*
Clague family, 919
Clapp, Lorinda, 72
Clapp, Thomas J., 72, 132
Clark, Abraham, 760
Clark, Alphin, 59
Clark, Edmund, 38
Clark, George, 715, 769
Clark, Harold T., 401
Clark, Lemuel, 59
Clark, Mervin, 144, 466
Clarke, James S., 1, 38, 948
Clarke, John H., 791
Clary, Robert E., 946
Clay, Henry, 247, 948
Clayton, John M., 247
Clayton Anti-Trust Act, 791
Cleaveland, Esther, 738
Cleaveland, Moses, 163, 223, 664, 734, 862, 924
  monument, 489
Cleburne, Patrick R., 946
Clemens, Laura E., 677
Clemmer, J. S., 89
Clendenin, David, 154, 247, 277, 428, 675, 712, 713, 948

Cleveland, Charlotte U., 664
Cleveland, Chester E., 234
Cleveland, D., 946
Cleveland, James D., 196
Cleveland, Jane L., 234
Cleveland, Oren L., 948
Cleveland Academy, 106, 948
Cleveland Academy of Natural Science, 196, 247
Cleveland Advertising Club, 906
Cleveland and Buffalo Transit Company, 463, 746
Cleveland and Chagrin Falls Railway Company, 557
Cleveland and Cincinnati Telegraph Company, 778
Cleveland and Eastern Railway Company, 557
Cleveland and Eastern Traction Company, 557
Cleveland and Mahoning Valley Railroad, 179, 446, 948
Cleveland and Pittsburgh Railroad, 508
Cleveland & Youngstown Railroad, 578
Cleveland Area Church Federation, 993
Cleveland Art Club, 177, 936
Cleveland Arts Club, 606
Cleveland Associated Charities, 684
Cleveland Automobile Club, 910
Cleveland Baptist Association, 619
Cleveland Bar Association, 948
Cleveland Cap Screw Company, 943
Cleveland Centennial Commission, 490, 567

Cleveland Central Armory, 771
Cleveland Central High, 25
Cleveland Chamber of Commerce, 87, 635, 641, 996, 1048. *See also* Greater Cleveland Growth Association
Cleveland Chamber of Industry, 331
Cleveland Charter Commission (1913), 1042–1043
Cleveland, Cincinnati, Chicago & St. Louis Railway Company, 535
Cleveland Cinema Club, 637
Cleveland Clinic, 563
Cleveland, Columbus & Cincinnati Railroad, 604, 948
Cleveland, Columbus, Cincinnati, and Indianapolis Railroad, 508
Cleveland Conference for Educational Cooperation, 54
Cleveland Council of Sociology, 651
Cleveland Day Nursery and Free Kindergarten Association, 846
Cleveland Development Foundation, 939
Cleveland Electric Illuminating Company, 574
Cleveland Engineering Society, 771
Cleveland Female Baptist Sewing Society, 609
Cleveland Female Seminary, 106, 948
Cleveland Fire Department, 1047
Cleveland Firemen's Relief Association, 948

Cleveland Gaslight and Coke Company, 671
Cleveland Gatling Gun Battery, 612
Cleveland Homeopathic Medical College, 750
Cleveland Hospital Aid Society, 866
Cleveland Hospital for Women and Children, 948
Cleveland Immigration League, 791
Cleveland in a Nut-Shell, 49
Cleveland Institute, 216
Cleveland Institute of Homeopathy, 895
Cleveland Institute of Music, 54
Cleveland Insurance Company, 38, 771
Cleveland Iron Company, 558
Cleveland Iron Mining Company, 676
Cleveland Junto, 891
Cleveland Leader, 192
Cleveland Library Association, 1
Cleveland Light Artillery Association, 351
Cleveland Metropolitan Services Commission, 842
Cleveland Municipal Light Plant Association, 960
Cleveland Museum of Art, 54
Cleveland Museum of Natural History, 54, 813
Cleveland Music School Settlement, 930, 934
Cleveland News, 672
Cleveland Orchestra, 609
Cleveland, Painesville & Ashtabula Railroad, 404, 508
Cleveland Paper Company, 948
Cleveland Philharmonic Orchestra, 948
Cleveland *Plain Dealer*, 672, 969
Cleveland Post-War Planning Council, 641
Cleveland Public Library, 54, 818
Cleveland Railway Company, 768, 771, 1045
Cleveland School of Art, 54, 667
Cleveland Shipbuilding Company, 517
Cleveland State University, 910, 939
Cleveland *Sun and Voice*, 567
Cleveland, the Making of a City, 984
Cleveland True Democrat, 192
Cleveland Trust Company, 771
Cleveland-Twinsburg Plank Road, 668
Cleveland Union Terminal, 578, 662, 716, 768
Cleveland Woman's Club, 555
Cleveland Women's Press Club, 220
Cleveland, Youngstown & Eastern Railway Company, 557
Clifford, Paul, 92
Clinton, De Witt, 948
Clinton Line Railroad Company, 95
Cluseret, Gustave P., 946
Cobb, Oliver W., 948
Cobb, Howell, 946
Cobb, Phillip L., 967
Cochran, C., Jr., 717
Cochran, John, 352
Cochran, Robert, 352
Cochran, William Cox, 548

Cochrane, Arthur, 168
Cochrane, John, 946
Cockley, William W., 310
Codding, G. M., 132
Cody, William Frederick, 948
Coe, Andrew J., 948
Coe, Asher Miller, 413
Coe, Elisha, 482
Coff, Chester W., 946
Coffin, Stephen, 948
Coffinberry, Henry D., 562
Coffinberry, Maria D., 562
Cogswell, William, 948
Coit, Daniel L., 188, 231, 293, 665, 734, 736, 775, 862
Coit, Henry H., 775
Coit, Wheeler, 240
Coit, William H., 775
Coleman, Asa, 185
Coleman, Asaph, 185
Coleman, John W., 948
Coleman family, 364
Colfax, Schuyler, 400, 419
Colgreave, W. W., 675
Collacott, Louise A., 619
Colleges and universities
    Connecticut, 23, 32, 712, 796
    Indiana, 790, 854
    Kentucky, 769
    Massachusetts, 6, 791
    Michigan, 387
    New Hampshire, 23, 948
    New York, 609, 818
    Ohio, 80, 104, 111, 117, 181, 247, 276, 305, 308, 325, 363, 387, 422, 425, 434, 496, 503, 510, 512, 518, 531, 563, 619, 647, 709, 750, 771, 796, 815, 817, 832, 875, 897, 910, 932, 939, 948–949
    Pennsylvania, 31, 67, 249, 802
    Rhode Island, 160
    West Virginia, 434
Collier, Daniel Lewis, 948
Collins, David, 294
Collum, Richard S., 211
Colman, Dudley, 948
Colombia, 700
Colorado, 791
Colorado Infantry
    2nd Regiment, 946
Columbia Nantucket (merchant vessel), 197
Columbia University, 818
Columbus, Christopher, 766
Comegys, C. G. W., 454
Commentaries on American Law, 694
Commercial Bank of Lake Erie, 247, 580, 829
Commercial National Bank, 212
Commons, John R., 651
Communications
    radio, 637, 790
    telegraph, 447, 778, 959
Comstock, J. L., 878
Condict, Lewis, 247
Confederate States of America
    Army, 301, 322, 423, 451, 466, 474, 562, 705–706, 863, 928–929, 931, 946, 948
    Navy, 178, 323, 705–706, 946
Conkling, F. A., 247
Connecticut, 1, 43, 139, 173, 180, 247, 405, 494, 580, 695, 714, 919
    Canaan, 422
    Cheshire, 115, 141–142
    Derby, 281
    Durham, 543

East Haddam, 634
East Hartford, 279
Enfield, 947
Fairfield County, 354
Glastonbury, 185, 663
Goshen, 1
Greenwich, 354
Groton, 421
Haddam, 23
Hartford, 31, 174, 231, 278, 950
Hartford County, 527
Harwinton, 882
Killingworth, 233
Lisbon, 186
Litchfield, 167, 948
Litchfield County, 8, 421, 424, 725
Long Mill, 413
Middletown, 114
Middlesex County, 865
Milford, 849
Montville, 378
New Hartford, 244, 363, 807
New Haven, 32, 240, 543, 692, 796, 833, 849, 970
New Haven County, 115
New London, 188, 562
New Milford, 561
Norwich, 132, 240, 293, 339, 617
Plainfield, 186
Redding, 132
Salisbury, 1, 217
Saybrook, 677
Simsbury, 915
Southington, 59
Suffield, 1, 31
Suffield Township, 1
Wallingford, 326, 473

Windsor, 245
Connecticut Land Company, 1, 174, 223, 231, 279, 281, 543, 561, 568, 622, 734–738, 775, 949–950
Connecticut Militia
  1st Regiment, 1
Connecticut Volunteer Infantry, 466
  5th Regiment, 946
Conolly, Thomas, 765
Conservation, 990
Construction, 344, 945
  bridges, 326, 404, 635
  churches, 82, 329, 391, 420, 631, 635, 718, 753, 757–758, 872
  lighthouses, 421
  railroads, 396, 508
  residences, 590, 683, 753, 900
  roads, 421, 426, 611, 744
  schools, 40, 421, 758, 1016
Consumers League of Ohio, 930, 935, 1000
Conversational Club of Cleveland, 516
Conversational Club of East Cleveland, 138
Converse, Amelia, 271
Converse, John P., 247, 271, 412, 948, 983
Converse, Martha, 271
Cook, Edward T., 454
Cook, Elzar, 115
Cook, Eveline Bosworth, 681
Cook, John, 115, 446
Cook, Matthew Scott, 454
Cook, Merriman, 115
Cooke, Eleutheros, 247
Cooke, J. P., 70

Cooke, Jay, 985
Cooke, Philip St. George, 946
Cooper, Samuel, 706, 946
Corcoran, Michael, 946
Cornell, Ezra, 778
Cornell, Thomas W., 683
Cornell, Wait, 413
Cornwallis, Charles, 948
Cortelyou, George B., 355, 897
Costa Rica, 700
Cotter, Charles S., 575
Coughlin, Charles E., 783
Coughlin, Thomas, 791
Cowan, Christopher, 299
Cowan, Mrs. Christopher, 299
Cowing, Hattie J. A., 398
Cowles, Isaac, 712, 738
Cowles, Ralph, 665, 948
Cowles, Solomon, 738
Cowles, Thomas, 139
Cox, Jacob D., 548, 946, 948
Cox, James M., 897
Cozad, Justus L., 680
Crandall family, 515
Crane, O. J., 144
Crane, Thurston, 181
Crawford, Frederick C., 943
Crawford, T. R., 353
Crawford, William, 24, 507
Crawford, William Harris, 744
Crawford, Ziba, 619
Crawford Door Company, 943
Cree, Thomas K., 619
Creighton, William, 715, 769
Creighton, William R., 144, 466
Cresson, Elliott, 247
Crickmore, H. G., 466
Crile, George Washington, 563, 901
Crile, Grace McBride, 563

Crime and punishment, 181, 791, 881. *See also* Civil War, prisons
Crissey, Forrest, 899
Criswell, J. M., 619
Critchley, Fawcett & Company, 921
Crocker, Jedediah D., 337
Croghan, William, 299
Crooke, Philip S., 946
Crookshank, N., 166
Crosby, Abijah, 132
Crosby, Abner, 235
Crosby, William G., 462
Cross and Baptist Journal, 325
Crosser, Robert, 791
Crowell, John, 247, 883
Cuba, 76, 400, 563, 897
Cull, Frank X., 791
Cullen, E. M., 927
Cullitan, Frank T., 790
Culver, Oliver, 166
Cumback, William, 948
Cumberland Road, 744
Cunningham, Cyrus, 691
Curtin, Andrew G., 946
Curtis, Eleroy, 948
Curtis, George Camp, 600
Curtis, Henry B., 590
Curtis, Lillie Tryon, 321
Curtis, Mattoon Monroe, **518**
Curtis, Samuel R., 946
Curtis, William Eleroy, 766
Cushing, Erastus, 433
Cushing, Henry K., 433
Cushing, Henry Platt, 793
Cushing, J. P., 70
Cushman, E. H., 17
Cutler, Jervis, 99
Cutler, Lysander, 946
Cutler, Manasseh, 69, 70

Cutter, Orlando, 1
Cuyahoga Community College, 939
Cuyahoga County Auditor, 1031–1032
Cuyahoga County Centennial Celebration, 172, 594
Cuyahoga County Charter Commission (1950), 790–791
Cuyahoga County Conservation Council, 990
Cuyahoga County Court of Appeals, 641
Cuyahoga County Court of Common Pleas, 948, 1033
Cuyahoga County Grand Jury, 1035
Cuyahoga County Historical Society, 1
Cuyahoga County Medical Society, 948
Cuyahoga County Military Committee, 466
Cuyahoga County Treasurer, 1036
Cuyahoga County Union Central Committee, 201
Cuyahoga County War Service League, 948
Cuyahoga Forge, 132
Cuyahoga River, 1, 46, 176, 635, 791, 868
Cuyahoga Valley, 663
Cuyahoga Steam Furnace Company, 517, 1037
Czolgosz, Leon, 86

D. W. Anderson & Company, 132
Dabney, Thomas S., 301
Daggett, Nathan, 406, 482
Dahlgren, John A. B., 946
Dahlgren, Ulric, 946
Dairy products, 613
Dallas, Alexander James, 744
Dana, Charles A., 946
Danaceau, Saul S., 782
Darlington, Carey Allen, 482
Darrow, George, 948
Dartmouth College, 23, 948
Daugherty, Harry M., 897
Daughters of the American Revolution, 199, 259, 398, 493, 513, 567
Davey, Martin L., 791
Davis, Harry E., 827
Davis, Harry L., 771, 1048
Davis, Jefferson, 423, 706, 946, 948
Davis, Thomas, 642
Davis, Varina H., 946
Davis, Woodbury, 462
Davis family, 752
Dawes, Charles G., 897
Day, Arthur H., 641
Day, James B., 499
Day, L. W., 466
Day, Lewis, 948
Deane, Silas, 789
Dearborn, Henry, 789, 871
Deas, Zachariah, 946
DeBoes, Joseph A., 948
Debs, Eugene V., 768
Decatur, Stephen, 948
Declaration of Independence, Signers of the, 760
de Forest, Louis Effingham, 168
de Garondelet, Baron, 198
Delameter, Jacob J., 196
Delaware, 30
de Lemos, Manuel Goyoso, 198

de Lery, Joseph Gaspard Chaussegros, 215
Delta Building Loan & Savings Company, 380
DeMaioribus, Alexander L., 948
Deming, Abigail, 70
Deming, Arthur B., 140
Deming, Julius, 279
Deming, Moses, 948
Demmon, Isaac N., 387
Denison, John Evelyn (Viscount Ossington), 690
Denison, Lemuel T., 948
Denison University, 619
Dennis, Harold D., 948
Dennis, Howard, 86
Dennison, William, 419
Dentistry. *See* Medicine
dePeyster, J. Watts, 946
Devereux, Henry Kelsey, 508
Devereux, John, 508
Devereux, John Henry, 508
Devol family, 982
Dewey, George, 897
de Zea, Pedro, 946
Diamond Match Company, 355
Dibell, Edwin, 160
Dick, Charles F. W., 567, 897, 948
Dickinson, John, 789
Dickson, Artie M., 852
Die Wahre Separation . . . , 366
Dille, Howard R., 749
Dille, Lewis, 247
Disaster relief, 36, 897–899
District of Columbia, 129, 135, 363, 403, 737, 839, 843, 847
Dix, John A., 946
Doan, D. C., 166
Doan, Samuel, 92

Doan, Seth, 829
Doan, William H., 880
Dobbins, Daniel, 1
Doddridge, Philip, 299
Dodge, Grenville M., 946
Dodge, John, 948
Dodge, Rebecca, 181
Donaldson family, 994
Donalson, Israel, 769
Donelson, Daniel S., 946
Donnenwirth, G., 1028
Doolittle, Henry, 396
Doolittle, William Frederick, 402
Doolittle Family in America, 402
Dorsey, Daniel A., 948
Dorst, J. H., 76
Doty, Edward W., 1043
Doty, James Duane, 222
Doubleday, Abner, 946, 948
Douglas, James C., 247
Dow, Neal, 462, 946
Draper, Lyman C., 338, 948
Drowne, Henry T., 948
Drowne, Solomon, 948
DuBois, W. E. B., 827
Dulles, John Foster, 674
Dunbar, William, 198
Duncan, Andrew J., 710
Duncanson, D. J., 923
Dunlap, John, 507
Dunning, William A., 897
DuPont, Samuel F., 946
Dwight, Benjamin, 278
Dwight, Margaret Van Horn, 692
Dwight, Theodore, 247
Dyer, Albion M., 568
Dyer, C. S., 592

E. A. Brown & Brothers Company, 412

E. C. Blackman & Company, 613
E. Grasselli & Son, 965
E. I. duPont de Nemours Company, 965
Eagle River Mining Company, 707
Eames, Hayden, 791
Earle, Homer, 948
Early, Jubal A., 946
Early Settlers' Association of Cuyahoga County, Ohio, 356
Early Settlers' Association of the Western Reserve, 902
East Cleveland Literary and Scientific Circle, 62
East 105th Street Canteen, 471
Eastburn, Isaac H., 801
Eastburn, James H., 801
Eastburn, Thomas F., 801
Eastern Cuyahoga County Horticultural Society, 17
Eastern Ohio Traction Company, 557
Eastman, Harry L., 961
Eaton, Cyrus S., 791
Eaton, William, 948
Eberhard, John G., 750
Eccles, Marriner S., 791
Eckhard & Steler Funeral Directors, 948
Economic Cooperation Administration, 674
Economic life and conditions
 California, 53
 Cuba, 400
 Mississippi, 108
 national, 247, 272, 563, 690, 769, 771, 791, 825, 897–899, 947
 New York, 696, 947
 Ohio, 31, 181, 185, 247, 272, 278–281, 295, 338, 366, 382, 389, 407, 422, 432, 438, 448, 456, 500, 580, 591, 616, 663–665, 681, 711, 722, 732, 734–738, 758, 773, 796, 802, 825, 843, 848, 854, 882, 889, 912, 914, 919, 924, 941, 947, 963, 970, 974, 983, 991, 1007, 1031–1032
 Tennessee, 437
 Vermont, 224
 See also Banking and banks; Farming and farms; Industry and manufactures; Labor and unions; Land deeds, surveys, and records; Merchants; Transportation
Eckman, William H., 177
Eckstein family, 580
Eddy, Richard E., 325
Edmiston, John, 951
Edmiston, Rebecca (Shaw), 951
Education
 educators, 6, 32, 325, 333, 387, 392, 406, 422, 434, 512, 518, 563, 635, 656, 667, 687, 693, 709, 742, 750, 774, 784, 796, 807, 818, 832, 856, 875, 882
 general, 54, 167, 947–948, 1002
 students, 5–6, 10, 31, 67, 305, 308, 363, 382, 387, 412, 503, 636, 647, 688, 693, 712, 729, 750, 790–791, 796, 802, 817, 828, 832, 836, 854, 874, 895
 schools (private), 101, 106, 384, 667, 741, 791
 schools (public), 25, 30, 173, 199, 316, 330, 363, 387, 425,

Education (*continued*)
    512, 555, 610, 613, 667, 750, 791, 919, 955, 1006, 1009, 1014–1018, 1020, 1024, 1027, 1030, 1037–1038, 1041, 1046, 1049–1052, 1058, 1065, 1071–1072, 1076–1077, 1079, 1086–1087, 1089–1091
  schools (Sunday), 7, 11, 30, 167, 256, 512, 609, 948
  See also Colleges and universities; Academies, institutes, and seminaries
Education Society of Richfield, 167
Edwards, J. R., 791
Edwards, John S., 1
Edwards, Lewis B., 948
Edwards, Rudolphus, 98
Egbert, Samuel L., 92
Eisenhower, Dwight D., 673–674, 756, 761
Eldredge, Alonzo, 753
Eldredge, C. M., 187
Eldredge, Hezekiah, 753
Eldredge, William, 188, 421
Electric Welding Products Company, 943
Eliot, Charles W., 387
Ellen, John S., 929
Ellet, Minnie, 570
Elliot, Marion Hall, 948
Elliott, Washington L., 946
Ellison, Ann, 940
Ellison, William, 940
Ellsey, William, 769
Ellsler, John A., 583
Ellsworth, Elijah, 219
Ellsworth, Martin, 738

Ellsworth, Oliver, 405
Ellsworth family, 919
Elwell, John J., 485
Elwin, Julia, 619
Ely, Ashley, 435
Ely, Darius, 435
Ely, Heman, 247, 502, 737
Ely, Justin, 502, 948
Ely, Lewis, 432
Ely, Merrick, 282, 432
Ely, Richard T., 651
Ely, William, 139, 278, 738
Emerson, Caleb, 145, 181
Emerson, George D., 181
Emerson, Harry I., 168
Emerson, Mary Dana, 181
Emerson, Oliver, 1055
Emerson, Ralph Waldo, 756
Emerson, William D., 181
Emery, C. F., 418
Emery, I. S., 948
Emery, Samuel M., 482
Emmerton, James A., 6
Emmitt, James, 948
Endicott, William C., 948
Engineering and engineers, 132, 404, 423, 497, 508, 611, 771, 926
England, 178, 563, 677, 683, 690, 733, 741, 804, 823, 833, 870, 905
England, John, 946
English, William E., 76
Ennis, Olive J., 592
Ensign, Seth I., 348
Entrican, George C., 830
Erie and Western Railroad, 662
Erie Land Company, 665, 734, 862, 948
Erie Literary Society, 796

Errett, Isaac, 387
Etwas fürs Herz, 366
Euclid Avenue National Bank, 640
Euclid Avenue Opera House, 554, 948
Euclid Innerbelt Association, 910–911
Europe, 563, 567, 600, 844. *See also names of individual countries*
Eustis, William, 154
Evans, Estwick, 948
Evans, George, 462
Evans, Thomas H., 384
Evans, William David, 551
Everett, Azariah, 132
Everett, Edward, 247, 756
Everhard, Mrs. Caroline McCullough, 385
Ewing, Mrs. Charles B., 935
Ewing, Thomas, 247, 948
Ewing, William, 70
Excell, Benjamin, 397
Exchange Brokers Company, 139
Expedition Railroad Line, 948

F. B. Stearns Company, 907
Facts, Fads and Fancies About Teeth, 200
Fairbanks, Abel W., 936
Fairchild, Daniel, 446
Fairchild, Lucius, 946
Fairfield Furnace Store, 366
Fairmount Theological Seminary, 27, 325
Fallis, John, 132
Fallis, Miriam, 482
Farley, James A., 790, 791
Farley, John H., 948

Farmer's Institute of Butler Township, 137
Farming and farms, 17, 31, 53, 83, 127, 132, 137, 202, 244, 282, 291, 318, 357, 426, 435, 454, 505, 528, 596, 619, 688, 775, 791, 828, 851, 854, 914, 919, 980
Farnsworth, Charles S., 410
Farnsworth, John F., 799
Farr, Eliel, 132
Farr, Joseph M., 363
Farrand, Harry M., 617
Farrand, Jared, 617
Farwell, Mary M., 271
Fasig, William B., 417
Fasig-Tipton Company, 417
Faudel, Henry J., 885
Faulkner, William, 602
Fearing, B. D., 592
Fearing, Paul, 181
Felch, Allan Shepard, 948
Felch, William Farrand, 172
Fellows family, 371
Female Charitable Society, 286
Fenian Brotherhood, 642
Fenn College. *See* Cleveland State University
Fenn, Sereno P., 949
Fenton, Alcinus Ward, 296, 466
Fenton, John, 132
Fenton, Myra F., 62
Ferguson, C. W., 863
Ferguson, Mrs. M. S., 863
Ferris, Weston, 946
Fess, Simeon D., 771
Fessenden, William Pitt, 178, 272, 462, 624, 756
Fessler, Mayo, 1043
Field, Cyrus West, 948

[373]

Field family, 697
Fillmore, Millard, 107, 203
Financial Crises and Periods of Industrial and Commercial Depression, 897–898
Findlay College, 363
Findley, Howard N., 948
Findley, Samuel, 932
Finley, E. B., 229
Firelands, 219, 223, 247, 338, 421, 737
Firestone, S. J., 119
Firestone, Solomon J., 358
First Farmer's Club of Butler Township, 137
First National Bank of Cleveland, 640
First New Jerusalem Society of Chillicothe, 68
First Ward Civic Association, 526
Fish, Stuyvesant, 897
Fitch, Mrs., 78
Fitch, Edward H., 364
Fitch, John, 139, 707
Fitch, Orramel H., 840
Fitch, Richard, 154, 247
Fitch, T. M., 619
Fitch, Winchester, 364
Fitch, Zalmon, 46, 139, 247, 279
Fitzgerald, James W., 642
Fleming, Thomas W., 948
Flewellen, A. J., 474
Flint, James, 345
Florence Academy, 249
Florida, 198, 423, 563, 764, 947
Florida Volunteers, 466
  2nd Division, 451
Flournoy, N. A., 946
Floyd, John B., 946
Foard, Andrew J., 474
Foch, Ferdinand, 948

Foos, Nelson, 948
Foot, David, 247
Foote, Herschel, 948
Foote, William L., 695
Foot(e) family, 623, 752
Foraker, Joseph B., 419, 567, 897
Ford, Horatio, 401, 557
Ford, Seabury, 247, 796, 948
Ford Motor Company, 943
Fording, David, 3
Forest City Live Stock and Fair Company, 508
Forney, John Wien, 948
Forrest, Nathan B., 423
Forster, Thomas, 948
Forsythe, Benjamin D., 595
Fort Bull, 215
Fort Donelson, 707
Fort Fayette, 469
Fort Garrison, 469
Fort Leavenworth, 755
Fort Oswego, 215
Fort Pitt, 299
Fort Powell, 323
Fort Shiloh, 707
Fort Sumpter, 121
Fortnightly Musical Club, 934
Fosdick, George, 70
Fosdick, Nicoll, 247
Foster, Charles, 387, 567, 592
Foster, John W., 897
Four-In-Hand and Tandem Club Company, 208
Fowler, William, 70
Fox, Gustavus V., 946
Fox, Josiah, 335
Fox, J. S., 9
France, 206, 410, 502, 563, 596, 678, 727, 790, 833, 985
Franklin and Warren Railroad, 31, 396

Franklin Club, 86
Franklin College, 308
Franklin Institute (Kentucky), 31
Franklinton Turnpike Road Company, 52
Frank, Waldo, 709
Frankfurter, Felix, 897
Franklin, Benjamin, 433, 948
Frary, George Spencer, 646
Frary, Ihna Thayer, 682
Fraternal and patriotic societies, 29, 31, 64, 79, 88, 165, 199, 259, 276, 398, 415–416, 493, 513, 544, 559, 567, 576, 653, 723, 781, 790–791, 920, 946
Free Trade Club, 948
Freeman, F., 66
Freemasons, 31, 88, 165, 544
Freese, Abraham, 1
Fremont, John C., 666, 948
French, B. B., 948
French, Clinton, 707
French, John, 400
French, Samuel G., 946
French and Indian War, 215
Friebolin, Carl D., 964
Friedman, Stanley S., 401
Frisbie family, 364
Frissell, Henry M., 100
Fritz, Robert Owen, 764
Frost, Adelaide Gail, 817
Fuller, John W., 576
Fur trade, 31, 55, 470
Furry, John Hamilton, 645
Fusco, James, 791

Gahn, Harry C., 791, 831
Galbreath, Samuel, 119
Gales, Stephen, 139
Galland, Isaac, 948
Gallatin, Albert, 421, 948

Gallegher, P. C., 948
Galloway, James, 948
Galloway, Samuel, 454, 948
Gannett, Alice P., 930
Gano, John S., 346
Gardiner, J. B., 948
Gardner, Ira W., 881
Gardner, Philander B., 535
Garfield, Abram, 818
Garfield, Eliza Ballou, 803, 948
Garfield, Harry A., 818
Garfield, Helen Newell, 968
Garfield, Irvin McD., 818
Garfield, James Abram, 129, 229, 272, 400, 592, 685, 688, 755, 818, 948
  residence, 632, 803
  monument, 632
Garfield, Mrs. James A. (Lucretia Rudolph), 387, 632, 818, 948
Garfield, James R., 296, 387, 818, 897, 948, 968
Garfield, Mary, 818
Garfield family, 751
Garlick, Theodatus, 195–196
Garretson, George Armstrong, 913
Garrison, Lindley M., 897
Garvin, Charles Herbert, 798
Gary, Elbert H., 683, 897
Gaskill, Joseph W., 236
Gates, Horatio, 789
Gates family, 667
Gates Mills Milling Company, 667
Gatlin, R. C., 946
Gayer, Echlin P., 811
Gaylord, E. F., 132
Gaylord, H. R., 426
Genealogical History of the Kelley Family Descended from Joseph Kelley of Norwich, Connecticut, 845

General Relief Committee, 36
Gentlemen's Driving Club of Cleveland, 508
George B. Ogden & Company, 132
George Rust and Company, 538
George Washington Bicentennial Committee, 401
George Worthington Company, 558
Georgia, 90, 144, 236, 447, 466, 474, 551, 607, 679, 786
    Atlanta, 451, 519
    Bryan County, 863
    Chickamauga Park, 764
    Lytle, 764
    Resaca, 679
    Savannah, 270, 303, 948
    Ways Station, 863
Georgia Volunteer Infantry, 270, 466
    8th Regiment, 863
    19th Division, 451
Gerlich, J. H., 479
German Baptist Mission, 325
Germany, 497, 596, 674, 750, 833, 874
Gerould, Henry, 72
Gibbs, Ebenezer L., 948
Gibbs, F. C., 619
Gibraltar, 585
Gibson, George, 507
Gibson, John, 507
Gibson, Mina S., 847
Gibson, W. H., 948
Giddings, Joshua R., 180, 247, 400, 412, 419, 577, 691, 797, 948
Gilbert, Asa, 278
Gilbert, Barclay, 656
Gilbert, Mary Lukens, 656
Gilbert, Samuel A., 946
Gilchrist Transportation Company, 841
Gill, Elizabeth M., 619
Gill, Robert G., 619
Gillet, Asa, 426
Gillmore, Quincy A., 946
Gilman, Benjamin Ives, 948
Girty, Simon, 24
Gist, States Rights, 946
Gladden, Washington, 897
Glass, Carter, 791
Glenny, William, 946
Goddard, Charles, 247
Goddard, John, 592
Goddard, Nathaniel, 70
Godfrey, John M., 948
Godkin, E. L., 387
Goethe-Schiller Monument Association of Cleveland, O., 479
Goff, Frederick H., 135, 771, 791
Golden Eagle (passenger ship), 537
Goldman, Emma, 86
Goldrick, Peter, 948
Goldsmith, Jonathan, 421, 900, 948–949
Goldsmith, Lucia A., 948
Gompers, Samuel, 897
Gongwer, W. Burr, 790, 791, 844
Goodman, Alfred Thomas, 507, 808
Goodman, Thomas, 166
Goodrich, Julia W., 948
Goodrich, William H., 948
Goodrich Social Settlement, 930
Goodwin, Caleb, 738
Goodwin, Emery, 807
Goodwin, George P., 946

Goodwin, Levi, 738
Goodwin family, 807
Goodyear Tire and Rubber Company, 716
Gordon, Eleanor, 363
Gordon, Jonathan, 132
Gordon, Richard B., 592
Gordon, William R., 482
Gorham family, 811
Gorgas, Josiah, 706
Gorgas, William C., 897
Gosselin, A. E., 215
Gould, Hannah Flagg, 948
Gowdy, Ryan, 933
Graham, George, 739
Graham, Robert, 280
Grand Army of the Republic, Department of the Ohio, 89, 100, 260, 524, 535, 549, 552, 603, 627
Grand River, 46, 421
Grange, 291, 467
Granger, Francis, 406
Granger, Gideon, 180, 421, 543, 712, 736, 924, 950
Grant, Jesse R., 948
Grant, Ulysses S., 203, 400, 465, 666, 705, 946, 948
Granville College, 325, 815
Granville Literary and Theological Institution, 325
Grasselli, Caesar A., 965
Grasselli, Eugene R., 965
Grasselli, Thomas S., 965
Grasselli Chemical Company, 965
Gray, A. Donald, 995
Gray, H. N., 619
Gray, Henry, 946
Gray, Martin E., 83, 329, 619
Great Lakes, 30, 132, 404, 538, 581, 599, 791, 841, 922–923. *See also names of individual lakes*
Greater Cleveland Council of Churches, 993
Greater Cleveland Growth Association, 996
Greater Cleveland Growth Board, 996
Greece, 585
Greeley, Horace, 247, 272, 400, 948
Green, John P., 987
Greene, Edward B., 168, 756
Greene, Nathanael, 714, 756, 789, 948
Greenman, N. W., 946
Greenville and West Milton Turnpike Company, 228
Greenwalt family, 667
Gregory, Edgar B., 837
Gregory, Enoch, 887
Gregory, Sarah Mumford, 837
Gregory XIII (pope), 949
Gridley, A., 132
Grierson, Benjamin Henry, 948
Gries, Moses J., 651
Griffith (steamship), 580
Griffith, B., 619
Grinnell, William, 645
Griswold, Dudley, 114
Griswold, Solomon, 862
Griswold, Stanley, 338, 924
Groll, George C., 177
Gross, William L., 447
Grossman, George, 177
Groton Avery Clan, 49
Guatemala, 563
Guilford, Linda Thayer, 106
Guitteau, Judson, 543

Gunn, Alexander, 948
Gurley, Mary Alice, 363
Gurley, Ralph R., 247
Gwinett, Button, 741

Hagerman, James John, 599
Haines, S. S., 592
Hale, Andrew, 663
Hale, Charles Oviatt, 663
Hale, Gideon, 948
Hale, Jonathan, 663
Hale family, 681
Hall, Gordius A., 562
Hall, J. M., 62
Hall, Nathan K., 247
Hall, R., 44
Hall, Renselear Russell, 893
Hall, Richard, 326
Halstead, N., 592
Hamilton, J. E., 592
Hamilton, Paul, 878
Hamilton Seminary, 160
Hamlen, H. H., 62
Hammond, Charles, 247
Hammond family, 681
Hampson, James, 562
Hampton, Taylor, 662
Hampton, Wade, 946
Hancock, John, 760
Hancock, Winfield Scott, 946
Hanna, Benjamin, 514
Hanna, Daniel R., 208
Hanna, Howard M., 208
Hanna, Leonard, 514
Hanna, Marcus A., 246, 355, 514, 567, 897, 948
Hanna, Robert, 514
Hanna, Seville, 948
Hard, Curtis V., 678
Hard, Dudley J., 678

Hardee, William J., 946
Harding, Florence K., 948
Harding, Warren G., 168, 948
Hardy, Frank A., 466
Harkness, Florence, 824
Harlan, James, 948
Harman, Grace Fleming (Mrs. Ralph A.), 727
Harman, Ralph A., 727
Harman, Sue Wade, 727
Harmar, Josiah, 507
Harmon, Elias, 31
Harmon, John, 247, 622, 712
Harmon, Julian, 31
Harmon, Martin S., 31
Harmon, Orrin, 31, 622, 737
Harper, Alexander, 732, 970
Harper, Alexander J., 985
Harper, J. C., 592
Harper, James A., 1, 46
Harper, Rice, 46, 691, 985
Harper, Robert, 247, 985
Harradence, W. F., 724
Harrington, George, 948
Harris, Andrew L., 897
Harris, Charles, 769
Harris, George B., 948
Harris, Isham G., 946
Harris, W. T., 387
Harrison, Benjamin, 387, 948
Harrison, Benjamin F., 451
Harrison, Marvin Clinton, 989
Harrison, William, 30
Harrison, William Henry, 154, 247, 534, 878, 948
Hart, Albert Bushnell, 401
Hart, Albert Gaillard, 531
Hart, Henry, 878
Hart, Luke E., 790
Hartt, Dudley N., 791

Harvard University, 6, 791
Harvey H. Brown & Company, 809
Haskell, Coburn, 189
Haskell, Jonathan, 948
Haskell Golf Ball Company, 189
Hathaway, Asahel, 139
Hauser, Elizabeth J., 768
Hawaii, 563, 567
Hawley, Abel, Jr., 482
Hawley, Emma Boutelle, 625
Hawley, George W., 426
Hawley, T. B., 1
Hawley, Timothy R., 426
Haworth, Paul Leland, 946
Hay, Clara Louise (Stone), 948
Hay, John, 634, 897, 948, 1001
Hayden, Amos Sutton, 948
Hayden, Aurelia, 882
Hayden, C., 882
Hayden, Ferdinand V., 687
Hayden, M. M., 132
Haydn, Hiram Collins, 948
Hayes, Ralph A., 948
Hayes, Rutherford B., 419, 454, 592, 824, 948
Hayes, Mrs. Seth, 935
Hayes, Webb C., 215
Hayne, Arthur Perroneau, 948
Hayslip, John, 602
Hazen, William B., 946
Head, B., 132
Heald, William, 948
Heard, Charles M., 196
Hearne family, 371
Heart, Jonathan, 1, 507, 948
Heath, William, 714
Heaton, Jacob, 210
Heaton, James, 715
Heazel, Francis J., 790

Heckewelder, Anna, 176
Heckewelder, John, 1, 176, 860, 949
Heckewelder, Sarah, 176
Hedrick, Elizabeth, 592
Hegins, Amelia Drum (Mrs. Charles), 847
Hegins, Charles, 847
Heintzelman, Samuel P., 666
Henderson, James Patterson, 802
Henderson, John Brooks, 946
Henderson, John M., 117, 1070
Henderson, Leon, 791
Henderson, Matthew, 802
Hendry, Samuel, 691, 991
Henry, C. E., 387
Henshaw, Joshua, 665
Herkomer, Herman, 936
Hermitage Furnace, 51
Herold, Peter M., 458
Herrick, Caroline P. (Mrs. Myron T.), 573, 596
Herrick, Elbert, 948
Herrick, Elise A., 948
Herrick, J. F., 100
Herrick, Myron T., 573, 574, 596, 683, 780, 897, 985
Herrick, Parmely Webb, 596
Herrick, Parmely Webb, Jr., 596
Herrick, R. R., 212
Heth, John, 948
Heyward, Thomas, 760
Hickok, Ezra William, 591
Hickox, Eri, 948
Hicks, Charles, 198
Hicks, Elias, 335
Higgins, David, 23
Higgins, Eunice, 23
Higginson, Thomas Wentworth, 948

[379]

Hildreth, Samuel P., 69, 948
Hildt, George H., 541
Hill, Daniel H., 946
Hillsboro Crusade Sketches and Family Records, 333
Hinckley, Samuel, 231
Hinde, Thomas, 294
Hindman, Thomas C., 946
Hine, Hezekiah, 892
Hine, Homer H., Jr., 467
Hine, Homer H., Sr., 247, 468, 712, 715
Hinsdale, Burke Aaron, 387, 632
Hinzmann, William, 874
Hiram College, 387, 817
Hiram Eclectic Institute, 688
Hiram House, 972
Hirsch & Andrews, 894
History of Dentistry in Cleveland, Ohio, 200
History of Fuller's Ohio Brigade, 576
Hitchcock, Ethan A., 948
Hitchcock, Frank H., 897
Hitchcock, Henry Lawrence, 796
Hitchcock, Peter, 247, 370, 675, 713, 796
Hitchcock, Peter, Jr., 796
Hitchcock, Peter Marshall, 796
Hitchcock, Reuben, 179, 584, 796
Hobart family, 321, 919
Hobby, Oveta Culp, 674
Hocking River, 52
Hodge, Alfred A., 567
Hodge, Maranda S. (Mrs. David L. Wood), 567
Hodge, Orlando John, 567
Hodge, Velorus, 567
Hodge Genealogy, 567
Hodges, George W., 786

Hodges, Marana, 786
Hodges, W. R., 879
Hogan & Wilson, 132
Holbrook, Daniel, 738
Holcomb, Henry, 825
Holden, A. F., 208
Holden, L. Dean, 208
Holden, Liberty E., 87
Holland, 935
Holland Land Company, 1, 735
Holley, John Milton, 1
Holloway, J. F., 517
Holloway, William, 948
Holly, Alphonso, 722
Holly, Morris I., 890
Holmes, Oliver Wendell, 756
Holmes, Theophilus H., 946
Holmes, Uriel, Jr., 543, 736, 950
Holt, Hamilton, 897
Holt, Joseph, 946
Home Gardening Association, 930
Hood, John B., 423, 474, 946
Hooker, Edward, 738
Hooker, Joseph, 465
Hoover, Herbert, 596, 674
Hopkins, Richard E., 946
Hopper, Daniel D., 855
Hopper, Delina (Woodrow), 855
Hopper, Isaac T., 335
Horse racing and breeding, 208, 279, 417–418, 508, 948
Hosford, Henry H., 697
Hospitals. *See* Public welfare
Hostetler, Joseph C., 844
Hotchkiss, Silas, 278
Hotels, inns, and taverns, 132, 241, 279, 364, 377, 408, 611, 1011
Houghton Mifflin Company, 827
House, Elizabeth J., 62

Hover, Ezekiel, 1, 247, 948
Hovey, Alvin P., 946
Howard, D. R., 9
Howard, Nathaniel, R., 674
Howard, Oliver Otis, 946, 948
Howard family, 321
Howe, Charles S., 635, 651
Howe, Frederick C., 930
Howe, Henry, 419, 948
Howe, Thomas, 247, 412
Howells, William D., 948
Howland, Charles Roscoe, 981
Howland, Joseph, 231
Howland, L. Paul, 897
Hoyt, Charles, 517
Hoyt, James Humphrey, 208, 670
Hubbard, Aaron, 668
Hubbard, Elijah, 859
Hubbard, Henry, 247
Hubbard, Lydia, 754
Hubbard, Nehemiah, 139, 859
Hubbard, William, 862
Hubby & Hughes, 268
Hudson, David, 1, 247, 862
Hudson, David Oviatt, 832
Hudson, William N., 154
Hughes, Adella Prentiss, 609
Hughes, Charles E., 897
Hughes, Langston, 709
Hughes, Rosemary, 804
Hughes, Samuel, 391
Hulburd, Calvin T., 799
Hull, Andrew, 141, 278
Hull, William, 428, 948
Humboldt Mining Company, 707
Humiston, Ransom F., 216, 864
Humphrey, George Magoffin, 673–674
Humphreys, Andrew Atkinson, 946

Humrickhouse, George, 313
Humrickhouse, Thomas S., 313
Hundley, D. R., 946
Hunsberger, Darius F., 857
Hunt, Jessie, 769
Hunt, William E., 353
Hunt, William H., 594, 657
Hunt, William S., 132
Huntington, Benjamin, 132
Huntington, C. P., 221
Huntington, George C., 1062
Huntington, Hannah, 194
Huntington, Julius C., 1, 166
Huntington, Marvin, 412
Huntington, Samuel, Jr., 194, 421, 468, 543, 712, 734, 738, 924, 948
Huntington, Samuel, Sr., 760, 948
Hurd, Frank H., 539
Hurd, Rollin C., 539
Hurlbut, George, 698
Huron River, 176, 391
Hussey, Payne & Company, 921
Hutchins, John, 247
Hutchinson, Clarence H., 611
Hyatt, Elisha, 482
Hyatt, Mary (Mrs. Thomas J.), 593
Hyatt, Thomas J., 593
Hyde, Alvan, 412
Hyde, Gustavus A., 671
Hydraulic Steel Company, 771
Hygiea Female Athenaeum, 33

Iddings, Hiram, 438
Iddings, Hiram A., 438
Iddings, Richard, 438
Illinois, 313, 595, 769, 815
  Bloomington, 206, 315
  Cairo, 447

Illinois (continued)
  Chicago, 36, 535, 595, 662, 766, 896
  Clinton County, 580
  Griggsville, 636
  Iroquois County, 940
  Paw Paw Grove, 664
  Pecatonia, 669
  Perry, 636
  Pittsfield, 636
  Quincy, 9
  Sheldon, 801
Illinois Artillery
  1st Regiment, 940
Illinois Volunteer Infantry, 466
  76th Regiment, 801
  77th Regiment, 834
Illinois Militia, 636
  52nd Regiment, 740
Illustrated London News, 724
Imboden, James D., 946
Immigration, 71, 206, 642, 791, 846, 897–899, 930, 941, 972, 1040, 1048
Improved Order of Red Men, 415
Independence and Parma Plank Road Company, 660
Independent Knights of Temperance, 31
Independent Order of Good Templars, 920
India, 817
Indian Ocean, 94
Indiana (territory), 162
Indiana, 30, 129, 325, 454, 509, 815, 931
  Bristol, 854
  Crawfordville, 168
  Fort Wayne, 285, 878, 895
  Indianapolis, 508, 680
  Knox County, 162
  Lake Cottage, 363
  La Porte, 656
  Richmond, 363
  Vincennes, 162
  Wayne County, 614
  West Union, 947
Indiana: Morgan Raid Commission, 931
Indiana University, 854
Indiana Volunteer Infantry, 466, 614
Indianapolis and St. Louis Railroad, 680
Indianapolis, Pittsburgh and Cleveland Railroad, 680
Indians, 1, 30, 32, 40, 42, 55, 99, 127, 129, 162, 206, 215, 219–220, 247, 299, 415, 433, 469–470, 507–508, 580–581, 589, 629, 680, 707, 734, 777, 794, 868, 878, 886, 897–899
Industry and manufactures
  automobile, 508, 716, 791, 907, 943, 989
  aviation, 943
  chemical, 716, 965
  coal, 132–133, 327
  general, 114, 189, 319, 326, 355, 366, 425, 546, 579, 596, 686, 771, 791, 825, 943–944, 947, 957, 959, 983
  iron and steel, 51, 132–133, 327, 497, 502, 517, 558, 599, 641, 674, 683, 716, 765, 771, 809, 943, 1001, 1037
  light and power, 574, 948, 960
  lumber, 538, 683
  nickel, 683
  oil, 581, 880, 921, 948

paper, 948
rubber, 716
shipbuilding, 517, 767
textile, 777, 791, 853, 915
Ingels, Howard P., 791
Insurance, 31, 38, 107, 210, 320, 517, 538, 771, 796, 841, 948
International Congress of Aviation, 594
International Nickel Company, 683
Interparliamentary Union, 897–899
Inventions and inventors, 139, 189, 449, 497, 517
Iowa, 129, 503
Iowa Volunteer Infantry, 466
Ira H. Owen (steamer), 923
Ireland, 52, 642, 733, 948
Irish American Club of Cleveland, 642
Irish Emigrant Aid Society of Ohio, 642
Irish Parliamentary Party, 642
Iron Age, 771
Iron Point Mining Company, 133
Irvin, Westley, 590
Irvine, William, 507
Irving, Washington, 756
Isaac Leuty & Company, 44
"Islander," 448
Isthmus Pacific Railway Company, 700
Italy, 585, 727, 733
Ives, Butler, 618

J. F. Rust and Company, 538
J. R. & W. P. Lee, 894
Jackson, Andrew, 203, 436–437
Jackson, Andrew II, 414
Jackson, J. G., 871
Jackson, James Frederick, 684
Jackson, John K., 946
Jackson, Sarah, 414
Jackson, Thomas Jonathan (Stonewall), 946
Jackson, William H., 946
Jackson & Great Northern Railroad, 301
Jackson Iron & Steel Company, 641
Jacobs, Asa, 1013
Jamaica, 870, 876
James G. Martin & Company, 495
Jamison, Robert H., 791
Janesville Gazette, 587
Jefferson, Thomas, 203, 948
Jefferson College, 249, 802
Jenkins, George K., 30, 482
Jennings, James R., 301
Jennings, N. R., 301
Jennings, S. C., 1
Jennison, William, 50
Joc-O-Sot, 433
John Huntington Polytechnic Institute of Cleveland, 667
Johnson, Andrew, 203, 624, 799, 946
Johnson, Austin, 429
Johnson, D., 432
Johnson, Henry N., 621
Johnson, Horace, 429
Johnson, J. K., 366
Johnson, J. W., 592
Johnson, James, 313
Johnson, John, 313
Johnson, John A., 247
Johnson, Joseph, 313
Johnson, Leverett, 623
Johnson, Levi, 1

Johnson, M. B. H., 592
Johnson, Phinehas, 738
Johnson, Tom L., 567, 651, 768, 844, 897, 904, 918, 948
Johnson, William K., 313
Johnston, A., 387
Johnston, A. (from Connecticut), 217
Johnston, Alvanley, 790
Johnston, Charles, 247
Johnston, J. T., 881
Johnston, John W., 543
Johnston, Joseph Eggleston, 423, 474, 706, 946
Johnston, Josiah S., 423
Jones, Andrew B., 703
Jones, Benjamin T., 434
Jones, Catlitt, 482
Jones, Charles M., 703
Jones, Henry C., 170
Jones, John Paul, 789
Jones, Robert M., 946
Jones, Day, Cockley & Reavis, 716
Jordan, Charles R., 445
Jordan, Stephen, 445
Jordan, Thomas, 946
Journalists, editors, and publishers, 33, 192, 325, 330, 333, 365, 387, 419, 503, 525, 567, 655, 709, 724, 766, 827, 837, 840, 856, 906, 932, 958, 969, 1019. See also Writings and writers
Journey to Ohio in 1810, 692
Judd, William, 507
Judson, Katherine B., 821

Kaiser, Peter H., 314
Kaiser-Frazer Corporation, 791
Kansas, 129, 202, 313, 503, 680, 755

Kasota (steamboat), 132
Kauffman, Catherine, 363
Kearney, Philip, 666
Keim family, 836
Kelley, Addison, 382
Kelley, Alfred, 107, 114, 166, 247, 421, 715, 829
Kelley, Alfred S., 382
Kelley, B. F., 666
Kelley, Datus, 107, 382, 1062
Kelley, Edwin, 107
Kelley, Hannah, 382
Kelley, Hermon A., 382, 845
Kelley, Irad, 107
Kelley, Moses, 297
Kelley, Sarah, 382
Kelley family, 1
Kelley's Island Literary Society, 448
Kelley's Island Wine Company, 382
Kellogg, Frank B., 897
Kellogg, Martin, 665
Kellogg-Briand Pact, 596
Kellogg family, 824
Kelsey, Edward E., 456
Kemp, H. S., 9
Kemper, James Lawson, 946
Kendall, Amos, 778, 948
Kennedy, John F., 790
Kent, Edward, 462
Kent, James, 694
Kenton Milling Company, 262
Kentucky, 325, 370, 454, 509, 595, 679, 730, 759, 769, 852
  Augusta, 121
  Crab Orchard, 951
  Danville, 447
  Logan County, 949
  Louisville, 224

Pleasant Hill, 947
Pleasantville, 954
South Union, 947
Kentucky Military Institute, 31
Kentucky Volunteer Infantry, 466
Kerr, Daniel, 247
Kerr, John, 52
Kerr, John S., 325
Kerr, Joseph, 769
Kershaw, John, 449
Kershaw, Joseph Brevard, 946
Ketchum, Hiram, 462
Kewish, Mary D., 919
Keys, Erasmus D., 946
Kilbourne, Byron, 948
King, Henry C., 897
King, Horatio C., 946
King, Joseph G., 715
King, Julius, 62
King, Lewis, 42
King, William S., 946
King's Daughters Society of Berea, Ohio, 550
Kingsbury, Andrew, 139
Kingsbury, Harmon, 412
Kingsbury, James, 65, 736
Kinsman, Frederick, 179, 632
Kinsman, Jeremiah, 186
Kinsman, John, 186, 247, 665
Kinsman, Robert, 186
Kinsman & Potter, 132
Kirby, Ephraim, 543
Kirke, Henry M., 451
Kirker, Thomas, 338, 871
Kirkpatrick, Abraham, 299
Kirkpatrick, John, 948
Kirtland, Henry T., 326
Kirtland, Jared, 278, 326
Kirtland, Jared Potter, 195–196, 242, 247, 543, 667, 948

Kirtland, Lois, 326
Kirtland, Nancy M., 326
Kirtland, Polly, 326
Kirtland, Turhand, 1, 46, 141, 164, 278, 326, 712, 734, 736, 738
Kirtland Society of Natural Sciences, 195
Kirwin, Patrick J., 790
Klotz, Robert, 946
Knapp, William Herman, 806
Knights of Columbus, 790
Knights of Honor of the State of Ohio, 29
Knights of Labor, 781
Knowlton family, 697
Knox, Henry, 714, 948
Knox, Philander, 897
Kohler, William, 946
Kosciuszko, Tadeusz, 789
Kossuth, Louis, 31, 948
Kurtz, Charles L., 670
Kurtz, David J., 943
Kyle, George J., 619
Kyser, James, 344

Labor and unions, 30, 35, 116, 127, 132, 160, 206, 361, 396, 447, 454, 465, 486, 497, 599, 612, 614, 641, 690, 708, 753, 768, 777, 781, 791, 830, 838, 842, 854, 897–899, 922–923, 938, 943, 948, 988–989, 1000, 1002
Labouchere, Peter Caesar, 690
Lacey, Ezra, 50
Lacey, John, 280
Lacey, William H., 50
Ladies Aid Society of Brocton, O., 84

Ladies Literary Circle, 649
La Durantaye, 24
Laird, John, 312
Lake Carriers' Association of West Virginia, 841
Lake Erie, 1, 46, 107, 176, 375, 382, 421, 463, 580, 626, 646, 824, 936, 948
Lake Erie Chemical Company, 716
Lake Erie Female Seminary, 796
Lake Shore Crude Oil Transportation Company, 921
Lake Shore Railroad, 508
Lake Superior, 536, 581, 676, 707
Lake Superior Iron Ore Company, 809
Lamberton, Robert C., 598
Lancaster, C., 338
Land companies, 1, 69–70, 102, 174, 181, 223, 231, 240, 279, 281, 295, 494, 520, 543, 561, 568, 622, 634, 665, 667, 714, 734–738, 775, 862, 948–950
Land deeds, surveys, and records, 1, 31–32, 46, 50, 52, 65–66, 70, 72, 98, 107, 114–115, 139, 141, 143, 159, 161, 163, 167, 169, 174, 180–181, 186, 188, 198, 202, 222–223, 228, 231, 240, 245, 247, 261, 263, 278–279, 281, 293, 295, 297, 299–300, 312–313, 317–318, 325–327, 336, 338, 348, 352, 354, 366–368, 375, 382, 391, 404–405, 408, 412–413, 421, 425–426, 436, 445–446, 449–450, 454–455, 459, 461, 472, 478, 484, 489, 494, 501, 523, 527–528, 531, 543, 555, 567, 569, 580, 589, 601, 604, 605, 609, 611, 618–619, 622–623, 630, 633–634, 665, 667–668, 680, 695, 700, 704, 711, 714–716, 722, 725, 734–735, 737–738, 747, 751, 754, 769–770, 775, 777, 779, 796, 806, 809, 839, 848, 850, 867–869, 877, 880, 887–888, 892, 899, 919, 942, 947–950, 955, 959, 966, 983, 986, 997, 1008, 1012, 1018, 1029–1030, 1059–1060, 1068, 1071
Landon, Joseph, 1
Landrum, Amanda (Mrs. Obed J. Wilson), 121
Landrum, George W., 121
Lane, Benjamin, 580
Lane, Charles F., 605
Lane, James Henry, 946
Lane Theological Seminary, 365, 600, 948
Langton, Levi, 59
Langworthy, Isaac P., 946
Lansing, Robert, 897
Larkin, Abel, 202
Larkin, Edwin, 202
Larkin, Stillman, C., 202
Larkin, Susannah, 202
Laronge, Joseph, 791
LaSalle, Robert Cavelier, Sieur de, 24
Latham, Allen, 299, 633
Lathrop, Daniel, 665, 862, 948
Lathrop, Edward S., 946
Lattimore, William, 278
Laubie, Peter A., 948
Laurens, Henry, 789
Lausche, Frank, 790
Law, Evander McIvor, 946

Law, Jonathan, 142
Law, William, 141, 738
Law, William, Jr., 141, 738
Law, lawyers, and jurists, 3, 15, 31, 51, 65, 117, 132, 139, 141, 162, 170, 180–181, 192, 194, 202, 206, 219, 222, 224, 229, 247, 261, 263, 278–279, 284, 297, 312, 314, 333, 338, 343, 368, 382, 400, 405, 412, 419, 425, 440, 446, 454, 462, 467–468, 489, 503, 539, 556, 577–578, 580, 592, 604, 622–623, 641, 647, 654, 667–668, 670, 694, 706, 711–712, 716, 728, 769–770, 788, 790–792, 796–797, 824, 828, 843, 861, 865, 897–899, 919, 929, 948, 958, 961, 964, 973, 977, 983, 987, 989, 991–992, 1002–1003, 1011, 1013, 1022–1023, 1025, 1028, 1033–1035, 1037, 1050, 1055–1057, 1065, 1070, 1073, 1080, 1082–1083
Lawler, Edward P., 410
Lawrence, Asa A., 810
Lawrence family, 512
Lawton, Alexander R., 946
Leach, Charles F., 296
League of Nations, 596, 918
Lear, Tobias, 154
Ledyard, Nathaniel, 421
Lee, Fanny J., 363
Lee, Richard Henry, 760, 948
Lee, Robert E., 423, 705–706, 946
Leete, Ralph, 788
Leete, William H., 788
Leete family, 512
LeFevre family, 512

Leffingwell, Christopher, 240
Leffingwell, William, 240
Legal Aid Society, 930
Leggett, Mortimer Dormer, 525, 879
Lemke, William, 783
Leonard, Francis M., 873
Leonard, J. E., 619
Leroy, James E., 323
Leroy and Burton Plank Road Company, 948
Letcher, John, 946
Leuty, Isaac, 44
Lewis, Charlotte S., 914
Lewis, Frances Esmond Durdin, 848
Lewis, Gleason F., 643
Lewis, Mrs. Joel, 299
Lewis, John L., 674
Lewis, Martha J., 363
Lewis, R. G., 633
Lewis, Wheeler, 154
Lewis, Wilbert W., 914
Lexington (whaling vessel), 94
Liberator, 656
Liberty Hall Academy, 948
Librarian Society of Cleveland, 948
Libraries and historical associations, 1, 22, 32, 52, 54, 86, 183, 214, 356, 411, 458, 472, 507, 547, 568, 625, 654, 691, 707, 723, 824, 902, 947–948, 980, 985, 1005
Licking County Pioneer, Historical, and Antiquarian Society, 980
Licking Land Company, 102
Life of Major General George H. Thomas, 218

Lincoln, Abraham, 129, 192, 203, 624, 666, 705, 946, 948–949, 952
Lincoln, Mrs. Abraham (Mary Todd), 666
Lincoln, Benjamin, 789
Lincoln, Robert Todd, 952
Lincoln, Sarah Bush, 641
Lincoln Club of Cincinnati, 592
Lindbergh, Charles A., 596
Lindsay, Robert, 574
Literary and debate societies, 12, 25, 52, 59, 62, 104, 119, 138, 206, 216, 226, 243, 258, 283, 307–308, 316, 448, 510, 516, 649, 651, 685, 738, 796, 891, 935
Little, Lyman, 861
Little Miami River, 589, 633
Livestock, 508, 1018–1019, 1021, 1059, 1075, 1080–1081
Livingston, John, 949
Livingston, Philip, 760
Lloyd, James T., 791
Locher, Ralph S., 976
Lockemer family, 667
Lockwood, Henry H., 705, 946
Lockwood's Corners Literary Society, 12
Lodge, Henry Cabot, Jr., 674
Lodge, Henry Cabot, Sr., 897
Loeb, William, Jr., 897
Logan, John Payne, 451
Lomus, B. J., 347
Long, Clement, 832
Long, David, 829
Long, E. C., 619
Long, John D., 897
Long, Mary S., 175

Longfellow, Henry Wadsworth, 756
Longstreet, James, 423, 946
Longworth, Nicholas, 897
Looker, Othniel, 154
Loomis, Clara Byrde, 512
Loomis, Mrs. Elatus G., 513
Loomis, Elias, 404
Loomis, Elisha Scott, 512
Loomis family, 919
Lorain Iron Company, 502
Lord, Anna, 754
Lord, Asa Dearborn, 856
Lord, Richard, 295, 517, 634
Lord, Samuel Phillips, 634, 862, 948
Loring, Charles, 70
Loring, Daniel, 948
Lossing, Benson John, 18
Lotteries, 31, 738
Louisiana, 99, 188, 198, 301, 322, 425, 447, 451, 488, 705, 776, 834
Louisiana (U.S. gunboat), 946
Louisiana Militia, 322
Louisiana Volunteer Infantry, 466
Lovell, Mary B., 16
Low, George J., 592
Lowe, D. F., 592
Lowell, James Russell, 756
Lower, William E., 563
Lowey, Mark P., 946
Loyal American League, 372
Ludlow, Arthur Clyde, 948
Lusher, Robert M., 301
Lybarger, Donald F., 973
Lyman, Carlos Parsons, 839
Lyman, D. B., 948
Lyman, Darius, 247, 983

[388]

Lyman, David, 413
Lyman, Theodore, 70
Lynn, James, 318
Lyon, Sidney S., 946
Lyttle, Bertelle M., 637

M. A. Hanna & Company, 674
McArthur, Duncan, 338, 948
McArthur, Rial, 154, 461
MacCarthy, H. O'C., 642
McCaslin, A. A., 820
McCausland, John, 946
McClellan, C. H., 946
McClellan, George B., 465, 666, 946
McClernand, E. J., 76
McClernand, John A., 946
McClung, D. W., 592
McClung, John W., 948
McCook, Alexander McDowell, 948
McCormick, Medill, 897
McCulloch, Henry E., 946
MacDonald, Harriet M., 721
McDonald, Sir John Alexander, 683
McDougall, Alexander, 714
McDowell, David, 92
McDowell, Irvin, 666
McDowell, William Osborne, 948
Macedonian, 325
McFarlan, Alexander B., 708
McFarland, Robert P., 948
McGiffert, James Henry, 948
McGinnis, George F., 879
McHenry House, 364
McHenry, James, 948
Machinery, 771
McIlrath, Alexander, 241

McIlrath Tavern, 241
McIntosh, Henry P., 683
Mack, John T., 215
Mackall, William W., 946
McKeehan, Homer H., 1045
McKinley, David, 601
McKinley, Helen, 948
McKinley, John, 601
McKinley, William, 86, 596, 634, 670, 683, 710, 766, 948, 987
McKinley, Mrs. William (Ida), 596, 710
McKisson, Robert E., 897, 948
McLain, Thomas J., 446
McLaren, James, 683
McLaughlin, Alexander, 52
McLaws, Lafayette, 946
McLean, C. R., 608
McLean, John, 247, 948
McMahon, James, 519
McMeekin, Hannah, 488
McMeekin, John, 488
McMichael, Stanley L., 948
McMullen, George W., 683
McNeal, George, 1028
McRae, Milton A., 592
McSweeney, John, 320
MacVeagh, Franklin, 766
McVeigh, R. B., 619
Madison, James, 203
Madison, Joab, 948
Madison College, 932
Madison Farmers' Association, 980
Maine, 4, 178, 462, 556, 735, 946, 947
Maine Volunteer Infantry, 466
Malden, William H., 948
Mallory, Stephen R., 946

Maloney, Mrs. D. H., 935
Manchester, Daniel Wilbert, 948
Manigault, Arthur M., 946
Manion, Dean Clarence, 790
Mann, George C., 387
Manry, Robert A., 905
Mansfield, Jared, 223
Mansfield, Joseph K. F., 946
Mansfield, L. K., 326
Manx Street School, 610
Mapes, George Carleton, 100
Maple Leaf Land Company, 520, 667
Maps, 1, 161, 299, 366, 410, 453, 457, 612, 629, 662, 667, 678, 705–706, 735, 739, 775, 814, 824, 910, 948–949, 986, 1012
March, Daniel, 777
March, George, 777
March, Oliver, 777
March, Stephen, 777
Margry, Pierre, 581
Marietta & Cincinnati Railroad Company, 948
Marietta & Pittsburgh Railroad, 1067
Marietta College, 181
Marietta Gazette, 181
Marietta Historical Association, 145
Marion, Francis, 789
Markley, Alfred Collins, 726
Marks, M. A., 651
Marshall, James C., 210
Marshall family, 697
Martin, Susanna (Mrs. Isaac Backus), 28
Marvin, Charles, 738
Maryland, 30, 110, 154, 269, 445, 482, 562, 699, 738, 810, 928

Maryland Artillery
  Baltimore Battery, 928
Maryland Volunteer Infantry, 466
Maschke, Maurice, 296, 897
Mason, James, 751
Mason, John, 470
Mason, Mary L., 363, 751
Massachusetts, 43, 187, 391, 405
  Beverly, 647
  Boston, 70, 384, 412, 454, 656, 894
  Brimfield, 278
  Cambridge, 705
  Dorchester, 661, 777
  East Bridgewater, 345
  Falmouth, 905
  Framingham, 671
  Freetown, 482
  Hampshire County, 888
  Hancock, 947
  Harvard, 947
  Ipswich, 69
  Lee, 132
  Longmeadow, 168
  Marblehead, 508
  Newburyport, 482
  Newton Center, 160
  North Adams, 647
  Peabody, 513
  Plymouth, 363
  Shirley, 947
  Sutton, 777
  Tyringham, 947
  Williamsburg, 616
  Worcester County, 777
Massachusetts Bay Colony, 877
Massachusetts Anti-Slavery Society, 948
Massachusetts Historical Society, 948

Massachusetts Volunteer Infantry, 466
Massie, Henry, 769
Massie, Nathaniel, 769
Mastick, Asahel, 281
Mastick, Benjamin, 281
Mastick, Benjamin, Jr., 281
Mastick, Cynthia, 281
Mastick, Edwin B., 281
Mastick, Elliot, 281
Mastick, Joseph, 281
Masury, Joseph, 647
Matchett, W. H. 242
Mathematics books, 52, 456, 482, 542
Mather, Flora Stone, 930, 1001
Mather, James, 754
Mather, Samuel (1851–1931), 897, 1001
Mather, Samuel, Jr., (1771–1854), 736, 754, 859
Mather, Samuel L. (1817–1890), 196, 676
Mather, Thomas, 754
Mathews, John, 948
Mathews, John G., 374
Matthews, Mary L., 644
Matthews, R. S., 946
Maule, Mary K., 946
Maumee and Sandusky Road, 426
Maumee River, 247, 507
Maurer & Mills, 872
Maxwell, Mrs. J. W., 17
May, Edward Tuckerman, 70
May, Henry Knox, 70
May, John, 70
May, Otto, 177
Mayfield Lyceum, 44, 667
Mayhew, Ira, 856
Maylin, Thomas, 948

Maynard, Charles S., 506
Mead, Hobby, 354
Mead, Jabez, 354
Mead, Jeremiah, 354
Mead, Sarah, 354
Mead, Shadrach, 354
Mead, Titus, 354
Meade, George G., 465, 946, 948
Meagher, Thomas Francis, 948
Means, Robert, 769
Meason, Isaac, 715
Mechanics and Citizens Institute of Cleveland, Ohio, 39
Medical Society of Ohio, 109
Medicine
  dentistry, 200, 586
  education, 5, 67, 109, 117, 242, 433, 496, 948
  general practice, 72, 132, 255, 433, 473–474, 498, 531, 562–563, 667, 675, 706, 798, 802, 895
  homeopathy, 750, 895, 948
  medicines, 366, 505, 650, 739
  See also Public welfare
Mediterranean Sea, 573
Meigs, Josiah, 739
Meigs, Montgomery C., 946
Meigs, Return J., 338, 428, 675, 924, 948
Melhinch, Mrs. William, 213
Memminger, Christopher G., 946
Memorial of William Spooner 1637 . . . , 399
Menace, 791
Menelaus (British warship), 269
Menning, Joseph, 781
Mentor and Willoughby Plains Temperance Society, 83
Mentor Library Company, 183

[391]

Mercer Academy, 238
Merchant, Aaron, 737, 806, 997
Merchant, Ahaz, 737, 997
Merchant, Corwin C., 737, 806, 997
Merchants, 44, 51–52, 70, 98, 107, 110, 131–132, 188, 197, 254, 268, 272, 277, 279, 281, 313, 319, 326, 366, 382, 405, 408, 412, 425, 446, 458, 470, 495, 537, 539, 558, 562, 748, 767, 810, 816, 820, 847, 877, 894, 916, 933, 949, 963, 974, 1022, 1034
Merkel, Peter, 425
Merrell, Catherine, 363
Merrick, Charles H., 650
Merrick, Myra K., 650
Merrick, R. L., 650
Merrill, Charles C., 406
Merrill, Horace, 132
Merritt, Edward A., 208
Metcalf, Bryce, 948
Metcalf, George P., 828
Mewett, Alfred, 667
Mexican War, 315, 423, 540, 562, 567, 580
Mexico, 315, 563, 567, 612, 678
Miami Baptist Association, 324
Miami Canal, 404
Micheaux Film Corporation, 827
Michigan (territory)
  Port Lawrence, 878
Michigan, 30, 36, 50, 580, 595, 600, 707, 737, 847, 849
  Ann Arbor, 392
  Detroit, 215, 618, 750, 841, 847, 943–944
  Ishpeming, 676
  Jonesville, 837
  Marquette, 676
  Michilimackinac, 55
  Newport, 599
  Pontiac, 48
  Saginaw, 538
  Saginaw City, 50
Michigan Engineers
  1st Regiment, 181
Michigan Supreme Court, 222
Michigan Volunteer Infantry, 466
  29th Regiment, 475
Michigan Welding Products Company, 943
Miles, Erastus, 829
Mill Creek Iron Works, 51
Millard, Royal, 1056
Millard family, 807
Miller, Halsey D., 376
Miller, Joseph K., 168
Miller, Margaret (Spangler), 168
Miller, Melancton, 92
Miller, Otto, 168, 436
Miller, Ray T., 790–791
Miller, Thomas J., 910, 937
Miller, William, 946
Milliman family, 300
Milling and mills, 262, 326, 395, 502, 667, 853, 912, 915
Mills, Isaac, 738
Mills family, 919
Milwaukee Iron Company, 599
Mining and mines, 132–133, 567, 581, 674, 683, 707, 767, 791, 861, 948
Minnesota, 770
Minnesota Volunteer Infantry, 466
Minshall, Mrs. T. Ellis, 658
Miró, Esteban, 198
Mishimens, Isaac, 357

Missionary Society of Connecticut, 481
Mississippi, 108, 188, 198, 488, 607, 698, 730, 828
Mississippi Marine Brigade, 759
Mississippi River, 198, 454, 759
Mississippi Valley, 99, 127, 487
Mississippi Volunteer Infantry, 466
Missouri, 50, 343, 497, 532, 535, 662, 680, 705, 810, 839, 896
Missouri Compromise, 715
Missouri Volunteer Cavalry
  3rd Regiment, 810
Missouri Volunteer Infantry, 466
  32nd Regiment, 810
Mitchell, Samuel, 878
Mittleberger, Augusta, 101
Mittleberger School, 101
Moffitt, S., 927
Monell, Ambrose, 683
Monroe, Charles W., 475
Monroe, James (president), 203
Monroe, James, 419
Montague, Gilbert H., 791
Montgomery and Clendenin & Company, 277
Monuments, 460, 479, 489, 632, 808, 948
Moody, Joseph E., 946
Moody, William H., 897
Moore, Augustus, 948
Moore, David, 630
Moore, Isaac, 454
Moore, Jonathan B., 946
Moore, Joseph, 630
Moore, Marion Louise, 389
Moore, Nathan, 336
Moore, Nathaniel, 630
Moore, William, 630

Morehouse, H. L., 619
Morgan, Daniel Edgar, 641
Morgan, Elias, 231
Morgan, George, 562
Morgan, George W., 562, 946
Morgan, James, 119
Morgan, James Morris, 562
Morgan, John (physician), 562
Morgan, John (trustee, Connecticut Land Company), 231
Morgan, John H., 370, 931
Morgan, Lewis, 421
Morgan, Marianne, 255
Morgan, May, 318
Morgan, Theophilus, 318
Morley, J. E., 943
Morning Musical Club of Cleveland, 97
Morris, Calvary, 181
Morris, Mrs. Gouverneur, 536
Morris, I. G., 132
Morris, Justin G., 459
Morris, Robert, 756, 760, 948
Morris Plan Bank, 791
Morrison, James, 948
Morrow, Jeremiah, 924
Morse, Edwin, 326
Morse, Eldredge, 326
Morse, Elkanah, 326
Morse, Emery, 326
Morse, Franklin, 326
Morse, Freeman H., 178
Morse, Henry K., 326
Morse, Samuel F. B., 778, 948
Morse and Kirtland Company, 326
Morse Bridge Company, 326
Morse family, 752
Morton, John, 760
Morton, Oliver P., 931, 946
Mosby, John S., 705, 946

Moses, Louis A., 749
Moses, Olive Crane, 749
Motion pictures, 637, 827
Mott, Richard, 247
Moulton, C. W., 592
Mount Holyoke Female Seminary, 854
Mowatt, Sir Oliver, 683
Mowry, William A., 387
Mullen, A. B., 462
Municipal Traction Company, 771
Murdock family, 515
Murray, Elijah, 273, 948
Music and music societies, 52, 54, 97, 257, 291, 360, 366, 439, 456, 554, 609, 650, 672, 750, 791, 825, 934, 947, 948
Muskingum River, 46, 69
Myers, George A., 246
Mygatt, Comfort S., 247, 718
Myrick, Herbert, 791

Naked Truths About Mormonism, 140
Nash, George K., 592, 897
Nash, James M., 522
Nathan, Robert, 709
National Air Races, 943
National Aircraft Show, 943
National Anti-Suffrage Association, 385
National Association for the Advancement of Colored People, 827
  Cleveland branch, 1002
National Bank of Commerce, 913
National Baptist Congress, 324
National Conference on Christians and Jews, 641

National Probation and Parole Association, 791
National Society of the Colonial Dames of America in the State of Ohio, 653
National Society of United States Daughters of 1812, Ohio Chapter, 398
National Sewer Pipe Company, 355
National Union for Social Justice, 783
National War Savings Committee, 403
National Wildlife Federation, 990
Near West Side Development Association, 911, 937
Nebraska, 447, 680, 971
Neff, Elizabeth C., 785
Neff, Peter (librarian), 37, 654
Neff, Peter (merchant), 110
Neff, Sarah, 654
Negroes, 246, 466, 656, 791, 798, 810, 827, 895, 909, 930, 941, 975, 987, 1002, 1004. *See also* Slavery
Nelson, Alexander, 392
Nevada, 567, 581, 861
New Granada, 700
New Hampshire, 16, 278, 390–391, 409, 412, 878, 947
New Hampshire Volunteer Infantry, 466
New Harbour Company, 295, 634
New Jersey, 30, 43, 139
New Jersey Volunteer Infantry, 466
New Lisbon Tippecanoe Club, 312

New York, 43, 69–70, 181, 192, 500, 537, 595, 600, 625, 644, 700, 735, 849
  Benton, 830
  Bridgehampton, 168
  Brookfield, 445
  Brooklyn, 330
  Buffalo, 377, 463, 746
  Canandaigua, 363, 737
  Colonie, 953
  Collins, 48
  Geneva, 830
  Groveland, 947, 953
  Hannibal Ville, 482
  Herkimer County, 98
  Kindara, 48
  Lawton Station, 48
  Madison County, 160, 445
  Monroe County, 232
  Mount Lebanon, 947
  Nassau Island, 630
  Nelson, 696
  New York City, 44, 894, 944, 946
  Onondaga County, 616
  Ontario County, 232
  Oswego, 318
  Perry, 4
  Pompey, 616
  Queens County, 630
  Queensbury, 887
  Rochester, 363, 753
  Rome, 482
  Saratoga, 454
  Schoharie County, 668
  Sodus, 947
  Utica, 854
  Warren County, 887
  Watervliet, 947, 953
New York Bulletin, 613
New York, Chicago, and St. Louis Railroad, 662, 896
New York Evening Post, 771
New York Homeopathic Physician's Society, 948
New York Independent Volunteers, 451
New York Militia, 162
New York National Freedmen's Relief Association, 84
New York State Geological Survey, 793
New York Volunteer Infantry, 162, 466
  19th Regiment, 342
  49th Regiment, 659
  127th Regiment, 705
  136th Regiment, 828
Newark and Shawnee Coal & Iron Mining Company, 133
Newberry, Henry, 245
Newberry, Roger, 862
Newcomb family, 340
Newman, T. F., 463
Newman family, 371
Newport, Thomas, 446
Newton, E. Swift, 805
Newton, Eben, 247, 843, 948
Newton, Noah, 223
Newton Theological Institute, 160
Newton Theological Seminary, 815
Newville, John, 299
Nicaragua Canal, 897
Nichol, Thomas M., 502
Nicholls, Francis R., 946
Nichols, John, 406
Nicholson, John, 132

[395]

Nickel Plate Road: The History of a Great Railroad, 662
Nicklin, Philip H., 181
Nicolet, Jean, 24
Nightingale, Florence, 948
Nightingale, Samuel, 110
Niles, Hezekiah, 247
Nixon, Richard M., 674
Nixon, William Penn, 592
Nolan, John H., 790
Northrop, John W., 90
Northrop, Lucius B., 946
Norris, Geal Grover, 742
North Carolina, 451, 946, 948
North Carolina Gold Mining Company, 948
North Carolina Volunteer Infantry, 466
Northeastern Ohio Teachers' Association, 948
Northern Ireland, 948
Northern Ohio Dental Association, 586
Northern Ohio Opera Association, 791
Northern Ohio Sanitary Fair, 213
Northwest Territory, 1, 34, 51, 181, 214, 373, 513, 739, 867, 878
Norton, Aaron, 154
Norton, Daniel, 139
Norton, Laurence Harper, 401, 983
Norton, Robert Castle, 760–761, 789
Norton family, 970, 985
Norwalk Seminary, 392
Notre Dame University, 790
Nott, George R., 833
Nutting family, 697

Nye, Horace, 948

Oberholser, Harry C., 813
Oberholtzer family, 512
Oberlin College, 897, 948
Odell, Jay, 680
O'Flaherty, Edward, 642
Oghema Niagra, 794
Ogle, Robert, 261
Ohio, 3, 30, 41, 43, 45, 58, 70, 83, 99, 105, 119, 174, 181, 184, 194, 199, 259, 299, 302, 309, 325, 333, 353, 363, 365, 392, 419, 427, 480, 497, 507, 509, 514, 534, 581, 586, 589, 596, 600, 604, 625, 633, 641–642, 655, 670, 706–707, 714–715, 737, 739, 754, 768–770, 773–774, 788, 791–792, 796–797, 831, 838, 847, 849, 868, 873, 897, 924, 949, 962, 970, 978, 985, 999
Adams County, 602, 1006–1007
Akron, 355, 608, 683, 815, 986
Albany, 948
Alliance, 3, 126
Antrim, 932
Ashland, 434
Ashland County, 704, 948, 1008–1009
Ashtabula, 161, 404, 508, 824, 840
Ashtabula County, 43, 61, 143, 234, 298, 426, 450, 564, 691, 694, 732, 742, 754, 859, 865, 912, 970, 991, 1010–1018
Ashtabula Township, 180, 412, 1012
Athens, 80
Athens County, 202, 948

Aurora, 32, 132, 693
Austin Township, 1084
Austinburg, 60, 112
Avon Lake, 515
Bainbridge Township, 1065
Batavia, 161
Bath, 461, 663, 681
Bear Run, 334
Bedford, 63, 72, 132, 916
Bellaire, 434, 460
Bellevue, 431
Berea, 374, 425, 510–512, 535, 550, 605, 948
Berlin Centre, 725
Bethel, 157
Birmingham Township, 1060
Black River Township, 1072
Bloomfield, 132
Bloomington, 649
Bloomville, 372
Boardman, 165, 272, 386, 446, 561, 738
Boardman Township, 1084
Braceville, 161
Brecksville, 1, 161, 689, 830, 885
Brecksville Township, 1035
Bridgewater, 261
Brimfield, 47
Bristol Township, 1084
Brocton, 84
Brookfield Township, 1084
Brooklyn, 264, 445
Brooklyn Township, 634, 1034, 1037
Brunswick, 605
Bucyrus, 227, 229, 1028–1029
Burton, 112, 115, 141–142, 278, 281, 796
Butler County, 132

Butler Township, 137, 1024
Cambridge, 82, 252, 407, 415–416
Cambridge Township, 1067
Canal Dover, 327
Canfield, 93, 217, 247, 286–288, 336, 338, 383, 523, 718, 843
Canfield Township, 1075–1076, 1084
Canton, 13, 363, 566
Carroll County, 458, 948, 1019–1020
Carrollton Township, 1019
Castalia, 979
Celina, 263
Center Township, 1023, 1025
Centre Township, 1019
Chagrin (now Willoughby), 496, 1071
Chagrin Falls, 232, 345, 557, 667, 854
Chagrin Township, 888
Champaign County, 148, 151, 1021
Champion (now Painesville), 279
Chardon, 48, 120, 132, 161, 406, 441, 667
Charlestown, 7, 132, 420
Chester, 48, 132, 156, 555
Chesterville, 776
Chillicothe, 52, 56, 68, 127, 131–132, 142, 202, 259, 265, 294, 454, 769, 948, 1081
Chippewa Lake, 256
Cincinnati, 27, 33, 82, 110, 121, 181, 188, 324–325, 346, 365, 368, 399, 482, 508, 535, 592, 604, 778, 944, 948

Ohio (*continued*)
  Circleville, 266
  Claridon, 244
  Clermont County, 1022
  Cleveland, 1, 25, 35–38, 43, 45, 53, 62, 71–73, 79, 86–87, 91, 96–98, 101, 106–107, 116, 132, 139, 142, 149, 166–168, 177, 182, 188–189, 192, 195–196, 200–201, 205, 208–209, 212–213, 216, 239, 254–255, 268, 284, 296–297, 330–331, 344–345, 350–351, 363, 372, 376–377, 383, 393, 395, 397, 401–402, 404, 408–409, 411, 417–418, 421, 433–434, 439, 471–472, 479, 481, 485, 489–491, 493, 497–498, 508, 512, 514, 516–517, 520, 526, 531, 535, 537–538, 544, 546–547, 551, 553–555, 558, 560, 562–563, 567, 572, 577–580, 582, 596, 603–607, 609–612, 619, 623, 632, 635, 637, 639–643, 648, 650–652, 654–655, 667–668, 670–671, 676, 678, 680, 682–684, 686, 695, 701, 707, 716–717, 722–723, 727, 731, 745–746, 749–751, 753, 756–758, 762, 764, 767–768, 770–771, 775, 778, 781–783, 785, 790–791, 794–795, 798, 804, 808–809, 814, 816, 819–820, 822–824, 827, 829, 831, 835–836, 838, 841–842, 844–846, 850, 858, 861, 866, 869, 872, 874, 880, 891, 897, 901–902, 906–910, 913, 918, 920–921, 926, 930, 934–937, 939, 941, 943–945, 948–949, 957, 959–960, 962–964, 969, 972–977, 979, 985, 987–990, 992–993, 995–996, 1000–1003, 1005, 1031–1032, 1034, 1038–1048, 1053
Coitsville, 161
Coitsville Township, 1084
Colebrook, 691
College Township, 706
Collinwood, 48, 100
Columbia, 605
Columbiana County, 137, 169–170, 312, 361, 1023–1027
Columbus, 2, 30, 52, 363, 383, 410, 508, 604, 856, 944, 948
Concord, 161
Concord Township, 46, 1063
Conneaut, 132, 364
Conneaut Township, 1013
Copapa, 605
Coshocton, 313, 353, 366, 504, 540
Covington, 486
Crawford County, 1028–1030
Cuyahoga County, 53, 71, 114, 132, 153, 167, 281, 339, 375, 398, 404, 445, 466, 483, 580, 605, 611, 623, 634, 641, 774, 780–782, 790, 806, 865, 888, 945, 961, 966, 973, 997, 1003, 1031–1059
Cuyahoga Falls, 497
Dalton, 250
Damascus, 226
Dayton, 363, 396, 443, 706, 815, 882
Deerfield, 282
Deerfield Township, 1084
Delaware, 276, 363
Delaware County, 955

Delta, 380
Dover, 155, 617
Dover Township, 1089
East Cleveland, 138, 241, 337, 478
East Cleveland Township, 1046
Edgerton, 260
Edinburgh, 383
Eldredge, 188
Elizabethtown, 214
Elk Township, 1090
Ellsworth, 161
Ellsworth Township, 1084
Elyria, 29, 43, 85, 171, 419, 502, 700
Elyria County, 74, 448, 621
Erie County, 979, 1060–1062
Euclid, 17, 112, 132, 235, 438, 775, 942, 1034
Fairfield, 854
Fairport, 571, 812
Fairview, 932
Farmington, 452
Fayette County, 488, 1063
Findlay, 136
Florence, 261
Florence Township, 1061
Fowler, 161
Fowler Township, 1084
Franklin, 31, 75, 159, 396, 528
Franklin Township, 1084
Franklinton, 52
Gallia County, 202, 1064
Gallipolis Township, 1064
Gambier, 654, 706
Garrettsville, 442, 572
Gates Mills, 520, 667
Geauga County, 50, 115, 139, 244, 340, 807, 873, 888, 983, 1065–1066, 1068

Geneva, 112, 441
Glendale, 399
Grand River, 112
Grandon (now Fairport), 279
Granville, 324, 693
Granville Township, 102
Green Township, 1063, 1084
Greene Township, 1086
Greenville, 228, 373
Greenwich, 132
Guernsey County, 407, 932–933, 1067
Guilford, 161
Gustavus, 40, 881
Hambden, 50, 535
Hamilton Township, 334
Hardin County, 703
Harpersfield Township, 970
Harrison County, 237, 308, 353
Hartford Township, 1084
Hayesville, 307, 381
Highland County, 715
Hillsboro, 333
Hiram, 818, 938
Hiram Township, 1084
Holmes Township, 1030
Howland, 161
Hubbard Township, 1084
Hudson, 1, 95, 112, 167, 832, 914
Hudson Township, 1084
Huntsburg, 807
Huron, 85, 188, 638
Huron County, 188, 191, 994
Independence, 758, 885
Independence Township, 1035
Ironton, 788
Jefferson, 132, 146, 347, 441, 591
Jefferson County, 484, 501

Ohio (*continued*)
  Jefferson Township, 691, 1014, 1063
  Johnson's Island, 370, 620, 646, 946
  Kelley's Island, 107, 382, 448, 621, 1062
  Kent, 75, 449, 497
  Kenton, 262, 300
  Kingsville, 160, 234, 289, 298, 441, 912
  Kinsman, 699
  Kirtland, 406, 856
  Knox County, 654, 706, 963
  Lafayette, 754
  Lake County, 132, 253, 321, 503, 691, 919, 1068–1071
  Lakewood, 401, 513, 565, 800
  Leffingwell, 161
  Lenox Township, 1014
  Leroy Township, 919
  Liberty, 161
  Liberty Township, 1084
  Licking County, 102, 915, 980
  Liverpool, 161, 412, 581, 775, 828
  Logan, 290
  Logan County, 151
  Lorain, 85, 638
  Lorain County, 398, 527, 529, 605, 696, 865, 1072
  Lost Creek, 147
  Lower Sandusky, 346, 713
  Lucas County, 865
  McComb, 896
  Mad River Township, 148
  Madison, 43, 132, 441, 691
  Madison County, 882
  Madisonville, 633

Mahoning County, 336, 446, 843, 1073–1077
Mantua, 31
Margaretta Township, 979
Marietta, 132, 145, 181, 186, 339, 815, 878, 948, 1067
Marion Township, 1063
Marlboro, 593
Marseilles, 353
Massillon, 122
Mayfield, 44, 520
Mayfield Township, 667, 1049
Medina, 182, 258
Medina County, 114, 167, 256, 293, 500, 581, 605, 754, 828, 1078
Meigs County, 202
Mentor, 132, 152, 183, 632, 803
Mentor Township, 888
Mercer County, 263
Mesopotamia, 143, 839
Miami County, 151, 157, 486
Middleburgh Township, 617
Milan, 391
Millersburg, 204, 434, 748
Millsford, 143
Monroe, 161
Monroeville, 759
Montgomery County, 52
Morgan County, 477
Morgan Township, 426
Mount Pleasant, 30, 109, 128, 275, 335, 482
Mount Vernon, 230, 359, 539, 590
Mount Washington, 815
Munson, 48
Muskingum, 339
New Athens, 308

New Dorset, 143
New Hope, 332
New Lisbon, 88, 169, 292, 312, 784, 1026
New Lyme, 691
New Market, 279
New Philadelphia, 505
Newark, 125, 133, 408
Newburgh, 65
Newburgh Township, 1034–1035, 1050–1052
Newbury, 161
Newton, 161
Newton Township, 1084
Newville, 802
North Bloomfield, 412, 545, 773
North Eaton, 650
North Olmsted, 413
North Ridgeville, 615
North Union, 947
North Washington, 703
Norwalk, 43, 339, 671
Oberlin, 644, 687, 828
Ohio City, 295, 491, 581, 634, 695, 701, 1053, 1059
Olivesburgh, 852
Olmsted Township, 1054
Orange, 685, 688
Orangeville, 396
Oxford, 636, 955
Painesville, 43, 91, 132, 142, 404, 421, 441, 467, 503, 508, 571, 711, 787, 825, 900, 919, 929
Paint Township, 1063
Parkman, 161, 271, 983
Parma, 660
Parma Township, 1055
Pepper Pike, 631

Perry Township, 1027, 1068
Pettiquotting, 176
Pickaway County, 317
Pierpont, 143, 234
Poland, 141–142, 154, 326, 428, 738, 812, 948–949
Poland Township, 1084
Port Clinton, 379
Portage, 113
Portage County, 8, 20, 31, 159, 167, 282, 293, 383, 394, 420, 449, 527–528, 622, 694, 868, 892, 938, 983, 1079–1080
Randall, 418
Randolph, 19
Ravenna, 11, 14–15, 20–21, 132, 161, 219, 345, 434, 645
Ravenna Township, 1079
Richfield, 161, 167
Richland County, 802, 852
Richmond, 304–305
Rockport, 132, 281, 445
Rockport Township, 1056
Ross County, 1081
Royalton Township, 1057
Russell Township, 1066
Rutland, 202
St. Mary's, 497
Salem, 26, 89–90, 126, 129, 132, 150, 170, 210, 225, 362
Saltcreek, 482
Saltcreek Township, 1091
Sandusky, 43, 346, 370, 429, 470, 620, 886
Sandusky Bay, 448
Seaman, 444
Seneca County, 372
Seven Mile, 132
Seville, 257

Ohio (*continued*)
  Shalersville, 291, 892
  Shalersville Township, 1080
  Sharon Center, 500
  Sheffield, 754
  Smithfield, 109, 656
  Solon, 613
  South Euclid, 667
  Southington, 161
  Southington Township, 1087
  Springfield, 570, 948
  Stark County, 237
  Steubenville, 10, 109, 132, 304, 459, 501, 513, 569, 597, 888
  Stow Township, 1082
  Streetsboro, 702, 719–720
  Strongsville, 48, 405, 535, 605
  Strongsville Township, 1034
  Sullivan Township, 1009
  Summit County, 8, 12, 114, 132, 167, 233, 461, 608, 663, 966, 986, 1082–1083
  Superior, 261
  Tallmadge, 1, 348, 422
  Tallmadge Township, 1083
  Thompson, 873
  Tiffin, 300, 642, 944
  Toledo, 130, 158, 539, 662, 878, 907, 943–944
  Troy, 185, 815
  Troy Township, 1084
  Trumbull County, 40, 66, 93, 132, 143, 180, 243, 386, 523, 694, 712, 725, 747, 1084–1088
  Trumbull Township, 180, 412, 1015
  Tuscarawas County, 1089
  Twinsburg, 32, 233, 319, 352, 889
  Union Township, 1063
  Union Village, 947
  Unionville, 46, 364, 732
  Upper Sandusky, 341
  Urbana, 316, 815
  Urbana Township, 1021
  Utica, 915
  Vermilion, 1008
  Vermilion Township, 851
  Vernon Township, 1084
  Vienna Township, 1084
  Vinton County, 1090–1091
  Wadsworth, 114
  Waite Hill, 321
  Wapakoneta, 40
  Warren, 31, 46, 66, 112, 142, 180, 345, 396–397, 412, 580, 665, 692, 694, 797, 807, 812, 877, 883
  Warren County, 334
  Warren Township, 1084, 1088
  Warrensville, 65
  Warrensville Township, 65, 1058
  Washington, 488, 932
  Washington County, 181
  Washington Township, 1020
  Washingtonville, 458
  Watervliet, 947
  Wayne, 388
  Wayne County, 453, 704
  Wayne Township, 1063
  Weathersfield, 747, 1084
  Wellington, 283
  Wellsville, 292, 480
  West Milton, 228
  West Salem, 132, 207
  West Union, 81, 103, 482, 602
  Western Star (Summit County community), 114

Whitewater, 947
Willeyville, 1059
Williams County, 261
Williamsfield, 389
Willoughby, 104, 111, 117, 132, 152, 273, 329, 349, 391, 432, 492, 496, 619, 854, 1071
Willoughby Township, 1069–1071
Wilmington, 656
Windsor Township, 1016–1018
Wooster, 166, 306, 320, 363, 453
Wyandot County, 353
Xenia, 57, 933
York, 161, 754
Youngstown, 141, 272, 277, 326, 468, 557, 578, 712, 855, 1084
Youngstown Township, 1077
Zanesville, 357, 525, 562
Zoar, 366
Ohio & Erie Canal, 56
Ohio and Nashville Railroad, 948
Ohio Anti-Slavery Society, 61
Ohio Association Opposed to Womans Suffrage, 385
Ohio Baptist Education Society, 325, 618, 948
Ohio Bell Telephone Company, 731
Ohio Canal, 180, 247, 338, 404, 665
Ohio Cavalry
  1st Regiment, 764
Ohio Chickamauga and Chattanooga National Park Commission, 453
Ohio Company of Associates, 69–70, 181, 240, 494, 714

Ohio Constitutional Convention (1850), 338, 363
Ohio General Assembly, 184, 194, 300, 312, 333, 335, 338, 400, 412, 454, 489, 539, 562, 567, 592, 604–605, 641, 712, 715, 773–774, 796, 924, 983, 985, 1023
Ohio governors, 34, 507. *See also individual names*
Ohio, Historical Commission of, 172
Ohio Militia, 247, 338, 346, 428, 562, 643, 1023
  2nd Regiment, 504, 723
  4th Division, 77, 123, 267, 543, 665, 675, 713, 796
  20th Division, 883
  Regimental courts, 602
Ohio Monument Association, 948
Ohio National Guard, 370, 410
  8th Regiment, 678
  107th Regiment, 612, 678
  171st Regiment, 646
  Troop A, 985
  Cleveland Gatling Gun Battery, 612
Ohio Natural Resources Council, 990
Ohio Railroad Company, 91
Ohio River, 1, 52, 69, 275, 383, 454, 867, 878
Ohio River Land and Marble Company, 948
Ohio Society of the National Society of Dames of the Loyal Legion, 949
Ohio Supreme Court, 180, 507, 712, 792, 924
Ohio University, 80

Ohio Volunteer Cavalry
  2nd Regiment, 430, 466
  6th Regiment, 296, 466, 705, 839
  10th Regiment, 855
  12th Regiment, 170
Ohio Volunteer Infantry, 466
  1st Regiment, 679
  7th Regiment, 144, 466, 890
  8th Regiment, 650
  9th Regiment, 903
  10th Regiment, 134
  19th Regiment, 251, 358, 522, 772
  20th Regiment, 707, 796
  23rd Regiment, 710, 818, 929
  27th Regiment, 551, 576, 669
  30th Regiment, 541
  39th Regiment, 576
  41st Regiment, 453, 519, 531, 786
  43rd Regiment, 576
  49th Regiment, 300, 605
  51st Regiment, 530
  55th Regiment, 372
  59th Regiment, 466
  63rd Regiment, 576
  73rd Regiment, 127
  84th Regiment, 699
  89th Regiment, 454
  92nd Regiment, 903
  94th Regiment, 466
  96th Regiment, 776
  98th Regiment, 466
  101st Regiment, 466, 759
  102nd Regiment, 852
  103rd Regiment, 90
  104th Regiment, 236, 645
  105th Regiment, 248, 506
  115th Regiment, 466
  120th Regiment, 434
  121st Regiment, 776
  122nd Regiment, 252, 540
  126th Regiment, 593
  144th Regiment, 488
  150th Regiment, 314, 549
  163rd Regiment, 310
  164th Regiment, 857
  171st Regiment, 370
  187th Regiment, 311, 884
  Hoffman's Battalion, 620
  19th Ohio Battery Association, 239
Ohio Volunteer Light Artillery
  1st Regiment, 466, 476, 535, 575, 588
  14th Independent Battery, 503, 698
Ohio Watchman, 622
Ohio Wesleyan University, 276
Ohio Woman Suffrage Association, 385
Oldfield, Barney, 948
Olmsted, Aaron, 159
O'Mahony, John, 642
Onstott, Anna Long, 948
Oratory, 3, 30, 32, 40, 70, 78, 106, 172, 206, 210, 219, 229, 247–249, 300, 312, 316, 330, 333, 338, 345, 356, 362, 364–366, 387–388, 392, 397, 433, 453, 489, 512, 563, 567, 581, 596, 622, 641, 655, 673, 684, 691, 693, 728, 739, 766, 768, 770–771, 774, 783, 787, 790–791, 796, 798, 802, 815, 819, 822, 824, 854, 856, 873, 881, 891, 897–899, 901, 913, 948, 958, 961, 976, 980, 998, 1003, 1042

Order of American Knights, 946
Order of United American Men, 416
Oregon, 202, 618, 853
Ormsby, Robert McK., 224
Osborn, Ralph, 715
Osborn & Hammond, 916
Osborn family, 752
Otis, Charles Augustus, 208, 579
Otis, William A., 412
Otis Steel Company, 716
Overton, Seth, 738
Oviatt, Benjamin, 167
Oviatt, Elizabeth L., 167
Oviatt, Heman, 167
Oviatt, Hiram P., 942
Oviatt, Lucy Ann (Bullard), 942
Oviatt, Marvin, 167
Oviatt, Nathaniel, 167
Oviatt, Orson M., 167
Oviatt, Schuyler R., 167
Owen, Allison, 462
Owl Creek Bank, 230

P. & J. P. Hawes & Company, 894
P. D. Hall & Company, 132
P. M. Weddell & Company, 408, 537
Pacific Ocean, 94, 197, 661
Pacific Telegraph Company, 778
Page, S. B., 619
Page, Thomas N., 897
Paige Car Wheel Company, 508
Paine, Charles C., 737, 919
Paine, Edward, 1, 46, 247, 279
Paine, Eleazar, 919
Paine, Halbert E., 799
Paine, Hendrick E., 919
Paine, Henry, 919

Paine, J. W., 466
Paine, Thomas, 878
Paine, W. H., 946
Paine family, 571, 919
Painesville and Fairport Railroad Company, 571
Painesville Telegraph, 503
Palmer, Caleb, 1, 665
Palmer, Edward, 946
Palmer, William Pendleton, 705, 946
Panama, 700
Panama Canal, 791, 897
Parker, Charles, 1, 278
Parker, Ely S., 946
Parker, James M., 437
Parker, Peter, 269
Parker, Samuel W., 247
Parker, Tyler, 942
Parkman, Francis, 271
Parkman, Robert B., 46, 247, 278–279, 983
Parks Foster (steamer), 922
Parmelee, James, 208
Parmelee family, 889
Parsons, Emma, 817
Parsons, Enoch, 421
Parsons, Henry E., 859
Parsons, Mrs. Henry E., 515
Parsons, Margaret A., 791
Parsons, Mary A. R., 515
Parsons, Myrta, 817
Parsons, R. G., 604
Parsons, Samuel Holden, 240, 494, 714
Parsons, Willie L., 817
Patrick, Robert, 446
Patterson, Robert, 247, 948
Pattison, R. E., 325
Patuxent River, 269

Paul, Hosea, 966, 986
Paul, Hosea, Jr., 350
Paul Brothers, 986
Payne, Henry B., 683
Peabody, A. P., 387
Pease, Calvin, 180, 247, 279, 338, 412, 421, 712, 924
Pease, Seth, 1, 734–735
Peck, John J., 946
Peet, Stephen D., 69
Pegram, John, 946
Pendleton, William N., 946
Penfield, Charles, 62
Pennslyvania, 30, 43, 51, 302, 325, 445, 480, 534, 595, 655, 847, 949
  Allegheny City, 686
  Bethlehem, 176
  Cambridgeboro, 255
  Chanceford, 601
  Clarkesville, 531
  Crawford County, 234
  Earl, 779
  Easton, 132
  Elizabethtown, 802
  Ephrata, 779
  Erie, 847
  Erie County, 851
  Greensborough, 784
  Harrisburg, 666
  Lancaster County, 363, 779
  Lewiston, 124
  Ligonier, 280
  Ligonier Valley, 51
  Logstown, 507
  Long Run Settlement, 784
  Meadville, 397
  Mercer, 238
  Mercer County, 531
  Newcastle, 383
  Penn Line, 234
  Philadelphia, 69, 132, 211, 303, 363, 726, 848, 944
  Pickawillany, 507
  Pittsburgh, 268, 299, 508, 542, 578, 847, 680
  Sunbury, 847
  Venango County, 850
  Washington, 802
  Westmoreland County, 784, 948
  York, 659
  York County, 601
Pennsylvania and Lake Erie Dock Company, 948
Pennsylvania and Ohio Canal, 31, 66, 180, 948
Pennsylvania Militia
  4th Regiment, 559
Pennsylvania Volunteer Infantry, 451, 466
  57th Regiment, 598
  84th Regiment, 598
Pentland, E., 847
Pepoon, Joseph A., 787
Peppercorn, Beryl, 838
Pere Marquette Railway Company, 716
Perkins, Edwin, 466
Perkins, Emma M., 908
Perkins, Frances, 729
Perkins, Henry Bishop, 665
Perkins, Henry W., 946
Perkins, Jacob, 179, 665, 957
Perkins, Jacob Bishop, 208, 665, 729, 957
Perkins, Joseph, 665, 745, 957
Perkins, Ralph, 729
Perkins, Simon, 1, 46, 139, 154, 161, 180, 247, 278, 412, 421,

665, 675, 713, 734, 736, 948, 957
Perry, A. H., 221
Perry, A. L., 387
Perry, David L., 315
Perry, Horace, 38
Perry, Oliver H., 652
  monument, 489, 808
  victory centennial celebration, 576, 626, 814
Perry, Samuel V., 975
Perry family, 409
Peru, 949
Peter the Great (Emperor of Russia), 658
Phelps, Alfred, 400
Phelps, Isaac, 426
Phelps, L. M., 247
Phelps, Oliver (1749–1809), 180, 736–737, 948, 950
Phelps, Oliver (1796–1877), 737
Phelps, Oliver Leicester, 737
Phelps family, 811, 919
Phelps-Gorham Purchase, 737
Philadelphia Centennial Exposition, 363
Philbrick, John D., 856
Philippine Islands, 750, 897
Phillips, John, 563
Picket, Albert, Sr., 856
Pierce, Ebenezer, 412
Pierce, Franklin, 203
Piercy, H. D., 901
Pike, George, W., 464
Pike, Isabel, 464
Pike, Maria, 464
Pike, Zebulon Montgomery, 464
Pillen, Herbert, 791
Pillow, Gideon J., 705–706, 946
Pillsbury, Isaac Newton, 404

Pinchot, Gifford, 897
Pinney, John, 279
Pioneer Association of Whitewater and Miami Valley, 214
Pioneers Memorial Association, 547
Pitkin, Perley Peabody, 465, 956
Pittsburgh & West Virginia Railway Company, 578
Plant family, 697
Platt, Richard, 70
Pleasants, John P., 769
Plost, Louis, 768
Poland Literary Society, 948
Political parties
  Democratic, 312, 539, 715, 788, 790–791, 844
  Free Soil, 30, 462
  Know-Nothing, 715
  Liberty, 462
  National Republican, 70, 333
  Republican, 192, 338, 387, 462, 467, 503, 514, 592, 607, 624, 641, 655, 670, 673–674, 715, 774, 810, 897–899, 952, 962, 999
  Union, 201
  Whig, 41, 70, 247, 312, 333, 338, 412, 462, 534, 715, 948
Politics
  Ohio, 31, 46, 52, 71, 86, 181, 201, 246–247, 296–297, 300, 312, 338, 404, 412, 419, 448, 453–454, 467–468, 503, 514, 526, 534, 539, 567, 577, 580, 596, 604–605, 641, 655, 670, 675, 701, 706, 710, 712, 715, 768, 774, 780–783, 788, 790–791, 796–797, 802, 825, 827, 830, 835, 842, 844, 851, 882,

Politics (*continued*)
    897–899, 904, 918, 924, 957, 962, 964, 987, 991, 999, 1050
    National, 31, 70, 181, 246–247, 312, 338, 387, 400, 412, 448, 462, 503, 514, 534, 562, 577, 592, 596, 607, 624, 632, 666, 673–674, 690, 705, 710, 755–756, 760, 768, 771, 774, 776, 783, 790–791, 797, 803–804, 825, 897–899, 918, 952, 962, 987, 999
Polk, Leonidas, 301, 423, 706, 946
Pollard, James, 946
Pollard, Robert, 769
Pomerene, Attlee, 791
Pope, John, 666, 946
Pope, Nathaniel, 769
Portage County Bible Society, 20
Porter, Asahel, 623
Porter, Augustus, 1
Porter, David, 616
Porter, David D., 946
Porter, Fitz-John, 666, 946
Porter, Pliny, 616
Portland Vegetable Oil Mills Company, 853
Portugal, 585
Positype Corporation, 791
Post, Charles Asa, 560
Post family, 982
Potomac River, 269
Potter, Jared, 326
Potter, Julia, 363
Potter, Lyman, 412
Potter, Clark and Murphey Company, 767
Potts, Stacey, 139
Potts, William H., 139
Pownall, Thomas, 948

Pratt, John, 325
Pratt, Seth, 404
Prentice, Jonas, 494
Prentiss, Ellen Rouse, 609
Prentiss, Frederick J., 977
Prentiss, Loren, 609
Prentiss, Luther Richard, 65
Prentiss, Samuel B., 977
Prescott, William Hickling, 756
Presley, Jeremiah, 92
Presley, John, 92
Presley, Richard, 92
Preston, Charles, 62
Preston, Moses, 132
Price, Bird, 769
Prichard, George, 938
Probert, W. G. C., 168
Proctor, Frances, 412
Proctor, John R., 296
Prohibition, 774, 791, 897–899, 918
Protection Life Insurance Company, 31
Public welfare, 641, 791, 941, 949, 1029, 1037
    benevolent societies, 14, 63, 75, 84, 181, 286, 609, 615, 631, 866
    charities, 286, 535, 684, 745, 771, 809, 906, 910, 935, 1001
    hospitals, 213, 271, 451, 474, 493, 650, 659, 706, 823, 856, 866, 946, 948, 1079
    settlements, 745, 846, 930, 934, 972.
    See also Disaster relief; Labor and unions
Pugwash conferences, 791
Puerto Rico (also Porto Rico), 657, 897, 913

Pulaski, Casimir, 789
Punderson, Lemuel, 278, 738
Putnam, David, 240
Putnam, Douglas, 186
Putnam, Israel, 240
Putnam, Rufus, 494
Putnam, W. L., 178
Putnam, William Rufus, 70

Raddatz, William J., 906
Ramo-Wooldridge Company, 943
Ramsey, William T., 82
Randall, D. A., 325
Randolph, George W., 946
Randolph, W. J., 946
Ranney, Rufus Percival, 694
Rawlins, John R., 946
Ray, James D., 770
Rea, Paul M., 403
Reconstruction, 84, 213, 487, 799, 810, 828, 864, 946
Records of William Spooner and His Descendants, 399
Red Cross, American, 205, 485, 721, 727, 805, 1048
Redfield, Nathan, 1
Reed, Calvin G., 482
Reed, Henry E., 946
Reed family, 515, 628
Reeve, Tapping, 712
Reid, Abigail, 696
Reid, H. F., 793
Reid, Whitelaw, 387
Reindeer (merchant vessel), 275
Religion, 68, 345, 362, 389, 397, 426, 448, 550, 600, 609, 636, 707, 712, 739, 796, 815, 866, 873, 910, 993, 1089
   Baptist, 27–28, 120, 122, 146–152, 155–157, 160, 171, 181, 190–191, 274, 324–325, 332, 334, 347, 376, 378, 381, 441–444, 491, 572, 591, 609, 619, 638, 849, 872, 948
   Christian, 9, 390
   Congregational, 8, 19, 32, 60, 70, 75, 158, 167, 264, 328, 386, 388, 420, 452, 572, 615, 631, 689, 702, 718–719, 796, 825, 949
   Disciples, 14
   Episcopal, 639, 667, 738, 757, 771, 910
   Friends, Society of, 30, 128–129, 275, 302, 335, 361, 954
   Lutheran, 204, 266
   Methodist, 127, 392, 822
   Methodist-Episcopal, 7, 11, 73, 207, 227, 265, 289, 292, 306, 379, 431, 492, 566, 822, 888, 948
   Methodist Protestant, 202
   Millerism, 1, 31
   Missionaries, 1, 23, 28, 40, 43, 45, 74, 151, 171, 209, 219, 227, 237, 264, 286, 325, 379, 393, 481, 533, 639, 647, 720, 817
   Mormon, 140, 597
   Presbyterian, 2, 45, 57–58, 74–75, 81, 85, 103, 105, 110, 112–113, 206, 250, 256, 285, 288, 312–313, 329, 337, 353, 359, 391, 452, 481, 533, 570, 613, 667, 720, 787, 795, 819, 932
   Protestant Episcopal, 82, 654, 858
   Shakers, 947, 953–954
   United Brethren in Christ, 237

Religion (*continued*)
   Universalist, 4, 47, 341, 882
   Zoar, Separatist Society of, 366
Religious Examiner, 932
Remenyi, Joseph, 709
Renick, George, 132
Renick, George, Jr., 132
Renick, Josiah, 317
Republic Steel Corporation, 716
Revere, Paul, 789
Revolutionary War, 18, 23, 70, 162, 280, 398, 435, 507, 562, 633, 714, 756, 760, 777, 789
Reynolds, Joseph T., 454
Reynolds, Thomas C., 705
Reynolds, W. A., 948
Rhett, Robert G., 403
Rhoades family, 512
Rhoads, Charles, 619
Rhode Island, 53, 160
Rhode Island Volunteer Infantry, 466
Rhodes, Charles L., 179
Rhodes, J. H., 387
Rhodes, James Ford, 246, 400, 897
Rice, Cecil S., 897
Rice, Corinna, 298
Rice, Harvey, 489, 808
Rice, William, 50
Rice, William L., 208
Richards, William, 28
Richardson, C. R., 9
Richardson, George C., 705
Richardson, Henry A., 946
Richardson, William W., 457
Richmond, Thomas, 619
Richmond Classical Institute, 948
Richmond College, 305
Rickey, Joseph, 569

Riddle, Albert Gallatin, 297, 400, 604
Riddle, Joseph W., 70
Riggin, Isaac C., 454
Riley, James Watson, 263
Ripley and Locust Grove Turnpike Company, 948
Risdon, Orlando Charles, 730
Risley, Lake, 517
Ritchie, Samuel J., 683
Robb, Louisa (St. Clair), 51
Robbins, A. D., 613
Robbins, Ammi R., 219
Robbins, Charles W., 747
Robbins, Electa M., 747
Robbins, Josiah, 747
Robbins, Thomas, 1, 426
Robbins & Blackman Company, 613
Roberts, Frederick Sleigh, 948
Roberts, Marcus F., 614
Roberts, William R., 642
Robertson, Elijah, 948
Robertson, Felix H., 946
Robertson, William, 915
Robinson, Emily, 365
Robinson, Frederick John, 870
Robinson, George, 777
Robinson, Hannah, 777
Robinson, J. S., 592
Robinson, Marius R., 365
Robinson family, 751
Rockefeller, John D., 87, 745, 846, 880, 948
Rodney, C. A., 871
Rogers, James Hotchkiss, 672
Rogers, W. K., 592
Rogers family, 697
Romaine, F. O., 592
Roosevelt, Franklin D., 791

Roosevelt, Theodore, 246, 596, 897
Root, Elihu, 76, 897
Root, Ephraim, 231, 736, 862, 950
Root, Joseph C., 971
Root, Ralph R., 948
Root Genealogy Company, 971
Rose, William Ganson, 984
Rose, William Grey, 655
Rosecrans, William S., 535, 946
Ross, James, 948
Ross, Mrs. William, 636
Rouse, Benjamin, 609
Rouse, Mrs. Benjamin, 213, 609
Royce, Abner, 372
Royce, B. F., 372
Royce, Mrs. B. F., 372
Royce, Henrietta L. (Knapp), 372
Royce, William D., 372
Roys, Mary A., 854
Royston, Grandison Dulaney, 946
Rubinstein Club, 439
Rudd family, 667
Rudolph, Adelaide, 818
Rudolph, Joseph, 818
Ruggles, Almon, 247
Ruggles, Daniel, 946
Ruggles, John C., 301
Rural Retreat Literary Society, 119
Rush, Benjamin, 67, 948
Rush, Richard, 154
Russell, Benjamin W., 279
Russell, William, 247, 715
Russia, 497, 596, 658
Rust, John Franklin, 538
Rust, R. S., 425
Rust, King & Clint, 538
Rust, King & Company, 538
Ryan Gowdy & Company, 933

Sacco-Vanzetti trial, 596
Safford, A. P. K., 861
St. Clair, Arthur, 34, 51, 280, 507
St. Clair, Daniel, 51
St. Clair River, 30
St. John, Isaac M., 946
St. Lawrence River, 750
Salen, Charles P., 904
Salen, Peter, 904
Saltspring Sugar Estate, 876
Samuel Bissel Memorial Library Association, 32
Sandusky River, 1
Sandy & Beaver Canal, 404
Sarchet, David, 407
Sarchet, Moses, 407
Sarchet, Thomas, 407
Sargent, A. L., 380
Sargent, Winthrop, 507
Saunders, Arnold C., 785
Savain, George H., 94
Sawyer, Charles, 791
Scandinavia, 563
Scarr, Anne, 553
Scheiber, Jacob, 944
Schillinger, N. I., 482
Schley, William L., 927
Schnably, Rudolph, 132
Schuyler, Aaron, 512
Schuyler family, 515
Schwab, Charles M., 683
Schweinfurth, Charles F., 762
Science and scientists, 16, 195–196, 563, 581, 707, 750, 793, 813
Scioto River, 633
Scotland, 352
Scott, Frank Augustus, 771
Scott, John M., 206
Scovel, James Mattach, 946

Scovill, Edward Alexander, 620
Scovill, Philo, 377
Scripps, Edward W., 897
Seabrook, Isaac D., 946
Seaver, Rodney, 521
Secreto (whaling vessel), 94
Seddon, James A., 946
Sellers, James William, 659
Sells, Benjamin F., 540–541
Seminole War, 580
Settlements. *See* Public welfare
Severance, Solon L., 175, 640
Seward, John, 693
Seward, William H., 400, 946
Sexton, Franklin Barlow, 946
Seymour, Belden, 208
Seymour family, 980
Shakespeare, William, 906
Shaler, Amelia, 139
Shaler, Charles, 299
Shaler, Mrs. Charles, 299
Shane, Anthony, 878
Sharp, O. H., 1070
Sharpe, Jacob, 948
Sharpe family, 667
Shaw, Edward, 590
Shaw, Leslie M., 897
Shedd, E. E., 567
Shee, John, 470
Shelley, Mrs. John, 213
Shepard, Warham, 1
Shepardson, D., 619
Sheridan, Philip H., 466, 946
Sherman, Charles R., 738
Sherman, Henry S., 791
Sherman, James S., 897
Sherman, John, 272, 419, 567, 592, 634, 670, 897–898
Sherman, William Tecumseh, 756, 946, 948

Sherwood, Dr., 125
Sherwood, Isaac Ruth, 946
Sherwood, Mary E. W., 946
Sherwood family, 364
Shields, J. C., 239
Shields, James, 1074
Shinn, Joshua, 132
Shire, Michael, 512
Shocknessy, James W., 791
Sholes, Stanton, 1, 166
Shoup, Francis Asbury, 946
Shriver, David, Jr., 744
Shriver, Jacob S., 534
Shryock, John T., 525
Shumway, Handel M., 153
Shurtleff, G. K., 651
Sigel, Franz, 666
Sigourney, Charles, 247
Silbert, Samuel H., 1003
Sill, Margaret, 754
Sill, Mehitable, 754
Siller, Ernst J., 479
Simpson, John, 946
Sinks, Frederick N., 791
Skinner, Abraham, 279
Skinner, Augustus, 711
Skinner, J. S., 247
Skinner, Roderick, 711
Skinner, Roger, 543
Skinner, Thomas, 279
Slavery, 30, 84, 108, 129, 247, 301, 365, 414, 465, 487, 690–691, 715, 797, 864, 870, 876, 946
    abolitionism, 247, 365, 412, 422, 656, 852
    African colonization, 181, 338
    anti-slavery movement, 13, 31, 61, 126, 181, 210, 365, 422, 462, 656, 680, 948

Sloan, John, 247
Sloan, Robert R., 249
Sloane, John, 338, 543
Sloane, Jonathan, 247
Smith, A. F., 108
Smith, Alfred E., 768
Smith, C. L., 132
Smith, Catharine B., 128
Smith, Charles, 179
Smith, Charles B., 440
Smith, Charles Henry, 395, 576
Smith, Mrs. Charles H., 626
Smith, Correl, 772
Smith, Edmund K., 946
Smith, Gustavus W., 946
Smith, Henry W., 66
Smith, James Y., 946
Smith, Joel, 725
Smith, John, 507, 924
Smith, Mrs. Lucinda (Johnson), 576
Smith, Martin, 1
Smith, Preston, 946
Smith, Reuben F., 819
Smith, Robert, 592
Smith, Robert K., 946
Smith, Samuel, 154
Smith, Thomas Kirby, 946
Smith, William Henry, 592
Smith-Stanley, Edward (13th Earl of Derby), 690
Smoot, Reed, 140
Smucker, Isaac, 980
Smyth, Sarah Lanman, 849
Snelling, J. G., 619
Snow, Eliza R., 948
Soldier's Aid Society of Northern Ohio, 213
Soldiers' and Sailors' Monumental Association of Bellaire, O., 460

Sons of Liberty, 946
Sons of Temperance, 290
Sorter family, 667
Sosman, Frank A., 127
Sosman, George, 127
Sosman, John F., 127
Sosman, Lucretia Browning, 127
South Carolina, 403, 509, 551, 946
South Carolina Volunteer Infantry, 466
South Dakota, 313
Southington Philomathic Society, 59
Sowers, John, 486
Spafford, Amos, 1, 421, 878, 924
Spafford, Hiram, 132
Spalding, Rufus P., 604
Spangler, Michael, 168
Spanish-American War, 76, 493, 563, 678, 750, 764, 800, 913
Spanish governors, 198
Spaulding family, 752
Speed, James, 946
Spencer, George, 750
Spencer, Harry A., 750
Spencer, Nathaniel, 244
Spencer, P. R., 1, 691
Spirit of '76, 22, 472
Spooner, Emily, 399
Spooner, Thomas, 399
Spooner, William, 399
Sports, 96, 208, 520, 613, 790, 979
Spring Symphony, 826
Springfield Association for the Promotion of Temperance, 948
Sproat, Amasa D., 67–68
Squier, Ephraim George, 509
Squire, Andrew, 87

[413]

Squire, Elbert J., 466
Stage Memories of John A. Ellsler, 583
Stanard, B. A., 195
Standard Oil Company, 921, 948
Standard Oil of Ohio, 880
Standard Parts Company, 771
Standish Chain and Manufacturing Company, 497
Standish Chain Company, 497
Standish, Philander H., 497
Stanley, George A., 195
Stanley, George W., 738, 865
Stanton, Benjamin, 210
Stanton, Edwin M., 624, 946
Stark, Caleb, 878
Starkweather, E. B., 604
Starkweather, Samuel, 196, 247
Starling, William, 769
Starr, Ephraim, 862
Starr, Nathan, 114
Steadman, Mrs. Buckley, 1
Stearns, Frank B., 907
Steel Products Company, 943
Steele, John, 948
Steele, William, 847
Steiner, Abraham, 176
Stellwagen, C. K., 949
Stephens, Alexander H., 946
Stephens, J. A., 498
Sterling, Elisha, 195–196, 247, 255, 517
Sterling, Frederick A., 974
Sterling, James T., 466
Sterling, John M., 38
Sterling, Mary Emma (Betts), 974
Sterling Lindner Company, 949
Sterrett, John, 769
Steuben, Baron von, 789

Steubenville & Richmond Plank Road Company, 304
Steubenville Female Seminary, 10
Stevens, A. P., 17
Stevens, George E., 324
Stevens, John, 324–325
Stevens, Thaddeus, 799, 946
Stevenson, Adlai E., 790
Stevenson, Carter L., 706
Stewart, Alexander, 528
Stewart, Andrew, 744
Stewart, James E. B., 946
Stickney, Benjamin F., 878
Stickney, Two, 878
Stimson, Henry L., 897
Stockham, Addison F., 535
Stockwell, Cyrus H., 834
Stockwell, John N., 791
Stockwell family, 752
Stoddard, Amos, 154, 539
Stoddard, Henry, 539
Stoddard, Richard M., 1
Stokes, Ethel, 168
Stone, Amasa, 1001
Stone, Charles Pomeroy, 946
Stone, Randolph, 481
Stone, Thomas, 760
Stonex, Wilbur, 592
Storrs, Betsy, 139
Storrs, Lemuel, 223, 734, 738
Storrs, Lemuel G., 139
Storrs, William L., 139
Stoughton, Edwin H., 946
Stout, Samuel H., 423, 474
Stow, Joshua, 223, 734
Straight, Willard D., 897
Stratford Press, 906
Strawn, Jesse B., 225
Street, Titus, 738
Strickle, Abraham E., 946

[414]

Strickle, Elizabeth A., 33
Strong, Caleb, 405
Strong, Eleanor (Painter), 826
Strong, Emory, 405
Strong, Henry, 240
Strong, John H., 829
Strong, John S., 405
Strong, Luther M., 300
Strong, Newton G., 535
Strong, Warner, 405
Strong family, 751
Stuart, Robert, 55
Stuart-Wortley-Mackenzie, James Archibald (Lord Wharncliffe), 690
Sturges, Lewis B., 247
Sullivan, Dr. E. W., 642
Sullivan, Mark, 897
Sullivan, William, 642
Summers, Benjamin, 851
Sumner, Charles, 946
Sumner, S. S., 76
Sumner Society, 226
Sutliff, Milton, 797
Sutphin, Al, 790
Swaim, David G., 755
Swain, Rufus, 343
Swasey, Ambrose, 771, 926
Sweden, 497
Sweeney, John E., 791
Sweeney, Martin L., 783
Switzerland, 733
Symmes, John Cleves, 948

Taft, Frederick L., 780
Taft, Robert A., 579, 641, 791, 962
Taft, William Howard, 246, 592, 596, 897, 948
Talbot family, 667
Taliaferro, John G., 247
Tallmadge, Benjamin, 70, 338, 543
Tallmadge Academy, 422
Talmadge, W. C., 822
Tappan, Abraham, 1, 46, 691, 868
Tappan, Benjamin, 1, 247, 338, 404, 543
Tappan, Electra, 691
Tariffs, 715, 791, 897–899
Tashmoo (steamer), 463
Tate, Allen, 709
Taylor, Alexander A., 252
Taylor, Benjamin F., 330
Taylor, Ezra B., 503
Taylor, Harry K., 168
Taylor, James E., 466
Taylor, James Wickes, 728
Taylor, John L., 454, 715
Taylor, Lucy E. L., 330
Taylor, Philo, 829
Taylor, Mrs. R. M. N., 364
Taylor, R. W., 1045
Taylor, Thomas Hart, 946
Taylor, Virgil C., 850
Taylor, Zachary, 203
Taylor, Z. P., 62
Taylor family, 512
Teapot Dome scandal, 596
Teetor, Josie C., 592
Teller, Henry M., 897
Temperance, 15, 26, 31, 83, 106, 110, 152, 192, 210, 253, 273, 287, 290, 333, 462, 477, 483, 565, 745, 796, 920, 948
Temperance Society (Burton), 796
Temperance Society (Willoughby), 273

[415]

Tennessee, 188, 236, 488, 531, 535, 679, 730, 786, 839, 852
  Nashville, 495, 508, 948
Tennessee and Alabama Railroad, 508
Tennessee River, 750
Tennessee Volunteer Infantry, 466
Tenney, Samuel, 70
Terry, Ellen F., 213
Texas, 562, 607, 715, 786, 834
Texas Volunteer Infantry, 466
Thayer, Almon, 132
Thayer, Ebenezer, Jr., 70
Thayer, Lyman, G., 647
Thayer, Proctor, 647
Theodore E. Burton: American Statesman, 899
Theophilus Trent, 330
Thomas, George H., 218
Thomas, H. A., 466
Thomas, Isabella A., 854
Thomas, John J., 946
Thomas, Mary A., 854
Thomas, Susan A., 854
Thomas James & Company, 131
Thompson, Charles E., 943
Thompson, Charles T., 592
Thompson, Eliza Jane (Trimble), 333
Thompson, James Henry, 333
Thompson, Moses, 948
Thompson Products Company, 943, 989
Thorndike, Henry, 278
Thorne, Isaac G., 487
Thornton, Matthew, 760
Thwaites, Reuben G., 215
Thwing, Charles F., 771, 897, 908, 948
Thwing, Luther, 139
Thwing, Nathaniel, 556
Tiffin, Edward, 34, 338, 543, 739, 871, 924
Tiffin Manufacturing Company, 944
Tilden, Daniel R., 247
Tilghman, Lloyd, 423
Tinkerbelle (sloop), 905
Tobacco, 30, 748
Tod, David, 66, 179, 247, 446, 691
Tod, George, 1, 712, 924
Todd, George, W., 752
Toledo, St. Louis and Western Railroad, 662
Toledo Steel Products Company, 943
Tolles, S. H., 503
Tomlinson, Levi, 281
Tomlinson, Lewis, 281
Torrance, William G., 784
Tourgée, Albion W., 387
Townsend Amos, 71
Townsend, Frederick, 948
Townshend, Norton S., 297, 419
Tozier, Kathleen B. Seaman, 723
Tracy, Benjamin F., 683
Tracy, Edward D., 946
Tracy, Elisha, 924
Tracy, J. J., 221
Transportation
  automobile, 335, 682
  aviation, 594, 596, 943, 989
  canals, 30–31, 56, 66, 180, 184, 247, 338, 404, 665, 708, 897, 948
  railroads, 31, 70, 91, 95, 179, 221, 247, 301, 335, 394, 396, 404, 423, 508, 517, 535, 557, 578, 580, 592, 604, 612, 662,

[416]

680, 683, 700, 716, 768, 771,
791, 796, 896–899, 921, 948,
1045
rivers, 897–899
roads, 46, 52, 174, 180, 182,
228, 279, 304, 366, 383, 412,
421, 426, 611, 634, 660, 668,
712, 715, 744, 767, 773, 885,
948, 957, 1029, 1035
ships, 70, 132, 197, 268, 275,
326, 421, 463, 465, 508, 538,
648, 661, 746, 791, 809, 841,
921–923
stagecoach, 21, 812
Transylvania College, 769
Travels
  Africa, 563, 567
  Canada, 215, 454, 690
  Central America, 509, 563, 766
  Europe, 502, 563, 567, 573,
600, 607, 733, 766, 833, 844,
899
  Mexico, 563, 567
  South America, 567, 766
  United States, 1, 4, 23–24, 30,
32–33, 40, 43, 52–53, 69,
99, 129, 141–142, 163–164,
176, 187–188, 202, 215, 245,
271, 299, 303, 345, 369, 383,
454, 481, 507, 536–537, 553,
562, 618, 663, 680, 688, 690,
692, 717, 738, 750, 773, 784,
793, 796, 802, 807, 851, 899,
947, 951
Treaty of Greenville, 469
Trent, William, 507
Trevor, Samuel, 325
Trimble, Allen, 333, 468, 715
Trimble, William Allen, 715
Trimble, William Henry, 715

Triplett, George W., 946
Trowbridge, F. E., 592
Trowbridge, G. A., 363
Trowbridge, Orrin, 592
Trowbridge family, 512
Trudeau, Carlos, 198
Trueblood, Benjamin F., 897
Truman, Harry S., 791
Truman, William, 326
Trumbull, Eliza, 139
Trumbull, Henry C., 139
Trumbull, Jonathan (1740–1809),
494, 714, 789, 948
Trumbull, Joseph, 139
Trumbull & Ashtabula Turnpike
Company, 180, 412
Trumbull County Bible Society,
386
TRW, Inc., 943
Tryon family, 321
Tucker, Thomas T., 739
Tuckerman, Edward, 70
Tumulty, Joseph P., 897
Tupper, Sir Charles, 683
Tupper, Samuel, 470
Turner, Albert, 759
Turner, Charles Albert, 759
Turner, Daniel, 652
Turner, Dwight D., 948
Turner, Hannah (Covert), 759
Turner, Peter, 652
Turney, Asa, 132, 691
Turpin family, 371
Tuscarawas Coal & Iron Company, 327
Tuscarawas County Horticultural
Society and Farmer's Club, 505
Tuscarawas River, 46, 868
Tuttle, H. B., 39
Tuttle, Mrs. H. B., 866

Tuttle, H. H., 619
Tuttle, Herbert, 333
Tuttle, J. B., 619
Tuttle, Mary McArthur (Thompson), 333
Tuttle family, 919
Tweedy, A. H., 371
Twinsburg Institute, 32
Tyler, John, 203, 534
Tyler, Moses Coit, 400

Union Club (Cleveland), 913
Union Land Company, 738
Union Signal, 333
United Automobile Workers, 989
United Kingdom, 497
United Service Club of Philadelphia, 211
United Spanish War Veterans, 800
United States (whaling vessel), 94
United States
　foreign relations, 178, 509, 562, 596, 674, 727–728, 791, 897–899, 917
　general, 162, 497
　Army (1790–1860), 193, 373, 428, 469, 567, 595, 743, 847
　Army (1861–1865), 465–466, 532, 567, 666, 705–706, 726, 730, 755–756, 825, 839, 894, 927, 956
　Army (1866–1916), 730, 750, 755, 913
　Army (1917–1919), 410, 582, 678, 790, 893, 901, 917, 985
　Bank, 715
　Board of Immigration Appeals, 791
　Congress, 69, 71, 107, 129, 140, 338, 363, 400, 462, 494, 503, 539, 632–633, 670, 673, 710, 715, 739, 774, 783, 791, 799, 831, 897–899, 999
　Council on National Defense, 791
　Department of the Interior, 813
　Federal Children's Bureau, 791
　Federal Deposit Insurance Corporation, 791
　Federal Reserve System, 791
　Federal Securities Exchange Act, 791
　Freedmen's Bureau, 864
　General Munitions Board, 791
　Inland Waterways Commission, 897–899
　Monetary Commission, 897–899
　National Labor Relations Board, 943
　National War Labor Board, 641, 943
　National Waterways Commission, 897–899
　Naval Academy, 946
　Navy, 562, 567, 585, 652, 897–899, 917
　Office of Internal Revenue, 948
　Post Office, 46, 107, 247, 349, 366, 405–406, 412, 421, 446, 545, 665, 717, 738, 791, 873, 878, 892, 897–899, 948, 1075
　Presidents, 203, 363, 612, 761. *See also under individual names*
　Sanitary Commission, 213, 609, 946

Shipping Board Emergency Fleet Corporation, 791
State Department, 917
Supreme Court, 791
Treasury, 247, 403, 462, 673–674, 728
War Department, 917
War Emergency Relief Board, 199, 493
War Finance Corporation, 135
War Industries Board, 791
War Production Board, 641
Works Progress Administration
  Federal art project, 682
  Federal writers' project, 597, 608
  Historic American Buildings Survey, 682, 948, 978
  Ohio Historic Records Survey, 611, 945
U.S.S. *Brooklyn*, 946
U.S.S. *Cambridge*, 946
U.S.S. *Cyane*, 652
U.S.S. *Diana*, 759
U.S.S. *Kearsarge*, 178
U.S.S. *Metacomet*, 946
U.S.S. *New Ironsides*, 946
U.S.S. *Nonsuch*, 652
U.S.S. *Richmond*, 946
United States Christian Commission, 350
University of London, 804
University of Michigan, 387
University of Pennsylvania, 67
Updegraff, David L., 482
Upper Mississippi, 707
Upton, Harriet Taylor, 385
Urban League of Cleveland, 1004
Urban renewal, 910–911, 937, 939
Urbana High School, 316

V. C. Taylor & Son, 850
Vallandigham, Clement, 312
Vallandigham, Clement L., 312, 540, 948
Vallandigham, Elizabeth, 312
Vallandigham, George, 312
Vallandigham, James L., 312
Vallandigham, Mary E., 312
Vallandigham, Rebecca, 312
Vallette, Lavelle, 619
Van Buren, Martin, 203
Vanderburgh, Henry, 162
Van Doren, Mark, 709
Van Dorn, Earl, 423, 666
Van Dyke, A. C., 480
Van Horne, Thomas B., 218
Vanik, Charles, 790
Van Sittert, William, 814
Van Sweringen, Mantis J., 578, 763
Van Sweringen, Oris P., 578, 763
Van Sweringen Company, 716
Van Sweringen Railway System, 662
Van Tassel, Isaac, 40, 338
Van Tassel, Lucia (Mrs. Isaac), 42
Varian, Alexander, Jr., 679
Vassar College, 609
Venezuela, 652
Veragua, Duke of, 766
Vermillion Institute, 307
Vermont, 187, 224, 281, 429, 617
Vermont Militia, 154
Vermont Volunteer Infantry, 466
Versailles Peace Conference, 727
Veterans Reserve Corps
  4th Regiment, 810
Vinson, Robert E., 771
Vinton, Samuel F., 181

Virginia, 30, 181, 296, 372, 445, 451, 508, 534, 633, 650, 792, 839, 928
   Alexandria, 70
   Austinville, 946
   Bolivar Heights, 946
   Brady Junction, 956
   Camp Pratt, 659
   City Point, 350
   Manassas Junction, 863
   Pendleton County, 127
   Richmond, 221, 252
   Staunton, 946
   Suffolk, 946
   Winchester, 252
   York County, 30
Virginia Military District, 299, 633, 715, 769
Virginia Militia, 118
Virginia Volunteer Infantry, 466
Voorhees, G., 17

W. Bingham Company, 767
Wabash and Erie Canal, 30
Waddell, Joseph A., 946
Wade, Benamin F., 247, 400, 691, 797, 948
Wade, Edward, 247
Wade, Jeptha Homer, 778, 959
Wade, Jeptha H. (grandson), 959
Wade, Randall P., 959
Wade Park Committee, 909
Wadena (freighter), 648
Wadsworth, Elijah, 154, 338, 468, 543, 562, 675, 713, 718, 736, 860, 924
Wadsworth, Frederick, 93, 247, 338, 543
Wadsworth, James, 543
Wadsworth, James (from Geneseo), 543
Wadsworth, Wedworth, 543
Waite, Carl, 978
Waite, Frederick C., 982
Waite family, 321
Wakeman, Joseph, 421
Walker, Francis A., 387
Walker, Henry, 139
Walker, S. N., 425
Walker, William H. T., 946
Walker family, 515
Wallace, George, 829
Wallace, Lewis, 879, 946
Wallace, W. K., 917
Wallula (freighter), 648
Walter, Paul W., 962
Walton, Lucius C., 1083
Walworth, Ashbel, 46
Walworth, Ashbel W., 247, 421
Walworth, J. P., 604
Walworth, John, 1, 46, 188, 279, 421, 948
War of 1812, 18, 118, 154, 269, 277, 294, 338, 346, 398, 426, 428, 504, 562, 580, 602, 643, 665, 675, 712–713, 715, 723, 765, 847, 924, 947
Ward, Elijah, 888
Ward, Hubert Herrick, 853
Ward, Marion D., 852
Ward, P. H., 119
Warden, R., 461
Ware, Henry, 70
Warfield, W., 769
Warner, Adoniram Judson, 946
Warner, A. J., 124
Warner, Chauncey, 527
Warner, S. S., 529
Warner, Worcester R., 771

Warner and Swasey Company, 771
Warner family, 364
Warren, Julius E., 401
Warren, Moses, 1, 950
Washburn, F. S., 419
Washburn, George G., 419
Washburn, Israel, Jr., 462
Washburn & Anderson, 132
Washington, Booker T., 355
Washington, George, 24, 401, 714, 761, 789, 948
  bicentennial, 401
Washington and Jefferson College, 802
Washington Armament Conference, 596
Washington Benevolent Society, 181
Waters, Abner, 427
Waters, Alonzo, 100
Waters, Lucy, 427
Wau Lee, 116
Waugh, A. J., 329
Wayne, Anthony, 373, 469, 948
Wayne, Medina & Cuyahoga Turnpike Road Company, 182, 634
Weather and meteorological data, 132, 235, 244, 361, 383, 454, 555, 581, 598, 618, 671, 801
Webb, Edward A., 669
Webb, Libbie, 669
Webb, William S., 1062
Webster, Clark, 298
Webster, Daniel, 756
Webster, Hiram C., 298
Webster, John Howard, 409
Weddell, Horace P., 408
Weddell, Peter M., 38, 408–409

Weddell House, 408
Weeks, John W., 897
Weeks family, 364
Wehrschmidt, Daniel A., 177
Weidenthal, Leo, 472
Weidenthal, Maurice, 791
Weisheimer, Marie, 750
Weisheimer, William, 750
Welch, D. E., 363
Welfare Federation of Cleveland, 641, 846
Welles, Gideon, 400, 705, 946
Wellington Literary Society, 283
Wells, Bezaleel, 501
Wells, Earl H., 1043
Wells, Francis A., 501
Wenban, Sion L., 177
West Virginia, 30, 210, 578, 666, 683, 730, 946
Westenhaven, D.C., 651
Western Anti-Slavery Society, 126, 210
Western Baptist Education Society, 27, 325
Western Female Seminary, 636
Western Freed-Man's Commission, 487
Western Reserve Bank, 180, 247, 665
Western Reserve College, 247, 422, 503, 531, 647, 796, 832, 949
Western Reserve Historical Society, 1, 22, 32, 54, 86, 472, 507, 568, 625, 654, 707, 824, 947, 985, 1005
Western Reserve Horse Breeders Association, 948
Western Reserve Railroad Company, 394

Western Reserve Teachers' Seminary, 406, 856
Western Reserve University, 518, 563, 709, 771, 875
Western Spectator, 181
Western Star Seminary, 114
Western Union Telegraph Company, 447, 778
Weston, Effie Ellsler, 583
Weygandt, Carl V., 792
Whaling, 94, 661
Wharton, John A., 946
Wheedon, W. C., 62
Wheeler, Aaron, 154
Wheeler, Homer, 854
Wheeler, John H., 946
Wheeler, Joseph, 76, 946
Wheeler, Maro, 854
Wheeler family, 605
Wheeling and Lake Erie Railway Company, 948
Wheelock & Osborn, 916
Whinery, Elijah, 119
Whinery, Joshua, 119
Whipple, Jerousha, 696
Whitcomb, H. D., 221
White, Austin H., 854
White, Daniel Price, 946
White, George E., 665
White, John W., 279
White, Susan, 854
White, Walter, 827
White, William Porter, 771
White Motor Company, 716
White Sewing Machine Company, 771
White Star Line, 463
Whiting, Elisha, 180
Whiting, William H. C., 946
Whitlock, Brand, 768

Whitney, Alexander F., 768, 790
Whitney, Mrs. James W., 833
Whitney, William, 619
Whittier, John Greenleaf, 756
Whittlesey, Asoph, 59
Whittlesey, Charles, 1, 196, 581, 632, 707
Whittlesey, Elijah, 154, 860
Whittlesey, Elisha, 31, 46, 93, 107, 247, 338, 419, 468, 712, 718, 738, 843, 948
Whittlesey, Polly, 843
Whittlesey, William Wallace, 843
Wick, Caleb B., 670
Wickersham, George W., 897
Wickham, Ben B., 578
Wickham, C. P., 419
Wickham, Gertrude Van Rensselaer, 220
Wickham, William C., 946
Wickliffe, Charles A., 247
Wilcox, Aaron, 233
Wilcox, Frank N., 629
Wilcox, Moses, 233, 426
Wildeson, Henry, 482
Wildman, Zalmon, 247
Wiley, Aquila, 453
Willard, Archibald M., 22, 177, 472;
centennial, 472
Willard, Frances E., 333
William IV (King of England), 870
William Robertson & Sons, 915
Williams, A. C., 140
Williams, B. C., 592
Williams, Benajah, 232
Williams, Eliphalet, 139
Williams, Ezekiel, 738
Williams, Nathaniel, 494

Williams, Peter, 240
Williams, William, 760
Williams, Willoughby, 495
Williamson, George T., 604
Williamson, James D., 604
Williamson, Matthew, 604
Williamson, S., 592
Williamson, Samuel, 604, 829
Williamson, Samuel, Jr., 604
Willis, Frank B., 34, 897
Willkie, Wendell, 641
Willoughby College, 104, 111, 492
Willoughby Collegiate Institute, 492
Willoughby Female Seminary, 951
Willoughby Medical College, 117
Willoughby University of Lake Erie, 492, 496
Wills, William, 338
Willys Company, 907
Wilson, James B., 132
Wilson, John, 523
Wilson, Leonard, 76
Wilson, Mrs. Obed J. (Amanda Landrum), 121
Wilson, Woodrow, 246, 596, 727, 918, 948
Wilson family, 752, 980
Wilson Transit Company, 648
Winchester, J., 154
Windfall Lyceum, 258
Wing, Marie R., 992
Winslow, Isaac, 70
Winslow, Rufus K., 195–196
Winslow Bros., 894
Winslow Car Roofing Company, 508
Wintermute, Lewis H., Jr., 363
Winthrop, Thomas L., 421
Winthrop, William, 421
Winton, Alexander, 943
Wisconsin (territory), 222
Wisconsin, 36, 509, 581, 707, 770, 815
  Fox River, 222
  Green Bay, 222
  Houghton County, 367
  Iowa County, 318, 925
  Janesville, 587
  Lancaster, 644
  Marquette County, 367
  Milwaukee, 222
  Menasha, 222
  Ontonagon, 367
Wisconsin Cavalry
  2nd Regiment, 521
Wisconsin Militia
  Mineral Point Guards, 925
Wisconsin Volunteer Infantry, 466
  8th Regiment, 587
Wise, Henry Alexander, 946, 948
Witt, Peter, 651, 768, 791
Wolcott, Alfred, 1, 46, 141, 161, 665
Wolcott, Frederick, 543, 862
Wolcott, Laurens W., 740
Wolcott, Oliver, 948
Wolcott, Winifred, 616
Woman suffrage, 385, 918, 958
Woman's Christian Temperance Union, 253, 333, 483, 745
Woman's Foreign Missionary Jubilee Committee, 209
Woman's Foreign Missionary Society, 227
Woman's Temperance Society of Morgan County, 477
Woman's Veteran Relief Union, 136

Women's Baptist Home Mission Society, 171
Women's Christian Temperance Union, 565
Women's Home Missionary Society, 45
Women's Missionary Union of the Cleveland Churches, 393
Wood, Benjamin, 758
Wood, David L., 567
Wood, E. G., 776
Wood, Mrs. E. G., 776
Wood, Julius V., 776
Wood, Leonard, 897
Wood, Lucius V., 776
Wood, Reuben, 247
Woodbridge, Dudley, 240
Woodbridge, William, 247, 712, 739
Woodbridge family, 339
Woodbury, Levi, 247
Woodruff, Ephraim T., 388
Woods, John, 247
Woods, John L., 640
Woods family, 697
Woolsey, Benjamin, 492
Woolsey, Mrs. Kezia, 492
Woolson, Constance Fenimore, 1001
Woolworth, Aaron, 168
Woolworth, Chester, 168
Woolworth, Joseph, 168
Worden, John Lorimer, 946
Works of James Abram Garfield, 387
World War I, 135, 168, 205, 259, 403, 471, 563, 596, 612, 682, 721, 727, 771, 790–791, 893, 897–899, 917–918, 941, 948, 1048

World War II, 563, 612, 641, 674, 804–805, 935, 943
World's Columbian Exposition, 766
Worthington, Thomas, 338, 924
Worthington Female Seminary, 392
Wright, Aaron, 426
Wright, Albert A., 824
Wright, Ambrose R., 946
Wright, Benjamin A., 270
Wright, Clarissa (mother of Elizur Wright, Jr.), 422
Wright, Clarissa (sister of Elizur Wright, Jr.), 422
Wright, Elizur, Jr., 422, 948
Wright, G. Frederick, 824
Wright, Ira, 868
Wright, James, 422
Wright, Jesse, 592
Wright, John C., 247
Wright, Marcus J., 946
Wright, Nathaniel, 368
Wright, Sherman, 132
Wright family, 512
Writings and writers
 genealogy, 49, 402, 512, 514, 567, 616, 845
 history, 1, 3, 22, 24, 28, 49, 93, 106, 202, 218, 314, 321, 333, 347, 353, 364, 385, 387, 400, 466, 512, 531, 535, 548, 560, 567, 576, 580, 597, 608, 662, 666–667, 707, 766, 814, 821, 824, 879, 885, 897–899, 901, 980, 983, 1054
 journalism, 33, 181, 192, 330, 365, 426, 448, 503, 766, 837
 literature, 33, 78–79, 125, 128, 175, 283, 330, 400, 485, 499,

567, 686, 709, 751, 756, 807, 826–827, 881
  miscellaneous, 518, 583, 771
  science, 200, 509, 563, 707, 750, 798, 813
Wyles, John, 278
Wyllys, J. P., 507
Wythe, George, 760

Yale University, 23, 32, 712, 796
Yancey, William L., 946
Ydrad Boat Club, 96
Yerkes, Ada Watterson, 970
Yonts, George, 132
York, R. H., 208
Youndt (Yund, Yount) family, 779
Young, Barney J., 748
Young, H. E., 946
Young, John, 736, 738
Young, Robert R., 791
Young, Stephen M., 790–791
Young Ladies League for Temperance Education, 106
Young Ladies Seminary, 16
Young Ladies Temperance League, 106
Young Men's Christian Association, 130, 910, 949
Young Women's Christian Association, 910, 941
Young Women's Christian Temperance Union, 26
Younglove, Moses C., 196

Ziegler, August, 76
Zimmerman, Charles B., 791
Zoar Gessang-Verein, 360

[425]

*This book
was set in ten-point
Caledonia. It was composed,
printed and bound by Vail-Ballou Press,
Binghamton, New York. The paper is Warren's
Olde Style by the S.D. Warren Company, Boston.
The design is by Edgar J. Frank and LaWanda McDuffie.*